More praise for *Humanitarian Action and Ethics*

'An important and valuable book on the ethical challenges arising in humanitarian action. It highlights the complex range of challenges, while also presenting practical and constructive recommendations from authors who have worked on the front line of humanitarian crises.'

Bayard Roberts, London School of Hygiene and Tropical Medicine

'Powerfully depicts the ethical challenges pervading a world which deliberately generates so much human suffering through disasters and conflict. The chapters demonstrate what we can do to help, despite the moral entanglements of today's humanitarian labyrinth.'

Ilan Kelman, Institute for Risk & Disaster Reduction,
University College London

T0347901

About the Editors

Dr Ayesha Ahmad is a lecturer in Global Health at St George's University of London, and Honorary Lecturer at the Institute for Global Health, University College London. She specialises in gender-based violence and mental health in conflict and humanitarian crises.

Dr James Smith, MBBS, MSc, is a Research Fellow with the Health in Humanitarian Crises Centre at the London School of Hygiene and Tropical Medicine (LSHTM). He has worked as an advisor to MSF Operational Centre Barcelona (OCBA), and as a researcher with Médecins Sans Frontières' Research Unit on Humanitarian Stakes and Practices (UREPH), and continues to work as an emergency physician with the UK National Health Service (NHS).

HUMANITARIAN ACTION AND ETHICS

Edited by Ayesha Ahmad and James Smith

With a Foreword by Hugo Slim

ZED

Humanitarian Action and Ethics was first published in 2018 by
Zed Books Ltd, The Foundry, 17 Oval Way, London SE11 5RR, UK.

www.zedbooks.net

Typeset in Plantin and Kievit by Swales & Willis Ltd, Exeter, Devon
Cover design by Burgess & Beech
Cover photo © Andrew Testa/Panos

A catalogue record for this book is available from the British Library
ISBN 978-1-78699-268-0 hb
ISBN 978-1-78699-267-3 pb
ISBN 978-1-78699-269-7 pdf
ISBN 978-1-78699-270-3 epub
ISBN 978-1-78699-271-0 mobi

'Books change us. Books save us. I know this because it happened to me. Books saved me. So I do believe through stories we can learn to change, we can learn to emphasise, and be more connected with the universe, and with humanity.'

Elif Shafak

CONTENTS

ACKNOWLEDGEMENTS

Ayesha Ahmad

The book has been a huge undertaking and most definitely a wonderful global and cultural experience. The desire to develop a book such as *Humanitarian Action and Ethics* has been longstanding, and I am thoroughly grateful for all of those who have helped bring an idea into reality.

I fundamentally need to thank Dr Donal O'Mathúna, who provided the foundation for this book. I must also convey my gratitude to my 'Big Boss', Dr Carwyn Hooper, St Georges University of London, for the support, space and freedom to fulfil my academic dreams. I acknowledge with deep gratitude our chapter contributors for their gifts to our book, and my co-editor, Dr James Smith.

Finally, I give my eternal thanks to my parents for teaching me the importance of fighting for justice, morality, and equality, and especially to my father for encouraging me to 'break stereotypes' – quite a potent combination of skills for working in humanitarian settings. So many friends have supported me, as well as my dear sister Sara, the best 'chwaer. I cannot name all in person but they are always with me as I write. I hope that these words will not be the last words I give to them in a book.

James Smith

Foremost, I wish to express my thanks to Ayesha Ahmad, who not only extended the generous invitation to participate in this important project, but whose tireless desire to tackle injustice in every aspect of her work is a source of great inspiration.

I owe further thanks to Philippe Calain for his many insightful reflections, and for his continued guidance and encouragement. Many thanks are due to Amy Neilson, for similarly insightful reflections during the search for sense in the nonsensical, and for being a stellar physician – particularly in those moments when it mattered the most. To Simukai Chigudu and Ahmed Khan, for their friendship and encouragement, I owe a great deal.

Finally, I wish to dedicate my contribution to this book to the memory of John Jal, a wonderfully kind and humorous man, whose commitment to the delivery of medical care, and his belief in the future of South Sudan, was evident in each and every one of the ward rounds we shared together. He is deeply missed.

CONTRIBUTOR BIOGRAPHIES

Fosco Bugoni is currently enrolled on the first-level Professional Master's Programme in Migration Law and Policies at the University of Milano-Bicocca. He holds an MA in Anthropology and Ethnology from the University of Milano-Bicocca, and a BA in philosophy from the University of Milano-Statale. He is a volunteer with NAGA, a Milan-based non-profit organisation that provides legal advice and primary healthcare services for irregular third-country nationals. His research focuses mainly on migrations in the Italian context, particularly on the labour migration of Ukrainian domestic workers and on the role of small and medium-sized towns in the complex processes of integration of asylum seekers and refugees.

Philippe Calain is a medical doctor specialised in infectious diseases and tropical medicine. He also holds a doctorate in biology (virology). He has worked in Rwanda, Afghanistan and Laos, and is currently a senior researcher with the Research Unit on Humanitarian Stakes and Practices (UREPH) of MSF Switzerland. His research focuses on humanitarian medicine, public health ethics, global health governance, public health surveillance systems, pandemic preparedness and development theory.

Celeste Cantor-Stephens is an activist, researcher–writer, musicologist and musician, working in both English and French. She has been involved in the support of displaced people in various parts of France and the UK for several years. Celeste recently completed an MPhil at the University of Cambridge, with a thesis on human rights violations and the institutionalised abuse of exiled people at the Franco–British border. She is a performing musician, and has a special interest in the social, psychological and political roles of music in the world.

Dr Caroline Clarinval works at the World Health Organisation's (WHO) Regional Office in Cairo. In her current role as Regional Adviser for Emergency Response and Operations, she is responsible for the WHO's emergency response and operations across the Middle Eastern Region. Prior to taking up her current post, she worked at the Federal Office of Public Health in Switzerland, as well as at the Institute of Biomedical Ethics at the University of Zurich. She also spent a decade abroad working for the International Committee of the Red Cross (ICRC) assisting populations affected by conflict.

Matthew DeCamp, MD, PhD, is an Assistant Professor at the Johns Hopkins Berman Institute of Bioethics and in the Division of General Internal Medicine. A practising internist, his research includes both conceptual and empirical methods at the intersection of health policy and bioethics. His PhD (philosophy) described the impact of human rights theory on intellectual property policy and access to essential medicines, and he has a longstanding interest in global health ethics (with special emphasis on short-term global health training).

Carol Devine is a Humanitarian Affairs Advisor with MSF Canada, focusing on forced migration and the mapping of climate and health humanitarian responses. She was Program Director and Access to Essential Medicines Campaigner for MSF Canada and has worked for MSF in Rwanda, South Sudan and East Timor. Carol was former Program Manager at the Museum of AIDS in Africa, and a 2016 Fellow at Arctic Summer College researching circumpolar health.

Nermin R Diab, MD, CM, MPH, is a resident physician in internal medicine at the University of Ottawa. She completed her Bachelor's and medical degrees at McGill University followed by a Master's in Public Health at the Johns Hopkins School of Public Health with a concentration in epidemiologic and biostatistical methods. Her research interests are in the fields of global health, health policy, and pulmonary and critical care medicine.

Liyam Eloul is a trauma therapist specialised in displacement and complex emergencies. Ms Eloul has worked internationally with the UN, INGOs and local NGOs across the Middle East and North Africa region and in sub-Saharan Africa, as well as with refugees post-resettlement in the USA. Ms Eloul received her Master's degree in International Disaster Psychology from the University of Denver, her Post-graduate Diploma in Psychosocial Interventions for Refugees and Forced Migrants from the

Center for Migration and Refugee Studies at the American University in Cairo, and her Bachelor of Arts in Cultural Psychology from Queen's University, Ontario. Ms Eloul is currently a Clinical Advisor with the Center for Victims of Torture.

Morshid Farhat received an MD, MPH, and MBA from the Hebrew University in Jerusalem, and LLB (Law) from UNO College. He completed his residency programme in obstetrics and gynaecology at the Hadassah Medical Center in Jerusalem (2001), and since then has practised medicine in Hadassah Hospital and HMOs. He specialised in medical management and administration at the Hadassah Medical Center (2006–2008). Currently, Dr Farhat is deputy director general at Ziv Medical Center. Since 2007, he has taught medical ethics, health law, and public health ethics at Hadassah College. Dr Farhat's current research interests include healthcare decision-making, medical ethics, risk management, and ethics in humanitarian settings.

Jane Freedman is a Professor of Sociology at the Université Paris 8, Saint-Denis, and member of the Centre de Recherches Sociologiques et Politiques de Paris (CRESPPA). She previously held a Marie Curie Chair at the Sorbonne University where she led a major European research project on gender and asylum. Her research focuses on issues of forced migration, asylum and refugee policies, gender and gender-based violence. As well as researching widely on European and international asylum and refugee policy, she has researched and written on international interventions to prevent gender-based violence, in particular in the Democratic Republic of Congo. Recent publications include: *Gendering the International Asylum and Refugee Debate* (Palgrave Macmillan, 2015); *Gender, Politics and Violence in the Democratic Republic of Congo* (Ashgate, 2015); and *A Gendered Approach to the Syrian Refugee Crisis* (Routledge, 2017). In addition to her academic activities, she has worked with various international organisations and NGOs to carry out research and advocacy work on these issues.

Kory L Funk, MPH, received his MPH degree from the Johns Hopkins Bloomberg School of Public Health in 2017 with a concentration in health in crisis and humanitarian assistance. His research interests include humanitarian ethics and health behaviour change with an international focus.

Vickie Hawkins, following three years in Oxfam's Emergencies Department, joined MSF in 1998, working first as a Financial Coordinator in China and Pakistan. She went on to complete successive missions as Project Coordinator and Head of Mission in Pakistan, Afghanistan and Zimbabwe. Vickie became head of the MSF UK's Programmes Unit in 2005, leaving to work with MSF projects again in 2011 as Deputy Head of Mission in Myanmar. In May 2014 she started in her current role as General Director of MSF UK.

Lara S Ho, PhD, RN, joined the International Rescue Committee (IRC) in July 2007, working in Tanzania, Côte d'Ivoire, DRC and Switzerland. She is currently based in Washington, DC as the Deputy Director of the IRC's Health Unit, managing a team that supports programming and research in environmental health, nutrition, reproductive health, and primary healthcare for populations affected by crisis. Lara was a Peace Corps Volunteer in Mongolia and still serves on the board of Friends of Mongolia, a non-profit organisation founded by returned Peace Corps Volunteers. She holds an AB in History and Science from Harvard and Radcliffe Colleges, a BS in Nursing from Johns Hopkins University, and an MHS and PhD in International Health from Johns Hopkins Bloomberg School of Public Health.

Dr Peter Hughes, MBBAO, BCh, FRCPsych, MSc, is a London-based psychiatrist who has worked globally for fifteen years, including in low- and middle-income countries, and regions affected by conflict and humanitarian disasters. He was founder and chair of the College of Psychiatry's special interest group on Global Mental Health. He is also co-lead of the Kings Sierra Leone and Somaliland mental health links. He has been involved with the mhGAP programme since 2010 as both a trainer and reviewer, and was awarded Volunteer of the Year by the College of Psychiatry 2014. Dr Hughes has published widely on global mental health.

Matthew Hunt is an Associate Professor and the Director of Research at McGill University's School of Physical and Occupational Therapy, and a researcher at the Center for Interdisciplinary Research in Rehabilitation. His research interests lie at the intersections of ethics, global health and rehabilitation, and he is currently conducting research related to palliative care in humanitarian crises, the ethics of humanitarian innovation and research, and access to rehabilitation services. He co-leads the Humanitarian Health Ethics Research Group (humanitarianhealthethics.net).

Rachel Kiddell-Monroe is a lawyer and an activist, specialising in global health, governance and bioethics. She is a member of MSF's International Board of Directors. Joining MSF in 1992, Rachel headed MSF projects in Djibouti, Rwanda and the Democratic Republic of Congo, along with a regional humanitarian affairs initiative in Latin America. Rachel is currently Professor of Practice at McGill University as well as Special Advisor to the international advocacy group Universities Allied for Essential Medicines (UAEM).

Katarína Komenská finished her PhD in Ethics at the Faculty of Arts, University of Prešov in 2013. Curently, she is a research assistant at the Institute of Ethics and Bioethics, University of Prešov. There, she also leads lectures and seminars in environmental ethics, bioethics, and cultural anthropology. Her interest is based in bioethics (medical ethics, animal ethics) and its reflections through the scope of non-utilitarian consequentialism. Her experiences with the work in humanitarian and development aid organisations have had impact on her ethical reflections on disasters and humanitarian crisis. She has participated at several study and research stays: University of Bolton, United Kingdom; MDC (Max Delbruck Center for Molecular Medicine), Department of Bioethics, Berlin–Buch, Germany; Centre of Applied Ethics, University of Linkoping, Sweden; and has actively participated at numerous scientific events and venues (e.g. Croatia, the Netherlands, Denmark, Germany, United Kingdom, France, Hungary, Czech Republic, Georgia, etc.). In 2013, she was awarded *The Faculty of Arts, University of Prešov in Prešov Award* for her research and publication results.

Dr Wasim Maziak is the Chair of the Research Committee for the Syrian American Medical Society (SAMS) and Professor and Chair of the Department of Epidemiology, Florida International University. He is also the founder and director of the Syrian Center for Tobacco Studies (www.scts-sy.org), a pioneering research and capacity-building institution in the Middle East.

Paul McMaster is a semi-retired surgeon who worked in the field for MSF from 2006 to 2008 in the DRC, Burundi and Somalia. Following that, he was Specialist Advisor for MSF's Operational Centre Amsterdam (OCA) until February 2012. While at OCA, Paul visited more than thirty MSF projects across the globe, and led emergency teams during the conflict in Sri Lanka, and later Haiti, in 2010.

Jingru Miao is a second-year medical student at McGill University who is passionate about global health and medical ethics. He is currently the chief operating officer at HANY, a Montreal-based student-run organisation that helps newly arrived refugees by providing language instruction and opportunities to build social support networks. Coming from a background in physiotherapy, he is driven to contribute to humanitarian projects centred on orthopaedics and rehabilitation.

Toby Leon Moorsom is a lecturer at Lancaster University in the Department of Politics, Philosophy and Religion and teaches at their Accra campus. He has a long history of labour, anti-poverty, and global justice activism and his writings can be found in a variety of academic and non-academic forums.

Maëlle Noé is an illustrator, mediator, dialogue facilitator, conflict transformation coach and trainer. Maëlle bridges the arts and conflict transformation through training, coaching and dialogue, both online and in person, in North America, East Africa and Western Europe. She received her BA (Hons) in Illustration from the University of the Arts London, her MA in International Peace and Security from Korea University, Seoul, and her MA in International Communication from American University, Washington DC.

Claire F O'Reilly is a physiotherapist working in refugee health, with experience in conflict and development settings in the Middle East and sub-Saharan Africa. Ms O'Reilly is particularly interested in the treatment of chronic pain and the physical manifestations of emotional trauma. She holds a Bachelor of Science in Physiotherapy and is currently completing her Master's in International Public Health. Ms O'Reilly is a technical and policy adviser for physical trauma rehabilitation in the Middle East.

John Pringle is a nurse and epidemiologist with a PhD in Public Health and Bioethics. He is Assistant Professor at McGill University's Ingram

School of Nursing and Vice Chair of the Médecins Sans Frontières (MSF) Ethics Review Board.

Diana Rayes, MHS, is a global mental health researcher and public health professional, currently coordinating a project on humanitarian ethics inside Syria as part of an R2HC/ELRHA-funded collaboration between the International Rescue Committee, the Syrian American Medical Society, and the Johns Hopkins Center for Humanitarian Health in southern Turkey. Her interest is mental health in crisis, particularly among refugees and displaced populations.

W Courtland Robinson, PhD, is an Assistant Professor at the Center for Refugee and Disaster Response at the Johns Hopkins Bloomberg School of Public Health. He has been involved in refugee research and policy analysis since 1979. He is the author of numerous studies on refugee issues, particularly in Asia. His book *Terms of Refuge: The Indochinese Exodus and the International Response* (Zed Books, 1998) was selected by the Humanitarian Times as one of the ten best books for 1999. His current research activities include famine and distress migration in North Korea, demographic assessment methods in complex emergencies, and development-induced displacement.

Leonard S Rubenstein is Director of the Program on Human Rights, Health and Conflict at the Center for Public Health and Human Rights at the Johns Hopkins Bloomberg School of Public Health, and a core faculty member of both the Johns Hopkins Center for Humanitarian Health, and the Johns Hopkins Berman Institute of Bioethics. He has engaged in extensive research in the Syrian conflict and is principal investigator for a project on ethical challenges for humanitarian health organisations in situations of extreme violence. He founded and chairs the Safeguarding Health in Conflict Coalition.

Elisa Sandri has a Master's degree in Anthropology of Development from the University of Sussex, and a Bachelor's degree in Social Anthropology from SOAS – University of London. She has worked as a researcher for the Norwegian Refugee Council and the Mekong Migration Network (Thailand). She is interested in how social anthropology can contribute to the study of humanitarian crises and is planning to start a PhD to continue her research on grassroots humanitarianism.

Dr Hugo Slim is Head of Policy at the International Committee of the Red Cross (ICRC) in Geneva. Before joining ICRC in 2015, he was Senior Research Fellow at the Institute of Ethics, Law and Armed Conflict (ELAC) at the University of Oxford where he led research on humanitarian ethics and the protection of civilians. Hugo has combined a career between academia and practice. He was Chief Scholar at the Centre for Humanitarian Dialogue from 2003–2007 and Reader in International Humanitarianism at Oxford Brookes University from 1994–2003. Between 1983 and 1994, Hugo worked for Save the Children and the United Nations in Morocco, Sudan, Ethiopia, the Occupied Palestinian Territories and Bangladesh. His most recent books are *Humanitarian Ethics: A Guide to the Morality of Aid in War and Disaster* (2015 Hurst/OUP) and *Killing Civilians: Method, Madness and Morality in War* (2007 Hurst/OUP).

Dr Namrita S Singh, PhD, MSc, has expertise in global mental health and humanitarian response. She currently works on humanitarian health research projects in Ukraine and Syria. Her completed projects include evaluations of interventions to improve rural healthcare in India and Tajikistan, and mental health assessments of displaced persons in Georgia. Dr Singh's research is aimed at improving psychosocial health and collective resilience after displacement and conflict.

Dr Vanessa Okito Wedi is a South African medical doctor of Congolese descent, who has experience working in both low- and middle-income countries. She is a director of the Ona Mtoto Wako initiative ('see your baby' in Swahili), which aims to bring lifesaving antenatal care to pregnant women who are unable to access conventional healthcare structures in remote and rural parts of low- and middle-income countries. This project aims to tackle the leading causes of maternal and neonatal mortality by identifying women at high risk from the most common causes of maternal death, i.e. pregnancy-related hypertension, anaemia, HIV and malaria. Furthermore, she is the founder and leading director of a non-profit organisation called the Vagina Workshop that aims to empower and improve the sexual, social and educational awareness of young women and girls in lower-income countries.

Sidney Wong is the Medical Director of MSF's Operational Centre Amsterdam. He is currently Chair of the TBPractecal trial's Project

Management Team, and a member of MSF's Humanitarian Ethics Committee.

Jan Wörlein is postdoctoral researcher in Sciences Po Paris. He is currently working on risk politics and volcanic research in Martinique. His research fields concern the politics of humanitarian aid, the politics of disaster and Caribbean politics. He holds a PhD in sociology from University Paris-Nanterre and an MA in political science from Freie Universität Berlin.

Salman Zarka is General Director of Ziv Medical Center, Israel. Dr Zarka, a physician, graduated from the Technion Institute, and served as a Colonel in the IDF for more than twenty-five years in a variety of positions, the last of which was commander of the Military Health Services Department. During his military service, he developed and became the Commander of the Israeli Field Hospital for Syrian wounded until it was closed. Dr Zarka received a Master's degree in Public Health (MPH) from the Hebrew University, Jerusalem, and an additional Master's degree in Political Science from the University of Haifa. Since 2013 he has also been Senior Lecturer at the Hebrew University Medical School, and at the University of Haifa Public Health School, Israel. His main research interests span public health, infectious diseases, and military medicine, including hospital operations in emergency situations. Dr Zarka is the author of almost thirty articles in peer-reviewed journals, and has organised a number of international conferences.

Shlomit Zuckerman is a medical risk manager, lecturing on medicolegal issues to hospital medical and nursing teams, providing ongoing legal counselling. She is also in charge of research at the division of medical risk management of a governmental insurance company in Israel. She obtained an LLB from the Hebrew University (1998), and an MA and PhD in Empirical Bioethics from Case Western Reserve University in Cleveland, Ohio (2004, 2009). She has taught medical ethics, ethics and genomics, and public health ethics since she received her PhD. Her research interests include public health policy and decision-making, medical risk management, ethics in disaster and armed conflict, and standards of care in the face of scarce resources. She has published in journals including *International Journal of Neonatal Screening* and *Current Pediatric Reviews*, and co-authored a chapter on medical neutrality in *Military Medical Ethics for the 21st Century* (Ashgate, 2013).

FOREWORD: HUMANITARIAN ACTION AND ETHICS

Hugo Slim

The public ethics of humanitarian action is typically grandiose, even grand-standing. The horror of people's suffering in war and disaster means politicians and humanitarian agencies alike make humanitarian appeals that are urgent, unambiguous and confident in their ability to help. This loud aspect of humanitarian ethics is the call of the humanitarian imperative, which usually sounds something like this: 'The situation is terrible. We must act now to save lives. We will do so neutrally and impartially to ensure that we respond fairly and well. We are on the ground and will make the most of your money.'

This urgent ethical appeal is essential but, quite rightly, it is complemented more and more by a quieter voice of professional humanitarian ethics, which recognises that the ethics of humanitarian action is not as simple as it sounds. Calling for help is one thing. Actually helping people 'on the ground' is another. The ferocity of armed conflict, the sovereignty of States, and the permanent condition of working in non-ideal settings with insufficient resources means that humanitarian action is fraught with ethical difficulties. Affected people and humanitarian workers continuously face hard choices about what is right and what is best.

This book is an important contribution from the new voice of professional ethics in humanitarian action. All the authors of its chapters are concerned with the granularity of humanitarian ethics. There is no moral grand-standing here but careful analysis of the many ethical problems thrown up in today's humanitarian operations. Every chapter is a practical and constructive reflection on what is morally difficult when trying to improve the lives of people who have been deeply harmed by war and displacement, and who are doing everything in their power to survive and recover.

The book's concerns are well chosen and highly topical. Each chapter looks behind the public face of humanitarian action to the ethical questions that arise in doing it. We know only too well that healthcare facilities, ambulances, patients and staff are now regularly attacked. What do these attacks mean for the ethics of healthcare in such dangerous settings? Mental health is addressed in the book. How should we best respond to people's mental health problems when they reach almost epidemic proportion across large parts of the Syrian population? With limited resources, is it right to be driven by a highly individualistic human rights approach that aims to reach out to every vulnerable person? Perhaps it makes better moral sense to design a 'public good' response that focuses on select actors of influence who can improve general mental health even if this means focusing less on women and more on men.

Displacement, migration and volunteerism are also at the centre of several chapters. We have seen and applauded many thousands of volunteers rushing to help the increasing numbers of refugees and migrants arriving in Europe. But what is good and what is bad in such spontaneous manifestations of the humanitarian imperative, and what does this tell us about the strengths and weaknesses of first responders, and of a primarily empathic response? The perennial problem of programme closure and ethical exit is also well analysed to guide people as they seek to mitigate the worst effects of funding cuts and the reduction of services. Each one of these areas is ethically pressing today in the lived experience of affected populations and humanitarian workers.

Every field of human activity is ethically complicated. Despite the moral climate of high ideals that surrounds most human endeavour, real life takes place in an operational context of imperfect power, coercion, threat, lack of resources, competition and confusion. Humanitarian action is no exception. This book spells out the difficulties that arise when humanitarian action and ethics are thought about together, and it offers us solutions.

It is a great pleasure to commend this book to all those who finance, study or practically engage in humanitarian action. It will inform and improve the way you think and work. We must congratulate Ayesha Ahmad and James Smith for bringing together this valuable collection. The editors and contributors are part of an exciting new group of scholar-practitioners engaged in humanitarian action and each of their chapters has nudged the field of ethics and humanitarian action further forward, and kept it real in the process.

This is a book we need and I hope it will spur on further study of the ethics of humanitarian action.

Dr Hugo Slim
Head of Policy, International Committee of the Red Cross
Geneva, 17 September 2017

FOREWORD: ON THE FRONT LINES OF HUMANITARIAN MEDICAL ETHICS

Vickie Hawkins and Paul McMaster

A remote area of Somalia. It was shortly after midnight when a young woman in labour reached the Médecins Sans Frontières (MSF) hospital. She was bleeding heavily. An emergency Caesarean section would be needed. A risky, yet routine procedure. But, for the MSF team on site it presented a significant challenge. The gravity of the situation was discussed with the female patient but she wished for her husband to give consent on her behalf, which he would not do even with sensitive and careful explanation. As the bleeding became worse, the team had to face either losing both a young woman and child or persuading her to go against her husband's wishes – with possible consequences for her in the long term.

The Afghanistan–Pakistan border. The lines on the turbaned man's face told the story of a tough life. 'Tell the world', he said, as he sat beneath the flimsy piece of plastic sheeting that he and his family called home. 'Tell the world about the inhuman circumstances in which they keep us here.' He was one of 7,000 refugees trapped in a tight, dusty no-man's land between Pakistan and Afghanistan, after the Pakistani border had been closed. They could not go forward, and they would not go back to the violence from which they had fled. MSF had opened a transit clinic at the border post, which quickly turned into a more comprehensive service. Small amounts of food were being distributed by another NGO, but the water, sanitation and shelter were dire. There were already cases of measles and malnutrition rates were climbing. We had privately called on the Pakistani government to re-open the border and allow at least this small group to cross and access the official camps. But our private calls were having no impact. At what point did we start to publicly tell the story of these 7,000 Afghans and decry the situation? It would increase pressure on the government, but it could draw a negative response. They could block our access and prevent us from drawing more attention to the situation.

Port au Prince, Haiti. Following the earthquake in 2010 an MSF field team rapidly ran out of antibiotics and anaesthetic agents yet faced multiple cases of children requiring emergency surgery. They had to choose between delaying surgery, risking septic shock and the children's deaths, or operating in conditions that posed just as many risks. What was in the child's 'best' interest, and who would understand and consent to an intervention, since many of the parents had been lost in the quake? Was the significant increased surgical risk acceptable? As the surgeon in the team put it, 'I may be dammed if I do operate and probably the children dammed if I don't.'

As a humanitarian medical organisation, Médecins Sans Frontières/Doctors Without Borders (MSF) grapples with these ethical questions every day.

Our dilemmas start with the needs of individual patients. How do we help a woman asking for a termination of pregnancy in a country where cultural norms and legal restrictions officially prevent us from providing such a service, and could lead to closure of the project should we be found to have helped her? Or a fistula patient suffering the effects of a botched operation but who needs to be referred back to the same surgeon as the only obstetric specialist in the area?

We face dilemmas when we make decisions about projects. Do we provide lifesaving secondary healthcare in a camp, aware that it may give the government additional grounds to restrict residents' movements and avoid referrals to the nearest Ministry of Health facility? In an HIV programme, where demands for treatment far outreach what we can provide, how do we justify our process of triage that prioritises those with the most advanced HIV, sending away those who are less sick only for them to return months later emaciated and now sick enough to meet our criteria?

And we face dilemmas at an organisational level. How do we decide between giving priority to a new treatment for a fatal yet neglected disease that remains hugely expensive and with which we can treat only a limited number of patients, when we could dedicate the same level of resources to reaching hundreds of thousands cut off from primary healthcare in a conflict situation? And how do we decide when to speak out and condemn endemic persecution, violence and abuse, aware that by doing so we will likely cut ourselves off from a community forever?

In recent years, the role of ethics in our decision-making at all levels has taken greater prominence. Medical ethics already informs our clinical practice and underpins the medical research we undertake, which undergoes extensive ethical review. We involve ethicists in decisions about the design of our projects and the decisions we make about speaking out, in particular to advise us on the prospect of doing harm.

We are increasingly drawing upon procedural ethics as a way of helping decide how we prioritise our resources. Prioritisation discussions are often emotive and involve tensions between what different individuals find important. By applying procedural ethics in a decision-making process, we are not seeking to reach or impose an ethical consensus or displace the role that both instinct and experience still need to play in complex environments that regularly fail to conform to expectations. We are making decisions based on a process that is transparent, and that all involved can agree is reasonable and defensible, despite their differences.

An essential part of that process is our investment in preparing our staff to work through ethical questions. We are introducing ethical frameworks as part of our induction programmes, ensuring medics and senior managers feel prepared, and that those starting their journey with MSF are more aware of the harsh reality of impossible decisions from an early stage. For example, in conflict settings, a team can face immense challenges with numbers of patients that far outweigh their capacity. In such a setting, the decision-making process of triage is widely practised as the only way to manage an impossible situation and determine medical priorities, choosing which patients will undergo medical treatment first. To those not fully trained in triage, it can be almost impossible to manage and may be deeply distressing.

This is the truth of humanitarian work: the kind of decisions that individuals affected by humanitarian crises, and by extension those that seek to help them, are faced with are often of the 'tragic dilemma' variety: decisions that present you with no ethically right choice, that leave you grappling with that which is the least worst.

Vickie Hawkins, Executive Director MSF UK
Dr Paul McMaster
London, 6 November 2017

INTRODUCTION: *NARRATING* HUMANITARIAN ACTION AND ETHICS

Ayesha Ahmad

This book represents a *perfect storm*: of what happens when there are collisions between the good intentions of shaping our world to be a better place and the tensions of forming a universal rhetoric to describe the beliefs, values and ethics of *who to protect, how to protect and why to protect* lives, societies and cultures, during crises that threaten *who we are* and the *way that we live*. A humanitarian crisis, by virtue of its nature, embodies chaos, and the ensuing outcome is complex. The challenge for this book was to devise a space for narrating humanitarian action and ethics that does not hold simplicity as an end goal. Ethics is not about answers. Any form or presentation of ethics, in our context, represents a moral obligation to see the sublime in the way we treat humanitarian analyses – especially under the guises of tackling injustice, promoting peace and maintaining the sacredness of all human lives.

This edited volume seeks to capture a pluralism of themes, rich reflections and the diverse challenges that expose the complexity of *encounters with ethics* during humanitarian action. Against the backdrop of case studies, academic research, and reflections on humanitarian responses to various crises, we emphasise the importance of shifting discussions from conclusions to open-ended dialogues to bring ethics into the rhetoric of humanitarian action. As such, this book sought to create a space in which to convey written narratives of lived experiences, in-depth observations derived from fieldwork, and other critical analyses. We emphasise the need for the importance of *expanding* ethics, rather than *reducing* ethics. We invite a non-exhaustive critique of our values towards our human condition, especially during times of trauma, to come into play.

The book naturally converged into themes that focus on humanitarian action, namely action that aims to save lives, action with the goal of alleviating suffering, and what it means to protect human dignity during, and in the aftermath of, crises caused by conflict or disasters.

A unique feature of the book was the open exploration of the lived experience of humanitarian actors, and the proactive examination of the nature of relationships in humanitarian practice, i.e. relationships within and between humanitarian organisations, within affected communities, and between humanitarian actors and the recipients of humanitarian assistance. For this reason, it has always been our intention that this book should convey a range of personal experiences, empirical research and, exploratory conceptual work to approach both creatively and constructively the practical issues faced in contemporary humanitarian response as well as to scrutinise the theoretical frameworks in which principles of ethics are situated.

As the chapter contributions began to take shape, we discovered that only by offering an equal platform to contributors from a diversity of disciplinary backgrounds, each with their own methodological approaches and analytical tools, could we begin to capture the extreme complexity of ethical reflections when exposed to the fragility and precariousness of the human condition. However, as we began to examine individual contributions, we found fragmentation: epistemological tributaries that lacked a point of convergence at which they could be understood in their full, shared complexity. During this process, we began to appreciate that there remains a fundamental disconnect between the conceptual frameworks and the disciplinary experiences that seek to make sense of the various aspects of a humanitarian crisis. It is our hope that *Humanitarian Action and Ethics* conveys the paradoxical and contradictory nature of what it takes – and what is needed – to hold an ethical lens to contemporary humanitarian action, in its many forms, illustrating the interplay of locating and then responding to the ethics within humanitarian action, and, in turn, undertaking the deconstruction of an illusory vision of absolute goodness and justice.

The ways in which humanity is interpreted and enacted during disasters, conflict, and other forms humanitarian crisis, symbolise the essence of human life. In principle, humanitarian action is the epitome of a force that counter-acts death, destruction and degradation. Furthermore, humanitarian action is a normative category that prescribes quite a specific mode of being, namely that of action. In this sense, humanitarian action is primarily viewed and assessed by the presence of humanitarian intervention as an equaliser to the de-humanising scenes of devastation that form the popularised rhetoric of conflict and other crises. The entirety of humanitarian action is served through its tangibility – its physicality – and its ability to bear the unbearable. Yet, there is also a strong theoretical foundation, such as the principles of humanitarianism, which originally were the seeds for its growth in our global world, in providing aid to those in need during humanitarian crises, regardless of who or where the victims are.

Humanitarian actors are required to navigate uncertain and unprecedented terrains, yet understanding the infiniteness of the human condition is pressured into compact forms and categories under the weight of dominant, positivistic and ultimately, reductionist, discourses from medicine.

Conceptualising humanitarianism, and the ethics *of*, *in*, and *beyond* humanitarian response and its representative organisations and other actors, is challenged by such dominant and privileging discourses that essentialise the body of humanitarian action and ethics as a physical presence to outweigh devastation and destruction. The focal points for ethical reflection that we identify in this book are the fissures where, although not exhaustively, we define injustice, violence, harm, suffering, failure, and apathy over empathy. Importantly, it is vital that good intentions are unpacked from the phenomenological enactment of resultant interventions.

Ethical reflection, as a component of a much broader discourse on health, has been subject to an accelerated incorporation into the structures and systems of institutions, organisations, and guidelines that shape contemporary health practice. The isolation of sub-disciplines such as medical ethics or bioethics in scientific medicine is typically traced to the development of technologies that have altered the margins of human life. Yet this representation has created the view that ethics is a symbolic separation of the *ethical* from the actual: ethics thus continues to run the risk of being perceived as 'surplus'. We need to write *Humanitarian Action and Ethics* to describe the perspective of and focus on ethics in order to bring these together – it should be the case that ethics is conceptualised as inherent to any discourse pertaining to humanitarian action. The process of responding to the lack of conceptual and pragmatic space for ethical reflection requires confronting the unfamiliarity of ethics, and instead promoting the view that ethics is ever-present and never indistinguishable from humanity. Recognising the presence of an ethical issue, either at the individual interface between crisis-affected person and humanitarian responder, or at the organisational level, is a marker of conscience and conscientiousness. While we recognise that identification of an ethical problem does not in and of itself redress structural violence, remedy organisational inefficacies, rectify human rights violations, or overcome barriers to the provision of effective and equitable healthcare, we do see in ethical reflection a call to challenge, mitigate, and ultimately to change, the discourse of suffering.

Further normative questions arise about the future for the nature of humanitarianism. In the context of an interconnected world, the alienation and forming of the *Other* is at a crucial point in terms of the potential to exercise its diminishing. Understanding who is affected by humanitarian crises is now in an unprecedented sphere of relation due to migration and communication. The distance that often occupied the central space of the dichotomy between *us* and *them* is disappearing. Similarly, the global impact of humanitarian crises has given rise to more of a global incentive to understand the phenomena of human suffering in these contexts. The human stories, and the juxtapositions between suffering and the alleviation of it, are the ethical challenges that humanitarian action must accommodate.

Humanitarian ethics is vulnerable to the sensitivities of drawing attention to ethical complexities because of the pressures to provide good outcomes in emergency missions while maintaining respect for cultural legacies. Infusing ethics with societal frames of reference such as culture or gender is a further reason why we have called for a focus on ethics in humanitarian action through this edited volume. We hope to decrease conformity with the traditional ethical frameworks from positivistic and universal motivations in medicine which have been extended into humanitarian action. The nuances that our chapter contributors perceived and brought to light illustrate that the ethics of humanitarian action go beyond the standardised frameworks of medical ethics or traditional humanitarian principles. At the same time, we further hope to redress this balance and to increase freedom of engagement with ethical issues.

The limitations of the availability and accessibility of considering humanitarian action and ethics either in the form of this edited volume or in the form of adequate platforms in education, training, and practice, are in flux. There is potential for the direction of humanitarian action and ethics to be influenced. A better understanding of disasters and the factors that result in a humanitarian crisis is helping us to see crises on a continuum. In other words, the disaster is no longer an event but a complex, irreducible collection of social, (geo)political, historical, cultural and environmental processes.

To bring it together, then, the edited volume is a symbol of the voices of humanitarianism. The chapters echo the aliveness of the issues that are critically discussed and analysed in academic frameworks and theories. The open-endedness of the ethical questions that our contributors present underscores the continuation of the silenced or unquiet ethical dilemmas that are being encountered globally. The overlooking of or struggle to provide resources for examining ethics on the field during humanitarian action is also paired with the sensitivities that go hand in hand with the nature of the ethical interface of humanitarianism with conflicts and crises. We view our edited volume as a platform to continue to raise discussions of humanitarian action and ethics.

Our predecessor and author of one of our forewords, Dr Hugo Slim, International Committee of the Red Cross, has paved a solid foundation both for us and the future of humanitarian ethics. Our case studies present a continuation of Slim's in-depth theoretical exposé of the need to find ways to conceptualise, analyse, and understand the normative implications of humanitarian responses and interventions. We hope our edited volume goes some way to help scribe the ethics of humanitarian action into an acceptable format; and to promote a shift in culture and discourse towards recognising that ethics is a reflection on taking care of the ways in which we treat humanity, and that supressing or burying ethical issues is a form of turning a blind eye, which is ultimately the antithesis of humanitarian action. Humanitarian action and ethics, therefore, is our attempt alongside our contributors, to offer a conceptual intervention for understanding humanity in the face of adversity.

1 | DIFFICULT DECISION-MAKING, COMPROMISE, AND MORAL DISTRESS IN MEDICAL HUMANITARIAN RESPONSE

James Smith

Introduction[1]

Humanitarian actors are often faced with multiple and repeated pressures in challenging and dynamic contexts. The practice of humanitarian medicine in such situations regularly demands that staff make difficult decisions, which in turn can have significant ethical implications. In 'Compromised Humanitarianism' Cullity (2010: 155) draws on the same fundamental premise to ask, 'how can humanitarianism operate in such conditions [as it characteristically must] without itself becoming morally compromised?'

For an organisation like Médecins Sans Frontières/Doctors Without Borders (MSF), which actively 'rejects the idea that poor people deserve third-rate medical care and [in turn] strives to provide high-quality care to patients' (MSF, n.d.) making concessions during the implementation of programmes can be the source of profound moral discomfort.

As a partial response to the difficulties inherent in humanitarian decision-making, and in recognition of inconsistencies in the outcome of such processes over time and in different contexts, a growing body of scholarship has sought to explore the political and procedural factors that shape decision-making in humanitarian programmes (Fuller, 2012; Le Pape, 2011: 248; Michael & Zwi, 2002). This pursuit is perceived as a desire to better make, justify, and defend choices, and to minimise moral discomfort. Such efforts are further bolstered by repeated sector-wide calls for greater accountability and transparency in the development and implementation of humanitarian programmes (Clarinval & Biller-Andorno, 2014).

While it is widely recognised that a degree of compromise is inevitable in *humanitarian decision-making*, and the broader practice of medical humanitarianism, the development of ethically informed and experientially derived frameworks with which to approach such issues is as of yet incomplete. In recognition of the humanitarian's position as 'moral entrepreneur' (Brauman, 2012: 20), this paper draws from selected peer-reviewed publications, reports and presentations to situate current debates pertaining to humanitarian decision-making, compromise, and moral distress in medical humanitarian response.

The Humanitarian Predicament

The practice of humanitarian medicine is broadly characterised by the provision of immediate, yet often prolonged, assistance to crisis-affected populations. Given the scale, scope and dynamism of needs in such situations and the finite resources available to humanitarian organisations, staff are regularly pressed to make decisions related to both the allocation of resources at the project level, and the distribution of their programme of activities within a much broader national, regional and global spatial frame (Hunt, 2008; Calain & Schwartz, 2014). Additional contextual constraints such as suboptimal access, insecurity, and inadequate supporting infrastructure, and internal constraints such as shifting intra-organisational priorities, further complicate the ability to deliver medical humanitarian assistance.

Over the course of the last 45 years, Médecins Sans Frontières/ Doctors Without Borders (MSF) has provided 'emergency aid to people affected by armed conflict, epidemics, natural disasters and exclusion from healthcare' (MSF, ND). Following MSF's receipt of the Nobel Peace Prize in 1999, then MSF International President James Orbinski acknowledged the humanitarian's responsibility to respond 'wherever in the world there is manifest distress'. This core commitment is central to MSF's Charter, and is often recited as a constitutive component of the humanitarian identity.

However, irrespective of the strength of the commitment to alleviating suffering, the impetus to assist populations in need is rarely commensurate with the financial, human, and other material resources available to fully realise this commitment in any given context (Michael & Zwi, 2002). As such, with very few exceptions difficult decision-making has become a defining feature of medical humanitarian response. De Waal captures this sentiment in his own analysis of 'humanitarian's tragedies', when he describes the context in which humanitarianism is practised as 'a world in which human ideals fail to match the realities of the human condition' (2010: 130). Utilising a term first coined by Calabresi and Bobbitt, Heyse argues that the same discrepancy between the number of crisis-affected people worldwide, and the finite means with which to respond to their resultant needs, prompts humanitarian organisations to make 'tragic choices' (2013: 69–70).

In this respect, we can speak of the inevitability – though not necessarily an *acceptance* – of difficult decision-making, which in turn necessitates an exploration of the terms on which compromise is negotiated, and of its impact on those who are compromised. Such work inevitably derives from a growing body of research related to choices and decision-making (Fuller, 2006; Heyse, 2013), quality and standards of care (Brauman & Beck, 2017), and the principles and motivations that underpin medical humanitarian response (Rességuier, 2017; see Komenská, this volume).

The issue of compromise at the macro level – often reported in relation to access and negotiation, and the withdrawal of humanitarian activities – has been expounded elsewhere, and establishes an additional layer of complexity that cannot be overlooked in any comprehensive exploration of decision-making and compromise at the interpersonal – or micro – level. Nevertheless, authors have dedicated much effort to outlining such issues in other fora, and for the purpose of this paper, while reference is made in passing to macro-level issues, I simply signpost here some seminal comprehensive and empirically informed contributions (Rieff, 2002; Terry, 2002; Magone, Neuman & Weissman, 2012).

Multi-tiered Ethical Challenges

Existing research related to ethical issues in decision-making in humanitarian response can be broadly divided into three categories. The first encompasses literature that explores meta-level organisational decision-making processes (Heyse, 2013), with a focus on key themes such as priority-setting (Fuller, 2012), justice (Rubenstein, 2009), the fair distribution of resources (Hurst, Mezger & Mauron, 2009), legitimacy (Calain, 2012), accountability (Hilhorst, 2002), and solidarity (Tiller, 2016). At the meta-level, these questions are concerned with the decision to intervene in a given context, with subsequent attention paid to the consequence of such actions, and the opportunity cost of intervention. Related scholarly work has interrogated the accuracy and conduct of needs assessments (Bradbury et al., 2003; Darcy & Hofmann, 2003; de Geoffroy & Grunewald, 2008) and the decision to withdraw assistance (Abramowitz, 2016; see Hunt & Miao, this volume).

Decisions at both the meta (identity) and macro levels account for a multitude of competing priorities, against which the consequent composition of medical assistance can be determined. However, at the micro level – in this case, the level of the clinical encounter – meta- and macro-level decisions become less immediately relevant, as individual healthcare providers are faced with the challenge of delivering medical care to individual patients (see Figure 1.1). As such, a second category of research has emerged; qualitative studies have attempted to profile the challenges faced by staff in the delivery of medical humanitarian assistance, and have identified a number of key themes, along with possible solutions that may protect against 'moral distress' (Jameton, 1984), or assist in the dissipation of 'moral residue' (Webster & Baylis, 2000) (see Table 1.1).

Ethics at the Level of the Clinical Encounter

Hunt and colleagues have defined two recurrent features identifiable in many humanitarian crises in low-resource contexts: contextual

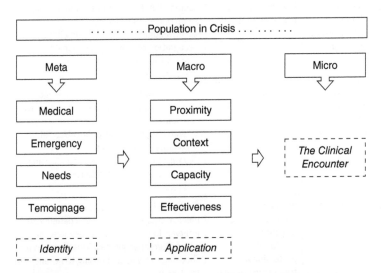

Figure 1.1 A schematic overview of key meta-, macro-, and micro-level considerations as related to a medical humanitarian organisation such as MSF.

TABLE 1.1 A summary of qualitative studies that have explored the moral experience and ethical challenges faced by humanitarian workers.

Study	Population	Key Findings
Gotowiec & Cantor-Graae (2017)	8 humanitarian healthcare providers	Four key themes: Ethics as a sense of right and wrong; Adversely bearing the burden of choice; Being held hostage by institutional constraints; and Difficulty in preparing for ethical challenges.
Asgary & Lawrence (2014)	44 medical humanitarians (MSF, IRC, ICRC, STC, ACF, WHO, UNHCR, etc.) (91% North American/European)	Personal responsibility to provide assistance; Identification with organisational mission; A broad mix of both positive and negative emotional responses; and A majority experience of burnout, and a diversity of associated coping mechanisms.
Nilsson et al. (2011)	16 employees of the Swedish Rescue Services Agency (managerial, operational)	A number of contextual factors affect humanitarian activities: formalities – laws, regulations, culture, safety aspects, media. 'The typical humanitarian assistance professional acts as a filter on this framework by interpreting the meaning of these conditions.'
Hunt (2009, 2010) (see also Hunt et al., 2012; Hunt et al., 2013)	18 Canadian professionals (15 healthcare, 3 HR/ management)	Five key themes identified: Motivations and expectations; Relational nature of humanitarian work; Steep power imbalances; Acknowledging and confronting limits; and Recognition of how organisational forms and structures shape the moral experience.
Schwartz et al. (2010) (see also Schwartz et al., 2012)	20 Canadian health professionals	Four main sources of ethical challenges: Resource scarcity and the need to allocate resources; Overarching historical/political/social/ commercial structures; Organisational policies and agendas; and Perceived norms related to roles and interactions.
Sinding et al. (2010)	20 health professionals (9 organisations, receipt of professional training in Canada)	Distinction between medication and medical equipment as either a patient care intervention, or as a scarce resource, for which alternative justifications are given for choosing to treat, or choosing to refrain from treatment

Hunt (2008)	10 humanitarian workers (9 medical, 1 NGO director)	Five themes identified: Tension between respect for local values and imposition; Barriers to providing adequate care; Differing understandings of health and illness; Identity of humanitarian workers; and Trust and distrust – interaction with local communities
Bjerneld et al. (2004)	20 Swedish medical humanitarians	Six themes identified: Positive feelings associated with humanitarian work; Frustration and stress – security, physical conditions, staffing, language barriers, isolation, poor planning; Lack of preparation; Perception of other actors – competency, structure; Factors affecting success – experience, diversity of skills; and Role of the NGO – recruitment, debriefing, guidelines.

insufficiency, which is to say a lack of the required personnel, material and financial resources, and infrastructure required to meet the needs of the local population; and dramatically increased population needs (Hunt et al., 2014). The so-called moral landscape of humanitarian response is further shaped by: cultural and power differences between staff and the local population, and within teams; organisational work practices that promote a culture of self-sacrifice in the face of overwhelming needs; and minimal regulatory oversight and a lack of clear guidance (Hunt, 2011). Given the imbalance between needs and means, humanitarians are pressed to practice a multidimensional 'ethics of insufficiency' of sorts, as they recalibrate their practice within a diversity of complex contexts. The aforementioned themes can thus be loosely categorised as follows:

Action Beyond Capacity: Humanitarian healthcare providers are regularly pressed to engage in the distribution of scarce resources. This is further exacerbated by often extensive population needs, for which medical activities constitute only a partial response. Capacity can be further constrained not only by contextual pressures, but by organisational decisions related to the staffing of programmes, and whether or not to invest in particular activities (Schwartz et al., 2010). This is pertinent in the case of vertical programmes that are artificially limited in scope (Devakumar, 2010), and emergency programmes that are similarly limited in scope, often as a result of logistical, security, and other barriers. In such circumstances, healthcare providers may be pressed to practice a form of triage, the terms for which may not be universally accepted by all members of a team. Important here is the way in which 'capacity' is interpreted by healthcare providers, and of the ways in which capacity and scarcity may be negotiated and disputed both between and within teams.

Action Beyond Culture: International humanitarian workers are transposed from often dramatically different healthcare environments, frequently without a strong prior appreciation of cultural differences or of variation in the socio-cultural dynamics of health, illness, death, and dying. As Hunt states, 'the moral dimension of humanitarian work is rendered more complex by the international and transcultural nature of this work' (2011: 606). If poorly understood and actioned, cultural dynamics can cause problems, particularly in relation to hierarchies of power and intra-team relations (Schwartz et al., 2010). Unsurprising is reference to cultural relativism in the available qualitative literature (ibid.). Importantly, cultural factors are shaped by individual subjectivities; existing research has focused predominantly on the experience of North American and European staff, whose socio-cultural experience may differ from that of colleagues who have lived, worked, and developed their professional expertise elsewhere.

Action Beyond Competence: Given the scale and scope of humanitarian needs, it is not uncommon for humanitarian healthcare providers to be pressed to make, and act on, decisions beyond their level of competence (Hunt, Schwartz & Fraser, 2013). Such is the often unexpected and rapidly changing nature of humanitarian crises. This is further problematised by a lack of clear regulatory oversight, and an absence of clear systems and processes for accountability (Hunt, 2011).

Acting Beyond Context: Humanitarian crises have a tendency to exist in close relation with existing or historic social and political systems and structures that perpetuate injustice, violence, and exploitation. Humanitarian healthcare providers may recognise the complex underlying causes of a humanitarian crisis, while constrained by the inherent limits of humanitarian response. This may pose an additional challenge for healthcare providers who must attempt to operate within the space afforded to medical humanitarian action in such settings.

Aspects of public health ethics are clearly identifiable in each of the above categories. To some humanitarian workers the challenge – arguably only partially reconcilable – manifests as a need to achieve some form of equilibrium between the rule of rescue, and the inevitable focus on aggregate populations and interventions that seek to best distribute medical assistance. Value pluralism, and the subjective weight afforded to individual values, principles, professional and organisational codes of practice, legal frameworks, and so on, naturally present a major challenge for humanitarian healthcare providers. These values and principles together comprise an ethical matrix of sorts, which is likely to be interpreted and actioned in a diversity of different ways dependent on the personal and professional experience of individual healthcare providers.

Exploring Difficult Choices and Moral Dilemmas

The plurality of principles and values available by which to guide isolated and cumulative actions can cause distress, particularly when such values appear to contradict one another (Fuller, 2003; Gotowiec & Cantor-Graae, 2017). MSF staff are continually reminded that 'the individual medical-humanitarian act ... is central to the work of MSF' (Le Pape, 2011). However, if this were truly the case, medical assistance would adopt an expansive characteristic, continually shifting and adapting to meet the needs of patients in an ever-increasing number of contexts worldwide.

Achieving 'health', as defined by the World Health Organization (ND), is an iterative process that is difficult to fully realise, even with the support of the most optimally resourced of health systems. As medical technologies and new forms of treatment emerge, health professionals are further pressed to adapt their practice in pursuit of the most effective treatment for their patients. If such an abstract circumstance were to exist, it may be possible to provide care with no concern for the opportunity cost and comparative implications of a singular, individualised care plan. However, individual health needs rarely exist in isolation. As such, healthcare practitioners, irrespective of their geographic location, are pressed to consider other features relevant to the provision of healthcare services to the wider community (Hunt, 2011). With this in mind, concern for decision-making processes, the fair distribution of resources for health, and the rationing of healthcare has come to be recognised as a constitutive component of contemporary medical practice. Notwithstanding such globally generalisable observations, the most apparent difference between decision-making in a rural healthcare facility on the dynamic frontline of a conflict-affected country, and decision-making in a well-resourced, financially solvent hospital in a high-income country is that thresholds for rationing are surpassed more rapidly in the former, and that pressure to make decisions is therefore experienced earlier and more intensively in the resource constrained context.

Such considerations naturally pose a challenge for humanitarian healthcare providers, whose commitment to a particular patient is destabilised by the need to share concern for other present and potential future patients. Similarly, this commitment is further tested by an inability to meet patient needs consistently and comprehensively in many contexts. As outlined earlier, the tension between individual and aggregate population needs is well established, and a source of repeated concern for many humanitarian healthcare providers. The need to make such choices can form the basis for a moral dilemma, from which may be derived moral distress and, if unresolved, ultimately moral residue.

Navigating the Semantics

Notably, Slim identifies a number of key distinctions between true moral dilemmas and what he refers to as tough choices (Slim, 1997). He identifies the following as tough choices that do not represent true moral dilemmas: a tough choice that wavers on uncertain evidence; a tough choice for which the moral reasons for or against action conflict with non-moral reasons; a tough choice between two good options; and choices that are not made between competing principles, but which are rather 'hellish choices'. In contrast, true moral dilemmas are defined by Blackburn as 'situations in which each possible course of action breaches some otherwise binding moral principle' (1994: 315).

Lepora takes this line of scholarship further in her study of compromise, defining compromise as a necessary trade-off between 'matters of principled concern – fundamental values, moral principles, personal agency, integrity, honour, rights, dignity' (2012: 3). The act of compromising necessarily requires the suppression of one or more matters of principled concern in order to satisfy another. As Hoffmaster and Hooker explain in their study of the selection process for renal transplantation, 'compromise aspires to satisfy each of the conflicting values, principles, or obligations partially and proportionately to its importance in the situation' (2013: 547).

Of note, Lepora also identifies a clear distinction between compromise and the following distinct processes: deliberation over interests of non-principled concern, presented as either an intra-personal choice or as a process of interpersonal bargaining; the correction and subsequent abandonment of a mistaken belief on further interrogation of the new or pre-existing information on which one's original position was determined; the full resolution of a dispute of moral importance, whereby the commonly agreed outcome leads to full settlement; the complete capitulation of a matter of principled concern in favour of another, which therefore eliminates the original source of tension; and the suppression of one party's principles by a dominant other, which represents a unilateral concession rather than a mutual compromise.

Beyond the semantic, these distinctions highlight the need for a thorough interrogation of the individual's experience of humanitarian action, and of their subjective interpretation of the values and principles that ultimately distinguish between tough choice, ethical challenge, or moral dilemma. For example, an issue that constitutes a moral dilemma for one member of staff may be perceived as a tough choice by another. Similarly, the rise of evidence-based practice and of protocol-driven care may lead to the abandonment of what Lepora terms a 'mistaken belief', and thus have the effect of reshaping what an individual would have once considered an act of compromise with moral consequence. With further qualitative examination, such speculative hypotheses can be better scrutinised.

Moral Distress and Its Impact

Pertinent to this line of enquiry is recognition that ethical challenges can have a detrimental impact on individual physical, emotional, and psychological wellbeing (Cardozo et al., 2012; Walsh, 2009). Notably, such consequences can also have a negative impact on the ability of healthcare providers to deliver patient care (Gotowiec & Cantor-Graae, 2017).

Of relevance in such situations is the concept of moral distress, which first emerged in the nursing care literature in the 1980s. Moral distress is defined as the result of a situation in which an individual is aware of the morally right cause of action, but is unable to act on such an awareness (Jameton, 1984). A two-phase process follows, in which an individual experiences initial distress, and later reactive distress, often referred to as moral residue. Such situations ultimately result in the compromise of an individual's moral integrity. While the term is rarely employed in such explicit terms in the humanitarian literature, the available qualitative studies illustrate the negative impact of aspects of the humanitarian experience on individual wellbeing. In their study of ethical challenges in humanitarian crises, Gotowiec and Cantor-Graae (2017) document a series of negative emotional responses among participants, including anger, frustration, outrage, sadness, and despair. In the same study, the authors capture the residual feeling of a resistance to continuing humanitarian work, while Nilsson et al. raise the profound concern that, 'by not paying attention to the consequences of moral stress, individuals might risk losing moral sensitivity and moral awareness' (2011: 66).

Such research raises the important question of the organisational duty of care to our staff, and of the extent of MSF's responsibility to minimise harm done to employees during the course of their work. More practical concerns relate to the impact of difficult experiences and the lack of resolution of morally distressing circumstances, on staff attrition and possible early departure (Gotowiec & Cantor-Graae, 2017). These issues continue to present a major human resource challenge for organisations like MSF, which continues to struggle to tackle the issue of staff retention.

Compromise in Medical Humanitarian Response

Recognising not only MSF's refusal to accept injustice, but also the inevitable need to make difficult decisions and their very real consequences for those who feel responsible for such decisions and their outcomes, how has the organisation defined its approach?

During the Nobel Peace Prize acceptance speech, Orbinski made the first explicit reference to MSF's commitment to an 'ethic of refusal': 'the refusal of all forms of problem-solving through sacrifice of the weak and vulnerable' (1999). This ethic of refusal is borne out of a history of repeated episodes of compromise, and represents a resistance to the unopposed domination of a single idea or action, which unchallenged could cause human suffering. Such an approach seeks to promote structural justice by refusing to bow to the systemic causes of inequality.

From Refusal to Resistance

The ethics of refusal has been further expounded by both Redfield in his profile of the history and ethics of MSF's humanitarian activities (2013), and separately by Rubenstein (2015: 143–70) in her study of cost effectiveness in the humanitarian programmes of international non-governmental organisations. Both authors identify gaps in the ethics of refusal as a framework with which to interpret the actions of humanitarian organisations, given that it has a tendency to supress the global governance responsibilities of large-scale institutions in favour of political reflexivity. Redfield reflects on the dual implications of an ethics of refusal when he asks,

> How can one resist the imperative to choose amid crisis, particularly when operating independently in the name of conscience? Or rather, how to select even as one 'refuses' to choose? If MSF follows an ethic of action as well as refusal, then it must engage, under protest as it were, but also in a manner that appears to favor the good. (2013: 167)

Rubenstein proposes an alternative framework that recognises that, insofar as crisis demands choices, and choices in turn demand selection in order to facilitate action, the global governance responsibilities of humanitarian organisations demand a greater emphasis on 'political judgement'. This is considered particularly pertinent for MSF, as one of the five largest humanitarian NGOs, as determined by total expenditure (ALNAP, 2015: 40). This proposed framework, an 'ethics of resistance', acknowledges the multiple and often conflicting responsibilities of humanitarian organisations, and necessarily prompts that they justify their actions – and similarly any corresponding inaction – in any given setting.

Resistance as opposed to refusal does not therefore constitute an outright rejection, but instead is an expression of a continuous struggle to identify a course of action that achieves optimum outcomes. Recognising that for MSF 'every decision is a singular act and not made by the mechanical application of principles' (2006), it remains that this ethic of resistance is to be practised at the level of the individual encounter, and defended as a healthy and productive tension at both the micro and macro levels of organisational decision-making.

Actualising Resistance in Medical Humanitarian Response

Importantly, such acts of resistance require continuous reflection and evaluation, with a commitment to transparency and accountability in the decision-making process, and clear articulation of how and why certain decisions were made. While it will remain impossible to avoid acts of compromise in many of the contexts in which MSF works worldwide, resistance allows individual members of staff, and the organisation as a whole, to remain committed to the provision of competent care and the treatment of patients with compassion and dignity. Herein lies a critical distinction between recognition of compromising contexts, and the compromise of principles. It should be reiterated that it is imperative to maintain a commitment to, and respect for, human dignity, even in the most austere of circumstances, while simultaneously recognising the inevitable limitations of certain forms of programmatic response.

While it is imperative that organisations like MSF work to minimise the need to make tough choices and to practice medicine in a compromised form, it is the plurality of experience within MSF, and the tension created by differences of opinion, opposing perspectives, lived realities, and individual and organisational priorities, that allow for the practice of forms of medical humanitarian resistance which force 'MSF to continually challenge the limits of its response' (Shanks, 2010: 20).

Note

1 An early version of this paper was presented at the Humanitarian Action & Ethics symposium, held at Sciences Po, Paris on 26–27 May 2016. This paper was written in part while the author was employed with MSF's Research Unit on Humanitarian Stakes and Practices (UREPH). The development of this paper benefited hugely from insightful conversations with Tammam Aloudat, Philippe Calain, Caroline Abu Sa'Da, Amy Neilson, and MSF colleagues in South Sudan, for which I am very grateful.

References

Abramowitz, S (2016), What happens when MSF leaves? Humanitarian departure and medical sovereignty in post-conflict Liberia. In: Abramowitz, S & Panter-Brick, C (eds) *Medical humanitarianism: ethnographies of practice*. Philadelphia: University of Pennsylvania Press.

ALNAP (2015), *The state of the humanitarian system*. London: ALNAP/ODI.

Asgary, R & Lawrence, K (2014), Characteristics, determinants and perspectives of experienced medical humanitarians: a qualitative approach. *BMJ Open*. 4: e006460.

Bjerneld, M, Lindmark, G, Diskett, P & Garrett, MJ (2004), Perceptions of work in humanitarian assistance: interviews with returning Swedish health professionals. *Disaster Management & Response*. 2: 101–8.

Blackburn, S (1994), *The Oxford dictionary of philosophy*. Oxford: Oxford University Press.

Bradbury, M, Hofmann, C-H, Maxwell, S, Venekamp, D & Montani, A (2003), *Measuring humanitarian needs. Needs assessment and resource allocation in Southern Sudan and Somalia*. HPG Background Paper. London: HPG-ODI.

Brauman, R (2012), *Humanitarian medicine*. Paris: MSF CRASH.

Brauman, R & Beck, M (2017), Médecins Sans Frontières and medical quality [online]. Available from: www.msf-crash.org/en/publications/medicine-and-public-health/medecins-sans-frontieres-and-medical-quality (accessed 29 November 2017).

Calain, P (2012), In search of the 'new informal legitimacy' of Médecins Sans Frontières. *Public Health Ethics*. Vol. 5 (1): 56–66.

Calain, P & Schwartz, L (2014), *How does MSF allocate humanitarian assistance: the place of ethical reasoning and social construction*. [Internal report]. Geneva: MSF.

Cardozo, LB, Crawford, CG, Eriksson, C, Zhu, J, Sabin, M, Ager, A, … Simon, W (2012), Psychological distress, depression, anxiety, and burnout among international humanitarian aid workers: a longitudinal study. *PLOS One*. 7: e44948.

Clarinval, C & Biller-Andorno, N (2014), Challenging operations: an ethical framework to assist humanitarian aid workers in their decision-making processes. *PLOS Currents Disasters*. DOI: 10.1371/currents.dis.96bec99f138 00a8059bb5b5a82028bbf.

Cullity, G (2010), Compromised humanitarianism. In: Horton, K & Roche, C (eds). *Ethical questions and international NGOs – an exchange between philosophers and NGOs*. Berlin: Springer.

Darcy, J & Hofmann, C-A (2003), According to need? Needs assessment and decision-making in the humanitarian sector. HPG Report 15. London: HPG-ODI.

de Geoffroy V & Grunewald F (2008), *Principle 6 of the Good Humanitarian Donorship Initiative: 'Allocate humanitarian funding in proportion to needs and on the basis of needs assessments'*. Plaisians, France: Groupe URD.

Devakumar, D (2010), Cholera and nothing more. *Public Health Ethics*. Vol. 3 (1): 53–4.

de Waal, A (2010), The humanitarians' tragedy: escapable and inescapable cruelties. *Disasters*. Vol. 34 (s2): s130–7.

Fuller, L (2003), *Many missions, one voice. Justice & integrity in MSF operational choices*. Amsterdam: MSF.

Fuller, L (2006), Justified commitments? Considering resource allocation and fairness in Médecins Sans Frontières. *Developing World Bioethics*. Vol. 6 (2): 59–70.

Fuller, L (2012), Priority-setting in international non-governmental organisations: it is not as easy as ABCD. *Journal of Global Ethics*. 1–13.

Gotowiec, S & Cantor-Graae, E (2017), The burden of choice: a qualitative study of healthcare professionals' reactions to ethical challenges in humanitarian crises. *Journal of International Humanitarian Action*. Vol. 2 (2).

Heyse, L (2013), Tragic choices in humanitarian aid: a framework of organizational determinants of NGO decision making. *Voluntas*. Vol. 24: 68–92.

Hilhorst, D (2002), Being good at doing good? Quality and accountability of humanitarian NGOs. *Disasters*. Vol. 26 (3): 193–212.

Hoffmaster, B & Hooker, C (2013), Tragic choices and moral compromise: the ethics of allocating kidneys for transplantation. *The Milbank Quarterly*. Vol. 91 (3), 528–57.

Hunt, MR (2008), Ethics beyond borders: how health professionals experience ethics in humanitarian assistance and development work. *Developing World Bioethics*. Vol. 8 (2): 59–69.

Hunt, MR (2009), Resources and constraints for addressing ethical issues in medical humanitarian work: experiences of expatriate healthcare professionals. *American Journal of Disaster Medicine*. Vol. 4 (5): 261–71.

Hunt, MR (2010), Moral experience of Canadian healthcare professionals in humanitarian work. *Prehospital and Disaster Medicine*. Vol. 24 (6): 518–24.

Hunt, MR (2011), Establishing moral bearings: ethics and expatriate health care professionals in humanitarian work. *Disasters*. Vol. 35 (3): 606–22.

Hunt, MR, Schwartz, L & Fraser, V (2013), 'How far do you go and where are the issues surrounding that?' Dilemmas at the boundaries of clinical competency in humanitarian health work. *Prehospital and Disaster Medicine*. Vol. 28 (5): 502–8.

Hunt, MR, Schwartz, L, Sinding, C & Elit, L (2014), The ethics of engaged presence: a framework for health professionals in humanitarian assistance and development work. *Developing World Bioethics*. Vol. 14 (1): 47–55.

Hunt, MR, Sinding, C & Schwartz, L (2012), Tragic choices in humanitarian health work. *Journal of Clinical Ethics*. Vol. 23 (4): 333–44.

Hurst, SA, Mezger, N & Mauron, A (2009), Allocating resources in humanitarian medicine. *Public Health Ethics*. Vol. 2 (1): 89–99.

Jameton, A (1984), *Nursing practice: the ethical issues*. Englewood Cliffs, USA: Prentice Hall.

Le Pape, M (2011), In the name of emergency: how MSF adapts and justifies its choices. In: Magone, C, Neuman, M & Weissman, F (eds) *Humanitarian negotiations revealed: the MSF experience*. London: Hurst & Co. Publishers.

Lepora, C (2012), On compromise and being compromised. *Journal of Political Philosophy*. Vol. 20 (1): 1–22.

Magone, C, Neuman, M & Weissman, F (eds) (2012), *Humanitarian negotiations revealed: the MSF experience*. London: Hurst & Co. Publishers.

Michael, M & Zwi, AB (2002), Oceans of need in the desert: ethical issues identified while researching humanitarian agency response in Afghanistan. *Developing World Bioethics*. Vol. 2 (2): 109–130.

MSF (n.d.), About MSF [online]. Available from: www.msf.org/about-msf (accessed 7 February 2016).

MSF (2006), *The La Mancha Agreement*. 25 June 2006, Athens, Greece.

Nilsson, S, Sjoberg, M, Kallenberg, K & Larsson, G (2011), Moral stress in international humanitarian aid and rescue operations: a grounded theory study. *Ethics & Behavior*. Vol. 21 (1): 49–68.

Orbinski, J (1999), *Nobel lecture: receipt of the Nobel Peace Prize 1999 by Médecins Sans Frontières*. Oslo, Norway, 10 December 1999.

Redfield, P (2013), *Life in crisis: the ethical journey of Doctors Without Borders*. Berkeley: University of California Press.

Rességuier, A (2017), The moral sense of humanitarian actors: an empirical exploration. *Disasters*. Published online: 28 April 2017. DOI: 10.1111/disa.12234.

Rieff, D (2002), *A bed for the night: humanitarianism in crisis*. London: Vintage.

Rubenstein, J (2009), Humanitarian NGOs' duties of justice. *Journal of Social Philosophy*. Vol. 40 (4): 524–41.

Rubenstein, J (2015), *Between Samaritans and states: the political ethics of humanitarian iNGOs*. Oxford: Oxford University Press.

Schwartz, L, Hunt, M, Sinding, C, Elit, L, Redwood-Campbell, L, Adelson, N, ... Ranford, J (2012), Western clinical health ethics: how well do they travel to humanitarian contexts? In: Abu-Sa'Da, C (ed.) *Dilemmas, challenges, and ethics of humanitarian action: reflections on Médecins Sans Frontières' Perception Project*. Montreal: McGill-Queen's University Press.

Schwartz, L, Sinding, C, Hunt, M, Elit, L, Redwood-Campbell, L, Adelson, N, ... DeLaat, S (2010), Ethics in humanitarian aid work: learning from the narratives of humanitarian health workers. *AJOB Primary Research*. Vol. 1 (3): 45–54.

Shanks, L (2010), *25 years of medical humanitarian action*. Amsterdam: Médecins Sans Frontières.

Sinding, C, Schwartz, L, Hunt, M, Redwood-Campbell, L, Elit, L & Ranford, J (2010), 'Playing god because you have to': health professionals' narratives of rationing care in humanitarian and development work. *Public Health Ethics*. Vol. 3 (2): 147–56.

Slim, H (1997), Doing the right thing: relief agencies, moral dilemmas and moral responsibility in political emergencies and war. *Disasters*. Vol. 21: 244–57.

Terry, F (2002), *Condemned to repeat? The paradox of humanitarian action*. Ithaca, NY: Cornell University Press.

Tiller, S (2016), Where is the love? [Online]. Available from: www.msf.org.uk/article/opinion-and-debate-where-love (accessed 29 November 2017).

Walsh, D (2009), Interventions to reduce psychosocial disturbance following humanitarian relief efforts involving natural disasters: an integrative review. *International Journal of Nursing Practice*. Vol. 15: 231–40.

Webster, GC & Baylis, FE (2000), Moral residue. Pp. 217–30. In: Rubin, SB & Zoloth, L (eds) *Margin of error: the ethics of mistakes in the practice of medicine*. Hagerstown, USA: University Publishing Group.

WHO (ND), Constitution of the WHO: principles. [Online]. Available from: www.who.int/about/mission/en/ (accessed 22 February 2017).

2 | MORAL ENTANGLEMENT AND THE ETHICS OF CLOSING HUMANITARIAN PROJECTS

Matthew Hunt and Jingru Miao

Abstract

Humanitarian organisations and their staff regularly make and implement decisions to close projects. Such decisions are often challenging, and may be contested within an organisation. They also have enormous ramifications for communities that are in receipt of assistance. In this paper, we consider what obligations humanitarian organisations hold towards recipients of aid when a decision is made to end a humanitarian project. We argue that humanitarian projects have intrinsic, as well as instrumental, value and thus create moral entanglements between humanitarian actors and local communities that require careful consideration due to the responsibilities that ensue. The extent of these entanglements is linked to the comprehensiveness of the humanitarian project in question, and the degree of vulnerability of the local community.

In light of these entanglements, the potential for harm to communities, and the disruption associated with closing a humanitarian project, humanitarian agencies need to assess what would constitute an ethical exit strategy for projects that they have elected to close. Such exit strategies should be carefully tailored to the type of project, the degree of moral entanglement, and the specificities of community and context. However, several overarching characteristics of ethical exit strategies can be identified. Basing our proposal on an analysis of the nature of relationships between providers and recipients of humanitarian aid, we argue that ethical exit strategies should reflect five commitments. In closing projects, humanitarian organisations should demonstrate respect for persons who have been recipients of their assistance and seek to minimise harm and disruption by acting in ways that are characterised by 1) transparency, 2) predictability, 3) adaptability, 4) participation, and 5) evaluation. In addition, humanitarian organisations have responsibilities towards their staff who will implement the closure of a project. These responsibilities include ensuring that relevant policies and resources are in place, and that training and support are provided to those who require it.

Closing projects is an inescapable aspect of humanitarian action; indeed, almost all humanitarian projects will eventually come to an end. Making and enacting such decisions is ethically fraught, and often a source of distress for humanitarian workers and local communities. Careful attention to ethical exit strategies that follow through on obligations towards local communities is therefore a vital component of ethical humanitarian action.

Introduction

> The 'exit strategy', the endgame, the 'when do we leave' is the most difficult, the most moveable, and the most emotive part of the equation. (Larry Hollingworth, 2003)

Non-governmental organisations routinely make and enact decisions to end projects. Indeed, such decisions are a necessary and unavoidable aspect of humanitarian practice. In some projects, the implementation of a decision to close is a relatively smooth process, especially when objectives have been met and the community has achieved greater capacity to meet their own needs. In other situations, such as those in which instability or decreased access make a project less tenable, such decisions are difficult to implement. Communities may feel uncertain about their futures and from whom they will receive needed help. For their part, humanitarian workers may feel that they are letting down a community that still requires assistance. Several commentators, as well as experienced humanitarian workers, have described ending projects as one of the most challenging components of humanitarian aid, and a recurrent source of concern (Redfield, 2013; Hollingworth, 2003; Hunt, 2008). When project closure is overly abrupt, inadequately planned or poorly implemented, a range of harms may result for communities. It is thus critical to examine the ethical implications of ending projects and consider how this can best be accomplished.

Drawing from a review of the literature, along with an analysis of narratives collected during qualitative research on humanitarian health

TABLE 2.1 Factors that contribute to decisions to end a project.

Factors	Associated Considerations for Choosing to Close a Project
Insecurity	Duty as employer to protect staff; Prudential reasons
Authorisation withdrawn by government or armed groups	Loss of neutrality can compromise access; Advocacy and criticism of local governments may cause expulsion
Lack human, financial or material resources to continue project	Shortages of resources; May be sudden or foreseeable
Objectives achieved	Stewardship of resources; Cost effectiveness
Project can be handed over to local agencies or another organisation	Sustainability; Cost effectiveness
Project is ineffective or inefficient	Stewardship of resources; Cost effectiveness
Local needs are no longer aligned with organisational mandate	Coherence and consistency
Aid co-opted or instrumentalised	Advocacy and integrity; Ethic of refusal; Seek to minimise harms for community
Greater needs exist elsewhere	Impartiality; Responsibility towards those who have yet to receive assistance

ethics (Hunt, 2008; Hunt, 2009), we examine ethical considerations associated with ending humanitarian projects. We begin by canvassing reasons why projects are ended. We then consider how projects are closed and explore the implications of these choices for local communities. We describe how moral entanglements are created between humanitarian workers and local communities, and how these entanglements give rise to graded obligations. Building upon this account, we identify characteristics of ethical exit strategies for the closure of humanitarian field projects.

Why Are Projects Closed?

To open elsewhere [the organisation] had to close [a project], and in opening, recognize that any project had a finite lifespan. (Peter Redfield, 2013)

In making a decision to end a project, organisations often weigh many factors, including 'push' factors (such as a deteriorating security situation, which pushes them to end a project early), 'pull factors' (such as the identification of communities with greater needs who have yet to receive assistance), and 'stay factors' (such as a sense of solidarity and commitment to continue helping a community that remains vulnerable and in need of assistance). In particular situations, one of these factors may be deemed most salient and tip the balance in favour of maintaining or closing a project. In other cases, competing arguments to maintain or close a project may lead to uncertainty or disagreement about the best course of action. In Table 2.1 we list key factors that may motivate a decision to close a field project, along with some associated considerations.

Unable to Continue

Several 'force majeure' situations can lead humanitarian non-governmental organisations (NGOs) to end a project. A prominent example involves situations of extreme insecurity, such as Médecins Sans Frontières' (MSF) decision to close projects in Iraq and Afghanistan in 2004 following fatal attacks on aid workers (Abu-Sa'Da, 2012; MSF, 2004). Another external situation leading to rapid termination of an aid project is a politically forced exit (Oswald & Ruedin, 2012), in which local governments or armed factions retract permission for a project, or expel the agency from the region or country. A lack of funding, supplies or human resources may lead to the interruption or cessation of activities. For example, the World Food Program (WFP) suspended food aid to 1.7 million Syrian refugees in 2014 due to a lack of funding (Cairns, 2015). Projects may also be ended if they cannot be staffed, such as a surgical project being discontinued because no anaesthetist is available.

Do Not Need to Continue

In other situations, a humanitarian organisation may judge that their project should be ended because its efforts are no longer needed. Ideally this occurs when projects have successfully achieved their objectives (such as reaching and sustaining targets for a malnutrition programme), or the local community's situation has improved sufficiently so as to render external interventions unnecessary (Heyse, 2013; Gardner, Greenblott & Joubert, 2005; Heldgaar, 2008). Projects may also be closed when an organisation identifies that other agencies are providing similar or overlapping services, or when local partners are identified who are capable and willing to take over a project. When communities develop the capacity to independently meet their own needs, or when governmental authorities are in a position to do so, external organisations should look to hand over programmes and to offer support to local actors.

Decide Not to Continue

In other situations, an NGO may decide to end a project judging that the reasons for so doing outweigh the reasons for continuing. This conclusion could stem from a resource standpoint, where projects are identified as being either ineffective or too expensive (Heyse, 2013), or from an outcomes standpoint, when an evaluation concludes that the project has little chance of meeting its goals within a reasonable timeframe (Davis & Sankar, 2006). Project managers and other decision-makers may also decide to end projects when local needs are no longer congruent with the organisation's mandate. Especially challenging situations arise when humanitarian organisations are confronted with situations in which their presence or projects have been co-opted or instrumentalised, and are thus inadvertently causing harm or in some way facilitating the wrongdoing of others. Such situations lead to vexing dilemmas for humanitarian organisations, which may decide to end a project based on an ethic of refusal (Rubenstein, 2015). Lastly, there are situations when a humanitarian agency may decide to end a project because needs are greater in other communities that have yet to receive assistance or that are more vulnerable (Fuller, 2006). This is also a challenging decision to make, in which a commitment to prioritise assistance for those most in need of assistance may conflict with obligations towards communities with whom organisations have already begun to work.

The analysis that we develop in the remainder of this paper focuses on situations where organisations have elected to end a project and have some degree of operational latitude to prepare for and implement such a decision in a measured and deliberate fashion.

How Projects Are Ended

Some projects are ended abruptly in the face of a 'force majeure' event. In other situations, a 'cut and run' ending is chosen (Lee &

Ozerdem, 2015). Though still common, especially in emergency relief projects, this type of project exit has been criticised for failing to consider continuity and sustainability, and causing harms such as the rupture of services upon which communities may depend (Lee & Ozerdem, 2015; Abu-Sa'Da & Mambetova, 2012). While disruption, uncertainty and even harm cannot always be avoided, these negative effects can be minimised through a more progressive approach to ending a project. As Rogers and Coates (2015) assert, hoping that all will work out is not a good enough plan for closing a project. The following three processes of project closure provide more measured and deliberate strategies for exiting: phasing down, phasing over, and phasing out (Levinger & McLeod, 2002).

Phasing down describes a period of gradual reduction in the deployment of resources by humanitarian organisations, in preparation for their eventual withdrawal (Rogers & Macias, 2004). Typically, this process precedes phasing over or phasing out. Where a sudden change of circumstances occurs, such as new flooding, drought or fighting, in a locale where phasing down has been initiated, the project can often be phased up to respond to the increased needs of the community.

Phasing over represents the transfer of programme activities to local institutions, communities, or organisations (Rogers & Macias, 2004) as part of a process of scaling back or completely exiting a project. Many organisations aim to end their projects by phasing over. As an experienced humanitarian worker expressed, 'we close a lot of projects not because they are finished – this work is never finished – but to hand them over because we have limits' (Redfield, 2013). Using this type of exit, humanitarian organisations can account for their limitations by promoting both local participation and sustainability of activities.

Phasing out entails ending a project without turning it over to the community, a local agency, or another humanitarian organisation (Rogers & Macias, 2004). This method is ideal for programmes that generate permanent or self-sustaining impacts (Gardner, Greenblott & Joubert, 2005), and allows time for agencies to review the durability of current interventions. For example, the reassessment of food security in a community affected by recurrent droughts is crucial in order to decide when to close a therapeutic feeding programme. Agencies can then integrate adjustments to the project accordingly, in order to promote the likelihood of long-term benefits, before complete closure of a project.

Implications of Closing Projects

Closing a humanitarian project may have enormous consequences. This is more likely to be the case when projects are longer in duration, more comprehensive in nature, and where communities are more vulnerable to future shocks or cyclical disasters. We highlight some key implications of ending projects for communities and humanitarian aid organisations.

The Wellbeing of Communities

The consequences for local communities when a humanitarian project is ended can be significant and wide ranging. Following the end of a project, there may be a disruption of services available to the community. For example, in Chad a number of consequences for the provision of healthcare services were reported once programmes were phased over to local authorities who could not match the level of care and free access previously provided by the humanitarian organisation: 'not only did patients lose access to their medical supply, the quality of care go down, and the number of doctors/medical personnel decrease dramatically, but the population also had to pay for all services and drugs' (Abu-Sa'Da & Mambetova, 2012). There are also economic and social impacts related to ending projects. Redfield (2013) describes how when he visited an MSF project that was being closed 'a sense of loss hung in the air throughout [his] conversations with local health authorities and the remaining personnel. MSF had not only provided care but also employment and a sense of bustling activity no one expected the government to match.' In another humanitarian project, a Canadian nurse described how before deciding to close the project they 'were running the local economy. Pulling out was such a big political thing and they were so upset after us because they were saying the situation will come again' (Hunt, 2008). As reflected in the above quotations, communities experience a range of feelings related to project closure, including fear of losing the gains that have been made, anxiety and uncertainty about the future, and a sense of being abandoned (Abramowitz, 2015; Ford & Bedell, 2002).

Organisational Consequences

How decisions to end projects are made and enacted has many implications for humanitarian organisations. Humanitarian workers may become frustrated or discouraged if they feel that decisions to end a project are not transparent or sufficiently justified (Hurst, Mezger & Mauron, 2009). Staff members, especially those closely associated with the project and the community, may resist decisions to close a project due to feelings of connection and solidarity with the community (Rubenstein, 2015). As a result, Redfield (2013) notes that 'the burden of decision usually falls to heads of mission and staff in the sponsoring headquarters'. In turn, this can create internal tension, and have an impact on morale and even on an organisation's self-identity if there is disagreement about such decisions. For example, a pattern of ending projects prior to completely achieving stated objectives may be seen as a form of failure, and lead to worries about the organisation's reputation (Davis & Sankar, 2006).

How projects are closed may also impact on external perceptions of an organisation. For example, the degree of transparency around decisions to close a project may be linked to the organisation's legitimacy, image and acceptance by communities (Fast, 2012), as well as how they are seen by governments, donors and other agencies (Abu-Sa'Da, 2012). Humanitarian organisations typically work in environments in which other aid agencies are present, and efforts to coordinate assistance between these organisations and with local partners have been increasingly prioritised in the humanitarian sector. Closing programmes without sufficiently communicating and coordinating with other organisations can lead to frustration, especially when these entities need to rapidly adapt their projects following another agency's departure. Local stakeholders may also view poorly planned and coordinated project closure as a 'showcase for "Western dominance" and evidence of a "patronizing attitude" towards local communities and other organisations' (Abu-Sa'Da, 2012), thus further undermining the departing organisation's legitimacy and acceptance. However, the likelihood that these negative consequences will occur is greatly influenced by how decisions to end projects are made and communicated, and how they are implemented.

Moral Entanglements and the End of Projects

In any [humanitarian] intervention you set up expectations and relationships, and these have to be dealt with [when deciding to end projects]. (Ford & Bedell, 2002)

As we have described, ending projects has implications for local communities, as well as for humanitarian organisations and their staff. In addition to the loss of services and the economic impact, the closure of a project also involves the end of relationships. Drawing on Henry Richardson's conceptualisation of moral entanglements, we identify sources of obligations that humanitarian organisations might hold towards local communities when they close a project.

Richardson (2012) developed the notion of moral entanglements to describe the interconnection and obligations that arise between researchers and research participants, particularly in study settings where there are few available resources and a high level of vulnerability. On this account, moral entanglements are created as the population comes to rely on the services provided through the study and when there is a high level of engagement and trust created between researchers and participants. Based on the degree of moral entanglement that has arisen, Richardson argues that researchers ought to uphold the special obligations of beneficence that ensue, including the duty to provide ancillary healthcare services.

Moral entanglements also arise between humanitarian organisations and the local communities served by humanitarian projects. These entanglements are greater when: 1) communities are more vulnerable, 2) they have come to rely on the project for basic services, and 3) there has been greater engagement between humanitarians and local communities. Vulnerability here can be understood in a general manner related to the susceptibility of being wronged or harmed (Hurst, 2008), but also in relation to the project and what it offers. Richardson (2012) links vulnerability to 'how much difference would getting the care in question make to the health or welfare of the participant?' In this sense, vulnerability is also associated with the loss of the project and services that it provided. The degree of reliance or dependence on the project is thus a crucial factor related to moral entanglement and the obligations that this generates. For example, the level of reliance will be high if a humanitarian organisation is the only entity that is available to provide assistance to a community in need. Whereas, if the local ministry of health or dozens of other agencies are present and are also able to meet local needs, reliance on that particular humanitarian organisation and its project is likely to be diminished. In this sense, concerns for sustainability and the harms that may result from the withdrawal of a project are greater if there are few or no other ways to ensure the provision of needed assistance. Finally, entanglement is linked to the level of engagement, which is in turn associated with the comprehensiveness of a project's reach and the duration of its presence. According to Richardson (2012), 'the longer and more intensely one interacts with someone, the more effort one must make not to treat that person as a mere means'. For instance, a humanitarian organisation that runs a large nutrition programme feeding thousands of children a day, as well as providing primary care services, will have become much more entangled with a particular community than if the project had focused exclusively on vaccination for a specific disease. In the former situation, an organisation's moral entanglements and corresponding responsibilities towards the community will be greater.

Several authors have provided accounts of how humanitarian organisations should weigh their responsibilities towards the communities they are currently working with when considering decisions to open and close projects. Fuller (2006), drawing on the work of Scheffler (2002), has emphasised that the intrinsic value of humanitarian projects, over and above their instrumental value, becomes more important as the degree of entanglement is greater and as the project generates feelings of hope, trust and solidarity within the local community, and with the humanitarian organisation. She argues that humanitarian organisations have significant obligations towards these communities based on the intrinsic value of the project, and that these obligations should be given weight in decisions regarding whether to close a project and initiate activities elsewhere. Aid recipients also identify the intrinsic value of humanitarian projects, and relationships with humanitarian workers, as important. Anderson et al. (2012) interviewed individuals who had received humanitarian aid to identify what they hoped to receive: in addition to 'significant positive and lasting change' in the economic and material conditions of their communities, they also wanted to experience a sense of solidarity, colleagueship and support with and from NGOs.

Rubenstein (2015) also describes the existence of special obligations towards communities who have received humanitarian assistance. She sees these obligations, however, as linked to a humanitarian organisations' governmentality, and the ways in which they adopt activities that would normally be the responsibility of a local government. She notes that in many settings, aid organisations have 'ongoing relationships with entire populations, exercise coercive power over them, and help to shape the background conditions against which they live' (Rubenstein, 2015). On Rubenstein's account, as NGOs take on more of these patterns of governmentality, their level of responsibility for the community increases and, especially their duty not to 'pull the rug out from under' aid recipients by abruptly exiting a project. They also have duties based on democratic, distributive, and humanitarian norms towards these communities that can be traced to their somewhat governmental role and interactions.

The concept of moral entanglements usefully draws together insights from both of these accounts; the responsibilities of humanitarian organisations are linked to both the roles they play and the power they exert in a given context, but also the relationships that they develop with local communities. High levels of entanglement provide a strong argument for the continuation of existing projects. However, there are still many situations when countervailing arguments might outweigh these stay factors, hence a decision to end a project ought to be made. In such situations, the concept of moral entanglements also suggests that humanitarian organisations have responsibilities to carefully attend to how they exit from projects that they have decided to close: that is, to identify an ethical exit strategy that attends to what is owed to local communities.

Ethical Exit Strategies

Exit strategies vary across organisations, communities and projects (Davis & Sankar, 2006). Some exits are poorly planned and implemented, resulting in the sort of harms described earlier. In other circumstances, project closure is carried out in ways that demonstrate respect for local communities, and that minimise negative impacts and disruption.

We believe that there are five general commitments that characterise ethical exit strategies, though how they are implemented will vary across settings. Ethical exit strategies will reflect commitments to transparency, predictability, participation, adaptability and evaluation (see Figure 2.1). As described above, responsibilities towards local communities are graded based on the degree of entanglement that exists. While some of the commitments described here apply equally across different project closure scenarios, such as being transparent about the reasons for ending a project, others will require greater

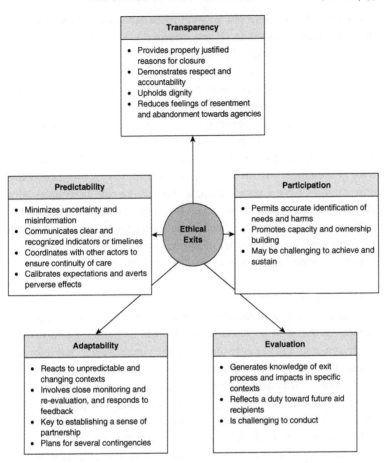

Figure 2.1 Five commitments associated with ethical exit strategies.

elaboration and attention, as when entanglements are greater, such as the amount of participation and planning that is required.

Transparency (of Reasons)

As Slim (2015) has noted, humanitarian workers frequently field questions from community members about why some individuals or groups are not receiving aid; indeed, he notes that answering such questions may be a significant part of their everyday work. In situations where a decision has been made to close or significantly scale back a humanitarian project, it is especially important that humanitarians provide frank and forthright answers when asked to explain why these decisions have been made (Hurst, Mezger & Mauron, 2009). Doing so demonstrates respect for those requesting the information, and also functions as a form of informal accountability towards those most directly affected by the decision: members of the local community and other stakeholders engaged in providing services. Rubenstein (2015) argues that enacting democratic norms such as transparency and reason-giving can 'contribute meaningfully to giving poor and disaster-affected people a greater sense of dignity and more control over their lives'. Given the consequences they bear when such decisions are made, communities have a very legitimate claim to be told their underlying rationale. Rogers and Macias (2004) also suggest that such transparency will reduce the likelihood of communities feeling resentment towards the organisation, but this is, of course, only likely to be the case if reasons provided are viewed as justified and not arbitrary.

Predictability (of Process)

The closure of a humanitarian project may create uncertainty and anxiety. It may also be accompanied by rumours and misinformation. Anderson et al. (2012) note that when the community is 'not informed about the timing or conditions of a project's ending, some feel abandoned'. Identifying the right time to end or scale back a project is therefore crucial, as is making clear the steps that will precede project closure. Exiting too early risks causing harm to communities that are still in a precarious situation, while exiting too late keeps agencies from helping other communities in need, and may also hamper local development (Lee & Ozerdem, 2015). Clear communication of timelines or indicators associated with project closure will help others to anticipate these steps and plan accordingly. Such clarity is also owed to local staff who work for the project (Gardner, Greenblott & Joubert, 2005). Where such information is not available, these individuals will be obstructed from making plans for further employment. It can also lead to frustration and competition (e.g. if it is not clear which staff will be retained as the number of staff are gradually reduced during a phased exit). In many settings, multiple humanitarian organisations are active and exit plans should also be communicated to these other agencies. Doing so will promote greater continuity of services for the community and avoid compounding the level of local disruption were multiple organisations to disengage at the same time. With greater predictability regarding the exit process, expectations will be better calibrated, and aid recipients, partner organisations, and local staff will be better able to prepare for the end of the project.

Participation

The IFRC (1994) Code of Conduct asserts that 'ways shall be found to involve programme beneficiaries in the management of relief aid'. Beyond being informed of why a decision was made (transparency of reasons) and how it will be implemented (predictability of process), there are strong reasons for humanitarian agencies to integrate an inclusive or participatory approach even when it comes to exit planning and the implementation of project closure. Including local staff and community representatives in exit planning is important in order to identify and address potential harms that may be less apparent to expatriate staff and managers of humanitarian organisations. Mitigating the relevant sources of risk will reduce the vulnerability of the community. Where a handover of services to another aid agency or local institution is planned, participation (in addition to clear communication of process) will be beneficial and contribute to better outcomes (Anderson et al., 2012). For example, engaging local agencies in a participatory fashion will support a handover, as the receiving agency will likely be more able and more willing if they have contributed to the planning of the process. Empowering local organisations not only builds capacity, but also transforms humanitarian relationships by reducing the dependence of communities on external aid (Oswald & Ruedin, 2012). To successfully hand over a programme, three elements must be considered and planned for: resource generation, local capacity, and motivation of those who will provide services to the community going forward (Davis & Sankar, 2006). There may also be situations when NGOs seek to handover a project to a somewhat unwilling group or entity. In these cases, working to support local groups to take over and sustain services is especially important. In some situations, humanitarian organisations may also be justified in pressuring local governments to provide services that they have been reluctant to deliver to a community (Rubenstein, 2015).

Several challenges exist for participation and partnership in exit planning: organisations may have different mandates, cultures and priorities (Lee & Ozerdem, 2015), as well as different capacities and expectations. As a result, an exiting organisation will need to accept the fact that the approach adopted by those to whom they have handed over the project may be different from their own. Where this involves a lower standard of care or reduced access to services, they may experience this as the need to compromise.

Adaptability

Careful and diligent planning is important for a successful exit. Humanitarian organisations also require the ability to adapt to the changing and unpredictable contexts in which humanitarian projects are situated. In this sense, sticking too tightly to planned timelines or the sequence of steps leading up to the closure of a project could unnecessarily cause added disruption or distress. Exit strategies should therefore be responsive to the unfolding of a project over time, and to feedback and input that is received from community stakeholders. In this sense, all exit plans should be provisional: 'flexibility is key to allow for the sense of partnership and mutuality, which is a precondition for the planning of a successful exit process' (Heldgaar, 2008). In practice, not only will plans need to be adaptable, multiple exit strategies may be necessary in order to prepare for a range of background scenarios (Gardner, Greenblott & Joubert, 2005).

Evaluation

The Core Humanitarian Standards (CHS, 2014) include the aspiration that 'humanitarian actors continuously learn and improve'. Integrating an evaluative dimension to project closures is a key contribution to ensure that learning occurs so as to improve future project exits. This can be difficult to implement, particularly when approaches to evaluation are more sophisticated and require returning to the community after project closure in order to assess its impact. Two key challenges for longitudinal evaluations are that funding cycles may not allow for an extended period of evaluation, and that aid agencies will have shifted their attention to other emergencies, and thus may not prioritise returning to a community to assess the legacy of the project and how it ended. However, generating such information (and developing case studies as a result) is necessary in order to inform humanitarian practice and policy. Such knowledge could be used to identify what strategies do and do not work, and can thus help to calibrate effective exit strategies. A commitment to such learning is also something that is owed to communities who will be assisted in the future.

NGOs' Responsibilities Towards Their Staff

In addition to obligations towards individuals and communities who have been recipients of aid, humanitarian organisations also have responsibilities to ensure that staff are equipped and supported to end projects. Humanitarian workers will benefit from having clear and relevant policies for project closure, particularly policies that provide sufficient latitude to ensure adaptability to changing circumstances, as described above. Preparation should include providing relevant training and the opportunity to consult with experts in this area, especially for field teams who have limited collective experience of closing projects. Where evaluation has been applied to assess the process and impact of past project closures, this knowledge can be used to inform the development of relevant policy and training initiatives. As a component of planning the end of a project, the organisation should also assess if particular security risks exist, and take steps to ensure their mitigation.

Davis and Sankar (2006) also suggest that NGOs should examine how project closure is seen within the culture of their organisation. For example, some organisations are very reluctant to close projects, even when objectives have been met, potentially generating concerns for cost effectiveness and distributive justice. Discussions around project closure and organisational culture can help to illuminate these practices and biases, and therefore contribute to a process of more open reflection and discussion (Rubenstein, 2015).

Conclusion

Closing projects is an inescapable component of humanitarian action and part of the work of every humanitarian organisation. As we have discussed here, the end of a project can be a very troubling and distressing situation for communities, for humanitarian organisations and their staff, and for local partner organisations. Depending on (and sometimes despite) the degree of planning and care with which an exit is organised, communities may feel let down or abandoned, and experience a sudden loss of services and support. For aid workers, the end 'of programs proves unsettling to humanitarian sensibilities' (Redfield, 2013) and may leave ethical residue: a sense that something of ethical significance has been given up when a decision is made to stop assisting a community that remains vulnerable or in need.

In these contexts, Richardson's notion of moral entanglements helps explain the nature of obligations around project exits and offers insight into how they should be discharged. From this perspective, the roles taken up by NGOs and the nature of the relationships established with local communities, along with attributes of the local community such as the degree of vulnerability and reliance, create special obligations (graded to the degree of entanglement) when a project is closed. Implementing an exit that is characterised by transparency, predictability, adaptability, participation and evaluation will promote the welfare and dignity of local communities.

References

Abramowitz, S (2015), What happens when MSF leaves? Humanitarian departure and medical sovereignty in postconflict Liberia. Pp. 137. In: Abramowitz, S & Panter-Brick, C (eds), *Medical humanitarianism: ethnographies of practice*. Philadelphia: University of Pennsylvania Press.

Abu-Sa'Da, C (2012), *In the eyes of others: how people in crises perceive humanitarian aid*. New York: Médecins Sans Frontières, Humanitarian Outcomes, NYU Center on International Cooperation.

Abu-Sa'Da, C & Mambetova, K (2012), Reversing the optics: MSF's Perception Project. In: Abu-Sa'Da, C (ed.) *Dilemmas, challenges, and ethics of humanitarian action*. Montreal: McGill-Queen's University Press.

Anderson, MB, Brown, D & Jean, I (2012), *Time to listen: hearing people on the receiving end of international aid*. Cambridge, MA: CDA Collaborative Learning Projects.

Cairns, E (2015), *For human dignity: the World Humanitarian Summit and the challenge to deliver*. Oxford: Oxfam International.

CHS (2014), *Core Humanitarian Standard on Quality and Accountability*. CHS Alliance, Group URD, the Sphere Project.

Davis, N & Sankar, M (2006), *A practice review of UNESCO's exit and transition strategies*. Paris: UNESCO.

Fast, L (2012), Programming, footprints, and relationships: the link between perceptions and humanitarian security. In: Abu-Sa'Da, C (ed.) *Dilemmas, challenges, and ethics of humanitarian action*. Montreal: McGill-Queen's University Press.

Ford, N & Bedell, R (2002), *Justice and MSF operational choices*. Amsterdam: MSF.

Fuller, L (2006), Justified commitments? Considering resource allocation and fairness in Medécins Sans Frontières-Holland. *Developing World Bioethics*. Vol. 6 (2): 59–70.

Gardner, A, Greenblott, K & Joubert, E (2005), *What we know about exit strategies. Practical guidance for developing exit strategies in the field*. C-Safe Regional Learning Spaces Initiative.

Heldgaar, J (2008), *Managing aid exit and transformation: summary of a joint donor evaluation*. Stockholm: Sida.

Heyse, L (2013), Tragic choices in humanitarian aid: a framework of organizational determinants of NGO decision making. *Voluntas: International Journal of Voluntary and Nonprofit Organizations*. Vol. 24 (1): 68–92.

Hollingworth, L (2003), Resolutions, mandates, aims, missions, and exit strategies. Pp. 267–83. In: Cahill, KM (ed.) *Emergency relief operations*. New York: New York University Press & the Center for International Health and Cooperation.

Hunt, MR (2008), Ethics beyond borders: how health professionals experience ethics in humanitarian assistance and development work. *Developing World Bioethics*. Vol. 8 (2): 59–69.

Hunt, MR (2009), Moral experience of Canadian healthcare professionals in humanitarian work. *Prehospital Disaster Medicine*. Vol. 24 (6): 518–24.

Hurst, SA (2008), Vulnerability in research and health care; describing the elephant in the room? *Bioethics*. Vol. 22 (4): 191–202.

Hurst, SA, Mezger, N & Mauron, A (2009), Allocating resources in humanitarian medicine. *Public Health Ethics*. Vol. 2 (1): 89–99.

IFRC (1994), *The Code of Conduct for the International Red Cross and Red Crescent Movement and NGOs in Disaster Relief*. Geneva: International Federation of Red Cross and Red Crescent Societies.

Lee, SY & Ozerdem, A (2015), Exit strategies. In: Ginty, RM & Peterson, JH (eds), *The Routledge companion to humanitarian action*. New York: Routledge.

Levinger, B & McLeod, J (2002), *Hello I must be going: ensuring quality services and sustainable benefits through well-designed exit strategies*. Newton, MA: Education Development Center Inc. for Organizational Learning and Development.

MSF (2004), MSF pulls out of Afghanistan. Press Release [online]. Available from: www.msf.org/en/article/msf-pulls-out-afghanistan (accessed 22 August 2017).

Oswald, K & Ruedin, L (2012), Empowerment sustainability and phasing out support to empowerment processes. In: OECD, *Poverty reduction and pro-poor growth. The role of empowerment*. Paris: Organisation for Economic Co-operation and Development.

Redfield, P (2013), *Life in crisis: the ethical journey of Doctors Without Borders*. Berkeley, CA: University of California Press.

Richardson, HS (2012), *Moral entanglements: the ancillary-care obligations of medical researchers*. Oxford: Oxford University Press.

Rogers, BL & Coates, J (2015), *Sustaining development: a synthesis of results from a four-country study of sustainability and exit strategies among development food assistance projects*. Washington, DC: FHI 360/Food and Nutrition Technical Assistance III Project (FANTA).

Rogers, BL & Macias, K (2004), *Program graduation and exit strategies: a focus on Title II food aid development programs*. Washington, DC: Food and Nutrition Technical Assistance Project, Academy for Educational Development.

Rubenstein, J (2015), *Between Samaritans and states: the political ethics of humanitarian INGOs*. Oxford: Oxford University Press.

Scheffler, S (2002), *Boundaries and allegiances: problems of justice and responsibility in liberal thought*. Oxford: Oxford University Press.

Slim, H (2015), *Humanitarian ethics: a guide to the morality of aid in war and disaster*. Oxford: Oxford University Press.

3 | THE OUTSIDER'S ROLE: ETHICAL REFLECTIONS FROM THE STUDY OF INTERNATIONAL–NATIONAL STAFF RELATIONS IN DEVELOPMENT AND HUMANITARIAN ORGANISATIONS

Maëlle Noé

Introduction

International humanitarian and development practitioners coming from donor countries often find themselves in the ethically challenging situation of having been hired for a job that does not reflect the best added value they can bring. This may paradoxically seem logical, given that their job situation is the product of the same inequalities they were officially hired to help alleviate. Readers may see this both as a problem and an opportunity: once conscious of the similarity between the dynamics in their workplaces and the dynamics they want to change, practitioners may be better equipped to clearly apprehend, and thus confront, this complex international humanitarian and development system, which has been relatively unchallenged and unaltered since its creation, while enhancing the overall quality of their work.

In this chapter, I present a condensed, reorganised and commented version of prior research[1] which explored the quality of relations between international and national staff in humanitarian and development organisation branches located in the East African region.[2] I gathered the data over six weeks in Nairobi, Dar Es Salaam, Bujumbura, Kigali, and Goma, through semi-structured interviews, facilitation of conflict-resolution skills training, informal conversations, and observations of organisational activities. Seventeen staff members from nine different organisations generously gave their time to be interviewed, fifteen of whom were nationals.

Interviewees participated in theory development as I chose a grounded theory research method, which means that instead of testing a pre-constructed hypothesis, theory gradually emerges through the data-gathering process. The result was a theory about the potential added value of outsiders, which, due to structural and behavioural factors, is not consistent with the implicit role differentiation between national and international staff in practice. Behind the question of relational tensions, we saw that international staff roles tend to detract from the value of national staff as insiders, reducing them to implementers rather than owners and designers of programmes intended to support their country's development. This situation creates unspoken discomfort, as both national and international staff may ask themselves, consciously or unconsciously: who is 'international development' really for?

In grounded theory, the literature is reviewed post theory extraction from the research. What I found in the literature review, which will be integrated throughout this discussion, is that authors have been describing the same role differentiation dynamics for over thirty years. Despite the publication of international resolutions about participation and ownership, such as the Paris Declaration on Aid Effectiveness in 2005 and the Accra Agenda for Action in 2008, the situations I observed in 2015 in Kenya, Tanzania, Burundi, Rwanda and the Democratic Republic of Congo showed a clear lack of evolution. The situation is ethically complex. The passive but immense strength of the status quo makes it challenging for even the most well-intentioned practitioners to effectively go beyond short-term pain alleviation and to contribute to constructive long-term change towards equality and dignity.

In this chapter, I set out to provide the reader with a clearer view into the systemic nature of the problem, a much-needed tool for anyone willing to challenge it. The diagram in Figure 3.1 represents the dynamics underlying the systematic devaluation of national staff

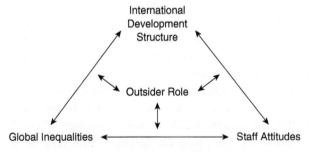

Figure 3.1 Interactions between levels constituting the international humanitarian and development system and the Outsider Role.

perspectives. Interactions take place on three levels: in relation to global inequalities, between donor and beneficiary countries on a macro level; international development structures at a programme level (hierarchies, salary differentiation, modes of operation, etc.); and staff attitudes at a micro level. This chapter will firstly present the ideal four outsider roles identified by interviewees, while highlighting the importance of high-quality listening, which is indispensable in predicting whether the presence of outsiders will add to or detract from collaborative efforts. It will then detail the relationships illustrated in Figure 3.1, using the focus on listening as a connecting thread, demonstrating the difficulty for internationals to fulfil their role as outsiders in a supportive manner in the current state of matters.

The Ideal Roles of the Outsider

Interviewees identified four roles that outsiders can play to support insiders:

Firstly, insiders see outsiders as a useful resource to provide a fresh perspective: 'If you are from an area there are things you see that outside people don't see, but vice-versa, if you are outside there are some things you see that when you are too close it's difficult to see' (Interviewee 1, Kenyan).[3] This statement resonates with how scholars have analysed the situation: being somewhat at a distance, outsiders' main advantage is that they may be better placed to see the big picture (Anderson, 1999; Suzuki, 1998; Vinhas, 2012).

Secondly, having relatively more freedom of speech or action, an outsider's status confers the ability to do things that insider could not do without undergoing more significant consequences. In Burundi, for example, as a national interviewee was pointing out, international staff are less likely to be killed, imprisoned or expelled when they touched on government-related issues. They are more likely to be only 'moderated' or 'unappreciated', because the interviewee's government depends on funding from the outsider's country of origin (10, Burundian). Internationals thus may find themselves being able to speak or initiate actions on injustices which they are not directly affected by and may not fully understand, but which their governments are connected to in ways that are not always clear or easy to leverage. These situations may be extremely frustrating for nationals, who tend to be better informed and who are directly affected in both the short and long term, but who find themselves unable to both speak up and maintain safety for themselves and their families. Above all, this questions what internationals can do about the different values donor countries place on human lives from their own countries versus human lives from the countries they have committed to give support to.

In addition to outsiders having more safety and freedom, Mukasa (1999) notes that the status of being from a donor country may also contribute to a certain degree of influence. She observed that outsiders 'used this influence to challenge a number of assumptions and beliefs amongst [local] communities'. For example, by employing women in their organisation, international organisations aim to raise the status of women (ibid.). She concludes that the lack of cultural awareness can affect a project both negatively and positively at the same time. This influence may not only be due to the financial ties between governments, but may also be the result of interiorised colonial ideology, as famously described by Fanon (1986).[4] Another reason for the disproportionate influence attached to internationals in some cases is that they may be viewed as impartial, because they do not share identities with any parties in local conflicts (Anderson, 1999; Schirch, 2013; Vinhas, 2012). The ethical question for the outsider here is how, when, and whether to use this influence at all: while it can sometimes constructively support insiders, using it may maintain and even reinforce this inequitable treatment.

Thirdly, being an outsider by default should make it easier to communicate with other outsiders back at headquarters who share the same language and culture, thus facilitating outsider–insider communication. Illustrating this, an American interviewee described the typical role of international programme staff: 'we basically do just regional assistance for whatever needs, generally it's proposal writing and report writing so a lot of times I'll take, or I'll get all the field reports submitted from Angola and compile them and fix some of the English,[5] compile them together, put them into a quarterly report that we need to submit to donors ... in some ways, one of the biggest value added is my being a native, a native English speaker' (7). In a similar vein, while giving her perspective on why internationals have higher-level positions, such as regional director, a Tanzanian interviewee noted: 'they know how to talk to [international donors]' (8). Similarly, a Burundian interviewee mentioned that European staff had come 'to support in fundraising' as they were 'in the process of contacting several local and international partners' (10).

The literature review concurred with this observation by interviewees and added that beyond communication skills, outsiders can sometimes have the advantage of benefiting from strong links to influential decision-makers in Western countries, what Schirch (2013) refers to as 'vertical social capital', allowing for better communication between headquarters and field-based entities (Mukasa, 1999). Being culturally (and physically) similarly to donors may also help to build donor confidence in 'cases in which there is a need for mutual learning and the breakdown of stereotypes' (ibid.).

Fourthly, outsiders have collected a different set of experiences and perhaps skills, which may be valuable to exchange with insiders: 'The ideal would be to complete each other, you come with what you know and you give it to national staff, and what national staff possess they give it to you, and you consider each other brothers' (17, Congolese). Outsiders may bring expertise, capacities, and/or comparative experiences (Schirch, 2013; Mukasa, 1999; Vinhas, 2012). Sometimes this could be just the experiences of dealing with a certain organisation's structure. It is arguable whether this exchange needs to be done by a person in a full-time position or whether it can be done in intermittent, perhaps even in virtual, exchanges. Outsiders, by definition, have something 'different' to bring to the picture that can be extremely constructive; however, it is not always easy to ensure that what is brought is relevant to insiders' needs, as we will explore in the next sections.

The Space for Listening

Reflecting on the roles outlined above, perspective, freedom of speech, communication with donors, and different skills and/or experiences, two points should be noted. Firstly, none of these bring any value whatsoever if high-quality listening is not present in the equation: if insiders are not listened to how valuable is the outsider's perspective? If insiders are not listened to, how valuable is the outsider's freedom of speech? If insiders are not listened to, whose message is the outsider communicating to donors? If insiders are not listened to, how relevant is the exchange of skills and/or experience (if there is any exchange at all)? The difficulty with this is three-fold: firstly, listening skills are often taken for granted yet very difficult to acquire; secondly, a minimum of relational quality and equity of treatment between listener and speaker is required; thirdly, there needs to be sufficient investment in time and appropriate space for it to happen.

The second point is that while this research looked at internationals and nationals, the status of 'insider' or 'outsider' can be defined in much broader terms. Internationals are not the only ones who can bring this outsider added value, of course, and being a national does not necessarily mean one has an insider perspective on the specific issue being dealt with. However, as we will see in interview extracts, being an international, especially a white one, does make a difference in terms of being trusted by donors and even unconsciously by nationals as 'people who know', regardless of whether anything objectively justifies this trust.

The two points above are interconnected: it is extremely difficulty for internationals to genuinely hear the perspective of nationals in a system which tends to systematically value international perspectives more than national ones, if the latter are solicited at all.[6] What results is a situation in which neither side benefits from the unique perspective offered by the other. The following example, shared by a Ugandan CEO,[7] strongly illustrates this unfortunate situation. Recalling her previous experience working with an international organisation, she told me: 'I felt like I was becoming dumber and dumber by the day. After one year, I shared this feeling with my older [national] co-workers, they had been through the same thing and had known it would happen to me.'

The following sections are broken down into the three interconnected relationships presented in Figure 3.1: the interaction between global inequalities and the structure of the development field, the interaction between this structure and staff attitudes towards each other, and the interaction between global inequalities and staff attitudes. In each section, we will examine how these interactions affect the quality of listening potentially conducted by outsiders, represented by the inner arrows of the diagram in Figure 3.1.

Global Inequalities – Structure

This section examines the relationship between global inequalities and the structure of the development field, which implicitly makes internationals seem indispensable and places them in leadership positions, and analyses the effects of this relationship on listening opportunities for those internationals.

Describing the structure of the international development field, interviewees often referred to its hierarchical disposition: 'Development work is diverse but layered, such that, hum, most project managers will be expats ... regional directors will always be foreign, they'll always be external, even when it's a national program ... and the rest, if they're trained, the rest will be nationals', a Kenyan interviewee cautiously expressed (5). 'Of course, at the higher level we have international staff' stated a Tanzanian interviewee (9). 'It's the structure of things' impassively observed another (8, Tanzanian), describing a seemingly immovable characteristic of international development. Authors have similarly noted that senior and higher-level management roles are generally filled by Westerners (Mukasa, 1999; Patel & McNamee, 2013; Vinhas, 2012).

This layered structure appears to be the result of the same global inequalities that international development sets out to address. For example, money typically channelled into the development industry comes from 'developed countries', and, as a Burundian interviewee factually noted: 'Most of the time, I would say around 80% of the time, the one who gives the money is the one who decides' (12). A Kenyan interviewee similarly explained: 'Funding organisations never trust anyone else with their money apart from their country-men, it's as simple as that' (5). Citing Dichter (1986) and Fowler (1989) to support her argument, Mukasa (1999) states that 'Donors were usually more willing to finance projects that are headed by expa-triates', adding that this often results in projects being initiated to suit donor requirements rather than to reflect local needs and aspirations (ibid.).

The aforementioned Burundian interviewee stated that 'as long as Burundians are not the ones to define their needs themselves, it means [donors] think that Burundians are not trustworthy'. Because this sentiment is pervasive and recognised, and because international development actors concede that it is not consistent with the aim of development, local participation has become a central theme in development.

However, while NGOs claim to have participatory management styles in theory, in practice, it is often not the case, or could mean very different things. Suzuki (1998) notes that the term 'participation' itself is very ambiguous, and managers may benefit from leaving it that way. Tendler (1982) categorised what US NGOs labelled participatory decision-making in three types: '(i) genuinely representative; (ii) top-down "sensitive" in which despite appearances of participation the

NGOs actually made the decisions in a relatively top-down manner, and (iii) local elite decision-making ... in which NGOs were criticised for responding to decisions made by local elites, which were taken by the NGO to be representative of all the poor'. The second of the three types is what has been written about most by the reviewed authors, what Chambers (1996) calls 'submissive participation' – '"they" participate in "our" project', where participating really means to implement (Schirch, 2013; Suzuki, 1998; Mukasa, 1999). In a situation where nationals are de facto implementers rather than designers, one could expect that little time is invested in listening to their perspectives, although logically they should be the ones leading the effort.

While this has been extensively talked about, the power structure remains the same, making it difficult to resolve the problem. For example, an interviewee stated that 'We are certified to adhere to [the international accountability label], which includes participation at every step of the projects'; then, later, while describing a specific project: 'the beneficiaries did not understand and did not see the benefits of the trainings [sic]' (11, Burundian), leading me to question what participation really meant. The interviewee simply replied that, indeed, their organisation had to make some progress in that area.

This structure also increases the disconnect between international staff and the reality that they are, in the context, hired to make decisions about. An international interviewee in the 'relatively unique' situation of having spent half his time in remote areas of the country during his first year on the job, which had decreased to a third at the time of the interview, expressed how even he, once back in a capital city for a while, sometimes forgets why his correspondents in the field might be having difficulties. Talking about the organisation's decision-making processes, which involve higher-level gatherings in the sub-region's capital cities, he expressed regret at the fact that: 'A lot of things get lost. For sure I, having been involved in the discussion, can contextualise some things, and you know sometimes people understand, you know they're not, unreasonable people, they understand when you explain to them, but often due to the magnitude of our programming, we can't go into all of the details of the matter and sometimes it's just ... yeah.' He also observed that the bigger the projects get, the less the people at the top understand what they are really about, losing touch with what is hidden behind development jargon and the impact on real life very quickly (2, Canadian).

'Some of them don't even go to the field',[8] lamented a Tanzanian interviewee, while reflecting on the burden they can be when they do, as they may feel excluded due to not understanding the local language, but putting in effort to include them in the conversation detracts from the quality of her work: 'if you only speak English you feel like you are out, and even if I go with someone, who speaks English, I can't wait to do translation while I'm supposed to listen well [...] and communicate with these people' (8). This seemingly contradictory sentiment poses the ethical question of whether internationals have their place in this picture at all.

Citing Dichter (1989), who had already argued back in 1986 that: 'whilst it may have been the case that local skills were not available a few years ago, it is no longer a reasonable argument to make. Rather, it is a weakness on the part of the NGOs' recruitment methods that fails to identify local skills' (Dichter, 1986), Mukasa (1999) makes the case that hiring internationals is more cost than benefit, at best. Yet, fourteen out of the fifteen national interviewees seemed resigned to the perspective that, because they are nationals, they will always play a subordinate role: 'As much as we work hard, we are capped, you see', shared a Kenyan interviewee (5).

The way in which interviewees discussed the idea of international–national staff ratio also reinforced the notion that the presence of international staff, often at the top of the hierarchy, is viewed as inevitable. They discussed it mostly out of concern for the financial costs: 'instead of coming with twenty internationals, if you come with two or three expatriates, isn't it, maybe at the managerial level, who will hire at the local level and maybe give a training, a skill and that will reduce the budget' (17, Congolese).

Of course, organisations without international staff do exist and thrive, but they need to be extremely assertive to maintain their independence. The fifteenth national interviewee, who worked at an internationally funded but 100 percent nationally staffed organisation in Burundi, recounted an example of this: an international donor once included the condition that international staff should lead the project for which they would be sending funds. It would have cost '$5000 plus $2000 per month, plus housing, transport, hotels ... this is not the kind of support we want'; the donor then threatened to withdraw everything. He concluded: 'they want money, they don't care about the country, they think "I am giving money, it is normal that I send someone, maybe unemployed, from Belgium"' (12, Burundi).

This questioning of donor motivations was also reported by Mukasa (1999), who observed in her field research that instead of internationals being hired for specifically needed skills, it was often their pre-existing skills and interests that dictated which projects were to be implemented. She suggested that their incentive may be first to make a good impression and enhance career development back home, then only secondly to contribute to positive change in the country they happened to currently work in. Even in cases where internationals were supposed to transfer relevant skills, they 'rarely worked on this basis, instead, they worked on a management basis which meant in practice that they retained overall control, rarely devolving it to locals' (MS, 1992 in Mukasa, 1999: 12).

The dynamic between global inequalities and the structure of the field, examined in this section, contributes to a system that implicitly considers internationals from donor countries as more qualified and trustworthy; gives them control; tasks them to make decisions based primarily on their perspectives; views them as the experts and from a standpoint that is very much disconnected from the realities they are working to alleviate. These conditions offer little space or incentive for listening to and prioritising insiders' perspectives.

Structure – Attitudes

This section examines the relationship between the structure of the development field – which implicitly values internationals more, as we have started to see, but which also restrains them through rigid procedural elements – and international and national staff attitudes, and analyses the effect of that relationship on the quality of listening opportunities for staff.

Describing the unjustified attitude of superiority perceived in some international staff, an interviewee explained: 'One thinks he is more intelligent, stronger even, but you arrive on the field and they also have studied almost the same schools as you, of course university differs but it's almost the same content, but you get a salary superior to that of locals so you have a tendency to think that you are better' (17, Congolese). With this succinct description, he explained the psychological effect of being more valued financially: some start to feel that they must be more valuable intellectually as well. The salary differentiation coupled with the hierarchy which often places internationals on top, as described earlier, can hinder the quality of listening by internationals: if they listen they will tend to listen very narrowly, looking for specific details geared to help them, the experts, solve the problem, rather than investing time in the type of listening that can support insiders to clarify what problems they are dealing with and how they want to proceed.

Reflecting on this type of attitude and comparing his experience of having worked with nine different organisations, an interviewee explained that: 'If you send us on the field, not with good mood but with tyranny, we'll go to the bar, we'll eat, and we'll decide what we'll write in the report. When staff is included, each one feels responsible. It's really a huge difference, here people stay in their offices until 9 PM, nobody tells them to, the whites have all gone home, the nationals stay, each according to the evolution of their work, it's not the whites who will stay, and we aren't paid for extra time, but because you know where you're going, you force yourself to' (10, Burundian). With this illustration of two extremes, this testimony highlights the effects of questionable ethical uses of biased power structures, while posing the question of a disparity in incentives between insiders and outsiders, as discussed in the previous section.

In addition to the nationality-based hierarchy, the topic of frustration at the salary differentiation came up on a variety of occasions. The first was to illustrate a reason for potential relational tension due to the perception that those who were paid more were not those who worked more. A human resources interviewee shared that: '[nationals] say that internationals are super paid, it's already the starting point of a conflict. Even if it is latent, we feel that it is there. It can be psychological too, when someone tells themselves that ah, my supervisor, only because he is an expat he has this but I do almost all of the work' (14, Congolese).

The second occasion was an expression of how those being paid more were not necessarily the most skilled staff members either: 'I discovered that in information technology, there are a lot of expatriates which were, allow me, terrible! Excel, terrible, power point, terrible, database, terrible!', so the interviewee had to train them while they get 'ten times more salary' (17, Congolese). Thirdly, as mentioned in the first section, to express concern about the vast budget needed to hire internationals: 'Each expatriate will need a house, a villa, a villa that will cost maybe more than $1500 or $2000, you see, he has allocations, he needs to have gardeners, this and that, all this nibbles on the budget of program execution' (17, Congolese). This frustration is even greater when it is not clear why internationals should be needed for a specific position; for example, an interviewee rhetorically asked: 'an assistant position, why internationalise it, while there are those [nationals] who can, who have the capacities?' (14, Congolese).

Interviewees also mentioned the training aspect in relation to the frequent turnover of international staff: 'Sometimes we get people, [...] internationals, who are very good, they know the work and they do it very nice, but sometimes we get a boss who doesn't know anything. We have to train them and by the time they are going to know [it is] already time for them to go and you get another one. Those are the frustrating things' (8, Tanzanian). Mukasa (1999) also noted that because of these turnovers 'Often, it was local staff who "showed expatriate staff the ropes"' rather than local staff learning from internationals. Nonetheless, local staff were simply not brought into senior positions, raising concerns about the 'level of ownership' of the programme by local staff. Some felt they were not adequately included in the decision-making process.

This can turn into more than frustration in some cases: a national staff member trained an international intern, coming from London, who was paid a $900 stipend a month as a monitoring and evaluation assistant. Three months later, the intern obtained the position above his. The international's salary thus went up to $3500 a month, while his remained at $1500. The national staff member ended up leaving the organisation and working in another country (14, Congolese). This case strongly illustrates how insiders can be treated as less valid and valuable people, so much so that they can ultimately decide to deprive the organisation of their insider value and to become an outsider in another country, even knowing that they are unlikely to be treated as well as an outsider coming from a donor country would be.

It is difficult to know whether the attitudes of superiority observed in some international staff precede or follow the psychological impact of being more valued by the structure or each other's influence, as they also vary on an individual basis of course, but interviewees noted other examples of such attitudes reflected in daily interactions. For example, another interviewee reported that in one organisation training participants,[9] a number of international staff ignored greetings from national staff. An attempt at team-building through football games for the entire staff was celebrated by this interviewee for having a good number of internationals attending the first time (14, Congolese). When the researcher attended the following weekend's game with an international intern, who was profusely thanked for being there, only two other internationals were present, neither of them staff from that organisation.

Mukasa (1999) similarly observed in her field study that layering did not just mean that internationals got higher positions and higher pay: even those lower on the hierarchical scale were treated differently from nationals at the same level. Referring to examples such as vehicle rules and eating meals separately, she illustrates this separation: 'The expatriate staff had their meals prepared for them by the domestic staff and ate in the main residential dining room. Other differences included the different sets of rules for the use of vehicles between the two sets of staff.'

The example of the football game cited earlier showed that the difference in treatment did not seem to be only between national and international staff. A chief of party national interviewee explained that as he went to get a drink with the team of drivers, they exclaimed: 'Ah! For the first time, we are acknowledged too' (14, Congolese). Similarly, while commenting on the difference that a higher educational level makes to people's attitudes: 'you will see in some organisation, people having very high level jobs are not so much interacting with the lowest staff' (13, Kenyan). Another interviewee also noted that having worked in a bigger organisation influenced the attitudes of national staff towards one another (1, Kenyan). These examples of devaluing colleagues based on social identities such as nationality, level of education or hierarchical status, not only hint at poorer opportunities for quality listening and thus quality work, but also relate missed opportunities to use the intra-organisational microcosm as a starting point to contribute to the evolution of humanistic values, such as dignity and equality, that humanitarian and development staff aspire to spread.

Internationals who are mindful about implementing such values in the way they treat their colleagues can run into other types of obstacles to quality listening due to the structure they are in. One obstacle is that being placed at a higher level in the hierarchy can make it especially difficult when the cultural expectation in relation to authority is to be given orders rather than asked for one's perspective. Vinhas (2012), for example, shared his frustration as an international staff member in

Pakistan, Haiti and Liberia, when his vision of a more democratic NGO management came up 'against the demand for a more authoritative management by national staff themselves'.

While I did not observe this kind of demand during my research, interviewees highlighted other ways in which the structure can make it difficult for international staff who have a more inclusive attitude to translate that into action. Procedural aspects, for example, often not only impact opportunities to listen, but also make it difficult to make use of the information gathered through listening in a timely manner. This can happen during the implementation of a project: an international interviewee expressed frustration at the standardised procedures that are applied to community projects, where the organisation tries to control as many variables as possible for better measurement of impact: 'It is really lost opportunities [to be] taking away all the flexibility that our field staff could have' when those staff have a heightened awareness of the context. For example, staff may know that to include a specific person in a meeting could make a big difference and lead to the change desired, but to respect procedure this person cannot be included (2, Canadian).

It can also happen during the needs assessment. Schirch (2013) refers to the problem of self-fulfilling prophecies in conflict-assessment trips, coming in to look for evidence that 'their branded peacebuilding method could work' thus 'Not listening to [insiders'] ideas upfront during assessment and proposal writing, but rather only wanting to consult after the fact to get approval or seek local partners as "implementers" of foreign designed projects.' She gives the example of donors pushing for social dialogues between tribes when local CSOs have clearly expressed the major drivers of conflict as being government corruption and the need for land reform, but foreign donors were 'reluctant to listen to local NGOs since they had already gone through a long process of developing policy goals, getting budget lines approved, and sending out request for proposals' (Schirch, 2013).

In addition to the reversed chronology of this process, the language used throughout is seen by some as exclusionary and disconnected from reality. A Kenyan interviewee expressed her frustration about the disparity between the vocabulary used in proposals and the realities she faces: 'I mean you look at those proposals, it's just jargon and, I don't know what are you talking about what are you saying, can you break it down into a language that is simplistic and something tangible. That is very hard, you know, you look at some of the job descriptions for a local person for example, it just doesn't make sense, it just doesn't make sense, there is nothing, at the end of the year you can't say I have achieved this much' (1). Both these language and timing issues (writing the proposal request, for example, prior to listening to nationals' perspectives) reduce opportunities for nationals' perspectives to be heard.

In this section, I examined the dynamic between the structure of the field and staff attitudes, observing that this dynamic contributes to a system which, by implicitly valuing international perspectives over national ones, can affect attitudes of staff towards one another in ways that contradict the humanistic values upon which their work is based. Such a system can also limit the incentive for internationals to remain involved in the long term and thus the incentive for high-quality listening and observation before deciding on solutions, and limit the possibilities for those who do make the effort to listen to effectively include insiders' perspectives.

Attitudes – Global Inequalities

This section examines the relationship between international and national staff attitudes and global inequalities, a relationship which combines extremely tough local economic contexts with a persisting colonial hangover, and analyses its effect on the quality of listening opportunities for international staff.

Reflecting on the perceived attitudes of donors and international staff, an interviewee concluded that: 'As long as Burundians are not the ones to define their needs themselves, it means they think that Burundians are not trustworthy.' Later on in the interview, speaking of a particular foreigner, he categorised him as: 'one of those who think that if a white doesn't direct things' (12, Burundian).

These remnants of colonial ideology are reflected on in a note by Schirch (2013) that most outsiders not only lack understanding of local contexts, 'They also may not trust insiders. Outsiders often come from countries that once held colonial policies that viewed local people as "subjects" or even as less than fully human.' The People in Aid (2007) report also indirectly expresses this by giving the following advice in their recommendation for the Kenya case study: 'Trust them – that they are capable of accomplishing their mission.' Whether these remnants of colonialism come from the staff themselves, since they come from countries where racism persists, or insidiously seep into their minds from the structure which was inherited from those times (in France, for example, the first development and cooperation staff were colonial agents repurposed after independence (Meimon, 2007)), nobody speaks about the issue openly, and it affects the attitudes of both sides.

'They don't listen because they know, they think they know better, so at the end of the day [...] we are not getting into the root of the problem, we are not addressing what is needed, they just address things based on some theory that they've done,' expressed a Kenyan interviewee (1). Reflecting a similar sentiment, Schirch (2013) observed that situations in which insiders are left out of the decision-making process result 'in local people seeing donor-driven programs as illegitimate, wasteful, and even neo-colonial – reflecting a we-know-what's-best-for-you approach'.

Illustrating the continuity of the impacts of these colonial policies, a Congolese interviewee expressed that: 'Some expatriates, they think that the black race is still inferior to the white race, while they arrive on the field and they find the opposite, you will realise that you think you are a genius but you get to the field and you find that there is someone more competent than you are, that makes wonders more than yourself' (17). The adverb 'still' in this sentence seems to be a symptom of the internalised inferiority previously referred to. Another interviewee reflected on this interiorising: 'It just comes down to dependence, that we've been accustomed, it's, it's there, even in us, even though we may not accept it, like you see this person you expect that, yeah, they are your saviour, you know they are there to make all the right decisions for you and to help you, and you are there just to receive it.' This leads to 'a lot of spectatorship there, [...] you're just waiting for them to make decisions, when you should really be proactive in terms of deciding what it is you want to do' (1, Kenyan). This implies that internationals not only hold financial control but sometimes psychological control too, and that both sides may lack objectivity in assessing the relevance of individuals' perspectives.

This also means that even if an individual is mindful of such dynamics, their interlocutor may not be, making it difficult to overcome as an obstacle to quality listening, especially as the financial and psychological aspects can combine. An international interviewee reflected on this struggle: 'Sometimes they will uh, they can quickly, while I'm asking a question they can quickly give in to what I'm saying or the idea that I'm suggesting while, I'm rather going to ask a question for them to define why they are doing this or that, not saying do this or that, but why do you want to take such a decision with such an activity, or such activity for such programming. Sometimes they will say "oh you're right, we should take this direction" while no, no, that's not what I want to say, I just want to, there is a reason there why you want to go in that direction, I don't want to imply that my idea is better than yours, that I am putting your idea into question' (2, Canadian).

Reflecting on similar dynamics, and moving away from the interiorising theory, a Kenyan interviewee offered: 'I don't know if it is to avoid confrontation or, or because, because at the back of your mind you think that they know what it is that they want to do, so ...' (1). One of the many reasons for this behaviour, suggested the Canadian interviewee, could be that these are more junior staff who know that they are coming from either the global or regional headquarters, and thus may fear repercussions if they express different views (2, Canadian). Illustrating this fear of repercussions in a context where alternative job opportunities are scarce, the interviewee who was most vocal about his frustration at the international–national ratio and racist attitudes, for example, expressed his views while not forgetting to express appreciation for international non-governmental organisation (INGO) job creation, 'since the government is failing miserably in this aspect' (17, Congolese). Similarly, after expressing her frustration about nationals being capped, an interviewee somewhat contritely said: 'I think that's good enough for us, because any development person, any genuine development person will want to make a difference in someone's life [...] as long as we are satisfied I think it's not a problem [...] if you are making an impact in someone's life then that's fine' (5, Kenyan).

Verifying these indirect messages, Mukasa (1999) reported that she was often told a Lugandan proverb which roughly translates to: 'The monkey does not tell on the forest that feeds it' meaning that 'Local staff [...] saw themselves not as equal partners in the program but as subordinates.' Vinhas (2012) also notes this, regretting local staff's wealth of knowledge and experience not being utilised because they would rather avoid expressing different ideas or opposition if this would risk loss of their job. Suzuki (1998) hypothesises that this lack of local expression is the result of a mix of apathy (expecting not to be listened to) and fear of raising their voices (fear of loss of job or negative treatment).

This section examined the mutually reinforcing dynamic between staff attitudes and global inequalities. The author observed that both the tough local economic conditions and remnants of colonial ideology detract from incentives for transparent communication between national and international staff, particularly for national staff perspectives to be expressed and valued.

Conclusion

This chapter set out to achieve two ethically focused tasks using prior research on international–national staff relations in humanitarian and development organisations in the East African region. The first one to present the four ideal outsider roles, namely: a fresh perspective, freedom of speech, communication with donors, and exchange of experiences and/or skills, while highlighting that without quality listening, internationals run the risk of removing rather than adding value. The way in which they can remove value from their collective efforts is by impeding on insiders' roles and suffocating their perspectives, whether intentionally or not, rather than effectively supporting them.

The second task was to demonstrate the difficulty of achieving high-quality listening in practice, given the system that humanitarian and development practitioners operate in. I did this by breaking this system down into the relationships between three of its levels, from macro to micro: global inequalities, the structure of the humanitarian and development field, and staff attitudes towards each other, and by looking at how each of these interconnected relationships (as shown on Figure 3.1) affect the quality of listening.

In the first relationship, that between global inequalities and the structure of the field, interviewees and fellow authors concurred that global inequalities – the same inequalities that practitioners work on alleviating – make the hiring of internationals from donor countries implicitly indispensable and systematically place them in leadership positions. I observed that this creates a situation in which internationals from donor countries are considered more qualified and more trustworthy, experts in 'development', which implies that they should be listened to rather than listen themselves. This situation pressures them to make decisions quickly, which allows little or no time to invest in quality listening to a diversity of insider perspectives. This situation also undermines whatever connection they might develop to field realities by being present in the country, since being mostly at their offices or in meetings speaking with people who share their language and disconnected jargon, further restricts their opportunities to listen to people living the realities that they are hired to impact.

In the second relationship, that between the structure of the field and staff attitudes, interviewees and fellow authors observed that since the structure implicitly values internationals from donor countries more, by compensating them better, staff often unconsciously integrate the idea that their perspectives must be more valuable. The frequent turnover also reduces the incentive for highest quality listening and observation prior to offering their outsider perspectives. Meanwhile, the structure also restrains their flexibility through rigid procedural elements. This higher implicit value again creates a situation in which international staff from donor countries end up (if they did not start that way) expecting to be listened to rather than the other way around, while the rigid procedural elements in the way the programmes are run limit the possibilities for those who do not fall into this insidious trap to include the perspectives of insiders to whom they have made the effort to listen.

In the third relationship, that between staff attitudes and global inequalities, interviewees and fellow authors observe that the combination of extremely tough local economic contexts and a colonial hangover, sustained by ongoing global inequalities both financial and of consideration,[10] make it difficult for national staff to feel safe to express themselves freely, when their financial survival, should they lose their jobs, will not be supported by the government as it might be in Western countries with government safety nets and better job markets. Therefore, should internationals try to listen, they may not actually be told the whole truth, for example, that a certain project would be a waste of resources; such a situation would, of course, have severe ethical implications. The fact that both national and international staff are sometimes still influenced by interiorised colonial ideology dictating that white people are superior, again restricts listening and speaking opportunities, because if white internationals from donor countries are considered to know better, they should be listened to rather than the other way around.

What this demonstrates is that, as someone who chooses to read a book on the ethics of humanitarian action would suspect, good intentions are not enough. If practitioners want to contribute to long-term change while somewhat blindly doing their best to alleviate short-term pains, rather than run the risk of participating in maintaining the status quo, they must challenge the system they are in, starting with being mindful of their own thought-processes and behaviours. I hope that this chapter will help readers see the situation more clearly, enabling them to channel their energy in a way that aligns as closely as possible with their values and vision of an ethical world.

Notes

1 Research for a thesis at Korea University, Master's of Arts in International Peace and Security at the Graduate School of International Studies titled: Redefining the Role of International Staff in International Development: How Inappropriate Insider–Outsider Role Definitions Perpetuate Structural Violence in East Africa and the West.

2 Interviewees from non-governmental and governmental organisations are not always differentiated in this discussion. Although the two can have very different modes of operation, the dynamics described by the staff were extremely similar. This could be the result of the snowball sampling method.

3 Note that the interviews with Congolese, Burundian and Canadian interviewees were carried out in French, and translated by the author in a very literal fashion. Note that interviewees are indicated by a number in parentheses: (1), (10).

4 When white people and black people have unconsciously integrated the racist ideology supporting colonialism: that the white 'race' would be superior to the black one.

5 Note that it is the English that is corrected, rather than a local language translated to English.

6 An interesting supplement to this research, which focused on the classic case of full-time hiring of internationals from donor countries, would be research on alternative ways to include outsiders' perspectives into development efforts, such as within sub-region or international professional exchange programs.

7 Context note: she was not interviewed, but reacting in informal conversation to this research as it was first presented.

8 While staff at headquarters define the field as the country in which the program is carried out, the interviewees refer to the field as outside of the national office, the specific location at which the program is implemented.

9 Referring to conflict-resolution skills training I facilitated during the research.

10 Still of cruel actuality, as noted by the Human Rights Commissioner of the European Council in 'Afrophobia: Europe should confront this legacy of colonialism and the slave trade' (Muižnieks, 2017).

References

Anderson, Mary B. 1999. *Do No Harm: How Aid Can Support Peace—Or War*. London: Lynne Rienner Publishers.

Bryant, Anthony, and Charmaz, Kathy. 2007. *The Sage Handbook of Grounded Theory*. London: Sage Publications Ltd.

Bush, Robert A Baruch, and Folger, Joseph P. 1994. *The Promise of Mediation: Responding to Conflict Through Empowerment and Recognition*. San Francisco: Jossey-Bass Publishers.

Chambers, Robert. 1996. The Primacy of the Personal. In *Beyond the Magic Bullet: NGO Performance and Accountability in the Post-Cold War World*. Eds Edwards, Michael and David Hulme. 241–53. Connecticut: Kumarian Press.

Corbin, Juliet, and Strauss Anselm. 2008. *Basics of Qualitative Research: Techniques and Procedures for Developing Grounded Theory*. 3rd edn. London: Sage Publications Ltd.

Dichter, T. 1986. Who Runs the Show? Staffing Patterns Overseas. Norwalk, CT: Technoserve Inc.

Dichter, T. 1989. Issues Critical to a Shift in Responsibilities Between Us Pvos and Southern NGOs. Washington, DC: USAID.

Fanon, Frantz. 1986. *Black Skin, White Masks*. London: Pluto Press.

Fisher, Ron. 1977. *Sources of Conflict and Methods of Conflict Resolution*. The American University. www.communicationcache.com/uploads/1/0/8/8/10887248/sources_of_conflict_and_methods_of_resolution.pdf (Accessed 10 November 2014).

Fowler, A. 1989. Why Is Managing Social Development Different? NGO Management, No 12, pp. 18–20.

Hardiman, Rita, Jackson, Bailey, and Griffin, Pat. 2000. *Readings for Diversity and Social Justice*. New York: Routledge.

Koutonin, Mawuna Remarque. 2015. Why Are White People Expats When the Rest of Us Are Immigrants? *The Guardian*: www.theguardian.com/global-development-professionals-network/2015/mar/13/white-people-expats-immigrants-migration (Accessed 10 January 2018).

Lawry, Lynn. 2002. *A Guide to NGOs for the Military: A Primer for the Military About Private, Voluntary, and Nongovernmental Organizations Operating in Humanitarian Emergencies Globally*. The Center for Disaster and Humanitarian Assistance Medicine: https://fas.org/irp/doddir/dod/ngo-guide.pdf (Accessed 6 April 2015).

Meimon, Julien. 2007. *The Invention of French Development Aid: Discourse, Instruments and Practices of a Hegemonic Apparatus*. Sciences Po, Research in Question – No. 21.

MS. 1992. *MS in the South: Partnership and Development*. Draft of Principles Paper. Copenhagen: MS.

Muižnieks, Nils. 2017. *Afrophobia: Europe Should Confront this Legacy of Colonialism and the Slave Trade*. Council of Europe Commissioner for Human Rights: www.coe.int/en/web/commissioner/-/afrophobia-europe-should-confront-this-legacy-of-colonialism-and-the-slave-trade (Accessed 25 July 2017).

Mukasa, Sarah. 1999. *Are Expatriate Staff Necessary in International Development NGOs? A Case Study of An International NGO In Uganda*. LSE Research Online. http://eprints.lse.ac.uk/29092/1/int-work-paper4.pdf (Accessed 7 April 2015).

Oktay, Julianne. 2012. *Grounded Theory*. New York: Oxford University Press.

Patel, Swati, and McNamee, Marie. 2013. The Challenges of International Pay. Compensating A Changing Global Talent Pool. *Insidengo. Interaction Monthly Development Magazine* (31): 15–16.

People in Aid. 2007. Motiver Le Personnel Et Les Volontaires Des ONG Travaillant Dans Le Sud. People in Aid. www.peopleinaid.org/pool/files/pubs/motiver-le-personnel-et-les-volontaires-des-ong-travaillant-dans-le-sud.pdf (Accessed 6 April 2015).

Schirch, Lisa. 2013. *Conflict Assessment & Peacebuilding Planning: Toward A Participatory Approach to Human Security*. London: Kumarian Press.

Suzuki, Naoki. 1998. *Inside NGOs: Managing Conflicts Between Headquarters and the Field Offices in Non-Governmental Organizations*. London: Intermediate Technology Publications.

Vinhas, Stéphane. 2012. Expatriés Et Nationaux: Les Deux Faces D'un Même Projet. *Revue Humanitaire* (33): http://humanitaire.revues.org/1417 (Accessed 5 April 2015).

Zarif, Tayyaba. 2012. Grounded Theory Method: An Overview. *Interdisciplinary Journal of Contemporary Research in Business* (4.5): 969–79.

4 | THE MORAL MOTIVATION OF HUMANITARIAN ACTORS

Katarína Komenská

Introduction

The distinctive characteristics of disasters and the way that they differ from everyday situations puts substantial pressure on those who respond to them. From the disaster ethics literature, there are three distinctive features of disasters proposed (WHO, 2002; Sumathipala et al., 2010; Zack, 2011; Geale, 2012; O'Mathúna, 2014). Firstly, disasters negatively impact the lives of individuals and society as a whole. Such incidents extend beyond the boundaries that delineate individual lives and thus demand a broader – often global – perspective. Secondly, disasters are acute and unstable; the different phases of a disaster can change quickly, and in a non-linear fashion, along with the ethical frameworks deemed most appropriate for decision-making. What may be considered morally justifiable in one moment (e.g. walking past an injured person in search of your child in the immediate aftermath of an earthquake) may be deemed morally unacceptable in another (e.g. the same situation, but some days later once the situation has stabilised). Finally, despite the fact that humanitarian ethics deals with situations common to the everyday experience of individuals in society (e.g. deception and the need for honesty and transparency, altruism and egotism, and so on), in disaster settings such issues are amplified given the dramatic contextual backdrop. With these three factors considered, the importance of ethical reflection in disasters is clear. Nevertheless, the process remains complex and challenging.

As mentioned, disasters are understood as unpredictable situations that often cause extensive damage, destruction, and suffering, and which cannot be dealt with by local communities in isolation. Humanitarian actors are therefore prompted to respond and to make ethical decisions in complex and dramatic settings, ultimately dealing with issues spanning fields as diverse as those of politics, economics, gender, culture, psychology, ethics, and morality. In humanitarian ethical inquiry it is necessary to approach certain moral questions: how do people become involved in humanitarian action, and what drives them to promote their moral values into the form of tangible humanitarian actions? This chapter draws from informal interviews with volunteers and other humanitarian actors working in Adaševic/Šid in Serbia, Rōzske in southern Hungary, and Idomeni in Greece, and from others responding to the recent European refugee crisis, during which the motivating factors for involvement in humanitarian action were examined from an ethical perspective (2015–). The aim of this chapter is to present some of the ethical challenges faced by volunteers and other actors, while considering the place of moral motivation in humanitarian practice.

Ethical Challenges for Humanitarian Actors

The complexity of disasters is challenging for humanitarian responders insofar as they must regularly make decisions with an ethical dimension. Commonly these decisions concern the allocation of limited resources (Geale, 2012), the political and social vulnerability of crisis-affected people (Zack, 2011), or the perceived neutrality of humanitarian action (Fink, 2004). Humanitarian actors must deal with these multiple and changing challenges on an everyday basis. This chapter does not seek to explore each of these issues comprehensively, but instead offers an overview of potentially ethically challenging situations, with a focus on the importance of understanding one's moral motivation in such circumstances.

It is important to note that humanitarian workers are not exclusively professionals (i.e. from healthcare, emergency response, military, or managerial disciplines). This raises not only questions regarding their training and professional skill set but also regarding their ability to recognise the potentially negative impact of their actions in humanitarian contexts. As Thoma and Bebeau (2013) observe, 'professionals tend to be more aware that ethical considerations are explicit in their roles and learn early in their training and socialisation that one must be ready to provide justifications for their actions', and as such are better placed from the outset to evaluate ethically challenging situations.[1] If humanitarian workers do not have the prior experience or skill set required to recognise the needs of crisis-affected people or the necessity of triage,[2] it becomes difficult for them to prioritise their actions. Irrespective of an individual's desire to act to the best of their ability on behalf of others, ignorance of the potential impact of emergency relief, or of the need to set priorities in certain contexts, may have a net negative consequence. This may be viewed as an issue of insufficient moral sensitivity and moral judgement in disaster settings.

An additional ethical challenge may present when individuals are faced with situations that conflict with their personal ethical frameworks. In the context of humanitarian crises, the need to make decisions despite resource limitations and relative professional inexperience can be demanding of individuals offering their services. Those people who respond to, or are in some way connected with, disasters (i.e. crisis-affected people, healthcare staff, other humanitarian aid workers, and military personnel) often report disillusionment and a form of ethical frustration as a result of the need to repeatedly make difficult ethical decisions (Lepora, 2012). Volunteers on the Balkan Route have often dealt with such a state while eyeing the never-ending stream of boats, buses, or trains carrying refugees, a situation which pushed them to overestimate their strength (both physical and mental). Based on external factors (e.g. limited resources, an absence of skills in crowd-management, and cultural elements), elementary tasks, for example the distribution of clothes, become more difficult, which often contrasts strongly with the primary motivation 'to help', when situations might have led to the rejection of support to an individual or group. This frustration is born of a challenge to the long-established, traditional ethical frameworks of volunteers that would otherwise have guided the resolution of such situations. For these reasons, new models may be required to mitigate the risk of disillusionment and frustration: the ethical 'trauma' that results from the need to morally compromise when making difficult ethical decisions (Goodstein, 2000).

Many authors are sceptical about whether it is possible to use traditional ethical frameworks, with their unique axiological perspectives and justifications for ethical decision-making, in the context of disasters (Schwartz et al., 2012; Leaning & Guha-Sapir, 2013; Wagner & Dahnke, 2015). This scepticism is the product of a disconnect between the prevailing deontological understanding of professional ethics (e.g. patient autonomy and the value of dignity), which may exist in strong tension with the ethical frameworks preferred in the formulation of effective tools for decision-making in humanitarian medicine (Schwartz et al., 2012). One of the first attempts to develop such an ethical framework began with the intention of producing a value-neutral and effective tool for decision-making by healthcare professionals responding to disasters (Leaning & Guha-Sapir, 2013). Such a consequential (utilitarian) approach – from which certain emergency relief tools have been developed – has its limitations, which in turn are challenged by appeals to common sense morality (Heinze, 2005), or by a need to consider the values of dignity, the moral right to life and its protection, and humanity (Komenská, 2017).

Finally, an important issue to consider in relation to humanitarian ethics is the extent to which morality may be derived from action. The suffering invariably generated by disasters is unlikely to dissipate without some form of intervention: certainly not with distant empathy and sympathy alone. Relief from pain and trauma is thus achieved by the conscious actions of an individual or a collective of actors who choose to become involved in disaster relief and humanitarian response.[3]

In relation to the aforementioned issues, decision-making in humanitarian action must be subject to ethical reflection. Two prominent questions must be addressed. Firstly, how does the moral agent identify the 'right' course of action during disasters and emergencies? Secondly, why and how does it happen that the moral agent acts upon this recognition of right over wrong? The former question relates to the formation of moral judgement, and focuses on decisions between what is right or wrong, good or bad. The latter question addresses the issue of what motivates an individual to enact moral decisions. The relationship between these two aspects of moral action will be introduced during the remainder of this chapter, with special attention paid to the issue of moral motivation in humanitarian action.

Moral Motivation in Humanitarian Action

People engaged in humanitarian action generally do so out of a strong motivation to help others. Unlike the motivation that drives other forms of professional activity, it is less common that the motivation for humanitarian action should be attributed to a concern for financial gain (either among volunteers, or paid professionals and experts). While it can be argued that this motivation occasionally results from an individual's desire to develop their professional expertise,[4] once the various challenges and difficulties associated with humanitarian action are considered, it is difficult to see such desire as a primary motivation (rather as an outcome secondary to other choices and motivations). We must therefore look elsewhere for more complex reasons that explain the motivation to engage in humanitarian response. To do so requires an exploration of the morality of those involved in humanitarian action, and of their willingness to do 'good'.

For the purpose of this chapter, it is important to recognise volunteers as one of the largest groups of humanitarian actors.[5] Nevertheless, this group is relatively under-studied, which raises necessary questions of the values that motivate their participation in humanitarian action. This disparate group is generally understood as comprising people who offer their time, energy, and expertise to help those in need without expecting any kind of benefit in return, be that financial, material, or otherwise.[6] In recent years, volunteering has been recognised as an important way to promote democratic values, social inclusion, humanism, and civic (frequently at a global level) participation. However, volunteers in humanitarian crises often operate on their own with limited or no support or coordination from the humanitarian sector's 'big players' (e.g. MSF, UNHCR, UNICEF, and the IRC). Nevertheless, these volunteers are an important and necessary component of disaster relief; they are often the most flexible of those involved, adapting easily to new challenges and changing pressures generated during humanitarian crises, and at a local level they are often initially best placed to interact directly with, and gain the trust of, crisis-affected populations. The 'Czech team',[7] as a coordinating group for volunteers on the Balkan Route (since 2015), has come to represent an example of successful humanitarian volunteering. The group was able to effectively modify its activities and services according to the changing political, organisational – and even meteorological – conditions during the refugee crisis.

A substantial proportion of those who volunteer in humanitarian crises are first responders.[8] They are often local people who already live and work in the area affected by crisis. Whether they are ordinary citizens or professionals (e.g. firefighters, police officers, emergency medical personnel), these first responders typically demonstrate a strong emotional bond to the community and the affected context, and therefore feel an obligation to offer protection, in such a way that this connection may be considered the first type of moral motivation for voluntary participation. This is exemplified by the story of the Maketū community in New Zealand, whose beaches and shores were badly affected by the Rena Oil Spill in 2011. Shortly after the spill the local community began to volunteer for clean-up shifts. The authors of a study on the volunteer response recognised the cultural context, belief systems, and customs as a source of motivation for the locals and other volunteers (Smith et al., 2015).[9] These volunteers were motivated by a close bond that they shared with the wider community, which was expressed as a form of spatial partiality.

Midgley's definition of the 'moral community' with its series of concentric circles may prove insightful here. A moral community is defined by considering two main features. Firstly, members of a moral community are grouped in concentric circles (such as by family, social class, nation, species, and, most broadly, biosphere). Motivation to help and support other members of the moral community is affected by an individual's belonging to one or more of the concentric circles, and the distance of the circles from the main circle, which represents the 'self' (Midgley, 1998). Secondly, Midgley declares that these concentric circles are not 'impenetrable social barriers', but that they can be modified by considering other, special moral claims (ibid.). These claims often arise from the emotional experience of social proximity and of individual bonds. For Midgley, the moral bond to protect those with whom we have a close emotional relationship is stronger and therefore of greater moral acceptability.

It may seem natural to view motivation for humanitarian actions in this way, but alone this framework does not offer a sufficiently robust analysis. Local volunteers may be the largest collective group of responders during a humanitarian crisis but they are not (and cannot be) the only responders. It should not be forgotten that a humanitarian crisis is a form of disaster which, by its definition, requires support from actors external to the affected community or region (O'Mathúna, 2014). Silk claims that virtue ethics has the potential to expand the scope of spatial partiality (perhaps to that of a universal applicability), such that people may be 'more willing to exercise beneficence with respect to those on another continent' (Silk, 2000). Were the emotional motivation for action to be based only on the localised generation of sentiment and empathy, then humanitarian response would be limited. At the very least, an attempt at achieving impartiality is required in order to facilitate humanitarian action: an impartiality that will enable non-affected moral agents to act rationally and responsibly to the needs of crisis-affected people. Impartiality also allows moral agents to: more objectively consider the need for and criteria that define triage;

make decisions on a cost-benefit basis; and consider the wider moral implications of their actions.[10]

The second form of 'ethical'[11] motivation stems from the current status of ethics within society. While on one hand, certain professionals, public figures, and politicians have downplayed the value of ethics in relation to professional conduct, a popularised form of ethics has become increasingly fashionable in contemporary culture. Bilasová has written of 'the search for new models in post-moral society and humanity' (Bilasová, 2008), of which a number of such models are now recognised (e.g. 'green' management, 'ethical' consumption, and lobbying for human rights). As positive as this trend may be, the contemporary popularisation of ethics raises additional moral and ethical dilemmas.[12] One such dilemma relates to the claim that ethics has been co-opted as a marketing tool, as a means by which individuals, companies, and organisations can preserve or enhance their social status. This fashion undoubtedly influences the choices made by moral agents, but not necessarily in a way that is deemed ethical (i.e. choices that derive from free, conscious, and responsible decision-making that intends to achieve what is good or right). Such decisions may be based on social expectations rather than on moral values and ethical considerations. This form of 'ethics' represents another form of external, anonymous authority, which leaves individuals under no obligation to consider the consequences or wider ethical implications of their actions.

Recently, humanitarian action and humanitarian volunteering have also adopted a fashionable and business-like form. Volunteers in search of a direct experience of suffering are driven by a compassion for, and empathy with, the 'suffering' and 'vulnerable' other (Ryška, 2014), with the media playing a pivotal role in this process (Silk, 2000; Calain, 2013). Ryška claims that volunteering has now become 'a historically unique and popular face of humanism' (Ryška, 2014). In some cases volunteering is now an activity for which people are willing to pay,[13] while in the most extreme cases it may take the form of 'humanitarian tourism'.[14] Volunteering that is motivated by a 'popular ethics' is easily identified in day-to-day volunteering (and in humanitarian action in general), of which there are numerous examples: the large number of volunteer blogs and pronounced social media use; the insistence of volunteers on morning or afternoon shifts that are busier and 'more visible' than night shifts; the avoidance of the hidden tasks involved in humanitarian action, and so on. Such volunteers have a tendency to aspire towards the heroic, and therefore attempt to work in the most 'attractive' positions: saving lives on the beach, working in the camp, and participating in food distributions. In contrast to this visible 'heroism', there is often an avoidance of other essential operational tasks, such as cleaning, other physically demanding jobs, and administrative support.

There is a practical ethical problem with this type of motivation in humanitarian action, as it is not often interiorised (in an axiological form) in the ethical decision-making process of the moral agent.[15] It is therefore difficult to sustain this form of motivation, with the effect that as soon as media coverage wanes, so too does the willingness to help.[16] Therefore, as in the case of partiality-motivated volunteering, action motivated by a popularised 'ethics' does not adequately explain the complexity of moral motivation for volunteering.

The third type of motivation for volunteering in response to a humanitarian crisis derives from the axiological preferences of the moral agent. Those who volunteer often do so citing religious beliefs (altruism and caring are core concepts in most religions) (Silk, 2000) or based on a particular political ideology (for example as a protest against a political system and its failures, or against the humanitarian aid system and the unjust distribution of aid). These volunteers see their motivation as value-based; their involvement is driven by values such as humanity, altruism, empathy, solidarity, and a desire to promote democracy, which may also be articulated in moral law (e.g. in the form of categorical imperatives or religious commandments) and understood as an individual's moral duty. This form of motivation is deontological in the sense that the moral values are absolute and are to be fully respected. Interestingly, those who volunteer on the basis of this type of motivation not only accept that it is their duty to honour the moral laws to which they subscribe, but that they are also obliged and motivated to promote these values and laws through their actions (de Colle & Werhane, 2007). This marks an important shift from the traditional understanding of a moral duty in deontological ethical theories, where doing 'good' is defined as honouring moral laws (with no explicit obligation to act upon them).

Nevertheless, this is also rather problematic in humanitarian contexts, as Lepora (2012), Heinze (2005), and Schwartz et al. (2012) have observed. There are various cultural and situational aspects of humanitarian action that must be reflected in ethical decision-making processes. Volunteers motivated purely by moral values may be incapable of relativising or prioritising these values when they come into conflict with aspects of their day-to-day humanitarian work (e.g. a deontological commitment to humanity and the dignity of refugees may come into conflict with an obligation to justly distribute limited time and resources). These conflicts may ultimately force volunteers to make decisions that they do not consider to be morally justifiable, which might in turn cause frustration and distress, with a negative impact on an individual's motivation to continue their work.

To summarise, the moral motivation for humanitarian action is understood and justified by individual actors in many different ways. However, in the theoretical discourse, two main positions in relation to moral motivation are distinguishable. Both of these positions attempt to explain the link between the intellectual and practical dimensions of morality: between moral judgement and moral action. One of these positions formulates its conclusions from non-cognitive arguments, interpreting moral motivation as a pro-attitude: a desire to do good. Supporting theorists would claim that the intellectual dimension of one's morality, or the ability to form moral judgements, is not a prerequisite to achieve moral action. In other words, it has been proposed that there is no direct link between moral judgement and moral action, and that the desire to do good is sufficient to fulfil an individual's moral ambition (Brink, 1997).

Such non-cognitive arguments may be discernable from the examples discussed earlier. Volunteers influenced and motivated by the popularity of 'ethics', for example, do not necessarily have a tendency to re-assess what is needed and what should be done. This might be considered an extreme case, but in such circumstances volunteers are unlikely to properly evaluate the situations in which they intervene, often do not have the skills to recognise the complexity of moral issues, and therefore might act without considering either what is right or what is needed. Similar non-cognitive arguments might be applicable in the case of local first responders, who may act out of their desire to help, and out of a willingness to protect their community, which represents a natural standpoint. Nevertheless, such natural feelings should always be subject to reason. Only by engaging with the intellectual dimension of morality are moral agents capable of defining what is right, and what course of action should be taken.

The converse position in the theoretical discourse is the cognitivist position, which emphasises the intellectual dimension of morality. For supporting theorists, moral judgements express beliefs formed by the rational and intellectual activity of moral agents. Moral action is therefore the product of an individual's recognition of a moral obligation: a moral duty without the pressure to transfer this duty into concrete action (Brink, 1997). In disaster settings, we must reject such an idea, since humanitarian action is derived from the practical dimension of morality, and is demanding of action from moral agents.

As Sterm suggests, with regard to ethics we must be concerned with 'the relation between the normative status of certain actions and the motivations of agents' (Sterm, 2012).[17] Moral rules, norms, and values recognised and accepted by a particular community and culture might help to define what is right and what is good (the reasons for, and formal criteria of, moral obligation), but attention must be paid to 'the thought of actions, and the doing of actions' (Sterm, 2012). Neither of these two approaches complies fully with the moral reality within which the moral agent must make decisions. For example, recognising someone's dignity does not guarantee that this ascribed value will be understood as one's obligation, or that it will be acted upon. Following the 'right' course of action is especially difficult in situations complicated by disasters. During these events, moral agents may easily be able to recognise what is 'right' and which values should be promoted, but be either unable or unwilling to fulfil their normative duties under the various pressures imposed by the crisis. Moral reality should therefore encourage the activity of moral agents (as an intention to do good), otherwise moral goals are likely to remain confined to the sphere of knowledge and theory. These examples exemplify the assertion that moral motivation must be analysed in a holistic manner: in a way that will emphasise moral agency, one's willingness to act, the ability to recognise moral obligation, along with the issue of moral development. Such a holistic approach is only achievable if the exploration of moral motivation captures the complex nature of the ethical decision-making process.

Moral Motivation and the Process of Ethical Decision-making

As discussed, in relation to humanitarian action, both dimensions of moral reality must be accepted in the process of ethical decision-making. Moral agents ought not only to recognise what is good or right, but also to put this into action. Despite this, there remains a gap between the terms on which moral judgement and moral action are defined. A review of the history of ethical thinking reveals that these two phenomena were linked rather intuitionally; it has been assumed that doing good is based on an acknowledgement of what is good or right, and that recognition of a moral obligation presupposes moral action. Nevertheless, there are many instances in which such a connection is undermined, for example in relation to the protection of the natural environment or the promotion of animal rights. Moral agents in general understand that they have a moral obligation to protect the environment (regardless of whether their values derive from an anthropocentric or non-anthropocentric worldview) but their actions do not necessarily correspond with an understanding of this moral obligation and situation. For example, they do not necessarily feel the drive to recycle, reduce the use of non-renewable resources, or use public transport rather than private cars, as a means of fulfilling a moral obligation to protect the environment.

During disasters and humanitarian crises, there are many such examples of the tension between moral judgement and action. Take for example the recent European refugee crisis, shaped by the negative stance taken towards refugees fleeing to Europe (since the spring of 2015), and the media coverage of this situation (Motal, 2015), along with the Hungarian referendum supported by the government to reject the quota set by the EU on accepting asylum seekers. Many European citizens understand the concept of human rights and the values of human dignity and humanity that should be universally promoted in a moral agent's actions. However, rational recognition of our moral obligation to assist victims of suffering and misery does not automatically translate to a willingness to act on this moral judgement.

In light of such observations, moral theorists began to focus on qualifying the relationship between moral judgement and moral action, approaching this supposed disconnect with an exploration of the process of ethical decision-making. According to Rest (1986), it was necessary to create a model outlining the complex inner processes that lead to moral action. Drawing from research in moral psychology and moral development, Rest formulated a four-component model for moral behaviour that captures the process of ethical decision-making.[18] The model consists of four components (or *capacities* required by the moral agent in order to make an ethical decision and ultimately perform moral action): moral sensitivity, moral judgement, moral motivation, and moral character (Armstrong et al., 2003). *Moral sensitivity* is defined as the ability to identify and discern problematic situations with an ethical dimension. *Moral judgement* is a skill employed by a moral agent in order to analyse the right course of action. *Moral motivation* involves a prioritisation of values, while *moral character* guarantees that the aforementioned components result in both moral development and moral action. Each of these components is interactive, cannot function in isolation, and collectively influences both the cognitive and affective dimensions of a moral agent's functioning (Bebeau, 2006).

Moral motivation is thus a core component of moral action, channelling the recognised notion of moral obligation (that results from one's moral sensitivity and moral judgement). Moral motivation captures the concern of moral agents for the needs of others, despite personal risk and inconvenience. It is 'the degree of commitment to taking the moral course of action, valuing moral values over other values, and taking personal responsibility for moral outcomes' (Armstrong et al., 2003).

Importantly, as with all other components of moral behaviour, moral motivation is considered to be a dynamic component of an individual's moral development: 'the relationship between moral understanding and motivation [is] not constant across the stage sequence, but ... is strengthened with development' (Thoma & Bebeau, 2013). At higher stages of one's moral development, moral judgements become increasingly internalised, and as such the motivation of moral agents becomes more consistent with their actions.

Rest's theoretical model for ethical decision-making may therefore have clear practical implications in relation to the moral motivation for humanitarian action. On one hand, it has been argued that in disasters and other humanitarian crises, the activity of moral agents (humanitarian actors of any sort) is elementary. The complexity of the four-component model shows that moral sensitivity and moral judgement offer little if they do not also urge the moral agent to act and to express their moral values in the form of concrete action. Moral motivation emphasises the role of these internal desires and commitment during the ethical decision-making process.

On the other hand, moral motivation should not be understood as an independent or superior component of the ethical decision-making process. This process also expects that the moral agent should recognise and accept their responsibilities in relation to action. As such, this assertion illustrates the limitations of some of the aforementioned types of humanitarian motivation. If the commitment to act is out of sync with an individual's moral sensitivity and moral judgement (as might be the case with untrained humanitarian actors, emotionally driven first responders, or humanitarian 'tourists'), then a commitment to do good may have negative consequences. Humanitarian actors should understand that their internal, emotional, or value orientation must be subject to reason and ethical consideration in any given situation. As such, Rest's model adequately depicts the complexity and interrelation between individual elements of the decision-making process.

Finally, Rest (1986) defines moral motivation as the preference of moral values (what ought to be done and what ought to be protected) over one's personal values (be they economic, professional, or personal). As has been stated earlier in this chapter, a commitment to place the needs of others above one's own, and to promote universal moral values such as humanity and solidarity, is complicated in the context of disasters. Given that ethical challenges are complex, dynamic, and often lack transparency, humanitarian actors are often disappointed by the role they play, the decisions they have to make, and the actions that they are prompted to take. In the light of these challenges, in order to continue their work, the degree of a humanitarian's commitment must derive from a strong personal value framework. Nevertheless, a humanitarian's motivation may change during the course of their participation in humanitarian activities as the terms on which they engage are significantly and repeatedly challenged. The four-component model recognises the dynamic nature of one's moral life as well as the course of one's moral development. Knowledge and an understanding of the processes that establish moral motivation (along with other components of ethical decision-making) are likely to accelerate the process of internalisation of moral obligations, to reduce moral distress, and to help in the making of ethically sound choices in humanitarian settings, with positive implications for the management and coordination of humanitarian activities.

This type of moral motivation can be also observed in the conduct of certain humanitarian actors. Usually, these actors have a longer history of involvement in the field of humanitarian and development work. As a result of their prior experience, they are able to refine their moral sensitivity in order to recognise ethical challenges in their work and instances where moral values and principles are in conflict in such situations. They also improve their capacity to pass moral judgements in cases of emergencies, sometimes even 'forgetting about the good, and do[ing] what is right', accepting the utilitarian pressures of humanitarian work without ignoring the significance of value-based justifications in their decision-making.

Such motivation is dynamic and can develop significantly over time. Experienced volunteers often refer to their initial motivation as a spontaneous feeling of empathy for victims of a crisis, or as value-based (many of the volunteers from the Czech Republic and Slovakia belong to the Catholic Church and are actively involved in its activities). After experiencing the humanitarian contexts in their entirety (e.g. operational, economic, political, cultural factors), and associated ethical challenges, these actors often reject external interpretations of their work as acts based on a particular duty (i.e. social, moral, or religious). In contrast, after recognising the needs of victims of crisis, the moral obligation itself often drives the urge to act. They claimed 'not to see any reasonable argument not to volunteer' and participate in the humanitarian action. Marián Cehelník, a coordinator of volunteers in Greece and Macedonia, explained his reasons and motivations during a talk on his experiences on the Balkan Route.[19] In his words: 'The problem is here. They are already here. The humanitarian crisis is in Syria, Turkey, etc., but it is also here, on our borders. We cannot close our eyes, look in different direction. We need to find a way how to answer the humanitarian needs responsibly.' Motivation, for such experienced humanitarian actors, is not idealised or naïve but is perceived rather in a practical, professional and humane way, cognitively recognised and internalised in the complex process of ethical decision-making. Moral obligation, together with the principles of humanitarian work, as well as the wider holistic and case-by-case ethical approach of humanitarian actors, are the moral basis of a deeply rooted and strong moral motivation.

Notes

1 Nevertheless, even professionally trained humanitarian workers will face 'unusual situations in which the professional ethics that apply in routine emergencies and health care situations may be tested' (Geale, 2012).

2 This does not apply only to members of the general public (local first-responders or volunteers), but also to first-time responders with no prior experience of, or training in, emergency response.

3 This should not be understood exclusively as professional or institutionally organised disaster relief.

4 For further reading, see Musick & Wilson (2008).

5 In numbers, local volunteers comprise the largest group of responders in humanitarian crises, particularly as they often act as first responders (Smith et al., 2015).

6 The United Nations lists three criteria that define voluntary actions: 'it is not undertaken for financial gain; it is undertaken of one's own free will; it brings benefits to a third party as well as to the people who volunteer' (Musick & Wilson, 2008). This definition is rather simplistic and may lead to inconsistences in the way volunteer work is understood (for more details see Musick & Wilson, 2008), but is sufficient for the purpose of this chapter.

7 Currently operating under the small non-governmental organisation PLNU (Pomáhame lidem na úteku).

8 Alongside local volunteers, other groups should be recognised: individuals who (either on their own or as part of small informal groups or more formally organised non-governmental organisations) arrive at the scene of a humanitarian crisis to assist with disaster relief. It is often only later that the so-called 'big players' develop the capacity to respond to the needs of crisis-affected people on a larger scale.

9 Another example of the impact of close community links is the story of Magdalena Verheyen, a nurse who responded to the tsunami disaster in Sumatra, Indonesia (see Dawson (2005)).

10 When reflecting on humanitarian action and the ethics of such action, it is necessary to formulate a value-neutral framework from which professionals can make effective decisions in relation to humanitarian intervention. See:

Leaning, J, Guha-Sapir, D (2013), Natural disasters, armed conflict and public health. *The New England Journal of Medicine*. Vol. 369 (19): 1836-42. Given the degree of overlap between challenges facing all humanitarian agents, be they professionals or local volunteers, the need for such frameworks should not be overlooked during discussions related to the norms and aspirations that guide humanitarian volunteers.

11 'Ethics' is used here to refer to ethics in its popularised sense, rather than in its more specific philosophical sense.

12 This topic deserves wider debate than is permitted here. For further details, see: Kalajtzidis, J (2016), Moral education and moral consumption. *Ethics and Bioethics (in Central Europe)*. Vol. 6(1–2): 39–44. Bilasová, V (2008), *Výzvy pre etiku v súčasnosti [Challenges of contemporary ethics]*. Prešov: Filozofická fakulta Prešovskej university v Prešove.

13 One such example are the now commonplace volunteering trips to the Global South where individuals pay for comfortable accommodation, food, a cultural and social programme, etc., while helping others.

14 Humanitarian tourism refers to a type of volunteering that is motivated by a volunteer's desire to meet new people, experience different cultures, improve language skills, visit new places, etc. Such volunteers are often unaware of their duties and responsibilities, and of what is irresponsible behaviour (not showing up for a shift, avoiding particular tasks, etc.), which may in turn create a hostile work environment.

15 The process of interiorisation of the world is an important part of one's identity development, which includes the interiorisation of values and norms that are linked to the development of cognition and moral character. Only moral agents who are fully morally

conscious are able not only to follow external societal norms, but to critically evaluate such norms, and interiorise and self-construct them in the form of a complex understanding of moral reality (Greenwald, 1988).

16 However critical this sounds, this initial – unstable – motivating factor may eventually develop (based on an individual's experience of humanitarian work) into a more morally defensible stance, based on a commitment to

humanity, dignity, solidarity, and shared responsibility.

17 'Normative' as either a consequential or deontological understanding of what is right.

18 This model has since been further developed and applied by Rest and others, including Darcia Narvaez, Muriel Bebeau, and Stephen Thoma (Thoma & Bebeau, 2013).

19 The debate took place in March 2016 at the University of Prešov, Slovakia.

References

Armstrong, MB, Ketz, JE & Owsen, D (2003), Ethics education in accounting: moving toward ethical motivation and ethical behavior. *Journal of Accounting Education.* Vol. 21 (1): 1–16.

Bebeau, MJ (2006), Evidence-based character development. Pp. 47–86. In: Kenny, N & Shelton, W (eds) *Lost virtue: professional character development in medical education: advances in bioethics.* Vol. 10. Oxford: JAI Press.

Bilasová, V (2008), *Výzvy pre etiku v súčasnosti [Challenges of contemporary ethics].* Prešov: Filozofická fakulta Prešovskej Univerzity v Prešove.

Brink, DO (1997), Moral motivation. *Ethics.* Vol. 108 (1): 4–32.

Calain, P (2013), Ethics and images of suffering bodies in humanitarian medicine. *Social Science and Medicine.* Vol. 98 (1): 279–85.

Dawson, S (2005), Touch of humanity. *Nursing Standard.* Vol. 19 (35): 24–6.

de Colle, S & Werhane, PH (2008), Moral motivation across ethical theories: what can we learn for designing corporate ethics programs? *Journal of Business Ethics.* Vol. 81(4): 751–64.

Fink, M (2004), *War hospital: a true story of surgery and survival.* New York: PublicAffairs.

Geale, SK (2012), The ethics of disaster management. *Disaster Prevention and Management.* Vol. 21(4): 445–62.

Goodstein, JD (2000), Moral compromise and personal integrity: exploring the ethical issues of deciding together in organizations. *Business Ethics Quarterly.* Vol. 10 (4): 805–19.

Greenwald, AG (1988), A social-cognitive account of the self´s development. Pp. 30–43. In: Lapsley, DK & Power, FC (eds) *Self, ego, and identity: integrative approaches.* New York: Springer.

Heinze, EA (2005), Common sense morality and the consequentialist ethics of humanitarian intervention. *Journal of Military Ethics.* Vol. 4 (3): 168–82.

Komenská, K (2017), Moral motivation in humanitarian action. *Human Affairs.* Vol. 27 (2): 145–54.

Leaning, J & Guha-Sapir, D (2013), Natural disasters, armed conflict and public health. *New England Journal of Medicine.* Vol. 369 (19): 1836–42.

Lepora, C (2012), On compromise and being compromised. *Journal of Political Philosophy.* Vol. 20 (1): 1–22.

Midgley, M (1998), *Animals and why they matter.* Athens: University of Georgia Press.

Motal, J (2015), Dehumanization of refugees in media as a case of moral disengagement. *Ethics & Bioethics (in Central Europe)*. Vol. 5 (3–4): 183–96.

Musick, MA & Wilson, J (2008), *Volunteers. A social profile*. Pp. 16–18. Bloomington: Indiana University Press.

O'Mathúna, DP (2014), Disasters. Pp. 619–39. In: ten Have, HAMJ and Gordijn, B (eds). *Handbook of Global Bioethics*. Dortrecht: Springer.

Rest, J (1986), *Moral development: advances in research and theory*. New York: Praeger.

Ryška, T (2014), Imaginace pomoci, rozvoje a humanitarismu [Imagining assistance, development, and humanitarianism]. Pp. 78–95. In: Gallayová, Z, Hipš, J & Urbanová, K (eds). *Globálne vydelávanie – kontext a kritika [Global education – context and critique]*. Zvolen: Technická univerzita vo Zvolene.

Schwartz, L, Hunt, M, Sinding, C, Elit, L, Redwood-Campbell, L, Adelson, N & da Laat, S (2012), Models for humanitarian health care ethics. *Public Health Ethics*. Vol. 5 (1): 81–90.

Silk, J (2000), Caring at a distance: (im) partiality, moral motivation and the ethics of representation. *Ethics, Place and Environment*. Vol. 3 (3): 303–9.

Smith, K, Hammerton, H, Hunt, S & Sargisson, RJ (2015), Local volunteers respond to the Rena oil spill in Maketu, New Zealand. *Kōtuitui: New Zealand Journal of Social Sciences*. Vol. 11 (1): 1–11.

Sterm, R (2012), *Understanding moral obligation: Kant, Hegel, Kierkegaard*. Cambridge: Cambridge University Press.

Sumathipala, A, Jafarey, A, De Castro, LD, Ahmad, A, Marcer, D, Srinivasan, S, Kumar, N, Siribaddana, S, Sutaryo, S, Bhan, A, Waidyaratne, D, Beneragama, S, Jayasekera, C, Edirisingha, S & Siriwardhana, C (2010), Ethical issues in post-disaster clinical interventions and research: a developing world perspective. Key findings from a drafting and consensus generation meeting of the Working Group on Disaster Research and Ethics (WGDRE). *Asian Bioethics Review*. Vol. 2 (2): 124–42.

Thoma, SJ & Bebeau, MJ (2013), *Moral motivation and the four-component mode*. Pp. 54. In: Heinrichs, K, Oser, F & Lovat, T (eds) *Handbook of moral motivation: theories, models, applications*. Rotterdam: Sense Publishers.

Wagner, JM & Dahnke, MD (2015), Nursing ethics and disaster triage: applying utilitarian ethical theory. *Journal of Emergency Nursing*. Vol. 41 (4): 300–6.

WHO (2002), *Disasters & emergencies: definitions*. Training package. Addis Ababa: World Health Organization.

Zack, N (2011), Digging deeper into ethics for disaster. *Review Journal of Political Philosophy*. Vol. 8 (2): 36–54.

5 | MAKESHIFT HUMANITARIANS: INFORMAL HUMANITARIAN AID ACROSS EUROPEAN CLOSE(D) BORDERS

Elisa Sandri and Fosco Bugoni

During the European 'refugee crisis' a myriad of grassroots organisations and private citizens began providing humanitarian aid to refugees across the continent.[1] This humanitarian assistance, despite being informal and independent of governments or international agencies, effectively administered aid and established significant networks of support. In this chapter, we focus on grassroots humanitarianism, or 'volunteer humanitarianism' (Sandri, 2016; 2017), in the 'Jungle',[2] the informal refugee camp in Calais. Humanitarian aid in the Jungle was almost entirely delivered by volunteers who were not professionals in this field, hence informality and improvisation played a central role in the delivery of aid. Although aid in refugee camps is often understood as an extension of the state's surveillance and disciplinary power (Diken, 2010; Pinelli, 2015; Sczepanikova, 2013; Whyte, 2011), the Jungle represents an interesting exception to the existing literature on camps, particularly in the European context. As we will illustrate, this is due to the fact that the Jungle was not administered by authorities or aid agencies, refugees were able to perform some acts of citizenship inside the camp, and volunteers refused to collaborate with local authorities in the coercion of refugees into bureaucratic systems. Nonetheless, the deliberate neglect of the humanitarian problem in Calais and the strategies of 'violent (in)action' (Davies, Isakjee & Dhesi, 2017), ultimately reaffirmed the authority of the state.

In this chapter, we focus on the work of volunteers from the summer of 2015 – when Calais once again became a spontaneous migration hub – to the demolition of the camp in October 2016. The research focused on volunteers and on their contribution to informal humanitarian aid. As such, the refugees' experience is mentioned only in brief. The chapter will discuss the work of one grassroots organisation, Lotus,[3] based in the UK but mainly active in France from July 2015 to November 2016.

Lotus provided medical aid in the Jungle, alongside other services such as the construction of shelters and the provision of support to young people. Interviews were conducted with members of the organisation, some of whom were medically trained and others who carried out a variety of tasks, from sorting donations to distributing hot drinks. One of the authors was also a member of the core group of Lotus volunteers. As a result of this direct involvement with the camp, the research directly engaged with questions of ethics, morals, and power, collocating fieldwork within the fields of knowledge production and of action (Scheper-Hughes, 1992, 1995; Hale, 2006). The picture that emerges can be considered an ethnography from the 'inside', for we have interpreted the practices of the organisation, while also creating those same practices (Maeckelbergh, 2009; Mosse, 2005). Contextualising humanitarian practices with ethnography reveals complexities that are often overlooked, such as the role of humanitarian actors and, in this case, of volunteers (Rozakou, 2012).

The chapter is structured as follows: first, we provide a brief overview of the context in which the Jungle came about. From there we outline the characteristics of the informal humanitarian response conducted by grassroots organisations in the Jungle, focusing specifically on Lotus and its provision of medical aid. Finally, we illustrate some of the tensions that arose between grassroots organisations and the state during the provision of assistance to refugees.

The Jungle: 'A Camp Full of Refugees'

In 2015, over one million people fled their countries and arrived on Greek and Italian shores following extremely dangerous journeys (UNHCR, 2015). The numbers represented a significant increase in migration to the European Union, with this year marking the beginning of the so-called 'European refugee crisis', despite the fact that the vast majority of newly displaced people during this period were hosted in countries such as Jordan and Turkey (Al Jazeera, 2016). As Calhoun (2010) argues, the notions of humanitarian 'crisis' or 'emergency' are symbols that carry strong values and a moral imperative to act. On the other hand, they also describe an emergency as something unpredictable and sudden, which breaks a supposed normality, and which needs to be contained with tougher policies. This nexus of care and control (Fassin, 2005) is evident in the European Union's (EU) overall border policy, from the practices of 'humanitarian rescue/sovereign capture'

(Pallister-Wilkins, 2017), to the practices of reception and evaluation of asylum claims (Sorgoni, 2016).

In the case of the Jungle, the camp serves as a symbol of the European asylum regime's crisis in its response to a longstanding issue. The history of this border as a focal point for migration dates back to the 1990s (King, 2016; Rigby & Schlembach, 2013; Rygiel, 2011; Walters, 2008). At the time, hundreds of refugees from Kosovo, Kurdistan and Afghanistan camped in Calais, waiting to cross the Channel to reach the UK. The French government decided to open a reception centre – the Sangatte Centre – managed by the French Red Cross, which provided short-stay accommodation (Fassin, 2005). However, the centre was closed in 2002 due to the British and French governments' fears that the centre acted as a pull-factor. International norms for refugee protection were largely ignored by the government, and humanitarian organisations condemned the lack of institutional assistance (Millner, 2011). Following Sangatte, migration did not cease, but instead refugees established small informal settlements in and around the town of Calais. In 2015, what came to be known as the 'new Jungle' developed as an informal settlement on wasteland just outside Calais. Local authorities did not give legal permission to occupy the land, but informally 'offered' the area to refugees as long as they stopped camping in the town (King, 2016). Rather than a refugee camp, the Jungle resembled 'a camp full of refugees' (Rubinstein, 2016). The space was completely bare, situated between the motorway and some houses. Refugees had to walk a number of kilometres to reach the first shops and to access services.

Since the early 2000s, a few local organisations have provided basic assistance to refugees in the form of food and clothing. However, with the rapid growth in the number of refugees,[4] these organisations struggled to deal with the increasing needs of the camp's residents. Grassroots organisations and ordinary citizens from across Europe (but in large part from the UK) started to bring donations to the camp. Volunteers' motivations were mixed: some were activists advocating for open borders and migrants' rights; some were not interested in politics but wanted to express solidarity with people stuck at the border; and others were linked with established volunteer organisations, trade unions or religious groups.

This new wave of volunteers built semi-permanent shelters, legal centres, women's and youth centres, a library, a performance space, and so on. Refugees also contributed to the life of the camp, by setting up cafés, restaurants, places of worship and barber shops. Within a few months, volunteers, together with the residents of the Jungle, were able to run services and recreational activities, and offer a degree of protection against the hardships of living in a makeshift refugee camp. Nevertheless, suffering and despair were evident and many refugees made reckless attempts to illegally cross the border to reach the UK, at times losing their lives. Unofficial records report that, between 2015 and 2016, over thirty people – including minors – died while trying to cross the border (CMS, 2017).

The Jungle was eventually dismantled at the end of October 2016 with the use of bulldozers, teargas and other forms of violence. Camp residents were forced to flee once again and face an uncertain future. Some refugees were sent to reception centres across France, while others aggregated in much smaller and hidden camps, but the majority went to sleep in the streets of Paris, which in turn became 'the new Calais' (Nossiter, 2016). The evictions in Calais only temporarily dispersed the problem,[5] causing further destitution for refugees and exacerbating tensions between volunteers and the authorities.

Makeshift Humanitarians and Medical Aid

Hundreds of people offered to volunteer in the Jungle from the summer of 2015, when the living conditions in the camp began to deteriorate in conjunction with a dramatic increase in the camp population. Aid was centred around donations from the public and on the work of volunteers who, for the majority, had never previously worked with refugees or in a humanitarian emergency. Lotus volunteers were not selected following an interview process, and they did not receive training before going to the camp. Due to 'easy access' to the Jungle from the UK, volunteers typically committed to the work on a casual basis, in their spare time. Apart from the medical staff, volunteers usually helped where they were needed and generally used their common sense when carrying out tasks in the camp.

Lotus, as with many other grassroots organisations in Calais, did not have a mission statement at the outset. Only after some time working in the camp did the group decide to take on specific tasks and responsibilities, defining their mission. For example, initially Lotus worked in the camp distributing donations, then focused on the provision of medical aid, and lastly changed scope again to provide support to young people. The absence of a defined mission statement, and the rapid changing of objectives throughout the months, meant that different organisations were often unknowingly providing the same services. This created confusion among camp residents and at times also led to a waste of resources.

Nevertheless, the informality of grassroots aid enabled groups to meet the immediate needs of the camp residents, as aid was provided quickly without reliance on bureaucratic systems. Financial donations to Lotus were channelled exclusively as aid, as volunteers did not receive remuneration for their work. Improvisation, informality and occasional participation were central components of volunteer humanitarianism. It can be stated that volunteers created an alternative to the 'humanitarian machine', as they provided humanitarian aid outside institutional frameworks and without the expertise of humanitarian aid workers (Sandri, 2017).

However, grassroots organisations, including Lotus, could only assist with basic forms of aid, as they did not have the capacity or the expertise to deal with more complex situations in the camp. For example, criminal activity was a significant issue in the Jungle, as gangs of criminals moved to the camp to exploit refugees, finding a fertile ground for their activities. Forced prostitution, the abuse of minors, and violence escalated rapidly. These were problems that volunteers could not deal with as they did not want to put themselves at risk. Despite the various appeals made by volunteers and refugees to the local authorities, the police did not intervene to remove the gangs from the camp, effectively allowing criminality and exploitation to continue. Safeguarding measures were completely absent and grassroots organisations were simply not able to prevent ill-intentioned people from entering the camp and taking advantage of refugees. Volunteers themselves were unaccountable; anyone could enter the Jungle and there was no system in place to check who was working in the camp.

Due to their lack of experience, and despite their efforts to work professionally, volunteers often made mistakes, such as promising donations that could not be delivered or by unintentionally triggering trauma during a conversation with a refugee. The work also retained a paradoxical element since volunteers, who were conscious of the fact that their presence could be seen to exonerate higher institutions of their responsibilities, did not want to put refugees' lives at risk by leaving Calais. Irena, one of the Lotus volunteers, put it clearly: 'You try to help but it's never enough and it will never be enough because institutions should be in there helping. But stopping is not an option either.'[6] In addition, the emotional burden that this work created, and the feelings of helplessness generated in the context of such a dramatic situation, were central to the volunteers' experience. However, opportunities to receive counselling and moral support were scarce.

Médecins Sans Frontières (MSF) and Doctors of the World (MDM) were two of the very few international humanitarian non-governmental organisations (NGOs) present in the camp. MSF provided medical services, organised rubbish collections, built some infrastructure, and filed legal cases against police brutality (MSF, 2016a). The already overstretched MSF medical clinic was only open for consultation during week days. After observing a great need for medical aid during the weekend as well, the Lotus founder reached out to friends and acquaintances in the medical profession to ask if they could help. She was able to put together a team of doctors and nurses and, thanks to the help of a group of volunteer builders, they opened the Lotus medical clinic in October 2015.

The Lotus medical team saw an average of one hundred people every weekend, witnessing a diversity of conditions that included: scabies, chest infections, sexually transmitted diseases, crisis pregnancies following incidents of rape, injuries caused by police brutality, broken bones caused by failed attempts to cross the border, and presentations of longstanding conditions such as diabetes. Along with these presentations, cases of post-traumatic stress disorder (PTSD), depression, and other mental illnesses were noted, for which little or no support was available in the camp.

Simple medical supplies such as plasters, pain-killers and dressings were provided as donations, and as such often could not be dispensed continuously throughout the months due to a temporary lack of contributions. Medical staff could not prescribe medicines to treat serious conditions because they did not have the authority, and because they wanted to avoid refugees misusing the drugs. Doctors and nurses could only provide first aid, medical triage, and advice. Despite these limitations, and the fact that the medical staff were not trained to respond to a humanitarian emergency, the clinic provided a stable service, and Lotus soon became one of the most respected grassroots organisations in the camp. As the founder and leader of the organisation stated:

We started to really become specialised not just medically, but we worked alongside solicitors, dealt with safety issues, becoming a more trusted advisory service in the camp. It meant that if someone came through the doors [of the clinic], they wouldn't just be treated medically but they'd almost be seen by lots of different services.[7]

The success of the Lotus medical clinic was also attributable to the fact that it was run by a grassroots organisation. Lotus proactively turned the clinic into a safe space, stressing the fact that the group was working independently of the state or aid agencies. Lotus staff were against documenting the names of the people who accessed their services, and they did not ask for documents. This had obvious drawbacks for the delivery of medical care in the clinic, as doctors and nurses could not follow up on patients and they had no records of the number of people seen. However, refugees accessed the clinic more willingly as they did not fear being reported to authorities. This approach was very different from other organisations working in the camp, as the founder of the group recalled:

Unfortunately, [the NGOs providing primary medical care] lost their relationship with the refugees because they started asking for some form of identification, and obviously the news spread like wildfire. Refugees were avoiding to see those who were offering primary care, and there was no other alternative apart from us back then.[8]

In some cases, international humanitarian organisations in other crisis settings have been the unwitting gatekeepers of the state, by collaborating with governments not only to help, but also to govern, the afflicted population (Agier, 2010; Feldman & Ticktin, 2010; Nguyen, 2010; Redfield, 2005; Redfield & Bornstein, 2010). This is particularly relevant in relation to the medical humanitarianism that arose in France during the 1990s that sought to address the domestic 'social emergency' of the '*sans-papiers*' (Ticktin, 2006). In that context, humanitarian practice and its bureaucratic apparatus was involved in 'unexpected or unplanned ways to determine who qualifie[d] as a refugee, citizen or native [...] and to discipline people once they acquire[d] refugee status' (Ticktin, 2014: 279). However, in the case of Lotus, by refusing to register refugees in their clinic the organisation asserted that their role was not one of policing but instead of protection of the camp residents. The organisation's provision of medical aid became an indirect way to challenge the authorities and their practices of control.

Evicting the Vulnerable: A 'Humanitarian Response'

The close cooperation between state institutions and humanitarian actors – already analysed in non-European contexts (Horst, 2008) – has also had the effect of outsourcing Europe's surveillance apparatus. This strategy responds to the political rationale that Foucault defined as 'governmentality', that is 'the way in which the conduct of groups of individuals has been increasingly involved in the exercise of the sovereign power' (Foucault, as cited in Fassin, 2009: 45). For example, in the Mediterranean, NGOs and commercial vessels have increasingly been co-opted to perform some of the functions of the state as the international community has retreated from its responsibility to protect (Heller & Pezzani, 2017; Pallister-Wilkins, 2017).[9] Moral and disciplinary projects have also been implemented, at times inadvertently, by the same volunteers who run unofficial reception centres and refugee camps (Pinelli, 2015; Rozakou, 2012). By imposing bureaucratic procedures on the informal process of welcoming refugees, the state has in some cases co-opted the work of volunteers and activists as 'positive' surveillance technologies, in the Foucauldian sense (Trubeta, 2015). For example, in PIKPA, the open reception centre in Lesvos, managed by grassroots organisations and activists, coastguard authorities forced volunteers to complete compulsory medical registrations for residents (ibid.).

Refugee camps and reception centres have been analysed, drawing mainly on Foucauldian terminology, as heavily institutionalised spaces, overloaded with *dispositifs* of surveillance and discipline, which borrow much of their architecture and organisational aspects from military and penitentiary models (Diken, 2010; Sczepanikova, 2013; Turner, 2015; Whyte, 2011). By warehousing refugees at the margins of the state, camps assumed a vital role as the gates of the political community, maintaining the 'national order of things' (Malkki, 1995) from the anomalous presence of such 'undesirables' (Arendt, 1973). This intent was evident in the response of the French state to the situation in Calais.

In January 2016, adjacent to the informal Jungle, authorities opened a reception centre built with converted shipping containers, which could host 1500 people. This new area lacked basic services such as running water, food distribution capacity, sanitary facilities, and communal areas. Authorities required fingerprints from the refugees in order to enter the containers, a requirement which was presented as an internal security measure. What this meant for refugees was that the right to shelter became conditional on their compliance with the state's chosen form of regulation, which involved their reintegration into the bureaucratic grids of the European asylum regime. According to European law, in order to claim asylum, refugees have to provide biometric records, including fingerprints, at their first point of entry into the EU. As per the Dublin Regulation, refugees without family ties in Europe can only legally claim asylum at their first point of entry in the EU. If they decide to carry on their journey, and their biometrics have already been registered in the EURODAC (the European finger-print database), they are returned to the country of arrival in order to complete the asylum assessment process.[10]

Very soon the containers became synonymous with insalubrity, roughness and loneliness. Many refugees preferred the Jungle to the containers, for they feared being put through a system that would jeopardise their chances of claiming asylum in the UK. Similarly to PIKPA in Lesvos, these containers embodied the Foucauldian 'positive power', for they were sites where coercion and surveillance served the state's interests. However, unlike the case of PIKPA, as a reaction to the mechanisms of control implemented in the form of fingerprinting and the poor conditions in the containers, volunteers began to protest and raised their concerns about the lack of facilities and safeguarding measures inside the centre. In addition, volunteers were not permitted access to the area and were unable to provide services there.

As the response to the containers had been negative, with a low uptake, at the end of February 2016 the south side of the Jungle, where three thousand people lived, was demolished with one week's notice. The authorities declared this a 'humanitarian response', designed to improve living conditions in the area (Boyle, 2017). This humanitarian justification for evictions resonates with what Fassin (2013: 40) observes as the paradox of invoking humanitarian reason, as 'the qualification "humanitarian" is such that it may be used extensively – and sometimes cynically – to legitimize any sort of action'.

For the last twenty years, authorities in Calais have oscillated between the provision of accommodation and the enforcement of evictions, requests for help from NGOs and the creation of obstacles to the work of volunteers. Constant tension exists at this crossroads between the authorities, locals, refugees and volunteers. This is also due to the fact that the Jungle represented a space that defied the sovereignty of the French state (Boyle, 2017), as refugees practised some acts of citizenship and assumed identities that were incompatible with their status as undocumented migrants. For example, they built their own shelters, created and named streets inside the camp, built recreational places, and generally self-managed the space. Refusing to enter the shipping containers and choosing to re-settle in other areas should also be interpreted as an act of citizenship. Refugees had the opportunity to recover some sense of community and social identity by getting rid (though only momentarily) of the bureaucratic labels that defined their position. As Boyle (2017: 31) puts it, the 'Jungle was the product of Anglo-French border policy but within its boundaries residents enacted their own social order beyond the realm of the French state'.

The work of the volunteers also played a part in challenging the role of the French and British states in Calais. Although the majority of grassroots organisations that formed in 2015 were not politically motivated, and their members did not define themselves as activists (noticeably differently from groups such as Calais Migrant Solidarity), they became very much involved in activism. Many of the grassroots organisations, such as Help Refugees, Care4Calais and Lotus came to the forefront of activism for refugees' rights in the UK, advocating for refugee protection and denouncing violent practices at the border. They organised campaigns, petitions and demonstrations and raised awareness about the issue at a time when both the French and British governments had neglected the camp. Activism was seen as the logical consequence of the humanitarian mission in Calais, as the situation in the Jungle had political roots in European migration policies (Sandri, 2017). Unlike MSF and other humanitarian NGOs, whose mandates do not incorporate the pursuit of justice or an improved social order (Redfield, 2005), volunteers took it upon themselves to oppose the strict migration regime and the violence perpetrated against refugees.

Nevertheless, local authorities and some of the local population displayed active hostility towards refugees and volunteers. The police repeatedly threw tear gas into the camp, attacked refugees when they left the Jungle and indiscriminately fired rubber bullets (MSF, 2016b; *The Guardian*, 2016). The main entrances to the camp were often patrolled by the police, and the CRS (Compagnie Républicaines de Sécurité – the French riot police) established check points around the camp, checking volunteers' cars and identification documents. The complete absence of the authorities inside the camp was noted in stark contrast to the presence of a substantial number of border guards and police officers at the Jungle's perimeter. The systematic abandonment that left the camp residents stranded can be understood with Foucault's definition of 'biopower', that is 'the power to foster life or to disallow it to the point of death' (Foucault, 1978). Only if we consider the carefully calculated reluctance to act – or 'violent inaction' (Davies, Isakjee & Dhesi, 2017) – as an extension of the agency of the state, can we recognise this camp as yet another site where biopower, surveillance and discipline were exercised. With recognition of these observations it becomes possible to expose forms of violence delivered by 'policies which seek to govern through the calculated withholding of the means to live' (ibid.: 8).

Conclusion

Despite its wretchedness, the Jungle was a space where tight communities were formed, and where important relationships were created between refugees, volunteers and activists. Refugees in Calais were met with general hostility from the authorities, but they also found volunteers and charitable organisations who provided help and support. As Fassin (2005: 365) argues, the case of Calais is 'paradigmatic of tensions between the discourses and practices of compassion and repression in the policies of immigration, and more specifically asylum, in Europe'.

The Jungle serves as an example of how refugees and grassroots humanitarian actors can find alternatives to the formal ways in which aid is normally administered, and mobility conventionally understood. As we discussed in this chapter, volunteer humanitarianism was characterised by a lack of expertise, informality and improvisation, together with a critique of the state and its practices at the border. We argued that the provision of aid in the Lotus medical clinic should be considered as a rupture from forms of governmentality and bureaucratic control, which by contrast have been enacted in other informal refugee camps across Europe. Furthermore, grassroots organisations in Calais openly challenged technologies of state surveillance by refusing to endorse the relocation of refugees into shipping containers provided by the local authorities. Volunteers became vocal opponents of the institutional handling of the issue in Calais and established networks of activism and advocacy for the protection of refugees.

While the grassroots response to the situation in the Jungle can be seen as an example of the way in which the delivery of some forms of humanitarian aid can be decoupled from the state's outsourcing of surveillance and disciplinary power, the state's inaction and deliberate neglect of this humanitarian issue can be interpreted as a biopolitical stance. Thus the implication is that, even while grassroots organisations did not actively cooperate with authorities, the state's mechanisms of control ultimately hindered the delivery of humanitarian assistance, without offering a viable alternative.

Notes

1 We use the term 'refugee' to refer to individuals who have left their own country in the strong belief that they cannot or should not return in the foreseeable future, as declared in Article 1 of the 1951 Geneva Convention, and by UNHCR (2006). This approach to terminology is not strictly legal, as we do not adopt the distinction between forced and voluntary migrants. However, the dichotomy between economic migrant and refugee has often proved to be empirically untenable, as migration is interwoven with different processes and motivations that cannot be understood separately (Casas-Cortes et al., 2015).

2 While recognising the problematic nature of the term, 'Jungle' has been widely adopted by camp residents, and is reflected here as an expression accepted by those living in the camp during the period in which interviews were conducted.

3 The organisation and the interviewees' names are pseudonyms.

4 According to a census carried out by Help Refugees, one of the largest organisations in Calais, the Jungle reached a peak population of 9,106 people in August 2016 (Help Refugees, 2016).

5 At the time of writing, ten months

after the eviction of the Jungle residents, there were more than 1,000 refugees in the area around Calais, who were again living outside with no access to shelter, toilets, food, or running water (Gentleman, 2017). A report conducted by the Refugee Youth Service has shown that some of the unaccompanied minors evicted from the Jungle are still on the move almost one year later (Taylor, 2017).

6 Irena, 31 May 2016.

7 Clara, 4 June 2016.

8 Clara, 4 June 2016.

9 This intent is clear in the 'Code of Conduct' that the Italian government imposed on all NGOs operating search and rescue missions in the Mediterranean. This eleven-point plan includes, among its most onerous requirements, the presence of law-enforcement officers on board rescue vessels, and the prohibition of the transfer of migrants to other vessels. Some humanitarian organisations, including MSF, refused to sign the Code of Conduct, criticising this attempt to exercise regulatory power over international waters, and the hampering of search and rescue missions in favour of the international community's retreat

from its responsibilities. For more details, see the letter signed by MSF on 31 July 2017 addressed to the Italian Interior Minister, Marco Minniti (MSF, 2017).

10 Along with the general tightening of EU member state policies on migration and asylum in 2015, a roadmap was drafted jointly by EU member states, Frontex, EASO (the European Asylum Support Office), Europol (the EU's law enforcement agency) and Eurojust (an EU agency tasked with judicial cooperation) to implement the so-called 'Hotspots approach' in Italy and Greece. The Hotspots approach, designed to streamline asylum procedures and register biometric data and fingerprints for any person accessing Europe illegally, aims to ensure full compliance with the Dublin Regulation and to deter the secondary movement of asylum seekers and refugees within the EU, effectively sealing Europe's internal borders (Heller & Pezzani, 2017). See in particular Articles 9 and 17 of EU Regulation 603/2013 ('Eurodac') (EU, 2013).

References

Agier, M (2010), Humanity as an identity and its political effects (a note on camps and humanitarian government). *Humanity*. Vol. 1 (1): 29–45.

Al Jazeera (2016), Ten countries host half of world's refugees: report [online]. *Al Jazeera*, 4 October 2016.

Arendt, H (1973) *The origins of totalitarianism*. Second Edition. New York: Harcourt, Brace.

Boyle, M (2017), Shelter provision and state sovereignty in Calais. *Forced Migration Review*. Vol. 55: 30–2.

Calhoun, C (2010) The idea of emergency: humanitarian action and global (dis)order. In: Fassin, D & Pandolfi, M (eds), *Contemporary states of emergency: the politics of military and humanitarian interventions*. New York: Zone Books.

Casas-Cortes, M, De Genova, N, Garelli, G, Grappi, G, Heller, C, Hess, S, … Tazzioli, M (2015), New keywords: migration and borders. *Cultural Studies*. Vol. 29 (1): 55–87.

CMS (Calais Migrant Solidarity) (2017), Deaths at the Calais border [online]. Available from: https://calaismigrantsolidarity.wordpress.com/deaths-at-the-calais-border/ (accessed 3 August 2017).

Davies, T, Isakjee, A & Dhesi, S (2017), Violent inaction: the necropolitical experience of refugees in Europe. *Antipode*. Published online 21 April 2017.

Diken, B (2010), From refugee camps to gated communities: biopolitics and the end of the city. *Citizenship Studies*. Vol. 8 (1): 83–106.

EU (2013), *Regulation (EU) No. 603/2013 of the European Parliament and of the Council of the 26th June 2013*. Brussels: European Parliament.

Fassin, D (2005), Compassion and repression: the moral economy of immigration policies in France. *Cultural Anthropology*. Vol. 20 (3): 362–87.

Fassin, D (2009), Another politics of life is possible. *Theory, Culture & Society*. Vol. 26 (5): 44–60.

Fassin, D (2013), The predicament of humanitarianism. *Qui Parle*. Vol. 22 (1): 33–48.

Feldman, I & Ticktin, M (2010), *In the name of humanity: the government of threat and care*. Durham: Duke University Press.

Foucault, M (1978), *The history of sexuality*. New York: Pantheon Books.

Gentleman, A (2017) Teargas, cold, no toilets: plight of refugees in Calais revealed. *The Guardian*, 10 August 2017.

Guardian, The (2016) Police and 'militias' attacking refugees at Calais, says charity. *The Guardian*, 13 February 2016.

Hale, CR (2006), Activist research vs. cultural critique: indigenous land rights and the contradictions of politically engaged anthropology. *Cultural Anthropology*. Vol. 21 (1): 96–120.

Heller, C & Pezzani, L (2017), Death by rescue [online]. Available from: https://deathbyrescue.org/ (accessed 3 August 2017).

Help Refugees (2016) Latest Calais census [online]. Available from: https://helprefugees.org.uk/news/latest-calais-census/ (accessed 2 August 2017).

Horst, C (2008), A monopoly on assistance: international aid to refugee camps and the neglected role of the Somali diaspora. *Afrika Spectrum*. Vol. 43 (1): 121–31.

King, N (2016), *No Borders – the politics of immigration control and resistance*. London: Zed Books.

Maeckelbergh, M (2009), *The will of many – how the alterglobalisation movement is changing the face of democracy*. London: Pluto Press.

Malkki, L (1995), Refugees and exile: from 'refugee studies' to the national order of things. *Annual Review of Anthropology*. Vol. 24: 495–523.

Millner, N (2011), From 'refugee' to 'migrant' in Calais solidarity activism: re-staging undocumented migration for a future politics of asylum. *Political Geography*. Vol. 30 (6): 320–8.

Mosse, D (2005), *Cultivating development: an ethnography of aid policy and practice*. London: Pluto Press.

MSF (2016a), France [online]. Available from: www.msf.org/en/where-we-work/france (accessed 4 August 2017).

MSF (2016b), France: refugees face 'slow death' in Calais' Jungle [online]. Available from: www.msf.org/en/article/france-refugees-face-%E2%80%98slow-death%E2%80%99-calais-jungle (accessed 4 August 2017).

MSF (2017), Codice di condotta: la lettera di MSF al Ministro dell'Interno [online]. Available from: www.medicisenzafrontiere.it/notizie/news/codice-di-condotta-la-lettera-di-msf-al-ministro-dellinterno (accessed 3 August 2017).

Nguyen, VK (2010), *Republic of therapy: triage and sovereignty in West Africa's time of AIDS*. Durham, NC: Duke University Press.

Nossiter, A (2016), Paris is the new Calais, with scores of migrants arriving daily. *New York Times*, 3 November 2016.

Pallister-Wilkins, P (2017), Humanitarian rescue/sovereign capture and the policing of possible responses to violent borders. *Global Policy*. Vol. 8 (1): 19–24.

Pinelli, B (2015), After the landing: moral control and surveillance in Italy's asylum seeker camps. *Anthropology Today*. Vol. 31 (2): 12–14.

Redfield, P (2005), Doctors, borders, and life in crisis. *Cultural Anthropology*. Vol. 20 (3): 328–61.

Redfield, P & Bornstein, E (2010), An introduction to the anthropology of humanitarianism. In: Bornstein, E & Redfield, P (eds), *Forces of compassion – humanitarianism between ethics and politics*. Santa Fe, NM: School for Advanced Research Press.

Rigby, K & Schlembach, R (2013), Impossible protest: noborders in Calais. *Citizenship Studies*. Vol. 17(2): 157–72.

Rozakou, K (2012), The biopolitics of hospitality in Greece: humanitarianism and the management of refugees. *American Ethnologist.* Vol. 39 (3): 562–77.

Rubinstein, J (2016), The Calais Jungle isn't a refugee camp, it's a camp full or refugees – and there's a huge difference. *The Independent*, 20 January 2016.

Rygiel, K (2011), Bordering solidarities: migrant activism and the politics of movement and camps at Calais. *Citizenship Studies.* Vol. 15 (1): 1–19.

Sandri, E (2016), 'Volunteer humanitarianism' across close(d) borders: volunteers and humanitarian aid in the 'Jungle' refugee camp of Calais. Unpublished Master's thesis, University of Sussex, Brighton, UK.

Sandri, E (2017), 'Volunteer humanitarianism': volunteers and humanitarian aid in the 'Jungle' refugee camp of Calais. *Journal of Ethnic and Migration Studies.* Published online 11 July 2017.

Scheper-Hughes, N (1992), *Death without weeping – the violence of everyday life in Brazil.* London: University of California Press.

Scheper-Hughes, N (1995), The primacy of the ethical: propositions for a militant anthropology. *Current Anthropology.* Vol. 36 (3): 420–1.

Sczepanikova, A (2013), Between control and assistance: the problem of European accommodation centres for asylum seekers. *International Migration.* Vol. 51 (4): 130–43.

Sorgoni, B (2016), Anthropology and asylum procedures and policies in Italy. Pp. 31–60. In: Tauber, E & Zinn, D (eds), *The public value of anthropology: engaging critical social issues through ethnography.* Bozen-Bolzano: BU Press.

Taylor, D (2017), Injured, hunted, lost: mapping journeys of refugee children aiming for UK. *The Guardian*, 13 July 2017.

Ticktin, M (2006) Where ethics and politics meet: the violence of humanitarianism in France. *American Ethnologist.* Vol. 33 (1): 33–49.

Ticktin, M (2014), Transnational humanitarianism. *Annual Review of Anthropology.* Vol. 43: 273–89.

Trubeta, S (2015), 'Rights' in the grey area: undocumented border crossers in Lesvos. *Race & Class.* Vol. 56 (4): 56–72.

Turner, S (2015), What is a refugee camp? Explorations of the limits and effects of the camp. *Journal of Refugee Studies.* Vol. 29 (3): 1–10.

UNHCR (2006), *The state of the world's refugees 2006: human displacement in the new millennium.* Geneva: UNHCR.

UNHCR (2015), Over one million sea arrivals reach Europe in 2015 [online]. Available from: www.unhcr.org/uk/news/latest/2015/12/5683d0b56/million-sea-arrivals-reach-europe-2015.html (accessed 4 August 2017).

Walters, W (2008), Acts of demonstration: mapping the territory of (non-) citizenship. In: Isin, EF & Nielsen GM (eds), *Acts of citizenship.* London: Zed Books.

Whyte, Z (2011), Enter the myopticon: uncertain surveillance in the Danish asylum system. *Anthropology Today.* Vol. 27(3): 18–21

6 | AMATEUR HUMANITARIANISM, SOCIAL SOLIDARITY AND 'VOLUNTEER TOURISM' IN THE EU REFUGEE 'CRISIS'

Jane Freedman

Introduction

The refugee or migrant[1] 'crisis' currently affecting the European Union (EU) has prompted a large mobilisation of volunteers to bring aid – in the form of food, lodging, medical aid, or even sea rescue – to 'migrants' attempting to reach and cross Europe. While this mobilisation may have demonstrated the need to reconsider, or at least nuance, some previously held beliefs concerning the anti-immigration sentiment harboured by many European citizens, demonstrating perhaps an unpredicted level of solidarity with refugees, it has also generated new situations in relation to these volunteers or 'amateur' humanitarians, and the role they play in providing basic necessities for the survival of refugees. In their efforts to 'mitigate the suffering of strangers' (Calhoun, 2008), these volunteers may clearly define their actions in terms that align with the common definitions of humanitarian action, but it is interesting to discuss the motivations, politics, and ethics that underpin their response. The fact that such a large number of 'amateurs' or volunteers have been involved in the response to the refugee crisis has also created some tension between such individuals and groups and the more 'professional' humanitarian organisation of United Nations (UN) agencies and large non-governmental organisations (NGOs): tensions that in themselves illustrate some of the contradictions inherent in these new forms of volunteer humanitarianism. This paper, based on empirical research carried out in Greece and in France in 2015 and 2016, including interviews with volunteers, members of humanitarian organisations and international organisations, and refugees themselves, will examine the various relationships that exist between these different groups, exploring the motivations of volunteers who offer help to refugees, their relationships with these refugees, and with the UN and larger

NGOs who have also delivered humanitarian relief during the crisis. The paper will also analyse whether the actions of volunteers have had the effect of obscuring the fundamental political roots of the crisis, and the failure of EU politicians and their policies to establish any lasting or effective means to protect refugees.

To begin this chapter, it may be interesting to describe a scene witnessed as an observer in the Grande-Synthe refugee camp near Dunkirk, in northern France. Médecins Sans Frontières (MSF) staff are touring the camp on a 'maraude' (a tour of the camp to reach out to refugees in need of help) to try and locate refugees who may be in need of medical treatment. They are accosted by a young English man – a 'volunteer' – who asks them to come and look at one of 'his' refugees, an Iraqi Kurdish woman, who is alone in the camp with her three young children. As the MSF doctors arrive at her tent, they ask the young man to leave them alone with this woman so that they can speak with her in private. He refuses: 'I've been looking after this woman since she arrived in the camp. I'm the one who's looking after her here.'[2]

This scene demonstrates some of the issues and difficulties provoked by the arrival of large numbers of volunteers to 'help' refugees arriving in Europe. Since mid-2015 when the massive arrival of refugees began to attract widespread attention in the European media and in the form of heightened political debate, thousands of volunteers have flocked to various European destinations to join efforts to help and support refugees. This mobilisation of volunteers to support refugees may be seen as a welcome sign of the fact that EU member states are mistaken in some of the assumptions they have made of the public response to refugees, and that public opinion is in fact not as 'anti-immigration' as some have supposed, but has instead manifested as a display of willingness to help the refugees. However, this mobilisation also poses problems that are both organisational and ethical. What is the role of these volunteers? How can we really understand their motivations? And how do their actions impact on both the various humanitarian organisations involved in the refugee response, and more importantly on the refugees themselves?

Situating the Refugee 'Crisis'

In 2015 more than one million refugees arrived in Europe, mainly from Syria, Afghanistan, Iraq and Eritrea, and in 2016, despite the closure of many European borders, and the EU–Turkey readmission agreement signed in March 2016 (EC, 2016), which made it more and more difficult for refugees to reach the EU, nearly 400,000 more refugees arrived across the Mediterranean and Aegean (UNHCR, 2016). The flow of refugees continues, though the official closure of the 'Balkan Route' means that refugees' journeys are increasingly made via Libya towards Italy, a journey which is arguably even more dangerous. Furthermore, following the closure of the Balkan Route, thousands of refugees have been stuck in Greece, unable to move on, and forced to remain in insecure camp conditions (Lovertt, Whelan & Rendon, 2017). Many more refugees have died at sea in their attempts to reach the EU, with estimates for 2016 indicating over 5000 deaths (UNHCR, 2016). Fleeing conflict and violence in their countries of origin these refugees take increasingly perilous and expensive routes to reach Europe, the journey made more difficult by the securitisation of EU migration policies and the closure of European borders (Freedman, 2016; Léonard, 2010; Lutterbeck, 2006). The labelling of this refugee flow as a 'crisis' in European political and media discourse can be seen to have had the impact of shifting EU immigration policies further from the politics of everyday bureaucratic control, and towards a politics of exception (Jeandesboz & Pallister-Wilkins, 2014), of the 'spectacular': a politics of border closures, the building of fences, and the destruction of camps (Freedman, Kivilcim & Özgür Baklacioğlu, 2017). It can also be argued that the crisis labelling helped to justify the move from a primarily political to a primarily humanitarian response (or at least a blurring of the two), and thus as EU leaders have failed to find any sustainable political agreement on the integration or relocation of refugees, the focus has shifted to how to respond to the basic needs of the refugees caught up in this 'crisis', with various initiatives launched, such as the rescue of refugees at sea and the provision of housing, shelter, food and medical aid. These new humanitarian initiatives come in addition to the efforts of a number of associations and organisations that have been working to support refugees and migrants in Europe for many years (Pette, 2016) – sometimes for decades – and which in some cases have been supplanted or crowded out by more recent humanitarian initiatives (Cabot, 2017). It can be argued that this focus on the 'humanitarian crisis' affecting refugees, along with widespread media images of refugees being rescued from unseaworthy boats or sometimes drowning, trekking by foot across hostile borders, and living in squalid camp conditions, has inspired the many thousands of volunteers who have flocked to various European destinations to 'help' or 'save' refugees, flooding the beaches of Greek Islands (Papataxiarchis, 2016), or wading through the mud in Calais. However, as pointed out earlier in this chapter, this huge volunteer response may represent a double-edged sword, both at times hindering the efforts of 'professional' humanitarians, and perhaps more importantly acting to mask or negate the political ramifications of the refugee 'crisis'.

It is impossible to establish any accurate statistics or data pertaining to the number, or the demographic makeup, of volunteers who have joined the refugee support effort. Yet observations and anecdotic evidence suggest that there are many thousands of such individuals, predominantly young people (although I also met several retired individuals among the volunteers), and European (with some North Americans also arriving to volunteer). It also seems that more women than men have volunteered, reflecting a specific gendered notion of volunteering and 'caring', as will be discussed later. Volunteers have come alone, in groups, or with friends, and have often organised their trips through social media networks such as Facebook and Twitter, with special groups set up to provide, in addition to news and photos of the refugee 'crisis', practical information about how to volunteer, along with travel and accommodation arrangements for volunteers and useful 'tips' from previous volunteers. Many volunteers have also set up blogs to write about and share their experiences, and have set up webpages through fundraising platforms such as GoFundMe to raise funds to pay for their travel to one or another of the sites at which they hope to volunteer (Cabot, 2017).

Motivations for Volunteering

At first glance, the motivations of volunteers engaged in refugee support activities in Europe seem to align with the classic goals of humanitarianism: to mitigate suffering and save lives, without making direct reference to the self as part of a humanitarian effort. When asked about their motivations for coming to Greece or to Calais, many of those I interviewed expressed the sentiment that they wanted to 'help' refugees. This rather vague notion of wanting to 'help' had been provoked in most cases by images seen on the television or in the newspapers of refugees undertaking the perilous sea crossing from Turkey to Greece, and struggling to survive in makeshift camps as they made their way through Europe. 'You just see those pictures on the television and it is so tragic, it pushes you to do something, to come and help',[3] said one young woman. Others pointed to newspaper articles and photographs that had encouraged them to come and volunteer. Members of French NGOs who have been working in Calais for many years dated the huge influx of volunteers very clearly to the newspapers' publication of the now infamous photo of Aylan Kurdi, the Syrian toddler washed up dead on a Greek beach in September 2015. 'As soon as that photo was published', said one, 'we were flooded by these young people coming over from England. I think they feel guilty.'[4]

In addition to expressions of wanting to 'help', many of the volunteers talked about needing to see what was happening with their own eyes, displaying a mix of compassion and curiosity (Papataxiarchis, 2016). 'I just wanted to come and see for myself', said one young man I met in Kos, Greece.[5] Another volunteer in Calais expressed similar sentiments: 'You see all those pictures on the television, and in the newspapers, and I just wanted to come over and see for myself and to find out what was really happening.'[6] The idea that volunteers wanted to see the refugee crisis implies that at the same time that the media brought the 'crisis' to public attention, there was generated a degree of scepticism among some members of the public that this same media could give them an accurate picture of what was 'really happening', and that they therefore needed to verify for themselves what the refugees were experiencing. The desire to find out what was happening was linked to the idea that this refugee 'crisis' was somehow a historic moment, of which those who were volunteering wanted to be a 'part'. The desire for such an experience can be understood as part of a wider quest for 'empathy', which has become commonplace in development and humanitarian discourse (Mitchell, 2016; Pedwell, 2012). However, while empathy may be seen as a way to overcome distance and 'othering', it may in practice act to fix and essentialise the giving subject and receiving object of empathy (latterly in this case the refugee).

This desire to see what was happening and to help also translated into a need to be seen to be helping, as volunteers constructed a personal narrative about their role in this 'historical' moment, and of their own contribution to the 'helping' of refugees. It seemed important for many of the volunteers to publicise their experiences of volunteering in order to mark their own individual part played in this moment by sharing their stories and photos on blogs, in Facebook posts, and similar, as manifestations of 'selfie humanitarianism' (Koffman, Orgad & Gill, 2015). Many of these posts recount the ways in which volunteers had gained personal satisfaction from what they believed was their role in 'saving' or 'helping' refugees. For example, one post on the Care4Calais Facebook page, highlights the positive impact a volunteer believes he had, and the 'uplifting' effect that this had had on him. In the post, he describes how he joined the Care4Calais group and travelled to France to work in the warehouse sorting and distributing donations to the residents of the 'Jungle'. He recounts being 'uplifted' by the 'smiling faces and gratitude' of the refugees in the camp who were grateful for the warm clothes, which could make a real difference to their lives in the camps during spells of cold weather.

Another volunteer recounts her pride at the reaction of her friends to her volunteering, and the approbation and praise that she has received from these friends who sent her messages such as 'the world needs more people like you'.[7] This kind of foregrounding of an individual volunteer's experiences can be read as part of a global phenomenon of what Razack (2007) terms 'stealing the pain of others', and of the utilisation of this pain to demonstrate oneself as a 'good' and 'ethical' person. The widespread use of social media by the volunteers can be seen as one way of receiving public approbation, which supports this demonstration of personal worth.

Other volunteers talked about their trips as an 'adventure' or 'something new', with the act of volunteering thus constructed as a means to partake in some kind of novel experience. One young woman working in the fashion industry who wrote a blog about her decision to volunteer in Calais talks about the fact that she is not a 'political' person or an 'activist', and that her main interests are makeup, fashion and celebrity. Prior to going to Calais, she had not travelled widely. She writes that she is not sure why she decided to go to Calais, but that the photos of Aylan Kurdi's body washed up on a beach were a strong motivating factor. As she found herself with some free time, she thought 'why not go and help?' This blog is interesting in that the volunteer explains her fears on discovering that most of the refugees in the Calais camp were men. She writes that by the time she discovered this it was too late to change her mind, despite that fact that she felt scared. She sought reassurance by telling herself that the trip would be an 'adventure' and an 'experience' (Her, 2016).

The fact that this 'adventure' is accessible and close to home for many volunteers (i.e. within Europe), and that it involves very little real 'risk' or 'danger' (in contrast to the imagined dangers of other humanitarian work in conflict zones, for example), makes this kind of volunteer adventure all the more appealing to many. The idea of 'adventure' and 'experience' also acts to reinforce the volunteers' perception of themselves as individuals doing something 'worthwhile' and 'making a difference' as outlined earlier. It can be argued that the resultant 'selfie humanitarianism', as illustrated by the numerous blogs, Facebook posts, and even 'humanitarian Tinder' (Mason, 2016), reinforces an individualised, neoliberal form of humanitarianism as 'charity', and as a project of self-realisation.

Gender and Caring: Saving the Children

The blog post quoted earlier, along with the responses of many interviewees, illustrate the mobilising power of images of children, and the way in which certain framings of the refugee 'crisis' that highlight the dangers to and vulnerability of women and children, might be attractive to volunteers who want to help or save those who they feel are 'innocent' and 'vulnerable'. Thus, the growing feminisation of refugee flows, with increasing numbers of women and children among new arrivals (Freedman, 2016; UNHCR, 2016), could also help to explain the increase in the number of volunteers coming to 'help'. For example, one volunteer in Calais recounted her distress at seeing the injustice of 'mothers sitting on the side of the road with their children looking powerless and broken' (Wilkinson, 2016). This desire to help the 'vulnerable' supports findings from existing research that has demonstrated the ways in which the framing of migration issues, and particularly the foregrounding of the vulnerability of child migrants and refugees, has an important impact on the creation of public sympathy for migrants and refugees, above and beyond opinions concerning migration policies and legislation (Anderson, 2010; Freedman, 2011). The desire to help children or babies is also evident in many of the photographs posted on Facebook and other social media platforms by volunteers, who are frequently pictured holding or surrounded by photogenic young refugee children. The privileging of women and children as those most in need or deserving of help, acts to reinforce the gendered representations of women and child refugees as passive and vulnerable 'victims', and to render invisible the suffering of male refugees, or in some cases to contribute to representations of the latter as undeserving or even 'dangerous' (Allsopp, 2017).

Furthermore, just as the object of this humanitarian sentiment has been gendered, so too has the volunteer: the individual 'helping' refugees. Again, it is impossible to provide accurate statistics for the number of men and women among those volunteering during the refugee 'crisis', but observations and interviews suggest that women outnumber men. Indeed, one leader of a refugee support group told me that new volunteers were 99 percent female.[8] The preponderance of women among volunteers can be attributed to traditional gendered norms and divisions of labour whereby women are given the tasks linked to care within society. Mostafanezhad (2013) argues that these tropes of female caring for 'other children' in the context of volunteer tourism are inscribed with a colonial history and ideology:

> Like their colonial counterparts, young female volunteer tourists, as well as their celebrity sisters, frequently care for and 'give back' to the world by educating and caring for children from the Global South. Indeed, this desire to 'give back to society' is a core theme in volunteer tourism, where young women seek to 'make the world a better place' by teaching English and caring for young children in the 'Third World'.

Volunteering as an Apolitical Act

While many volunteers seemed to be motivated by a desire to help or to 'see for themselves', fewer references were made to details of European refugee policy or the political situation more generally. Few of the volunteers I spoke to had any formal political affiliation or previous involvement with what they perceived as political activities (such as volunteering for a political party, or taking part in political demonstrations or rallies). In fact, their engagement seemed for the most part to be largely apolitical. A retired English teacher, one of the few elderly people volunteering in Calais, explained that she found she had spare time and was looking to find a way to be useful to others. She had never had any previous experience of working with migrants or refugees, and had never been a member of a political party or any other political organisation, though she did feel that her professional role as a teacher had involved helping the children with whom she worked. Others also explained that they had not had any prior formal political engagement, and had not previously paid any attention to national or European immigration policies, or their effects. When these volunteers discussed the politics of this refugee 'crisis' it was generally in very vague terms, deploring the fact that 'no one is helping these refugees', or that 'Europe is doing nothing', but without a precise understanding of, or view on, EU asylum and immigration policy, or of the national policies of the country in which they were volunteering. This depoliticisation of volunteer support can be seen of symptomatic of a more general depoliticisation of the 'crisis', as argued earlier, such that the principal solutions appear as 'humanitarian' – saving lives, providing basic necessities – rather than as a need to challenge the political structures, laws or policies that created the situation.[9] Furthermore, these volunteers had no conception that by engaging in humanitarian action they themselves may be engaged in a form of political activity. Much has been written about the interconnectedness of humanitarianism, control and repression (Kobelinsky & Makaremi, 2009) and it could be argued that in helping to 'save' refugees, the volunteers are in fact contributing to the continuation of a repressive and exclusionary European migration regime by hiding or softening the worst consequences of said regime. However, none of the volunteers that I interviewed expressed any concerns about the way in which their actions could have a wider impact on European policies or regimes, with their focus very much on the local activities in which they were involved, and on the ways that they perceived they had contributed to 'saving' or 'helping' refugees.

These feelings of wanting to help, or of feeling guilty and wanting to do something to expunge this guilt, are of course not unique to the current refugee crisis, and this mobilisation of volunteers should be situated within a broader expansion of what has been called popular humanitarianism or humanitarian tourism. Mostafanezhad (2014) explores the notion of popular humanitarianism within which 'a recurring story emerges around the Global North's aesthetic and individuating engagement with poverty in a consumable form in the Global South'. She documents the ways in which organised 'volunteer tourism' has emerged to allow volunteers from the Global North to travel to the Global South to take part in projects to 'help' those affected by chronic poverty or violence. While 'volunteer tourism' involves travelling to the Global South in order to participate in these acts of 'helping' or 'saving' people, the fact that the refugee 'crisis' has involved the movement of millions of these 'saveable bodies' to Europe itself, can be seen to have magnified this phenomenon as volunteers no longer have to travel so far, or to locations which may be perceived as dangerous, in order to enact their desire to 'help' or 'save'. For example, getting in a car or on a train and travelling to Calais, or taking a cheap flight to Greece, is in many ways far easier and cheaper than travelling to parts of Africa. The influx of refugees has thus allowed a substantial expansion of this form of volunteerism, as individuals from the 'Global South' have instead travelled to Europe. But while those being 'saved' are closer to the homes of those seeking to 'save', they are still constructed as the 'other', in the same way that African children have repeatedly been constructed as a saveable 'other' by the various advocacy activities of international organisations, NGOs, and celebrity humanitarians (Daley, 2013; Mostafanezhad, 2014). This 'othering' of refugees contributes to a reinforcement of what Malkki (1996) has described as their status as 'speechless emissaries', as a result of which 'refugees stop being specific persons and become pure victims in general' (ibid.). In this context volunteers see refugees not as fellow citizens with rights to be defended, but as the 'other' to be rescued or saved. Furthermore, this notion encourages volunteers to expect refugees to behave in a certain way in order to conform to this status of 'victim', with resultant disappointment if this is not perceived to be the case (e.g. if refugees are more actively demanding of their rights).

Having had no experience of contact with this refugee 'other', with the exception of images and reports conveyed by the media, the volunteers may create a specific and idealised view of what refugees should be like, which may result in 'disappointment' when they arrive in a camp and enter into direct contact with refugees. In some circumstances, this can result in sentiments or expressions of disapproval or disgust, provoked by the idea that the refugees do not behave as worthy objects of 'help' or of 'saving'. Several volunteers expressed feelings of dismay that the refugees did not clean up after themselves, threw litter, or even threw away clothes that had been given to them. 'To tell the truth', said one young woman in the Calais camp, 'I didn't think it would be as dirty as this. I know they don't have many facilities but they're making it worse by throwing rubbish everywhere, it's quite disgusting really.'[10] Others complained that the refugees were badly behaved during food distributions, and did not know how to queue properly. One group of UK volunteers tried to remedy this by insisting that the refugees queue up in an orderly line if they wanted any food. Those who refused had their meals withheld as a form of punishment until they joined the queue with the others.[11] Other volunteers expressed disappointment that the refugees did not seem as grateful as they expected them to be, and that they were not always pleased to engage with them in the way that they wished. At the Grande-Synthe camp it was possible to observe piles of discarded clothes which had been given to the refugees but which were not wanted or needed. Several volunteers I spoke to remarked on this, and criticised the fact that the refugees were not grateful for help, and were acting wastefully by discarding the clothes that had been donated to them.

These feelings of disappointment can also translate into a need to regulate and to control refugees' behaviour. In a blog recounting her experiences in Lesbos, one young female volunteer described her role in deciding which refugees were really in 'need' and who should receive distributions of clothes. She argued that everyone wanted new shoes and t-shirts, even if those that they were currently wearing were not wet or torn. But there were not enough new clothes to distribute to all of the refugees, so it was important to make a choice about who most needed or 'deserved' new shoes and clothes. She described her position as an arbiter, who had to say 'no' to those who were considered less needy or less deserving that others: having to 'smile and say no'. As a result, volunteers have adopted the position of judges of the refugees' situation, of their needs, and of the degree to which they are deserving of help.

Professional Versus 'Amateur' Humanitarians

The new influx of volunteers hoping to practice refugee support arrives in locations where there are, in many cases, already long-established NGOs and associations involved with similar activities. These new arrivals have provoked mixed reactions from the more 'professional' or organised refugee support groups. Some of the regular staff of humanitarian organisations involved in refugee response welcomed the arrival of the volunteers, both as an extra workforce to help with daily tasks with which they felt they had become overwhelmed following the arrival of so many new refugees, and as a symbolic sign of support for refugees that served to illustrate the fact that public opinion was not as anti-refugee as governments might have liked to imply. However, others underlined problems caused by this influx of volunteers, which according to them were both practical, organisational and ethical.

Organisational issues involved clashes between different organisations all trying to provide the same services to refugees, and particularly clashes over food distribution. During meetings of the Plateforme des Migrants (meetings designed to coordinate different organisations' activities within the camps around Calais) there were often arguments about the fact that too many people were trying to bring and serve food to the refugees, a situation that resulted in excess food being wasted and thrown away. For example, a member of Auberge des Migrants, an NGO based in Calais that has provided food and clothing for refugees and migrants in the region for over twenty years, explained that her organisation had worked out what quantity of food was needed, and also the best way to distribute this food to ensure that all refugees received a portion, but that these systems had been disrupted by the arrival of so many new volunteers, which in turn resulted in food going to waste.[12] On a similar note, in the Grande-Synthe camps I observed a clash triggered by the arrival of volunteers from England with a lorry fitted out with a kitchen that they wanted to use to cook for the refugees in the camp. On arrival they found no place to park and asked Salaam, a local organisation that was already distributing meals, to move their truck. When the members of Salaam refused to do this, one of the new arrivals from England began swearing at them at threatening them with violence: 'We've come all the way from England with this lorry of stuff for the refugees, and they won't move out of the way and let us in.'[13] Such clashes seem to stem from the volunteers' belief that they are doing a good thing and that it is they who 'know best' what is helpful for the refugees, while the more 'professional' humanitarians believe that they have the experience and expertise required to provide support for the refugees. Both in Calais and in Greece 'professional' humanitarians complained about the crowds of volunteers who were getting in their way as they tried to do their jobs: 'They are just everywhere and we can't get around them.'[14]

The influx of volunteers was also highlighted as a problem by the mayor of Lesbos, who was reported complaining about the negative impact of the arrival of so many volunteers on the island: 'I have seen many NGOs and individuals coming without official registration and showing no cooperation with our municipality. This causes everyone upset and these NGOs arouse doubt and mistrust among the residents of Lesbos. I would say their presence is disruptive rather than useful' (Nianias, 2016). The same article also quotes a resident of Lesbos who highlights the sometimes disruptive and confusing role of the volunteers, with many rushing into the water to try and 'save' refugees from boats, in a way that frightened the refugees, or by sharing incorrect information that caused confusion.

Beyond these clashes over food and clothes distributions, and instances of volunteers 'getting in the way' of humanitarian staff, there were concerns expressed over the motivations of the volunteers, and of the way in which they interacted with refugees. Some humanitarian actors expressed concern that 'anyone' could approach refugees, and that this lack of control could lead to abuse or exploitation. In fact, access to most of the refugee 'camps' has been fairly open and unrestricted – at least during the early stages of the 'crisis' – meaning that volunteers have been able come in and out without being stopped or subjected to an identity check. In the Greek islands, particularly before the establishment of the more regulated 'hotspots', anyone could enter the various locations where refugees were camping. Similarly, in Calais and the surrounding camps, while French security forces patrolled the perimeter of the camps to try to stop refugees getting out and boarding lorries on the motorway in an attempt to reach the UK (Freedman, 2017), there was no control or restriction over who entered in to the camps. Several volunteers seemed to have attached themselves to – or 'adopted' – individual refugees or families, and could be seen to have created relations that could be construed as relationships of control or dependence. It was common to hear volunteers talk of 'my' family, in reference to a refugee family with whom they had established contact and had been 'supporting' or 'helping'.

Helping the Suffering 'Other' or Encouraging Refugee Citizenship

While previous studies of the humanitarian response to refugee movements have employed a biopolitical framework to criticise the way in which humanitarians have fostered the protection of suffering bodies and have thus produced 'a limited version of what it means to be human' (Ticktin, 2006), others have shown how, by fostering refugee leadership and citizenship, humanitarian activists can encourage new forms of political agency and subjectivity (Robins, 2009). There are undoubtedly citizen-led initiatives in Europe that do try to foster and support refugees' own agency (Ataç, Rygiel & Stierl, 2016), but many others seem to reinforce the notion of refugees as victims who must be 'helped', and this helping may reinforce racialised and gendered constructions of refugees that dominate in media and political discourse. Returning to the original humanitarian ethic of alleviating the 'suffering of others' and saving lives, it is clear that the generally 'generous' motivations of volunteers should not be doubted, but that at the same time, the volunteers themselves, and the emotional appeals to which they respond, do not attempt to challenge established schemas of dealing with 'otherness'. Refugees remain objects of pity, who need to demonstrate their 'deservingness' in order to receive aid. As Kallius, Monterescu and Rajaram (2016) argue with regard to volunteers supporting refugees in Hungary during the recent crisis, rather than challenging the notion of belonging through inclusionary acts of citizenship, 'humanitarian volunteers targeted non-nationals as the primary subject of intervention in a way that foreclosed their agency'.

Conclusion

It would be difficult and perhaps wrong to argue that the fact that so many volunteers have rushed to participate in refugee support activities is a negative phenomenon, since it clearly shows that a substantial proportion of the European population believes that Europe should do more to welcome refugees, and that people from Europe (and from the global community) are willing to travel in order to try to deliver support to these refugees. Similarly, these volunteers do in general believe that they are acting with the best of intentions, and that their actions are motivated by a desire to help others within the framework of this humanitarian 'crisis'. In many cases these volunteers may bring additional help or support which is needed to meet the basic needs of refugees. Moreover, anecdotal evidence would seem to show that many people who volunteered for the first time during the refugee 'crisis' returned to volunteer again with refugees, or moved on to other forms of humanitarian activity in different locations. However, the frequently depoliticised nature of this volunteer support means that little focus is placed on the wider issue of migration in the European Union, and refugee policies, or on the volunteers' own role with regard to these broader trends and policies. Similarly, the volunteers do not tend to reflect in any depth on the causes of displacement, or on the responsibilities of their own governments and countries of origin as stakeholders in the perpetuation of the conflicts that cause refugees to flee and seek protection in Europe. Furthermore, the ways in which many volunteers perceive the status of refugees, and their own roles and relationships with the refugees, might be seen to reinforce dominant representations of refugees as dehistoricised and depoliticised 'victims', lacking their own agency or political subjectivities.

By acting in such an apolitical way, it may be argued that these volunteers have returned to the roots of humanitarianism, and to the claims of neutrality on which humanitarianism was founded (Barnett, 2005), but I would argue that this neutral and apolitical approach is no longer morally sustainable in a situation in which European governments could – and should – be held responsible for the way in which their actions (and non-action) have dramatically exacerbated the dangers and insecurity faced by refugees, leading in some cases to the death of refugees by drowning or by neglect of their basic needs. The problem is not the apolitical nature of volunteer humanitarianism, but the way in which it masks the responsibilities of political authorities and systems, which have created and maintained this situation of 'crisis'. As Brauman argues, silence cannot always be equated with neutrality (Brauman, 1998), as silence may be taken to illustrate or signify tacit approval of governments' actions (or non-action). In this case, the political silence of volunteer humanitarians allows governments and political authorities to evade their responsibility to protect refugees and to address the root causes of the crisis. Various researchers have argued that the work of humanitarian associations and NGOs perpetuates a system of repression, allowing for the prolongation of governments' politics of 'exception' with regard to refugees, with volunteer associations acting in many ways as the 'right hand of the state' (Kobelinsky & Makaremi, 2009). It can be argued that the volunteers, by not questioning this role, despite their best intentions further contribute to this politics of repression. Furthermore, by maintaining the distinction between refugees as 'suffering subjects' (Robbins, 2013) as a product of their 'otherness' and other groups who may be marginalised or excluded within society, volunteers contribute to the conservation of a more general model of neoliberal governmentality. This type of volunteer humanitarianism can thus be seen as part of a wider process of neoliberal governmentality and citizenship whereby individuals are encouraged to engage in individual acts of solidarity, compassion or charity, motivated by appeals to emotion, while at the same time being denied the opportunity to demand state-based or structural solutions to major social or political problems.

Notes

1 There has been debate about whether those arriving in Europe amongst the most recent arrivals on the Aegean and Mediterranean routes should be classed as 'refugees' or 'migrants'. Whilst the official categorisation of a refugee according to international law is based on the recognition of an asylum claim by a national jurisdiction, or by the status conferred by the United Nations High Commissioner for Refugees (UNHCR) in a refugee camp, it can also be argued that anyone fleeing violence or persecution and unable to stay in their country of origin is de facto a refugee. The term 'migrant' has been used by some people to imply that people on the move are not fleeing persecution, but are instead 'merely' economic migrants trying to enter the EU for their own economic gain. In this chapter, I have thus made the choice to employ the term 'refugee' to indicate that most of the people arriving in Europe during the current 'crisis' have been forced to flee their countries as a result of persecution, violence, or danger, and thus should be considered 'forced' migrants.

2 This scene was observed at the Grande-Synthe camp near Dunkirk, December 2015.

3 Interview in Kos, July 2015.

4 Interview in Calais, December 2015.

5 Interview in Kos, July 2015.

6 Interview in Calais, January 2016.

7 For these posts and more, see the Care4Calais volunteer chat group: https://www.facebook.com/groups/956020314476605/.

8 Interview in Paris, May 2017.

9 It should be noted that this research did not concern very specifically political organisations such as the No Borders movement, which has challenged European border and migration policies for many years, and which has organised interventions in Calais and at other sites across Europe. For the most part, new volunteers who have arrived in European locations to support refugees have not been involved with No Borders or similar movements of political contestation.

10 Interview in Calais, February 2016.

11 Scene observed at the Grande-Synthe camp, Dunkirk, December 2015.

12 Interview, December 2015.

13 Scene observed at Grande-Synthe camp, Dunkirk, January 2016.

14 Interview in Kos, July 2015.

References

Allsopp, J (2017), Agent, victim, soldier, son: intersecting masculinities in the European 'Refugee Crisis'. Pp. 155–75. In: Freedman, F, Kivilcim, Z & Özgür Baklacioğlu, N (eds), *A gendered approach to the Syrian Refugee Crisis*. London: Routledge.

Anderson, B (2010), *Where's the harm in that? Immigration enforcement, trafficking and the protection of migrants' rights*. Presented at: The Ethics of International Migration Management, Pompeu Fabra University, 26 April 2010.

Ataç, I, Rygiel, K & Stierl, M (2016), The contentious politics of migrant and refugee protest and solidarity movements: remaking citizenship from the margins. *Citizenship Studies*. Vol. 20 (5): 527–44.

Barnett, M (2005), Humanitarianism transformed. *Perspectives on Politics*. Vol. 3 (4): 723–40.

Brauman, R (1998), Refugee camps, population transfers and NGOs.

Pp. 177–95. In: Moore J (ed.), *Hard choices: moral dilemmas in humanitarian intervention*. Lanham, MD: Rowman and Littlefield.

Cabot, H (2017), *The dangers of humanitarian governance in Greece*. Presented at: Global Refugee Crisis Conference, UCLA, 8 May 2017.

Calhoun, C (2008), The imperative to reduce suffering: charity, progress, and emergencies in the field of humanitarian action. In: Barnett, MN & Weiss, TG (eds), *Humanitarianism in question: politics, power, ethics*. Ithaca, NY: Cornell University Press.

Daley, P (2013), Rescuing African bodies: celebrities, consumerism and neoliberal humanitarianism. *Review of African Political Economy*. Vol. 40 (137): 375–93.

EU (2016), EU–Turkey joint statement, 18 March 2016 [online]. Available from: www.consilium.europa.eu/en/press/press-releases/2016/03/18-eu-turkey-statement/ (accessed 19 August 2017).

Freedman, J (2011), The Réseau Education Sans Frontières: reframing the campaign against the deportation of migrants. *Citizenship Studies*. Vol. 15 (5): 613–26.

Freedman, J (2016), Engendering security at the borders of Europe: women migrants and the Mediterranean 'crisis'. *Journal of Refugee Studies*. Vol. 29 (4): 568–82.

Freedman, J (2017), 'After Calais': creating and managing (in)security for refugees in Europe. *Migration Studies* (forthcoming).

Freedman, J, Kivilcim, Z & Özgür Baklacioğlu, N (2017) *A gendered approach to the Syrian Refugee Crisis*. London: Routledge.

Her (2016), 9 things I learned volunteering in a refugee camp [online]. Available from: Her (2016), www.her.ie/life/9-things-i-learned-volunteering-in-a-refugee-camp-260215 (accessed 19 August 2017).

Jeandesboz, J & Pallister-Wilkins, P (2014), Crisis, enforcement and control at the EU borders. Pp. 115–35. In: Lindley A (ed.), *Crisis and migration: critical perspectives*. London: Routledge.

Kallius, A, Monterescu, D & Rajaram, PK (2016), Immobilizing mobility: border ethnography, illiberal democracy, and the politics of the 'refugee crisis' in Hungary. *American Ethnologist*. Vol. 43 (1): 1–13.

Kobelinsky, C & Makaremi, C (2009), *Enfermés dehors. Enquêtes sur le confinement des étrangers*. Bellecombe-en-Bauges: Editions du Croquant.

Koffman, O, Orgad, S & Gill, R (2015), Girl power and 'selfie' humanitarianism. *Continuum: Journal of Media and Cultural Studies*. Vol. 29 (2): 157–68.

Léonard, S (2010), EU border security and migration into the European Union: FRONTEX and securitisation through practices. *European Security*. Vol. 19 (2): 231–54.

Lovertt, A, Whelan, C & Rendon, R (2017), *The reality of the EU–Turkey Statement: how Greece has become a testing ground for policies that erode protection for refugees*. Oxford: Oxfam.

Lutterbeck, D (2006) Policing migration in the Mediterranean. *Mediterranean Politics*. Vol. 11 (1): 59–82.

Malkki, L (1996), Speechless emissaries: refugees, humanitarianism and dehistoricization. *Cultural Anthropology*. Vol. 11 (3): 377–404.

Mason, CL (2016), Tinder and humanitarian hook-ups: the erotics of social media racism. *Feminist Media Studies*. Vol. 16 (5): 822–37.

Mitchell, K (2016), Celebrity humanitarianism, transnational emotion, and the rise of neoliberal citizenship. *Global Networks*. Vol. 16 (3): 288–306.

Mostafanezhad, M (2013), 'Getting in touch with your inner Angelina': celebrity humanitarianism and the cultural politics of gendered generosity in volunteer tourism. *Third World Quarterly*. Vol. 34 (3): 485–99.

Mostafanezhad, M (2014), Volunteer tourism and the popular humanitarian gaze. *Geoforum*. Vol. 54: 111–18.

Nianias H (2016), Refugees in Lesbos: are there too many NGOs on the island? *The Guardian*, 5 January 2016.

Papataxiarchis, E (2016), Being 'there': at the frontline of the 'European Refugee Crisis' part 1. *Anthropology Today*. Vol. 32 (2): 5–9.

Pedwell, C (2012), Affective (self)-transformations: empathy, neoliberalism and international development. *Feminist Theory*. Vol. 12 (2): 163–79.

Pette, M (2016), Venir en aide aux migrants dans le Calaisis: entre action associative locale et crise migratoire internationale. *Savoir/Agir*. Vol. 36: 47–53.

Razack, S (2007), Stealing the pain of others: reflections on Canadian humanitarian responses. *Review of Education, Pedagogy, and Cultural Studies*. Vol. 29 (4): 375–94.

Robbins, J (2013), Beyond the suffering subject: toward an anthropology of the good. *Journal of the Royal Anthropological Institute*. Vol. 19 (3): 447–62.

Robins, S (2009), Humanitarian aid beyond 'bare survival': social movement responses to xenophobic violence in South Africa. *American Ethnologist*. Vol. 36 (4): 637–50.

Ticktin, M (2006), Where ethics and politics meet: the violence of humanitarianism in France. *American Ethnologist*. Vol. 33(1): 33–49.

UNHCR (2016), *Regional refugee and migrant response plan for Europe. January to December 2016*. Geneva: UNHCR.

Wilkinson, K (2016), Volunteering in Calais. *Critical and Radical Social Work*. Vol. 4 (1): 117–20.

7 | LA NOUVELLE FRANCE: INSTITUTIONALISED ABUSE, 'EXCEPTION' AND SPECTACLE IN THE EXILED/ VOLUNTEER RELATIONSHIP AT THE FRANCO–BRITISH BORDER

Celeste Cantor-Stephens

In April and May 2017, following years of involvement, I returned to Calais, northern France, to investigate abuse carried out by local and national authorities towards exiled people at the Franco–British border. This return was made in response to tales of increasingly abominable conditions, reported by those 'on the ground', notably since authorities bulldozed the unofficial refugee camp, often referred to as the 'Jungle',[1] in October 2016. This was a destruction of a space that, while dehumanising, precarious and unpredictable, provided some degree of consistency, shelter, food, water, friendship, and information, and maintained relatively safe women and children-only spaces. At the time, the sprawling shanty-town was inhabited by over 8,100 people (Wannesson, 2016a). Following its destruction, local authorities, assisted by the media, promoted images of Calais as a migrant-free town (Charrier, 2016), and public attention hugely diminished. Abuse did not. Less focus meant more obscurity; the exiled were exiled further, made 'invisible', and segregated into zones where their apparently exceptional existence could be treated with exceptional brutality.

Research was undertaken as an immersive critical political ethnography, and included time spent working alongside activists, volunteers and workers supporting exiled people in Calais. Semi-structured interviews were conducted with ten of these workers and two exiled people, augmented with numerous more informal conversations. Data also came from analyses of British, French and international politico-legal documents and practices.

Findings were unsettling, revealing severe human rights violations and extensive abuse of exiled people by national and local authorities, including regular, direct physical assaults by the French police. Research also identified ways in which institutions produce and control spaces and systems of abuse at the border, implicating the public, and perpetuating platforms for continued abuse.

This chapter considers this discriminating, (mis)educating place of Othering, capitalist spectacle, and exception, where 'rules' and rights can be violated. I discuss how such environments, images and practices, led by authorities, shape events and relationships, guiding perceptions of 'the migrant', fuelling anti-immigrant rhetoric as well as 'humanitarian' concepts, founded on notions of competition and the Other.

Guest Room

For almost a week, Jed has been sleeping in a cheap hotel in northern Calais. It's a quiet place to stay; he has barely seen anyone else inside the building, and the owners are pleasant enough. On 7 February 2017, he is violently woken in the middle of the night. Vigorous, heavy banging on the door accompanies shouts of 'Police!' Jed stumbles to pull on some pants just as two CRS[2] riot police burst in. Desperately searching his panicked mind, Jed cries 'Je n'ai parler pas français!' [sic], hoping this conveys his lack of French. One of the intruders looks squarely at him and declares: 'Albanian.' The other grasps the top of the large rucksack by the bed, and throws it to the floor. He points at a confused, tired Jed and then to the bag, and orders: 'Papers.' Intimidatingly, the police move and shout aggressively as Jed tries to explain that he doesn't have 'papers'.

But he does have a passport. He hands it to the police. They take a moment to look through it before, suddenly, becoming very polite. Jed is British. 'OK, you must leave,' they explain. 'We are closing the hotel, it's a crime scene.'

After the designated 15 minutes to pack his belongings, Jed makes his way out of the hotel. Nearing the exit another police officer stops him aggressively, shouting: 'You can't leave! Show me your papers!' The process repeats, the passport is produced, the once-threatening officer provides a courteous 'OK, you may go.' Down a now-barricaded alleyway leading from the hotel courtyard to the accommodation, Jed sees other officers heavily questioning someone. Shortly after 4 am he finds himself on the Calais streets, sheltering from the rain in doorways, until another hotel opens for guests at the seaside town.[3]

This hotel raid formed part of an operation to tackle a smuggling ring assisting Albanian and Iraqi people in their efforts to reach the UK (GD & AFP, 2017). While traffickers and hotel owners were profiting from others' desperation, many of those staying in the hotel – at six or seven to a room (Liberation, 2017) – were simply doing what they could afford to further their journey. For those able to pay the extortionate fees – in this case 10,000 euros according to one newspaper (Tissérand, 2017) – paying to reach a destination is often a final, desperate decision. Exiled from their former lives, unlike Jed these human-trafficking victims will not have been able to produce passports certifying a status as 'tourist': or at least as *Valid Documented Human.*

They will not have experienced the relief that Jed, a volunteer with a Calais-based charity, felt after his 'very first-hand ... experience' in which, for a brief moment, the police 'treated [him] just as they would treat [any migrant]'. All will have been subject, in differing ways, to local and national systems that on one hand create proud, culturally rich tourist destinations, and on the other are proudly exclusive, unafraid to condemn and differentiate according to conceptions of origin and belonging.

La Nouvelle France and the Invisible Other

Recent political events and discourses have emphasised nationality, patriotism, *'outsider* threats', and *'insider* strength'.[4] General and presidential elections in the UK (8 June 2017) and France (23 April, 7 May 2017), the Brexit referendum (23 June 2016) and consequent negotiations for Britain's departure from the EU (commencing 19 June 2017), a series of 'terrorist attacks' in France and the UK – spurring xenophobic and racist rhetoric and further 'acts of terrorism' (Dodd & Taylor, 2017) – and previously unseen levels of forced migration (UNHCR, 2015) – largely as a result of similar, larger-scale attacks in areas well-removed from France and Britain – have all been highly significant.

Alongside this, the French and British states, and certain local regions, appear to promote an impossible land. This place is modern, open and cosmopolitan, corresponding with an ever-moving, global-ised world; it is simultaneously exclusive, guarding, promoting and prioritising the nationalistic self over Others. This imagined space is full of contradictions: an abstraction that I have called *the paradox of La*

Nouvelle France (LaNF).[5,6] Here, mutually perpetuating manipulations of space and (dis)information, a kind of public and 'non-public' (mis) education (Dijstelbloem & Broeders, 2015), allow rules to differ between populations, and create a platform for abuse.

'Welcome to Calais!' cries Mayor Natacha Bouchart, thrusting her arms open as she stands in front of Calais' grand town hall (Ville de Calais, 2017; n.d.). In April 2017, a municipality-funded video announced that '1,000 British residents' would win a day-trip to Calais (Go, 2017a). Winners would witness the unveiling of a statue of Churchill and De Gaulle, a monument '[representing] the reconstruction of France [...] [an instrument] for reclaiming the [French] image'[7] (Demassieux, in *Voix du Nord*, 2016). Celebrating the apparent glory and bond between France and Britain, any hint of a non-white, non-European is almost hyperbolically absent from the cheerful video.

Within the glossy presentation of these 'idealised', welcoming nations is a none-too-subtle message of exclusion. Across the Channel, the UK government manifesto, selling a 'great nation [with] a glorious history', almost explicitly reserves the *unity* of this select national club for a certain group (Conservative Party, 2017: 10). Representative of this, the rubric 'A Country that Comes Together' *directly* precedes the subheading 'Controlling immigration' (ibid: 54). The *gain* of the *citizen* is key to this rhetoric, seemingly existing in opposition to the *non-citizen*. Throughout the Conservative policy statement, notions of healthy togetherness are juxtaposed with competitive, anti-outsider rhetoric: 'in matters of migration, [...] *Britain* must stay strong and *united* – and take a *lead in the world* to defend *our interests*' [emphasis added] (ibid.: 6).

From this perspective, as the exiled are pushed further away – made 'invisible' (whether chased to out-of-town woodland, erased from municipal videos, or forbidden from entering the country) – they simultaneously become very *present. They* are the threat against which *we* unite. The development of *LaNF* – be it France, the UK and/or Calais – is founded on the exploitation of a *particular* image; the presence – real or 'threatened' – of any 'foreign body' necessarily disrupts this 'unblemished' promoted vision, protruding, *hyper-present*. Within the *paradox of LaNF* is thus another *paradox of the 'invisible Other'*.

Sensationalist media and 'voluntourism' reflect this, with their invasive cameras eager to capture the 'rare sight' of the 'unknown'.

So-called *voluntourists* – combining humanitarian aid work with often-voyeuristic tourism – are often scorned by those more likely to identify as 'activists' in Calais, their actions perceived as an egocentric hindrance, rather than practical acts of solidarity. Voluntourism is rarely conducive to active, on-site change, but (perhaps unintentionally) further promotes Othering and the institution of *LaNF* from which this emanates. To some extent, then, this outwardly well-intentioned voluntary-humanitarianism-cum-tourism is a consequence and perpetuation of what appears to be a contrasting, more explicit anti-immigrant rhetoric; both thrive on the image of the Other. Arthur Thomas, a youth worker with the Calais-based Refugee Youth Service, told me of an unaccompanied minor who provided his testimony in the hope of beginning the asylum process. Afterwards, the 15-year-old asked: 'but, you didn't film me? [...] I don't understand; in Europe everyone films us [...] but they don't help.'[8]

The Bad Migrant/Good Refugee

'Invisibility' affords Othering a subtlety. The 2017 British government manifesto promised to redefine 'definitions of asylum and refugee' by focusing on 'people in parts of the world affected by conflict and oppression' and *not* those 'who are young enough, fit enough, and have the resources to get to Britain' (Conservative Party, 2017: 40). In short, the 'Good Refugee' is far away; the 'Bad Migrant' is *here*. The 'Good' therefore remain invisible, a practical impossibility, nonexistent except as a symbol of the would-be host country's 'generosity'. The 'Bad Migrant' *will* (the state promises) *be made* invisible, obliterated, but is *actually* hyper-present. Simultaneously, the distant *Refugee* is unfortunate *because* they are far from this great 'place of sanctuary' (ibid.: 40), while the 'Bad Migrant' unscrupulously deprives others of this benefit. Thus, the recurring yet impossible dichotomy of the 'illegal immigrant'/'deserving refugee' is furthered; the migrant who is here must *necessarily* be criminal. In reality, no person can *be* illegal, yet numerous state-enforced paradoxes reinforce this disparaging concept, ensuring that asylum seekers commit 'offences'. Under most circumstances, for example, to request asylum in the UK, one must have entered British territory; without official documents, the only way to do this is illegally. Such socio-political rhetoric confirms the manifesto statement; migrants who are *present* are unscrupulous law-breakers, while far away refugees are poor and helpless.

If, as Aristotle (n.d.) suggests, humans' innate political quality is demonstrated by being 'the only animal [...] endowed with the gift of speech',[9] we may select who we recognise as a political human by how we interpret the sounds that they make (Rancière, 2001). The 'Good Refugee' is far enough away (in distance, as well as in sentiment) that they cannot be truly 'heard'. Rather, their 'voice' is reconstructed in what we may selectively assume are 'only groans or cries expressing suffering [...] but not actual speeches demonstrating a shared *aisthesis*' (ibid., thesis 8). Thus the 'Good Refugee' becomes an apolitical Other, unworthy of true inter-*human* empathy and aid (such as refuge). Nonetheless, their *suffering* is sufficiently communicated that they can be pitied, deprived of the privileges of *our* land, while *La Nouvelle France* is aggrandised through the public declaration of support for these 'Poor Refugees'. Ironically, the '*Victim*-Other' (the *Poor Good Refugee*) is pitied *because* they are Other, that is, *because* they are *not* a member of *LaNF*. Image, rather than practicality, is key to this show, in which human rights policies are developed 'far away from the killing fields', in conference halls where victims are absent, although sometimes 'paraded for effect' (Mutua, 2007: 578).

Demonstrating the transformation of this rhetoric from anti-immigration to pro-humanitarianism, perhaps the most devastating example of the 'poor' *distant* (and non-existent) refugee is the *dead*. In September 2015 the image of the body of three-year-old Syrian Alan Kurdi washed up on a beach made headlines (Khan, 2015), and marked the beginning of an influx of journalists and volunteers to Calais. Yet Alan's was by no means a unique case; his own five-year-old brother died on the same occasion, and between September 2015 and February 2016 an average of two children *per day* are thought to have lost their lives crossing the Mediterranean (UNHCR, 2016). With these facts largely unreported in the mainstream media, the single image of the helpless child-refugee transformed the subject into a spectacle, a media, social and political tool. Thus this romanticised, fetishised Refugee featured in glossy magazines and social media *selfies* is likely (perhaps inadvertently) to be deprived of *humanness*, of their own will and reality. Instead they become a kind of *property* and expression of those who create and control their image, of those who subscribe to the patronising concept of 'saving the Refugee', further dehumanising and excluding this 'privileged object of humanitarian biopolitics' (Žižek, 2002: 91).

Spectacle and Competition

A sense of ownership and control prevails over the Bad Migrant/Good Refugee figure, emanating from a competitive, capitalist environment and its institutions. The society of *La Nouvelle France* is a *spectacle* (Debord, 1992). Built on false promises and misleading conceptions, it is an unattainable image of an impossible ideal, of consumption and abundance, promising fulfilment and unity. It embodies, in reality, the competition of a capitalist society, where unattainable images mediate social relations, and the *human* is usurped by the *thing* (ibid.). It is also 'a new kind of enjoyment', engendering 'new sacrifice' for a 'new need' that seduces the consumer to ruin (Marx, n.d.). The *spectacle* thrives on competition; since it is never achieved there must be something or someone in the way. Those nearest the 'head' of this *society of spectacle* – typically the elite and already-powerful (though also subjects and victims of the *spectacle*) – profit from the sale of an impossible vision to those who, in turn, compete with others to obtain it.

In the final round of the 2017 French presidential elections, right-wing, anti-immigration candidate Marine Le Pen won a majority in two of France's 101 departments; one of these was Pas-de-Calais (Ministère de l'intérieur, 2017a). The working-class, industrial area has some of France's highest rates of unemployment (Insee, 2017). In an interview, Arthur Thomas observed: 'Some [locals react] violently, persuaded that "these people" are coming to steal [...] that they're "parasites".' As workers were gradually made redundant at Calais's Tioxide chemical factory, looming over the out-of-town industrial area and woodland where the exiled often sleep, local authority figures such as MP Yann Capet publicly blamed the presence of migrants for economic difficulties (AFP, 2017; *Voix du Nord*, 2015; Wannesson, 2015), while failing to acknowledge that the job cuts and an imminent planned closure were part of multinational, multibillion-dollar Huntsman Corporation's long-term global programme (Huntsman Corporation, 2017; Reuters, 2014). Sabriya Guivy, also with Refugee Youth Service, bluntly attributes Le Pen's local popularity as '[down to Mayor] Bouchart. There has been such "brain-washing" about Calais losing so much money because of "these migrants" [...] the migrant crisis is being exploited.'

Thus, the *actually* unobtainable vision of *LaNF* appears *temporarily* (since we still believe in its reality) ruined by the arrival of outsiders (and, since this is a *competitive* society, not merely by their *arrival*, but by their *intention*). This promotes a *willed failure of the Other* in order to further one's *own* goal of obtaining the seductive image of the *spectacle* (*LaNF*). For those *otherwise* at the 'base' of the capitalist power hierarchy (such as redundant factory workers), the most feasible competitors are the still-less-privileged exiled. To be 'equal' with competitors and apparent 'thieves' of the idyllic vision would mean self-demotion to the level of the 'Bad Migrant', while differentiating oneself from this subjugated group permits individuals to regain power over the classification system, and over their own mobilisation. Drawing 'difference out of the undifferentiated' (Bourdieu, 1984: 479), the disadvantaged are set into competition with the disadvantaged, the less-well-off against the *even*-less-well-off. Although *LaNF* depicts idyllic unity, it paradoxically requires Othering to create competition, without which the *spectacle* (*LaNF*) cannot exist.

Simultaneously, although the exiled may be (perceived as) 'competitors', they are nonetheless *excluded*, their underprivileged position assumed to be outside the normative 'idyllic' aspirations of *LaNF*. Thus the *difference* of the Other expands, and the exiled become *a different kind of spectacle* (Mbembe, 2003); they are the subjects of '*spectacular*' conditions, a morbid display that could not happen to any '*normal* citizen'. The exiled thus becomes an Other who is both pitied and celebrated as they highlight the 'greatness' of *LaNF* and its apparent privilege, afforded to many, but not all. This is particularly true of the 'Poor Good Refugee', of the exiled who become a tool in the production of the *spectacle* of *LaNF*.

Thus while the *Poor Refugee* becomes a symbolic figure of pity, they are also one of comparison and competition. Without competition there is no *Nouvelle France*; without this *specific competitor* there is no 'Saviour Volunteer'. The exiled are the *spectacle-thing* through which individuals may 'prove' and promote *themselves*, along with, and *as a product of*, *LaNF*. Further, while inadvertently championing certain values of the capitalist-driven *Nouvelle France*, much of this self-promotion is explicitly positioned in opposition to 'anti-immigrant' discourse and its proponents: that is, to some extent, in *competition* with them, over the same issues and Refugee-*things*. Thus, the exiled risk becoming pawns in a larger society of competition.

This is not to suggest that activists and volunteers should *not* overtly oppose anti-immigrant rhetoric. On the contrary, in Rancière's terms (2001: thesis 10), consensus (i.e. lack of dissensus, of disruption, of standing up to be seen and heard) is the 'end of politics'; in other words, 'if you are not part of the solution, you are part of the problem'.[10] Yet as the semi-invisible and vulnerable exiled are impeded from demonstrating for their own rights, there is a risk that advocates, responding as a *necessary* 'nexus' between the state and abuse (Mutua, 2007: 578), fall into the same modes of functioning that drive the behaviours and events that they appear to oppose, furthering the apoliticisation, dehumanisation and self-advancing competition promoted by *LaNF*. Where the exiled outsider is associated with economic capital and struggle, and a neoliberal society 'interpellates individuals as entrepreneurial actors in every sphere of life' and 'relieves the discrepancy between economic and moral behavior' (Brown, 2003), it is almost *inevitable* that the 'good done' by the Saviour Volunteer becomes a form of competition, and the 'benefiting' Refugee a symbol of 'success'.

(Mis)information

Deception prevails at the Franco–British border. When the 'Jungle' shanty-town was demolished, many former inhabitants were promised that by cooperating, wearing wristband-tags and boarding buses to Centres d'Accueil et D'orientation (CAO)[11] (Refugee Youth Service, 2016), they would be withdrawn from the Dublin System of deportation and guaranteed asylum in France. Some regions kept to this agreement, but many have not (Migrants Erythréens, Soudannais et Sommaliens de Calais à Rennes, 2016). Aarif[12] told me, 'When they destroyed [the Jungle], they [said:] "When you go to [the] CAO you can have everything, you will get documents, you will have a house, everything, you can stay nicely." [In the CAO] the situation was very bad.' After two months Aarif returned to Calais.

Volunteers who witnessed the 'Jungle' demolition described how the presence of English-speaking Home Office officials, wearing tabards marked 'Official UK' (Wannesson, 2016b), led minors to believe that the buses would take them to England. Others were given departure dates to be reunited with family in Britain, only for them to be cancelled, and the children dispersed around France (Hunter & Pope, 2016: 4). As a result of what Arthur Thomas described as 'numerous, astonishing, scandalous false promises from the French and English states', interviewees reported an overwhelming mistrust among youths in Calais. Nadine Rubanbleu depicted minors as '[saving] themselves' by fleeing 'when they see someone [official] coming,' and legal worker Sabriya Guivy described 'the most difficult thing [as being] that [children] no longer trust the legal system [...] And they're right!'

The destruction of the shanty-town coincided with the closure of Calais's asylum office (Wannesson, 2016c), where people could once access information, as well as apply for asylum. Consequently, risk of arrest while travelling to the office in Lille discourages asylum-seeking and obstructs access to information on options and entitlements: preventing people from accessing rights, and from accessing the knowledge that provides the 'right to have rights' (Arendt, 1962). State provision of such information appears non-existent in Calais, where the exiled are encouraged to fear rather than to seek help from authorities. Arthur Thomas stressed the impact this has on children, whose 'very, very little knowledge of their rights' prompts 'a focus on "saving their own skins" and going to England, rather than [defending their rights]'.

One of the aims of long-term workers in Calais is thus to provide the information that is denied by the state, in the case of Refugee Youth Service '[allowing] children to become children again, and also become beings who are able to make proper choices, who have time and space to stop and assess the situation' (Sabriya Guivy). On one occasion, I witnessed a couple approach French activists to seek advice on travelling elsewhere after being prevented from entering the UK. Unusually, the individuals were citizens from within the European Economic Area, and had thus been *illegally* denied entry (UK Government, 2003). Without the assistance of the activists, this would not have been discovered.

Despite experience, access to information, and legal resources, those who support the exiled are also thwarted by institutionalised manipulation and deception. For example, following the destruction of the 'Jungle' in March 2017, the local authorities prohibited organisations from publicly distributing food, potentially depriving hundreds of this basic need (Go, 2017b). Following an appeal, Lille Administrative Tribunal overturned the ban, ruling that the mayor had infringed upon human rights (Tribunal Administrative de Lille, 2017). Consequently, Calais municipality heightened its regime of dispersing and arresting exiled people, forcing distributions out of town, to take place at the predominantly used Rue des Verrotières site. The police began monitoring this space, imposing time constraints on organisations; after an hour of distribution, police descend from their vehicles, conduct identity checks and arrest any undocumented person who lingers. At other times, the volunteers are targeted, each 'Western-looking' individual is asked for identification documents, without clear reasoning, and vehicles may also be searched (Wannesson, 2017). In May 2017, when these practices were systematised, the Refugee Community Kitchen was preparing around approximately 400 meals for each evening distribution. On one occasion, I attended with a volunteer legal worker who, when CRS police stormed the site, asked for proof of an order to shut down distributions. The police officer responded: 'Contactez le Ministère de l'intérieure!'[13] Workers from multiple organisations told me they had repeatedly asked for documents proving official orders, without any being produced: '[We ask] "on what basis?"' Sabriya Guivy tells me. '[They say:] "It's the orders." I can't see any written document about this.' The source of these injunctions appears unlocatable; each actor passes responsibility on to another, between police force, public prosecutor, mayor and prefecture, denying their own responsibilities, while abuse continues (Goudeseune, 2017). Nadine Rubanbleu expressed this incomprehensible situation: '[The police are] pawns. Whenever they do something [they say] "we're carrying out orders". Yes, well show us these "orders"; what are they, where?' Many interviewees identified the police as key sources of deception; '[they] play hugely with the effects of disinformation on people's rights,' said Arthur Thomas, explaining how officers had attempted to search a charity vehicle without a warrant.

Normalisation

Threads of *dis*information and *lack* of information are spun into images of the idealised *Nouvelle France*, and propagate notions of *normality* surrounding events. The opacities of juridical and asylum processes contribute to these seemingly impenetrable obstacles, and further open space for abuse. In Calais, I have frequently been asked a myriad of questions on the complex procedures surrounding asylum and deportation. Despite access to resources, and English and French fluency, the systems are so charged with exceptions and ambiguities that identifying satisfactory, dependable answers can appear impossible. Long-term workers struggle against these challenges, and like the exiled are deprived of means of disproving or rejecting the apparent *normality* of disruptions, injustice and abuse by authorities. As the routine mistreatment of exiled people in Calais has escalated, it is as if norms have adapted. Philippe Wannesson, a Calais-based activist, author and researcher of blog *Passeurs d'hospitalités*, confirms this, telling me that organisations rarely confront the authorities with legal, human rights issues, but appear to 'compromise', as if 'they don't dare to ask' through 'a kind of normalisation of the situation'. This is corroborated by a sense of helplessness; Clare Moseley explained how the police prevent food distributions '[which] they're not supposed to do, legally, but there's nothing we can do to stop them'.

Hostile Environment

Such events appear simply to have become part of the prevailing structure, echoing the 'hostile environment' promised by then UK Home Secretary Theresa May (Kirkup & Winnett, 2012), explicitly designed to make the lives of *certain* foreigners so difficult that they cannot bear to stay. Organisations supporting the exiled also become victims of 'hostilities'. On a visit to the Care4Calais warehouse, where workers sort donations into sprawling boxes of clothes and blankets, Clare Moseley re-emphasised to volunteers the importance of keeping the entrance area clear. 'The authorities will use that as an excuse to close us down', she warns, 'It's happened before near here.' On the other side of Calais, a long-term volunteer at the buzzing Auberge des Migrants warehouse echoes these words as she spins around, politely designating tasks, assessing order and space, needs, equipment, and deliveries. A health and safety inspection has been announced. Everything must be perfect; one criticised element and the warehouse might be shut down. Individuals are equally susceptible. '[Activists] have been arrested just for having a pen-knife in their bag [...] One friend was held for over 20 hours', recalls Nadine Rubanbleu. Another was stopped by police as she took an injured individual from a woodland camp to the hospital during the night; one of the two passengers had undone their seatbelt just moments before the car was parked, and the driver had been issued with three separate fines.

Yet it is undoubtedly the exiled who suffer the most from 'exceptional' mistreatment. Aarif, who had travelled from Afghanistan, told a familiar story: 'We feel really, you know, sad, because we [think:] "this is Europe; European [countries] have human rights, everything." But here is – we don't see any human rights in France.' Sabriya Guivy estimated that around 60 percent of children currently in Calais had left the state reception centres they were sent to following the destruction of the 'Jungle', having 'sampled [something that] wasn't the child protection service,[14] it was a thing done especially for Calais, a third-rate child protection service'. The concept of *LaNF* evokes protection and ample provision for all, depicted in such national systems of care. In reality this is reserved for some, while others are provided with a token replica, or deprived completely of care.

A host of social and legal structures are invalidated for *certain* foreigners at the Franco–British border. This is exemplified as the exiled in Calais are banished from the town centre to experience inhospitable living conditions in the woods and wastelands of the outskirts, denied essential resources, and physically harmed by civil 'forces of protection'. French law that ensures emergency accommodation to 'any homeless person experiencing medical, psychological or social hardship'[15] (CASF, 1956), also appears to have been nullified for those in Calais, despite the reality that such vulnerability is inherent to the asylum seeker (Toubon, 2015a; 2015b). Similarly, in 2003 the '*Loi Sarkozy*' (République Française, 2003) was created, allowing *foreign* detainees to be tried in courtrooms 'in direct proximity' to police-run detention centres, enabling an otherwise illegal procedure that could compromise the integrity of a trial. In Britain, similar *foreigner*-exclusive practices occur, including, for example, within a detention system where non-criminal migrants can be held *indefinitely*, while UK nationals suspected of 'serious crime' (such as murder) are detained without charge for a maximum of four days (UK Government, n.d.).

Exception

In this constructed space of 'citizens' and 'Others', two distinct worlds are created within one. While idealistic visions of a generous, shared land are promoted, 'exceptions' are made for those who are themselves constructed to appear as 'exceptions' to the image.

One Ethiopian man I met in Calais carried in his bag, among very few possessions, a Union Jack: a physical memento of his faith in all that is British. After several weeks, tiring of repeated arrests, detention and daily physical abuse from the Calaisien police at the British border, he left to begin the asylum process in Belgium.

In the glorified image of *La Nouvelle France* (equally representative of *New Britain*), abuse (of the undeserving) appears impossible. France and Britain were instrumental in the development of the conventions that define human rights (Bates, 2010), and are typically perceived as respecting of said conventions (Maplecroft, 2016). Yet violations can be most disturbing when they manifestly contrast – like the Other – with the neat image that has been constructed. Long-term workers expressed continuing outrage at events witnessed *in France*: 'children running around a shanty-town in sandals and t-shirts [...] living on the streets. And this is happening *in France*' (Arthur Thomas). Interviewees highlighted the incongruity of a country that 'supposedly [...] respects human rights' (Clare Moseley), and 'that claims to be [a place] of human rights, [but refuses] access to water, the right to wash, and the right to eat. Without mentioning shelter' (Dominique Mégard).

Simultaneously, it is the *contrast* with expectation that *allows* abuse – and further breaking from convention – to continue. Territorial boundaries (such as the Franco–British border) may be understood as *enabling* human rights and liberties; they delineate, for example, the boundaries of distributive justice and right to self-determination (Banai, 2013). Yet borders, therefore, also determine the *scope* (Caney, 2005) of these benefits: that is, *who* has – or does *not* have – the right to access them. The space within national borders is bound with normative material, such as forms of identification (Robertson, 2009), which provide a means of locating and limiting this scope. Notions of the global, cosmopolitanism and renewal – the *Nouvelle* – thus contrast with the nationalistic, homogeneous and traditional – the *France*.[16] While the Other is key to *LaNF*, s/he appears as a disruption to this 'perfect' homogenous vision: an 'exception'. Since they do not fit *within LaNF*, additional 'exceptional' space must be created to accommodate the 'exceptional' Other; these are the camps, detention centres, *not*-public spaces, out-of-town industrial areas and woodlands to which the exiled are banished. The '*state* of exception' (Agamben, 2005; Schmitt, 2005) – apparently caused by the presence of the Other – is the catalyst for these '*spaces* of exception', which equally conflict with the unblemished image of *LaNF*. Paradoxically, these 'exceptional' states and spaces are a *necessary component* of *LaNF*: an impossible, self-contradicting *spectacle*, it cannot *not* have exceptions. Since legal norms, rights and regulations require a consistent reference point – a 'homogenous medium' (Schmitt, 2005: 13) – to be assessed and put into practice, in 'exceptional circumstances', 'exceptional measures' may be applied. A 'state of exception' can be used to attack 'entire categories of citizens who for some reason cannot be integrated into the political system' (Agamben, 2005: 2). Thus the abuse suffered by exiled people at the Franco–British border becomes part of the self-perpetuating system (the unobtainable *Nouvelle France*); exclusion leads to states of exception (apparent 'abnormality'), which lead to spaces of exception (and 'exceptional measures'), leading to increased modes of exclusion.

Yet these spaces of exception are also the pages of magazines and social media sites, where 'public' figures – embodied 'beauty' or 'ugliness', extreme wealth and celebrity, 'perfect lives' and sob-stories, but certainly not 'normal' living human beings – are paraded. At the same time, the 'brave survivor' refugee, or the couple who '[jetted]-off' on an "incredible" trip to Greek refugee camp' (Blott, 2017) are also dehumanised, or become briefly superhuman.

Whose Lives? – Reflections

The paradoxes of *La Nouvelle France* emphasise an important question regarding responses to exiled people at the Franco–British border; *whose lives are we aiming to protect*? While the often-distant *romanticised* refugee is instrumentalised to promote the 'saviour's' own image, and others within reach are denied assistance, competed against or used as competitive status symbols, proponents of *LaNF* perpetuate and increasingly succumb to its illusions, while those most in need of refuge suffer to the greatest extent.

La Nouvelle France is the agentive creation of a system of discrimination, abandonment and mistreatment; it is a space that self-expands to allow further abuse. It is also a self-promoting (mis) education, by authorities, institutions and elites, demonstrating *how* the territory is run, and *who* is (not) worthy of its benefits and rights.

This chapter is by no means a dismissal of those who work to support the exiled at the Franco–British border, and in similar conditions elsewhere. Many of these individuals and groups not only undertake the much-needed work of would-be protecting host states, but are necessary to protect *from* these institutions. While some may be motivated by desires for self-aggrandisation, many – if not most – appear driven by an ethically-rooted response to perceived injustices.

Nonetheless, this chapter reflects upon the way in which rhetoric and policies promoted by state and local institutions implicate and guide the public, and can seep unknowingly into the actions and motivations of various humanitarian and other supporting workers. These actors are also met by a complex environment of *dis*information, seemingly impenetrable juridical systems, and direct attempts by authorities to disrupt their activities. Simultaneously, omnipresent hierarchical structures, visions of the ideal, and conceptions of belonging and norms, are likely to impact on actors of all types, regardless of their conscious intention.

As aid workers, perhaps having set out with an ethical stance, inadvertently fall into the harsh patterns driven by border institutions, they may end as contributors to the perpetuation of such systems, concealed as a single link in complex and infinite chain-structures of abuse (e.g. Young's 'structural injustice', 2006). The resulting behaviours are in turn likely to continue to drive the cycle of exceptions, of the competitive, misdirected and discriminatory *Nouvelle France*.

While it is thus imperative that non-governmental and independent groups and individuals continue to offer support to exiled people, this research suggests a need for a greater awareness of, and resistance to, wider prevailing structures, practices and discourses, which may be both explicit and subtle. It is crucial that these complex, underlying cultures of abuse are *directly* tackled at a systemic level; only in this way can their harmful perpetuation be addressed, and more effective support and collective change be realised.

La Nouvelle France

Walking, I am stopped at a drawbridge, lifting to let a small yacht through. I use the moment to take in the sounds, smells and sights in the north of Calais port-town. Further down the canal, the marina holds a mass of sailing boats, clinking and singing in the wind. I had forgotten, in the space since my last visit, how harsh this coastal weather can be, and struggling to walk against the elements sparks memories of shelters collapsing in the old camp. Things have changed in Calais, and in France, although it is hard to tell to what extent. It is the day after the French presidential election results. Local opinions differ on the change this will bring, but many are relieved that centrist Macron was – just – chosen over far-right, anti-immigration, and increasingly popular Le Pen.[17] A Frenchman, perhaps in his 70s, joins in the wait at the bridge. He comes casually over to chat. I tell him I have come from England. With a hint of irony, he retorts: 'Ah. Vous venez voir La Nouvelle France alors!'[18]

Notes

1 This term is problematic, not least for its representation of the camp's inhabitants as 'animals'. Nonetheless, it reflects living conditions, continues to be frequently used by exiled people, volunteers, and activists in Calais, and is well-known among the public. I use it for ease of understanding in this restricted discussion, held in inverted commas to reflect surrounding complexities.

2 Compagnies Républicaines de Sécurité (the French riot police).

3 Many thanks to volunteer Jed Tinsley for sharing his story.

4 The Conservative Party 2017 election manifesto, for example, was described as a 'plan for a stronger Britain' and reiterated the promise of 'strong and stable leadership' (Conservative Party, 2017).

5 I would like to clarify that my analyses are *not* made in reference to the historical French colonial area of La Nouvelle France, in North-America. It is nonetheless interesting to note that the socio-political conception of 'new' lands recurrently emphasises the concept of space *for certain people*, and *not* for Others.

6 I emphasise that *La Nouvelle France* is *not necessarily* indicative of France itself, or even of governmental nations, but of any territory fulfilling the criteria of *LaNF*. Here it refers especially to France, the UK, and Calais.

7 Translated from the original French.

8 Many of the interviews cited in this work were conducted in French. For clarity, they are provided directly in English here, except where significant to understanding.

9 Aristotle suggests that human political ability is expressed through 'speech'. I extend this to body language and other non-verbal communication. I also question Aristotle's argument that non-human animals perceive no more than pleasure and pain, recognising, however, that political activity, as typically understood, relies on human forms of communication.

10 This expression, in varying forms, is usually attributed to political activist Eldridge Cleaver (Ebony, 1988).

11 'Reception and Orientation Centres'; short-term accommodation for asylum-seekers, located in very diverse areas of France, and with very varied living conditions (Hunter & Pope, 2016).

12 Not his real name.

13 'Contact the Ministry of the Interior!' (the UK Home Office equivalent).

14 *La protection de l'enfance.*

15 Translated from the original French.

16 Whether France, Britain, Calais or any territory fulfilling the criteria of LaNF.

17 In 2012 Marine Le Pen won 17.9 percent of votes in the first round of presidential elections (Ministère de l'intérieur, 2012). In 2017, she won 21.3 percent, taking her to the second round against just one other candidate (Ministère de l'intérieur, 2017b).

18 'Ah. So you've come to see "the New France"!'

References

AFP (2017), Calais: fermeture de l'usine Tioxide avant fin 2017, 108 personnes sur le carreau [online]. France 3. Available from: http://france3-regions.francetvinfo.fr/hauts-de-france/nord-pas-calais/pas-calais/calais/calais-fermeture-usine-tioxide-fin-2017–108-personnes-carreau-1216631.html (accessed 24 August 2017).

Agamben, G (2005), *State of exception* (translated by Attell, K). Chicago and London: University of Chicago Press.

Arendt, H (1962), *The origins of totalitarianism*. Cleveland and New York: Meridian Books.

Aristotle (n.d.), Politics: part II (translated by Jowett, B) [online]. Available from: http://classics.mit.edu/Aristotle/politics.1.one.html (accessed 24 August 2017).

Banai, A (2013), Political self-determination and the normative significance of territorial boundaries [online]. Available from: http://eis.bris.ac.uk/~plcdib/territory/papers/banai_selfdetermination.pdf (accessed 24 August 2017).

Bates, E (2010). *The evolution of the European Convention on Human Rights: from its inception to the creation of a permanent court of human rights*. Oxford and New York: Oxford University Press.

Blott, U (2017), Worlds apart! Love Islanders Camilla Thurlow and Jamie Jewitt post about their 'incredible' trip to Greek refugee camp (while their co-stars 'charge thousands' to hit the party circuit). *Daily Mail*, 8 August 2017.

Bourdieu, P (1984), *Distinction: a social critique of the judgement of taste* (translated by Nice, R). Cambridge, MA: Harvard University Press.

Brown, W (2003), Neo-liberalism and the end of liberal democracy. *Theory & Event*. Vol. 7 (1).

Caney, S (2005), *Justice beyond borders: a global political theory*. Oxford and New York: Oxford University Press.

CASF, République Française (1956), Code de l'Action Sociale et des Familles (CASF) – Article L345–2–2 [online]. Available from: www.legifrance.gouv.fr/affichCodeArticle.do?idArticle=LEGIARTI000020444502&cidTexte=LE GITEXT000006074069 (accessed 24 August 2017).

Charrier, P (2016), Il n'y a plus de migrants à Calais [online]. LaCroix. Available from: www.la-croix.com/France/Il-plus-migrants-Calais-2016-11-17-1200803871 (accessed 24 August 2017).

Conservative Party (2017), *Forward, together – our plan for a stronger Britain and a prosperous future: the Conservative and Unionist Party manifesto 2017*. London: The Conservative Party.

Debord, G (1992), *La société du spectacle*. Paris: Éditions Gallimard.

Dijstelbloem, H, Broeders, D (2015), Border surveillance, mobility management and the shaping of non-publics in Europe. *European Journal of Social Theory*. Vol. 18 (1): 21–38.

Dodd, V, Taylor, M (2017), London attack: 'aggressive' and 'strange' suspect vowed to 'do some damage'. *The Guardian*, 20 June 2017.

Ebony (1988), Whatever happened to ... Eldridge Cleaver? Pp. 66–8. *Ebony*, March 1988.

GD, AFP (2017), Calais: un an avec sursis pour un hôtelier ayant hébergé des migrants [online]. BFMTV. Available from: www.bfmtv.com/police-justice/calais-un-an-avec-sursis-pour-un-hotelier-ayant-heberge-des-migrants-1166810.html (accessed 24 August 2017).

Go, M (2017a), Pour faire revenir les touristes anglais, la maire se met en scène dans un clip publicitaire [online]. *La Voix du Nord*. Available from: www.lavoixdunord.fr/163117/article/2017–05–15/pour-faire-revenir-les-touristes-anglais-la-maire-se-met-en-scene-dans-un-clip (accessed 24 August 2017).

Go, M (2017b), L'arrêté municipal visant à interdire la distribution de repas aux migrants signé [online]. *La Voix*

Du Nord. Available from: www.
lavoixdunord.fr/126090/article/2017–
03–02/l- arrete-municipal-visant-
interdire-la-distribution-de-repas-
aux-migrants-signe (accessed 24
August 2017).

Goudeseune, M (2017), Après la décision
de justice, comment se passent les
distributions de repas? [online].
La Voix Du Nord. Available from:
www.lavoixdunord.fr/149721/
article/2017–04- 17/apres-la-decision-
de-justice-comment-se-passent-les-
distributions-de-repas (accessed 24
August 2017).

Hunter B & Pope, R (2016), An uncertain
future [online]. Available from: www.
infomie.net/IMG/pdf/uncertain_
future_report_1_.pdf (accessed 24
August 2017).

Huntsman Corporation (2017),
Huntsman announces intention
to close remaining operations
at its titanium dioxide facility in
Calais, France [online]. Available
from: http://ir.huntsman.com/
phoenix.zhtml?c=186725&p=irol-
newsArticle&ID=2254694 (accessed
24 August 2017).

Insee (2017), Taux de chômage localisés
au 1er trimestre 2017 [online].
Available from: www.insee.fr/fr/
statistiques/2012804 (access 24
August 2017).

Khan, A (2015), Alan Kurdi's father on
his family tragedy: 'I should have
died with them'. *The Guardian*, 22
December 2015.

Kirkup, J & Winnett, R (2012), Theresa May
interview: 'we're going to give illegal
migrants a really hostile reception'.
The Telegraph, 25 May 2012.

Liberation (2017), Un an avec sursis
pour un hôtelier ayant hebergé
des migrants [online]. *Libération*.
Available from: www.liberation.fr/
direct/element/un-an-avec-sursis-
pour-un-hotelier-ayant-heberge-

des-migrants_64224/ (accessed 24
August 2017).

Maplecroft (2016), Human Rights Risk
Index 2016 – Q4 [online]. Available
from: http://reliefweb.int/report/
world/human-rights-risk-index-
2016-q4 (accessed 24 August 2017).

Marx, K (n.d.), Economic & philosophic
manuscripts of 1844. Third
manuscript: private property and
labor (translator unknown) [online].
Available from: www.marxists.org/
archive/marx/works/1844/epm/3rd.
htm (accessed 24 August 2017).

Mbembe, A (2003), Necropolitics
(translated by Meintjes, L). *Public
Culture*. Vol. 15 (1): 11–40.

Migrants Erythréens, Soudannais et
Sommaliens de Calais à Rennes
(2016), Open letter [online]. Available
from: https://passeursdhospitalites.
files.wordpress.com/2016/11/
communiquc3a9_migrants16–11.pdf
(accessed 24 August 2017).

Ministère de l'Intérieur (2012), Résultats
de l'élection présidentielle 2012
[online]. Available from: www.
interieur.gouv.fr/Elections/Les-
resultats/Presidentielles/elecresult_
PR2012/(path)/PR2012/FE.html
(accessed 24 August 2017).

Ministère de l'intérieur (2017a), Résultats
de l'élection présidentielle 2017
[online]. Available from: www.
interieur.gouv.fr/Elections/
Les-resultats/Presidentielles/
elecresult_presidentielle- 2017/
(path)/presidentielle-2017/index.html
(accessed 24 August 2017).

Ministère de l'intérieur (2017b),
Résultats de l'élection présidentielle
2017: France entière [online].
Available from: www.interieur.
gouv.fr/Elections/Les- resultats/
Presidentielles/elecresult_
presidentielle-2017/(path)/
presidentielle-2017/FE.html (accessed
24 August 2017).

Mutua, M (2007), Standard setting in human rights: critique and prognosis. *Human Rights Quarterly*. Vol. 29 (3): 547–630.

Rancière, J (2001), Ten theses on politics (translated by Bowlby, R, Panagia, D). *Theory & Event*. Vol. 5 (3).

Refugee Youth Service (2016), Child Protection Report for October–November 2016 [online]. Available from: www.calaisrefugeesolidaritybristol.co.uk/wp-content/uploads/2016/06/RYS-Child-Protection-Report-III-1.pdf (accessed 24 August 2017).

République Française (2003), LOI n° 2003–1119 du 26 novembre 2003 relative à la maîtrise de l'immigration, au séjour des étrangers en France et à la nationalité [online]. Available from: www.legifrance.gouv.fr/affichTexte.do?cidTexte=JORFTEXT000000795635&categorieLien=id (accessed 30 August 2017).

Reuters (2014), Chemical maker Huntsman to cut about 900 jobs [online]. Reuters. Available from: www.reuters.com/article/us-huntsman-jobcuts-idUSKCN0JF2AU20141201 (accessed 24 August 2017).

Robertson, SL (2009), 'Spatialising' the sociology of education: stand-points, entry-points, vantage-points. Pp. 15–26. In: Ball, S, Apple, M & Gandin, L (eds), *Handbook of sociology of education*. London and New York: Routledge.

Schmitt, C (2005), *Political theology: four chapters on the concept of sovereignty* (translated by Schwab, G). Chicago: University of Chicago Press.

Tissérand, C (2017), Enquête sur les filières de passeurs: cinq gérants d'hôtels placés en garde à vue [online]. *La Voix du Nord*. Available from: www.lavoixdunord.fr/115239/article/2017-02-07/enquete-sur-les-filieres-de-passeurs-cinq-gerants-d-hotels-places-en-garde-vue (accessed 24 August 2017).

Toubon, J (2015a), Décision du défenseur des droits MDE-MSP-MLD-2015–154 [online]. Le Défenseur des Droits. Available from: www.gisti.org/IMG/pdf/ddd_dec_mld-2015–156.pdf (accessed 24 August 2017).

Toubon, J (2015b), Exilés et droits fondamentaux : la situation sur le territoire de Calais [online]. Le Défenseur des Droits. Available from: www.defenseurdesdroits.fr/sites/default/files/atoms/files/20151006-rapport_calais.pdf (accessed 24 August 2017).

Tribunal Administrative de Lille (TA Lille) (2017), N°1702397 [online]. Available from: www.fildp.fr/media/ta-lille-ord.-21-mars-2017-n-1702397.pdf (accessed 24 August 2017).

UK Government (2003), EEA nationals: EUN01. UK visas and immigration [online]. Available from: www.gov.uk/government/publications/eea-nationals-eun01 (accessed 24 August 2017).

UK Government (n.d.), Being arrested: your rights [online]. Available from: www.gov.uk/arrested-your-rights/how-long-you-can-be-held-in-custody (accessed 24 August 2017).

UNHCR (2015), Worldwide displacement hits all-time high as war and persecution increase [online]. Available from: www.unhcr.org/uk/news/latest/2015/6/558193896/worldwide-displacement-hits-all-time-high-war-persecution-increase.html (accessed 24 August 2017).

UNHCR (2016), With growing numbers of child deaths at sea, UN agencies call for enhancing safety for refugees and migrant [online]. Available from: www.unhcr.org/uk/news/press/2016/2/56c6e7676/growing-numbers-child-deaths-sea-un-agencies-call-enhancing-safety-refugees.html (accessed 24 August 2017).

Ville de Calais (2017), Opération touristique – Spot ITV! [video]. Available from: www.youtube.com/watch?v=bwDvnJUqiCU (accessed 24 August 2017).

Ville de Calais (n.d.), Welcome to Calais [online]. Available from: www.welcome.calais.fr/en/prize-draw-competition-rules (accessed 24 August 2017).

Voix du Nord (2015), Bernard Cazeneuve annoncé à Calais en mars prochain [online]. *La Voix du Nord*. Available from: www.lavoixdunord.fr/archive/recup%3A%252Fregion%252Fle-ministre-de-l-interieur-bernard-cazeneuve-annonce-a-ia33b4858n2665370 (accessed 24 August 2017).

Voix du Nord (2016), Calais: une statue de Winston Churchill et du Général De Gaulle pour séduire les Britanniques [online]. *La Voix du Nord*. Available from: www.lavoixdunord.fr/archive/recup%3A%252Fregion%252Fcalais-une-statue-de-winston-churchill-et-du-general-de-ia33b4858n3387352 (accessed 24 August 2017).

Wannesson, P (2015), Inquiétude 3: impasse politique [online]. Available from: https://passeursdhospitalites.wordpress.com/2015/09/17/inquietude-3-impasse-politique/ (accessed 24 August 2017).

Wannesson, P (2016a), Bidonville de Calais: recensement d'octobre [online]. Available from: https://passeursdhospitalites.wordpress.com/2016/10/22/bidonville-de-calais-recensement-doctobre (accessed 24 August 2017).

Wannesson, P (2016b), Des mineur-e-s dispersé-e-s dans toute la France et dans l'incertitude [online]. Available from: https://passeursdhospitalites.wordpress.com/2016/11/05/des-mineur-e-s-disperse-e-s-dans-toute-la-france-et-dans-lincertitude/ (accessed 24 August 2017).

Wannesson, P (2016c), Pas d'asile à Calais [online]. Available from: https://passeursdhospitalites.wordpress.com/2016/12/15/pas-dasile-a-calais/ (accessed 24 August 2017).

Wannesson, P (2017), Quand les autorités hésitent et cognent [online]. Available from: https://passeursdhospitalites.wordpress.com/2017/04/21/quand-les-autorites-hesitent-et-cognent/ (accessed 24 August 2017).

Young, I (2006), Responsibility and global justice: a social connection model. *Social Philosophy and Policy*. Vo. 23 (1): 102–30.

Žižek, S (2002), *Welcome to the desert of the real: five essays on September 11 and related dates*. London and New York: Verso.

8 | ETHICAL CHALLENGES AMONG HUMANITARIAN ORGANISATIONS: INSIGHTS FROM THE RESPONSE TO THE SYRIAN CONFLICT

Kory L Funk, Diana Rayes, Leonard S Rubenstein, Nermin R Diab, Namrita S Singh, Matthew DeCamp, Wasim Maziak, Lara S Ho and W Courtland Robinson

Background

Decision-making for humanitarian health organisations in armed conflict, where combatants often violently interfere with humanitarian operations, is fraught with ethical challenges. Health workers often find themselves confronted with dilemmas where answers consistent with humanitarian values and standards do not exist, requiring what Hunt et al. (2012) describe as the need to choose a 'least-worst option'. De Waal (2010) refers to these challenges as among humanitarianism's 'inescapable cruelties', and argues that they are an unavoidable consequence of working at odds with the interests of powerful forces of war.

Increasingly, the ethical challenges that humanitarian health workers face are the result of direct attacks on healthcare facilities and health workers themselves. In 2016, attacks against health workers were recorded in twenty-three countries (SHIC, 2017). Although determining recent trends in attacks against health workers is difficult, in part due to the lack of standardised reporting (ibid.), it is clear that such attacks are not a new phenomenon (Abu-Sa'Da et al., 2013; Pedersen, 2002).

During the ongoing Syrian Civil War, health workers have been systematically targeted. The war has decimated the Syrian health system, which had seen a steady improvement in health outcomes in the preceding decades (Kherallah et al., 2012; Save the Children, 2014). In April 2011, pro-government forces began arresting doctors, paramedics, and patients in protest areas (Fouad et al., 2017), and in July 2012, the Syrian government passed 'anti-terrorism' laws that effectively criminalised the provision of medical aid to opposition groups (OHCHR, 2013). By September 2013, an estimated 15,000 doctors had fled Syria; by November 2016, that number had increased to 27,000 (Al Dardari, 2016; Iacopino, 2014). The World Health Organization estimated that more than half of Syria's hospitals were either closed or only partially functional by the end of 2016 (WHO, 2017). A review of data from multiple sources by Fouad et al. (2017) found that, as of March 2017, the number of health workers killed in targeted attacks had risen to 814, of which 723 were attributable to the Syrian Government and its allies. The same data also found that attacks on health facilities in Syria steadily increased between 2013 and 2016 (ibid.).

Few studies have been conducted on the impact of attacks against health workers. In Yemen, Neuman (2013) observed – even before the current conflict, in which hospitals have been bombed – that Yemeni doctors live in a constant state of fear due to threats of violence, and explored the impact of this on health outcomes and public perceptions of health workers. In eastern Burma, Footer et al. (2014) documented how fear and insecurity among health workers have made it difficult to fulfil the right to healthcare in minority communities. While these studies provide some insight into how attacks targeting health workers generate serious ethical challenges concerning obligations to act with neutrality and impartiality, to ensure quality of care, and to serve all in need and ensure the safety of staff, additional research is needed to better understand these issues and pathways to addressing them.

In light of this need, our study team, including members from the Johns Hopkins Bloomberg School of Public Health (JHSPH), the Syrian American Medical Society (SAMS), and the International Rescue Committee (IRC), sought to better understand the ethical challenges that humanitarian health organisations face in violent settings, and their implications for decision-making in such contexts. This chapter presents a preliminary analysis of themes and relationships from key informant interviews with managerial staff of humanitarian organisations operating in Syria. Interviews were conducted between January and March 2017 in Gaziantep, Turkey and Amman, Jordan, which serve as key hubs for organisations working in northern and southern Syria. The interviews formed part of the first phase of a two-year study entitled, 'Ethical challenges in humanitarian health in situations of extreme violence'.[1]

Methods

Key informant interviews (KIIs) were conducted using a semi-structured interview guide with staff members of organisations who are currently providing (or have provided) medical services inside Syria. The guide asked respondents about their role within their organisation, the services provided by their organisation, and what ethical challenges their organisation has faced while providing or supporting the provision of health services in Syria. Eight interviews were conducted in Arabic, four were conducted in both Arabic and English, and the remaining twenty-two were conducted in English. Interviews in Arabic were conducted and later translated into English by members of the study team fluent in both Arabic and English. No audio-recording equipment was used, as the goal of the KIIs was to capture major themes and guide the development of subsequent study phases, which will include in-depth interviews with field staff working in Syria and stakeholder workshops, with the ultimate goal of developing an ethical framework, tool, and guidelines to enable humanitarian health organisations to respond to complex ethical challenges in violent settings. Interview notes were recorded by hand or typed by the interviewer, and later transcribed electronically in English. Interview participation was restricted to qualified managerial staff who: were responsible for the coordination or administration of humanitarian health relief efforts inside Syria; were at least eighteen years of age; spoke English or Arabic; were accessible in Jordan or Turkey during the interview period of January to March 2017; and were willing to provide verbal, informed consent.[2]

Forty-one respondents (thirty-two males, nine females) took part in thirty-four interviews (nineteen in Turkey, fifteen in Jordan), representing twenty-seven organisations (sixteen international, eleven local) who were recruited from the list of members of the World Health Organization's Health Clusters in Amman and Gaziantep, and with the aid of additional snowball sampling. The majority of interviews were completed by an individual respondent, although two interviews in Turkey and two interviews in Jordan were conducted with more than one respondent present. Representatives of one multi-government and one United Nations entity were interviewed in Jordan, while the rest of the interviews were conducted with non-governmental organisations. Most of the organisations worked in opposition-controlled areas, although some worked in areas controlled by the Syrian government. Most of the organisations interviewed operate or support primary health centres inside Syria, with many supporting secondary healthcare services, outreach, logistics, and other health-related operations. Some of those interviewed were also responsible for health service provision to refugees or displaced persons in Jordan or Turkey, but it should be noted that these services were not the subject of the interviews.

Once all of the interviews were completed, a member of the study team analysed the interview transcripts using qualitative content analysis (Morse & Field, 1995) to identify challenges in general, and once this was completed, to focus more specifically on ethical challenges. 'Challenge' was defined as a difficulty encountered by an organisation during the course of their humanitarian health operations inside Syria, while 'ethical challenge' was defined more specifically as a challenge that made it difficult or impossible for an organisation to provide services consistent with humanitarian and bioethical principles. Descriptions of how organisations responded operationally to challenges were also analysed.

Once all of these challenges were identified, six themes were identified by a team member such that challenges could be grouped into thematic categories which described the context in which the ethical challenge arose, and which might be useful in the formulation of questions for the subsequent in-depth interviews that would hone in on ethical challenges faced by field staff inside Syria. These themes included: challenges related to targeted attacks; access restrictions; resource limitations; engagement with governing authorities and armed groups; cultural norms; and the demands of donors. Each challenge was matched to a single, most relevant theme, as determined by a team member. The ethical challenges described in this chapter were selected from this analytical process.

Results

Numerous ethical challenges were identified spanning a variety of themes. Challenges identified as stemming from physical attacks were most frequent, followed by those stemming from access restrictions, resource limitations, and the actions of governing authorities and armed groups. Challenges identified as stemming from cultural issues and donor behaviour were also present, but were less frequently reported. The ethical challenges experienced and reported by humanitarian aid organisations were sorted into the following themes:

Attacks Targeting Healthcare

Many challenges originated from targeted attacks on healthcare, by far the most prevalent concern among respondents. Targeted attacks may create ethical challenges related to the need for health organisations to balance the safety of their staff and patients while under attack, with the obligation to provide care to the communities they serve. Respondents reported instances in which workers were injured, kidnapped, killed or threatened with violence, as well as situations where their organisation's facilities had been deliberately and systematically targeted, so much so that some could anticipate where and when the next attack would take place. Multiple respondents gave insight into their resulting dilemmas:

> The trend of attacking hospitals has led to the moving of hospitals underground … We know they are targeting health care centers. Now communities are refusing hospitals and health care centers because they believe it will be bombed.[3]

> How do you make it a safer environment? Do you decrease length of stay? Do you decrease the number of health care workers working there? Do you decentralise decision-making? Some communities have protested and even burned down health facilities because of fear that it will be targeted and increase risk.[4]

Another respondent described how the destruction of health facilities creates a burden on resources for other facilities in the area:

> There was a point where … a nearby maternal and child health hospital had sustained attacks over the course of three days. Two [hospitals] were destroyed completely … This was horrible for us because of the added stress on our facility … Think about 30,000 people living in [a] camp with one maternal and child health hospital to cater to them, then it goes out of service.[5]

Multiple respondents raised concerns about what they referred to as 'risk transfer', whereby larger organisations reserve more dangerous tasks for smaller (usually Syrian) organisations in order to mitigate risks posed to their own staff. One respondent said:

> A lot of [international NGOs] don't have employees on the ground, but only work through partnerships with local people ... this is all done so that they don't assume their responsibility if something happens to them ... Staff are themselves being attacked and are traumatised, and these NGOs won't assume their responsibility.[6]

Restrictions on Access

Numerous challenges also arose from access restrictions. These included: the inability to physically transport materials or personnel into service areas due to the closure of the Jordanian and Turkish borders; denial of entry or passage by the Syrian government or other armed actors; and the inability to conduct in-person training or to monitor activities on the ground. These practices necessitated difficult choices about whose needs would be met, in what way, and how well, with constraints imposed by the combatants, rather than as determined by the needs of the communities.

One respondent described how restrictions on access contributed to a supply shortage, and how that may prevent the delivery of supplies to certain areas:

> In 2015, in Wa'er, I was buying from the black market. Where else can I get supplies? There were some big issues regarding malnutrition. We were only able to guarantee entrance of supplies after three months. Hard to reach areas are difficult.[7]

Restrictions on access also posed difficult questions about maintaining standards of care and accountability for these standards:

> We can follow up on medical procedures in Jordan, but who will assess that inside Syria? There is not any kind of accountability of those staff inside. We have stories about a nurse who is doing a laparotomy[8] – who will judge her at the end of the day? This is a huge problem in Syria.[9]

A respondent from a major donor expressed concern about dilemmas that arise when access limitations result in an inability to verify information germane to operations and to meeting responsibilities to communities:

As an organisation that is accountable to the public, we cannot just 'trust' people with funds. But we cannot verify needs assessments; we have to rely on third parties. Who is controlling distribution? Who decides who gets treated? Most of the doctors running these clinics say that they're open to all, but without access, it is difficult to verify that.[10]

Limitations on Resources

Other ethical challenges related to a lack of adequate resources and the implications this had on the ability to meet community needs. These challenges included those related to staff shortages, which resulted in the overworking of staff, or practices that were beyond an individual's scope of training and knowledge; hospitals operating over capacity; and gaps in service provision, such as a lack of gender-based violence interventions or psychosocial support for children. These challenges all raised concerns about adherence to obligations to provide quality care and deliver humanitarian aid.

Multiple respondents described scenarios in which a lack of specialists led to physicians operating beyond their scope of practice. One respondent gave the following example:

Staff availability is the biggest concern. Most of the staff have left Syria or fled inside the country. At the end of the day, that person needs money to support his family. At the same time, they cannot protect their family. Staff availability is very, very low. You will find a general surgeon doing a C-section or a general practitioner doing a normal vaginal delivery. You cannot abide by WHO or other standard guidelines.[11]

In addition to a lack of staff, hospitals operating beyond their capacity was also a common concern. The following respondent described difficulties with overcrowding after attacks on nearby facilities resulted in theirs being the only maternal and child health facility in the area:

We had a flu outbreak – eighty-five kids to twenty cribs. The corridors [of the hospital] were filled with people sitting on mattresses, waiting. We had to place two babies per incubator ... As a doctor, I know – I mean, I was trained that it is wrong for a hospital room to be crowded or to place two infants in one incubator. I have to make a decision based on the reality of the situation.[12]

A resource-limited environment also creates challenges for organisations that must set priorities and make decisions related to the equitable allocation and distribution of resources. One respondent described trying to work with beneficiaries in such situations:

> Our needs assessment might say 10,000 kits are needed, but only 5,000 are available. This can create a situation of people hating each other – 'Why did you get it and not me?' [or] 'Only IDPs, but not local residents?' ... Go and distribute something, and then come back and ask if [they] got something the first time, they will say no. But if you say, 'if you got something the first time, I will give you something else', they will say yes ... Even the medical facilities will lie about actual needs. You might train someone to do a facility assessment, and they go to the facility during the day and it is empty of equipment, but if they go back at night, it is full.[13]

Demands of Governing Authorities or Combatants

Additional challenges related to the actions of local or national governing authorities or fighters that could compromise organisational independence, neutrality and impartiality as well as medical confidentiality. Challenges falling under this theme included those related to: registration with the Syrian government; armed groups making demands about whom to hire or to whom to provide services, including the physical removal of trauma patients from facilities; armed groups asking for beneficiary information; or other challenges resulting from the influence of groups exercising authority that interfered with the ability to uphold the humanitarian principles and adhere to medical ethics.

Many respondent organisations were unregistered with the Syrian government and expressed concern about continuing to operate while not complying with the legal requirements to do so. They reported that the registration process can take years and involves providing the government with information about beneficiaries and staff that can compromise their security. One respondent described the risk this poses to their perception as a neutral and impartial organisation:

> You have to understand that even though we declare ourselves as a non-biased health organisation with no political standing, the mere fact that we are not 'pro-government' makes us [perceived as] 'the enemy' and 'anti-government'.[14]

Another respondent noted that registration might affect their organisation's standing with the local community as an impartial and neutral actor:

> Our credibility in Syria with beneficiaries and staff is that we are unaffiliated with the government. If we register, how does how our beneficiaries view us change? Working with the government is inherently political. They are trying to manipulate the humanitarian effort in their favour.[15]

Additional ethical issues arose as a consequence of interference with the obligation to provide impartial care. One respondent recounted the organisation's inability to follow through with needed treatment after an armed group removed a pro-government fighter who was receiving treatment from their facility:

> We couldn't do anything about it; we obviously couldn't refuse although [the fighter's] situation was critical ... We never knew what happened to him; we obviously were scared for our own safety. Who do we report to? The government? We are not registered: of course we can't do such a thing![16]

Another common concern was that demands from combatants not to treat certain individuals led to decisions about whether to comply or to shut down a facility due to an inability to provide impartial care. A respondent noted that this was a concern for both health workers and patients:

> Sometimes we have to shut down treatment facilities and hospitals because groups ask, 'who are you treating?' We are a humanitarian organisation, we do not say 'no' just because someone is a fighter on one side or the other. We do not ask their background ... We are not for one side or the other. Sometimes women will lie because their husbands are fighters. What do you do?[17]

Two respondents also noted the need to decide whether to adhere to the Syrian government's demand that organisations fabricate or censor information, rendering it difficult to assess actual needs on the ground. One respondent described the government's use of coercion to influence reporting, and the ethical dilemma this generated:

We have to go back and forth on humanitarian needs documents because the [Syrian] government asked us to change them. The government wants no mention of serious violations or ethical challenges. For example, [a major international organisation to which the respondent reports] has come back to us and said, 'the government is threatening our staff, we need you to change this'.[18]

Cultural Norms

Challenges arose from conflicts between the responsibility to meet women's needs equally and local cultural practices and attitudes towards women and women's health. Organisations reported that services oriented towards women, especially reproductive health and gender-based violence services, are often difficult to implement; male gynaecologists often face harassment and family planning interventions must be implemented in secret. On gender-related issues, one respondent said the following:

In women's hospitals, we need female doctors. For gender-based violence, we need female doctors … Female staff have their own issues – rape issues and risks at night when their work requires day and night shifts. Or a husband doesn't let his wife work, [or] a brother doesn't let his sister work.[19]

Donor Demands

Challenges also arose from donor demands that impeded independent decision-making and the use of judgement to meet the needs of beneficiaries. These demands included accountability standards and restrictions on how funding could be used that were not consistent with the reality of humanitarian aid delivery and cross-border access into Syria. These rules led to service gaps and a need to seek alternative funding to meet obligations to certain populations, and in some cases resulted in the denial of services to people. One respondent described the dilemma of deciding whether to work with external funders:

Documentation and transparency … it is hard to put up signs and be noticed. But donor[s] ask … for example, the donor wants invoices for purchased projects, such as buying diesel … we don't buy diesel at a shop; we get it from a barrel.[20]

Conclusion

The responses of those interviewed for this study provide a valuable insight into the circumstances in which ethical decision-making challenges arise, based on the perspectives of members of humanitarian health organisations operating inside Syria. While those circumstances are varied and complex, our analysis suggests that health organisations are most commonly confronted with ethical challenges that make it difficult to fulfil their obligations to act with neutrality and impartiality, practise independent decision-making, ensure the equal treatment of women, and deliver an acceptable quality of care.

We intend to conduct further research, including interviews with field staff, to understand the nature and impact of ethical decision-making challenges on healthcare delivery in the context of violence, and to explore ways in which humanitarian health organisations can mitigate these impacts.

Limitations

It should be noted that this study has certain limitations. The findings here represent only a preliminary analysis of key informant interviews from the first phase of a two-year study. In this phase, interview notes were recorded by hand, which could have affected clarity and completeness of the recorded content. The second phase of the study, which will include in-depth interviews, may provide additional insight into these challenges, how they come about, and what organisations can do to mitigate their impact or prevent such challenges altogether. In the second phase, interviews will be recorded, and member-checking will be carried out to improve the credibility of results. In addition, most of the respondents that participated in this first phase work with organisations that operate in opposition-controlled areas of Syria. Ethical challenges faced by organisations operating in government-controlled areas might differ from those detailed here. Finally, study findings pertain to the conflict in Syria; while this context offers an ideal case study for the investigation of ethical challenges associated with violence against humanitarian health workers, appropriate caution should be taken before generalising our findings to other contexts.

Implications

We hope that the information and insights drawn from our study may be of use to humanitarian health practitioners, policy-makers, and researchers alike, who seek to gain a better understanding of the types of ethical challenges that humanitarian health organisations face, along with how these challenges are contextualised. This analysis underscores the need for continued research in this area, and for the development of guidance to support humanitarian health organisations operating in violent contexts.

Notes

1 This analysis forms part of a research study funded by ELRHA's Research for Health in Humanitarian Crises (R2HC) Programme, which aims to improve health outcomes by strengthening the evidence base for public health interventions in humanitarian crises. The R2HC programme is funded equally by the Wellcome Trust and the UK Government (ELRHA, 2017).

2 The study protocol was approved by the Institutional Review Board (IRB) at the Johns Hopkins Bloomberg School of Public Health, as well as the IRB at the Jordan University of Science and Technology, and the Ethical Research Committee at Gaziantep University.

3 Interview in Amman, January 2017.

4 Interview in Amman, January 2017.

5 Interview in Gaziantep, February 2017.

6 Interview in January 2017.

7 Interview in Gaziantep, February 2017.

8 A surgical incision into the abdominal cavity, which is beyond a nurse's scope of practice.

9 Interview in Amman, January 2017.

10 Interview in Amman, January 2017.

11 Interview in Amman, January 2017.

12 Interview in Gaziantep, February 2017.

13 Interview in Amman, January 2017.

14 Interview in Amman, January 2017.

15 Interview in Amman, January 2017.

16 Interview in Amman, January 2017.

17 Interview in Amman, January 2017.

18 Interview in Amman, January 2017.

19 Interview in Gaziantep, February 2017.

20 Interview in Gaziantep, March 2017.

References

Abu-Sa'Da, C, Duroch, A & Taithe, B (2013), Attacks on medical missions: overview of a polymorphous reality: the case of Médecins Sans Frontières. *International Review of the Red Cross.* Vol. 95 (890): 309–30.

al Dardari, A (2016), Syria's long-term humanitarian and development challenges [video]. Middle East Institute's 70th Annual Conference. Available from: www.youtube.com/watch?v=68GBLTM4KNQ&feature=youtu.be&t=42m21s (accessed 6 July 2017).

De Waal, A (2010), The humanitarians' tragedy: escapable and inescapable cruelties. *Disasters.* Vol. 34 (S2): S130–7.

ELRHA (2017), Research for health in humanitarian crises [online]. Available from: www.elrha.org/work/r2hc (accessed 21 August 2017).

Footer, KH, Meyer, S, Sherman, SG & Rubenstein, L (2014), On the frontline of eastern Burma's chronic conflict—listening to the voices of local health workers. *Social Science & Medicine.* Vol. 120: 378–86.

Fouad, FM, Sparrow, A, Tarakji, A, Alameddine, M, El-Jardali, F, Coutts, A, ... Jabbour, S (2017), Health workers and the weaponization of health care in Syria: a preliminary inquiry for the Lancet—American University of Beirut Commission on Syria. *The Lancet.* Published online 14 March 2017.

Hunt, MR, Sinding, C & Schwartz, L (2012), Tragic choices in humanitarian health work. *Journal of Clinical Ethics.* Vol. 23 (4): 338–44.

Iacopino, V (2014), Attacks on medical care in Syria [online]. The Lancet Global Health blog. Available from: http://globalhealth.thelancet.com/2014/02/28/attacks-medical-care-syria (accessed 7 July 2017).

Kherallah, M, Alahfez, T, Sahloul, Z, Eddin, KD & Jamil, G (2012), Health care in Syria before and during the crisis. *Avicenna Journal of Medicine.* Vol. 2(3): 51–3.

Morse, JM & Field, PA (1995), *Qualitative research methods for health professionals.* Thousand Oaks, CA: Sage Publications.

Neuman, M (2014), No patients, no problems: exposure to risk of medical personnel working in MSF projects in Yemen's governorate of Amran [online]. *Journal of Humanitarian Assistance.* Available from: https://sites.tufts.edu/jha/archives/2040 (accessed 29 July 2017).

OHCHR (2013), *Assault on medical care in Syria.* Human Rights Council: 24 Session. Agenda item 4. A-HRC-24-CRP-2. Geneva: Office of the United Nations High Commissioner for Human Rights.

Pedersen, D (2002), Political violence, ethnic conflict, and contemporary wars: broad implications for health and social well-being. *Social Science & Medicine.* Vol. 55: 175–90.

Save the Children (2014), *A devastating toll: the impact of three years of war on the health of Syria's children.* London: Save the Children.

SHIC (2017), *Impunity must end: attacks on health in 23 countries in conflict in 2016.* Safeguarding Health in Crisis Coalition, May 2017.

WHO (2017), *Syrian Arab Republic: annual report 2016.* Geneva: World Health Organization.

9 | HOME AND AWAY: ETHICAL ISSUES IN HUMANITARIAN AID TO SYRIANS IN ISRAEL

Schlomit Zuckerman, Morshid Farhat and Salman Zarka

Introduction

Six years into the devastating Syrian civil war, many Syrian patients[1] are still seeking urgent medical assistance, currently not available in their homeland. Notably, they are not considered refugees as they seek medical care as 'cross-border medicine' on the grounds of human crisis, following their own will. Their arrival at the healthcare facility in Israel is coordinated and logistically assisted by the Israeli Defence Force (IDF), and they go back home, on their request, once care is completed (and sometimes even before that). According to the World Health Organization's Health Resources Availability Mapping System (WHO, 2017) over half of Syria's 111 public hospitals, and half of its 1802 public healthcare centres are either closed or only partially functional. Media reports, citing research by Physicians for Human Rights, suggest that more than half Syria's 30,000 doctors have fled (Ellen, 2017). Several hospitals in the north of Israel have been providing medical care, on a humanitarian basis, to Syrian casualties since 2013, including the treatment of serious war injuries and infections, medical care for the sick, and aspects of antenatal care (Abbasi, 2017). This paper aims to shed light on the ethical issues related to the provision of medical assistance for these patients, with the aid of a humanitarian ethics framework. Before we delve into this ethical discourse, a brief description of the unconventional setting in which Israeli assistance is delivered to Syrian patients, and its divergence from the 'normative' setting of humanitarian action (if such norms exist), is offered.

In international humanitarian law, refugees are deemed to be those fleeing a dangerous warzone after suffering tremendous loss, and later arriving into a quiet and neutral place. In the case of Israel, the country has been in a state of war with Syria since 1948. Despite the day-to-day uneventful routine at the border between the two countries, tension occasionally builds up around the border, which is followed by military action. This situation leaves both patients and healthcare professionals (HCP) – at least temporarily – on two sides of an armed conflict. Moreover, even in times of peace at the Israeli–Syrian border, the Israeli Defence Force (IDF) plays a major role in the provision of care to patients. The IDF mediates the pick-up, transportation, and admission of patients to medical centres. From that moment onwards, the hospital takes over the patient's care. Discharge takes place on the basis of the health professionals' decisions. No one other than the medical team is involved in this decision. Moreover, patients are hospitalised above and beyond their medical need, that is, weeks or even months, in comparison to many local patients. Given the current scarce medical infrastructure in Syria, the medical team makes an effort to provide all possible care throughout the course of a patient's hospitalisation, unless the patient asks to be discharged earlier, which is oftentimes the case. Following a fully autonomous medical decision to discharge the patient, they are discharged. Given that they are not refugees sent back to their countries against their will, but rather cross-border patients, representatives of IDF chaperone them back to the Syrian border. Patient pick-up and return to Syria is coordinated by the IDF, taking into account patients' security and other personal needs. In other words, the IDF is in charge of bringing patients from the border to the hospital and returning them there once they are medically fit for discharge. This process is under the IDF's authority, as a logistics arm that protects the Israeli border, and in light of the fact that the IDF has exclusive access to and knowledge regarding what is going on around the border.

Ethical discourse related to patients seeking medical assistance in an enemy country is lacking. So too is the infrastructure or platform in international law necessary to discuss this unique humanitarian setting. The purpose of this chapter is to contribute to an ethical discourse, and perhaps to design such a normative platform in order to analyse this distinctive situation.

The Unique Setting of the Humanitarian Aid

In many – albeit not all – humanitarian actions the disaster or armed conflict takes place hundreds or even thousands of miles away from the countries that deliver medical relief teams. Thus, this form of aid comprises arrival in a disaster area and the construction of a medical facility to assist wounded civilians, in close proximity to the war zone.

Those relief teams are often out of their comfort zone, which in turn raises logistic and cultural obstacles to provision of care (Hunt et al., 2014) that team members must discuss and resolve in real time to ensure the provision of effective assistance. Such was the case for Israeli relief teams working in Haiti in the last decade (Merin, 2010). However, in the case of the wounded Syrians, given the geographic proximity of northern Israel to the war zone, medical care to Syrians is provided in several hospitals in Israel, all located in proximity to the Syrian and Lebanese borders (mostly Galilee Maaravi Medical Center in Nahariya, and Ziv Medical Center in Safed). Those hospitals also provide routine medical and ambulatory care to Israeli citizens and residents.

The ethical framework we propose to use in this case is derived from two guideline documents, both created by the Red Cross and Red Crescent (RCRC) humanitarian organisations. We have based our ethical analysis on guidelines created by the non-governmental, independent RCRC, because the state of Israel (including its medical centres) have declared neutrality in relation to the civil war in Syria. Therefore, we argue that the use of a normative platform created by a humanitarian organisation is suitable for the purpose of ethical analysis in this case, though it requires adjustments given the unique natures of the setting, as we will discuss throughout this paper. The first document which sets the ground for the ethical analysis of humanitarian assistance is the Fundamental Principles of the International Red Cross and Red Crescent Movements (the RCRC Principles), adopted by the 25th International Conference of the Red Cross in Geneva, 1986. The second document is the Code of Conduct for the Red Cross and the Red Crescent and NGOs in disaster response programmes (RCRC Code of Conduct), an elaboration of the RCRC Principles which was developed and agreed upon by eight of the world's largest disaster response agencies in the summer of 1994.

We will discuss how the ethical principles and values outlined in their documents apply to the case of Syrian casualties receiving medical care in northern Israeli hospitals. We begin our discussion by outlining the humanitarian imperative (Article 1 of the RCRC Code of Conduct), and investigate its relevance in relation to the provision of humanitarian assistance to Syrian casualties by Israeli HCP. We will then explore the principles that guide the ethics of humanitarian assistance. These principles include impartiality and proportionality of assistance (Article 2 of the RCRC Code of Conduct), neutrality (Article 3 of the RCRC Code of Conduct), the independence of relief teams (Article 4 of the RCRC Code of Conduct), along with the dignity-related principles –respect, participation, and consent of beneficiaries (Articles 5, 6, 7 and 10 of the RCRC Code of Conduct). Finally, we examine the principles of sustainability and accountability and discuss the complexity of accounting for both principles in this setting. We conclude by suggesting that the humanitarian imperative and dignity principles are well addressed in this context while neutrality, independence, and future-facing principles (sustainability and accountability) ought to be better addressed if the delivery of humanitarian assistance to Syrian patients is to continue. In order to regulate this unique situation, normative guidelines ought to be created. In the next section, we outline the issue of the humanitarian imperative in the context of humanitarian aid delivered to Syrian patients in Israel.

Setting the Stage: The Humanitarian Imperative

The fundamental principles of the RCRC movement, proclaimed in Vienna in 1965, comprise seven fundamental principles that guide RCRC's humanitarian work. The first element is 'humanity', which aims to alleviate human suffering wherever it may be found. The purpose of the principle of humanity is to protect life and health, and to ensure respect for all human beings. It promotes mutual understanding, friendship, cooperation, and lasting peace among all people. An adjusted principle, suggested by Hunt and colleagues (2014), is 'the ethics of engaged presence', which is focused on the recognition of shared humanity and vulnerability, and which characterises healthcare practice in a global frame. As the authors note, 'in settings of crisis or deprivation [shared humanity can] be obscured due to circumstantial inequalities and "dehumanizing effect"' (ibid.: 51).

The consequence of inequalities and the risk of dehumanising effects in relation to the case at hand is even more substantial, given the context. Israel and Syria had been longstanding enemies. Each side of the conflict carries the residual effects of a shared history of violence, and even at the present time, the border between the two countries is monitored and inspected by both sides. Hunt (ibid.) suggests acknowledging the imbalance of power between patients and humanitarians, and that this imbalance must be addressed in order to attend to patients' needs and suffering, and to treat them as moral equals. In the case we present, addressing this power imbalance is more complex than in most humanitarian settings, where international aid teams arrive in a setting with which they have no former acquaintance or shared history of animosity.

For Slim, 'the defined goal of humanitarian action is to save and protect individual lives so that they have the opportunity to flourish. It is not to determine how they should flourish and organise this flourishing ... the goal is life' (2015: 47). In our case, accounting for this vague definition of life as the 'goal', decisions made by hospital teams are indeed commensurate with the needs-based care provided to the patients (Abbasi, 2017). Thus, these decision-making processes not merely meet the goal of life, but also emphasise the quality of life. In the following section, we elaborate on this process of needs/emergency-based decision-making.

Impartiality and Proportionality

Impartiality, as defined by the second of the ICRC principles, refers to a stance that does not discriminate by nationality, race, religious beliefs, class or political opinion. It endeavours to relieve the suffering of individuals, with action guided solely by needs, and to give priority to the most urgent cases of distress. In accordance with Article 2 of the Code of Conduct of RCRC, 'aid priorities are calculated on the basis of need alone'. That is, the only thing that should determine the prioritisation of care to one person over another once they are admitted to hospital is their relative need: in extreme cases the question is who is more likely to lose their life without medical intervention. This doctrine plays a major role in the situation at hand, given the special circumstance of providing medical care to citizens of an enemy country, let alone combatants who are actively involved in the civil war. HCP provide care that is based on need or emergency criterion to any patient, which is extended to any Syrian patients arriving at Israeli health facilities.

This mechanism of needs-based decision-making amplifies the issue of the fair distribution of scarce resources. Rationalising resource allocation in this context is different from the other humanitarian responses. Syrian patients are transported from their home (indeed, a place of turmoil) to a foreign, 'enemy' country. They arrive at the emergency room of a regional hospital that must also deal with other urgent cases. Often their wounds necessitate urgent care and complex procedures, use of costly medical devices, intensive care for a certain time, and later, follow up by physicians and nurses. They compete with hundreds of thousands of Israeli citizens and other residents living in the hospital's catchment area to be prioritised for receipt of medical care in the hospital (Abbasi, 2017). In the case that their wounds require emergency care, less urgent elective procedures scheduled for Israeli patients must be rescheduled. Moreover, because they have no other place for medical transfer (such as community care facilities), the patients may stay at the hospital for a longer period of time, making continued use of hospital beds, which are scarce resource in the Israeli healthcare system.

This practice raises an important distributive justice quandary. As a recent article describing current Israeli bioethics states: 'a bioethics framework based on both a secular worldview and monotheistic tradition assumes that people not only have a basic right to healthcare but also have responsibilities and obligations towards their fellow citizens' (Jotkowitz, Agbaria & Glick, 2017: 2584). Why, therefore, should the state of Israel use its scarce resources (including hospital beds, the time and cost of procedures and use of devices, and the time and cost of medical care) on foreign, non-resident, wounded persons belonging to an enemy state? One may argue that people should receive assistance based on their citizenship or residency status. This question troubles Israeli HCP and citizens alike (Abbasi, 2017).

The Israeli bioethicist Michael Gross presents the following question, which in his view is a common intuition: 'Friends and family should aid one without expectation of reciprocity, often at great personal cost and when knowing that the same aid might benefit a stranger more. This is a common intuition. To think too hard about aiding a stranger when the life of one's family or friends are in danger is, as Bernard Williams famously puts it, one thought too many. Is medical care for enemy wounded also one too many?' For Gross, answering this question requires an understanding of the personal relationships among soldiers, namely the distinction between primary and secondary bonding. Gross, however, argues that the ethical demands on caregivers vary according to the strength of primary bonding. As primary bonds weaken and secondary bonds strengthen (as is the case here, given that physicians are not in a close/personal relationship with patients, either Syrian or Israeli), the universal duties of justice replace the parochial ethics of care. This, he emphasises, might be particularly true of physicians rather than medics (Gross, 2012: 78–79) That said, one may ask, what form does medical assistance take when the stranger is officially from an enemy country? We will discuss this issue in the section that follows.

The Principle of Neutrality

A practical aspect of humanitarian ethics is encompassed by the principles of neutrality and independence. The RCRC frames the former principle as follows: 'In order to continue to enjoy the confidence of all, the Movement may not take sides in hostilities or engage at any time in controversies of a political, racial, religious or ideological nature' (RCRC fundamental principles, the principle of neutrality). If this core humanitarian principle poses a challenge to NGOs in other humanitarian settings, it is an even greater challenge for the healthcare professional in an Israeli hospital faced with treating a wounded person from an enemy country.

That said, a recent qualitative study (Young et al., 2016) disputes these assumptions. As one might expect, wounded civilians and combatants are initially suspicious, and at times are hostile towards the Israeli soldiers who transport them from their homeland to a country that they have learned to fear. Similarly, Israeli HCP who provide care are ambivalent about the treatment of enemy patients. In the words of the Young et al. study: 'Assuming neutrality and complete objectivity was not only inappropriate in this study, considering our epistemology, but was also unrealistic considering the first author's in-depth experience living in Israel during a time of war (Operation Protective Edge)' (ibid.: 3). However, Young et al. found that both Israeli HCP and Syrian patients, and the patients' accompanying family members, changed their beliefs, using cognitive strategies that allowed both sides in the medical encounter to humanise one another, and to accommodate a new understanding of the relationship between them. Although Israeli HCP and Syrian patients often start by holding dissonant feelings, most overcame those feelings through a process of re-humanisation of the individuals with whom they interacted. This has also been the authors' insight. Encouraged by the dehumanisation to re-humanisation of patients and caregivers, we proceed to explore the application of the next principle: that of the independence of medical teams.

The Principle of Independence

The principle of independence, as interpreted by Article 4 of the RCRC Code of Conduct, states that national societies of the Red Cross must: 'always maintain their autonomy so that they may be able at all times to act in accordance with the Red Cross principles'. It is acknowledged that the pursuit of independence poses a significant challenge for humanitarian organisations in general given their shared concern that they should not become foreign policy instruments of donor governments. That said, it is clear that humanitarian action also necessitates cooperation given that humanitarian needs often arise in highly unstable contexts, where the ethical conduct of humanitarian action by various actors and organisations is necessary to avoid harmful implications for victims (Clarinval & Andorno, 2014). Pragmatically speaking, rather than calling for full independence one must seek an optimal balance between dependence and interdependence (Slim, 2015: 73).

Once again, the uniqueness of the context has an impact. If these challenges exist for 'traditional' humanitarian organisation in 'normative' humanitarian response, the situation is even more complicated when discussing the care of Syrian patients by Israeli HCP in local hospitals. In this situation, for medical action to succeed, an orchestrated balance between several actors: healthcare teams, the IDF, and Israeli governmental officials is required. Thus, full independence of HCP is particularly challenging. However, as far as medical decision-making goes, Israeli HCP provide care to all patients arriving at their facilities, without questioning their place of origin. Once the patient is admitted to the hospital, HCP are autonomous to make their own clinical decisions regarding the acute/emergency condition, as they consider suitable. Due to the well-known clinical routine and established practices, HCP in their usual clinical environment are arguably more independent than a traditional medical team assisting patients in a field hospital. By extension of the concept of HCP autonomy, it is important to discuss the following values, which stem from the classical bioethical principle of respect for patient autonomy.

Respect, Participation and Consent

Respect for patient autonomy, allowing patients to take an active role in decision-making regarding their care and future health, and obtaining consent for care, emerge from the concept of human dignity. This concept is a basic pillar of medical ethics and bio-law, which has generated thriving debate in the past two decades regarding the limits of dignity, and the definition and practical implications of the concepts of dignity and human rights (Barilan, 2014). For example, human rights scholars advocate that international assistance should not be viewed as charity, which currently allows people in the 'industrialised North' to feel compassionate about the very poor, without necessarily facing the suffering of those people. For Yamin, rights and obligations must locate us all – victims and caregivers – on the same political map, which requires that humanitarianism is viewed as a philosophy more complex than charity (Yamin, 2010).

To a greater extent than the principle of neutrality discussed above, these 'dignity principles', referred to in articles 5, 6, 7 and 10 of the RCRC Code of Conduct, are highly influenced by national and international political power, which defines the relationships between humanitarians (in this case the Israeli HCP), the Syrian patients, IDF officials, and the Israeli government. Given the political, social and cultural setting within which this interaction is embedded, application of those principles to the case at hand requires a careful balancing of the norms, values and beliefs that shape the lives of patients, caregivers, and other stakeholders alike.

On one side of the balancing scale again lies the historical animosity between the two countries and the chaotic reality patients (both combatants and civilians) have lived through since 2011. In addition, one must account for the traumatising experiences many of the patients have borne for several years, prior to their arrival at the hospital; the likelihood that they will return to similar experiences following discharge; and the significant health disparities between life at home in Syria and life away in an Israeli hospital. These parameters increase the vulnerability of patients and have direct implications for the respect they are granted by both IDF officers and HCP, and for their participation in decision-making processes regarding their individual futures. Perhaps most straightforward in this sense is the legal requirement for informed consent for treatment, outlined in the Patient's Rights Act of 1996.

On the other side of the scale stand the similar cultural, religious and ethnic origins of patients and caregivers. Due to these shared origins, values, beliefs and customs may be easier to accommodate. When a

Syrian patient arrives, an Arabic-speaking social worker provides them with the Qur'an, and makes them feel a little more at home. It is hoped this will make patients feel more empowered. Moreover, caregivers are well aware of the many potential clinical and cultural sensitivities of Syrian patients, and are thus well suited to provide skilful assistance and ultimately to meet patients' holistic needs (Hunt et al., 2014). Patients on the receiving end of care tend to be thankful for the professional care they benefit from while being treated in an Israeli hospital (Young et al., 2016).

The informed consent process (as opposed to the requirement for a mere signature on a consent form) in Israel is regulated by laws and guidelines. The Patient's Rights Act 1996 articulates in Clause 13 the requirement for informed consent for medical care and sets out exceptions to the requirement for consent in Clause 15 (i.e. when the patient cannot consent to care, the patient is resisting care, or in the event of a medical emergency). In those situations, consent is obtained from three physicians (in a medical emergency) or from an ethics committee (when a patient is resisting care). This law does not exclude non-citizens or non-residents, and therefore applies to Syrian patients as well. Explanations for treatment and consent forms are given in the patient's language, which in this case is Arabic.

In practice, informed consent is obtained from an adult patient who is legally competent; otherwise, HCP turn to the court, which appoints a proxy decision-maker for surgical interventions or other procedures that require oral consent. Obtaining consent in this context is not always straightforward. For example, when a Syrian teenager or helpless patient is treated and their parents are not accompanying them, or are not accessible, the hospital ought to turn to the court for approval of consent for each surgical intervention, in line with the Legality and Guardianship Act of 1962. In such a case, the teenager is hospitalised alone in a foreign country, surrounded by people with white gowns speaking a foreign language that the patient does not fully understand, where the mentality is different, and the question arises as to how informed the patient ultimately is, and how genuine their given consent. In addition, a legal quandary arises: what is the authority of an Israeli court to make decisions for Syrian citizens? We now consider the remaining set of principles for application in our ethical framework, namely, those principles that relate to the limits of care.

Sustainability, Accountability and the Standard of Care

The last set of principles, completing our proposed framework for humanitarian ethics in this case, relate to the character of humanitarian workers as providers of good stewardship, that is, those who deal with existing resources and think about the future of humanitarian assistance. Article 8 of the RCRC Code of Conduct states that, 'Relief aid must strive to reduce future vulnerabilities to disaster as well as meeting basic needs.' The essence of this Article aims to ensure more than just saving lives, but rather to ensure a better life and less physical and mental injury for victims in the present as well as in the future. This Article is concerned with the chronological limits of humanitarian assistance. Realistically speaking, Israel cannot do much to end or minimise the magnitude of the civil war in Syria, either at global policy level, or at local level. In relation to the more realistic goal of saving life and improving healthcare, despite the full cooperation of the IDF and HCP, when it comes to the overarching conflict between numerous combatant groups in Syria, the hands of HCP are pretty much tied.

Article 9 of the RCRC Code of Conduct states that, 'our programmes will be based upon high standards of professionalism and expertise', thus claiming that humanitarian agencies are committed to provide professional – rather than 'amateur' – assistance, even if amateurish efforts are well-intentioned. As Slim articulates,

> Ethics stretches across the past, present and future. What we
> have done and what we are doing with people creates legitimate
> expectations of what we will do for their future, and what we will do in
> the future if we are called upon again. People have sustainable claims
> and obligations. This sense of sustained humanitarian responsibility
> that stretches into the future seems morally right but cannot be
> limitless. (2015: 97)

In practice, as noted earlier, HCP in Israel provide a highly professional standard of care for all patients, regardless of their nationality, ethnicity or religious beliefs, based on medical needs (Abbasi, 2017).

The issue of accountability, and specifically the problem of limitations to the medical care delivered to patients, disturbs both HCP caring for Syrians, as well as humanitarian organisations in Israel (Ethics Committee of Physicians for Human Rights, 2015). Furthermore, while a professionalised and high standard of care is delivered to patients while at the hospital, the continuity of care is poor. They arrive at the hospital alone, with no medical records, and HCP often learn about their conditions solely from self-reported data. Once they leave the healthcare facilities and are brought to the Syrian border, medical care is abruptly cut off. At present, it is evident that care for such patients is compromised, if not stopped completely, given the very scarce medical infrastructure, facilities and personnel in Syria. For instance, a young patient who was discharged from the hospital with doses of insulin for her diabetes noted that she did not have a refrigerator at home to safely store the drug. In addition, given that identifiable documentation of medical care may expose patients or HCP to danger by exposing care given by the Israeli 'enemy', a letter with a fake patient name is provided. As such, patients admitted several times will receive different names for each episode of hospitalisation, and thus HCP are unable to gather a clear medical history. While this process confers legal protection to patients returning to Syria, medical risks are simultaneously generated.

Conclusion

The care of the Syrian patients by Israeli HCP in Israeli hospitals is a unique example of humanitarian medical assistance. Such care is provided to patients in adequately equipped and highly professionalised medical facilities. However, patients are mobilised from their homes to receive care. Once discharged from the hospital, they go back to the 'burning' war zone, where they face very poor living conditions, which in turn threatens the long-term sustainability of their state of improved health. In the current geopolitical environment in which this situation exists, there is an immanent risk in both providing and receiving care. The assistance of Syrian patients is not accepted by the Syrian regime and may be interpreted (as it has been in the past) as foreign intervention in the country's internal affairs, or as taking a side in the conflict. The principles of neutrality and independence, and the future-facing principles of sustainability and accountability are, therefore, far less easily applicable in this unique context. Historical narratives and current geopolitical tensions, along with the presence of many stakeholders, including patients (civilians and combatants), HCP and hospital management, the IDF, and the Israeli government, each with their own agendas, challenge adherence to the aforementioned principles.

We have shown in this chapter that Israeli HCP succeed in responding to the humanitarian imperative, and adhering to the dignity principles while treating patients arriving at their facilities, despite the many inherent obstacles. As Young et al. conclude in their qualitative study on this unique interaction:

> Healthcare providers expressed overwhelming medical humanitarian beliefs regarding their care for Syrian patients. Although it was sometimes a personal struggle to overcome and cope with the dissonant professional and personal beliefs, cognitive strategies allowed HCP and Syrian patient caregivers to humanise each other and benefit from the process. Participants in this research were able to lay aside personal differences for the purpose of healing and saving lives, even the lives of their enemies. (2016: 13)

If the delivery of humanitarian assistance for Syrian patients in Israeli hospitals is to continue, neutrality, independence and future-facing principles ought to receive greater attention. To meet this goal, we advocate for the design of specific guidelines, suitable for use in unique contexts such as this, and agreed upon by the relevant governmental agencies, physician and medical ethics professional organisations, and NGOs, at a national level. While we are aware that normative documents might widen the gap between discourse and the expectations of patients and caregivers on the one hand, and actual practices and experiences on the other (Rességuier, 2017), we believe that with a well thought through normative framework, HCP are better equipped to address the ethical dilemmas they face in the treatment of non-Israeli patients in Israeli hospitals.

Note

1 The terminology we use throughout this chapter is 'patients' rather than refugees, as these individuals arrive at the hospital to receive medical care and go back to their country. Until now, none of the patients has claimed asylum. Once they do, the hospital team will refer the claim to the appropriate authority, which is the state of Israel, to handle the claim. That said, the term 'patient' in this unique setting is inherently ethically and legally complex and does require greater analysis from health professionals and ethicists in the field.

References

Abbasi, J (2017), Israeli physician Salman Zarka, MD: caring for Syrian patients is our duty. *JAMA.* Vol. 317 (11): 1105–7.

Barilan, YM (2014), *Human dignity, human rights, and responsibility: the new language of global bioethics and biolaw.* Cambridge, MA: MIT Press.

Clarinval, C & Biller-Andorno, N (2014), Challenging operations: an ethical framework to assist humanitarian aid workers in their decision-making processes. *PLOS Currents Disasters.* 23 June 2014.

Ellen, F (2017), Six years into Syria's war, rebel areas face deepening medical crisis. Reuters. 16 March 2017.

Ethics Committee of Physicians for Human Rights (2015), Syrian patients: the dilemma of limited care [online]. Available from: http://cdn4.phr.org.il/wp-content/uploads/2015/02/מטופלים-סורים-דילמת-הטיפול-המוגבל.pdf (accessed 6 September 2017).

Gross, ML & Carrick, D (eds) (2016), *Military medical ethics for the 21st century.* Abingdon: Routledge.

Hunt, MR, Schwartz, L, Sinding, C & Elit, L (2014), The ethics of engaged presence: a framework for health professionals in humanitarian assistance and development work. *Developing World Bioethics.* Vol. 14 (1): 47–55.

Jotkowitz, AB, Agbaria, R & Glick, SM (2017), Medical ethics in Israel—bridging religious and secular values. *The Lancet.* Vol. 389 (10088): 2584–6.

Merin, O, Ash, N, Levy, G, Schwaber, MJ & Kreiss, Y (2010), The Israeli field hospital in Haiti—ethical dilemmas in early disaster response. *New England Journal of Medicine.* Vol. 362 (11): e38.

Rességuier, A (2017), The moral sense of humanitarian actors: an empirical exploration. *Disasters.* Published online 28 April 2017.

Slim, H (2015), *Humanitarian ethics: a guide to the morality of aid in war and disaster.* Oxford: Oxford University Press.

WHO (2017), *WHO Syria donor update, Q2 2017.* Geneva: World Health Organization.

Yamin, AE (2010), Our place in the world: conceptualizing obligations beyond borders in human rights-based approaches to health. *Health and Human Rights: An International Journal.* Vol. 12: 1.

Young, SS, Lewis, DC, Gilbey, P, Eisenman, A, Schuster, R & Seponski, DM (2016), Conflict and care: Israeli healthcare providers and Syrian patients and caregivers in Israel. *Global Qualitative Nursing Research.* Vol. 3: 1–15.

10 | THE EMERGENCE OF HUMANITARIAN FAILURE: THE CASE OF HAITI

Jan Wörlein

Introduction

The aftermath of the fatal 2010 Haiti earthquake disaster has been described as a period of the largest and most dense deployment of humanitarian relief since the emergence of the international humanitarian system (Verlin, 2014). The January 2010 7.0-magnitude earthquake, followed by a multiplicity of crises including the cholera epidemic, Hurricanes Sandy and Matthew, two electoral crises, and widespread drought, has resulted in an unprecedented influx of humanitarian actors to the country. The Haitian case is also seen as the archetype of what has been called 'humanitarian failure': the narrative of a humanitarian system failing to deliver aid in an efficient way (Karunakara, 2010; Farmer et al., 2012; Katz, 2013; Thomas, 2013; Biquet, 2014). This narrative of failure was not exclusively an external criticism, but was also widespread among humanitarian workers themselves (Binder, 2013). Even though the criticisms of inefficient aid are legitimate some of the underlying ethical challenges to the idea of humanitarian failure are rarely put forward. As Binder (2013) points out the idea of a humanitarian failure tells us more about failed expectations of a humanitarian system, than about its actual performance. This chapter offers for that reason an analysis of the conditions under which those expectations appear, to contextualise ethical debates about aid failure.

The 'humanitarian world' (Revet, 2011) became increasingly professionalised and institutionalised during the 1980s and 1990s, with growing 'competition and division of labor' (Dauvin & Siméant, 2002). This 'world' is today repeatedly confronted by the phenomena that the Haitian case crystallises: a great fluidity of actors in the 'field' as a result of short-term contracts; rapid turnover between headquarters and the 'field'; varying affiliations between different types of organisations as a result of consultancy contracts; and insecure working conditions (Schneiker, 2015).

For this reason, this chapter proposes to analyse the professional practice of humanitarian response in Haiti between 2010 and 2015 with the assumption that the fluidity of aid to Haiti is as much an obstacle as a resource for local agents. My focus is specifically the way in which crisis management actors in Haiti (re)produce the conditions of their actions using elements of their fragmented and changing environment. This will show how actors cope with the ethical dilemma of engaging in a system which they partially perceive as immoral.

For an Open Definition of Aid Actors and Aid

In contrast with functionalist and normative approaches that focus on failure, I seek to study the reasons why aid actors perceive themselves as part of the failure of the humanitarian system in Haiti. For this reason, I will refrain from proposing an external definition of such a humanitarian system in disarray, because those definitions tend to narrow the debate to efficient aid rather than open it to a historical but local perspective. I will rather conceptualise the humanitarian space in Haiti as defined and structured by its actors, and thus draw on Atlani-Duault and Dozon's (2011) anthropological perspective:

> humanitarian aid now simply defines activities which groups claim as being humanitarian aid and they intervene and organize for this purpose a system of intervention on other social groups.

However, as I am interested in the notion of the humanitarian system and its implications as organised space, I will focus on the dynamics of self-regulation within that space as well as on the impact of that space on the self-perceptions of aid actors in Haiti. I will ask under what structural conditions the perception of Haiti as a case of humanitarian failure is constructed. I consider the space of aid in Haiti as a social space in the sense that French sociologist Lilian Mathieu developed for the 'space of social movements': an intricate web of actors, who all share certain references, modes of action and social logics (Mathieu, 2012).

This analysis is based on six years of ethnographic research on humanitarian actors in Haiti, which was conducted between 2010 and 2016 as doctoral research in political sociology. Since it was impossible to map all the actors who worked in Haiti during that period, I chose to focus on aid coordination meetings. These meetings were excellent observation sites from which to understand how actors interact, how aid is conceptualised, and how social relations inside the aid sector are organised. My ethnographic fieldwork also included immersion with a group of humanitarian expatriates, as I rented a room in one of their houses during each of my field trips. This allowed me to gather ethnographic data on their daily lives, their travels, and their social relationships in addition to their work relations in the field of humanitarian assistance. Along with my observation of mechanisms for humanitarian coordination, I was, therefore, also able to conduct an ethnographic study of the humanitarian milieu in Haiti.

First, I will explain how humanitarian actors have become hegemonic in the 'field' to aid understanding of the conditions under which moral questions about aid delivery in Haiti appeared. I will then analyse the fragmentation of professional practices of humanitarian actors in the post-earthquake phase between 2010 and 2012 to show how a consensus about the morality of aid performance in Haiti eroded. Finally, I will briefly consider the evolution of the system until 2016 to point to the continuing ethical dilemma between a rigid but efficient system versus a more flexible and inclusive approach.

Building the Humanitarian Space in Haiti

Here I reconsider the unambiguousness with which the humanitarian narrative is imposed in Haiti by analysing both how humanitarian professionals shape their social space in the country and how they have structured the categories used to understand their actions. Atlani-Duault and Dozon remind us that the categorisation of certain activities as 'humanitarian' is recent: 'One can only ask oneself about this extension of an aid that is said and considered to be humanitarian to actions which, twenty-five years ago, could have been considered as relevant to development aid' (Atlani-Duault & Dozon, 2011). Based on this perspective, my first objective is to understand how aid interventions in Haiti adopted the title of 'humanitarian' assistance by gradually excluding Haitian state actors and naturalising moral expectations about what humanitarian actors should and can do in Haiti.

How Financial Exclusion of the Haitian State Led to Its
Institutional Marginalisation

The starting point is the so-called Dole amendment vote in 1995, after the assassination of a well-known Haitian lawyer (Mireille Durocher de Berlin). The Republican majority in the US Senate argues that the instability of the Haitian government makes it necessary to put approximately $50 million of planned aid on hold. The United States Agency for International Development (USAID), followed by other major donors, then ceases to directly fund Haitian state institutions and redirects a substantial part of the official development aid towards private aid organisations (Morton, 1997). The International Monetary Fund (IMF) decision to also put aid on hold in 1998 was linked to the privatisation process, which was under way but seen as going too slowly under the Aristide government (which came to power in 1994). Thus, the decision to stop funding the Haitian state was not taken because of issues of corruption or clientelism, as is often stated in the Haitian case (Gros, 2012; Schuller, 2008).

This withdrawal of budget aid had a snowball effect, because after the US Senate and the IMF put aid on hold, the Inter-American Development Bank stopped lending money to the country as well, in 1999, after Aristide temporarily suspended the Haitian Parliament. At the turn of 2000, the Haitian government was thus virtually no longer a recipient of financial flows for development assistance.

This situation allows private organisations to quickly become major aid actors in the country. The 1998 hurricanes – which provoked an increase in aid projects in the country – gave a structural advantage to humanitarian actors within the existing informal cooperation between state agencies and NGOs. The sudden increase in non-state actors made it necessary for the Haitian state to start cooperating more with them. As early as 1997, Haitian ethnologist Pierre-Etienne Sauveur attempted to warn about this power shift, when he wrote from a nationalist point of view that NGOs were 'invading' the country (Sauveur, 1997). He especially demanded that the Haitian government better oversee those new private actors.

An Inclusive System of Coordination

However, compared to the post-earthquake context, the Haitian government was at the time still formally present in the coordination of aid. Since 1994, the government, in cooperation with the United Nations, had developed a formal framework of coordination with the civil protection agency (DPC) within the Ministry of the Interior. When, in 1998, after Hurricane George, the larger international organisations, led by the United Nations Development Programme (UNDP), asked for more formal coordination of humanitarian aid in Haiti, the Haitian state was still a central part of the overall coordination mechanism of the National Plan for the Prevention of Disasters (PNGRD) developed by UNDP from 1998 to 2001 (Ministère de l'Intérieur et des Collectivités Territoriales, 2001). The National Committee for Risk Management and Disasters (CNGRD) was designed to coordinate relief efforts in case of a disaster with officials from Haitian ministries among its board. The National Plan gave only an advisory role to international NGOs within the so-called International Support Group.

In 1999, the system was renamed National Risks and Disaster System (SNGRD), without having yet operated. In 2008, the SNGRD was presented as an example of good practice at a global level in the United Nations strategy for the least developed countries. The system was viewed as exemplary, because of the 'proactive role of government' (Ferreyra, 2008).

The state was supposed to be a stakeholder at each level of the system. However, the 2004 political crisis and the occurrence of new emergencies led to the marginalisation of the Haitian state. On the one hand, the political crisis that led to the ousting of Aristide and caused riots throughout the country provoked the militarisation of international interventions in the country; on the other hand, the logic of emergency management consolidated the perceived morally desired space and need for humanitarian actors in international aid efforts in Haiti.

From Ad Hoc Conflict Management ...

As I have described, the emergence of humanitarian aid in Haiti was linked to the redirection of funds from the Haitian state to private actors, but also to the restructuring of risk management structures in the country. While the Haitian state had developed specific institutions since 1983, notably the Pre-Disaster and Relief Organization (OPDES), the simultaneity of humanitarian reform at an international level (from 2005) and the emergence of new crises in Haiti (from 2004) allowed for the institutionalisation of a 'humanitarian system' in the country.

In 2004, president Aristide fled Haiti for the second time after two coups destabilised the country. To deal with ongoing riots, the United Nations Stabilization Mission in Haiti (MINUSTAH) was deployed to maintain stability. As an integrated mission, its mandate also meant it could implement policies intended to assist the transitional government, including the delivery of aid. Immediately after the passing of resolution 1529 of the United Nations Security Council (United Nations Security Council, 2004), which gave UN forces a first, three-month mandate, an informal meeting of donors in March 2004 took the decision to create the Interim Cooperation Framework (ICF), which would involve both the MINUSTAH and the Transitional Government of Haiti. Its creation, as a supervision and coordination instrument to ensure the full cooperation of state officials in the peace process, was directly inspired by United Nations experiences in East Timor, Afghanistan, and Iraq, and its design was copied from the Joint Needs Assessment tool used in Liberia. The first draft was directly based on the one developed for the UN mission in Sudan (Campeau 2006). The tool had, therefore, been conceived as an instrument for post-conflict contexts, in which international supervision was central.

Based on thematic groups, which were later transformed into what the UN called 'sector tables', this system was overseen by the World Bank and the UN, and supported by the European Commission and the Inter-American Development Bank, but envisioned as a partnership arrangement with the interim government. Each 'sector table' (including international organisations, as well as bilateral and multilateral donors) was, for instance, led by representatives of the Haitian state (UNDG, 2006, 2004). Initially, the Haitian government is therefore structurally involved in the coordination of aid.

The system of sector tables was put to the test for the first time during Hurricane Jeanne in September 2004, when the question of coordinating the action of the Haitian government with that of incoming humanitarian agencies, as well as the interactions between those humanitarian agencies, arose. A new 'sector table' for humanitarian aid was therefore integrated into the system (ibid.). However, this system was not perceived as effective by humanitarian actors on the ground. It was considered a governmental device intended to control aid actors' activities, contrary to the frequently expressed need of humanitarian aid agencies for a horizontally organised coordinating body. This is the reason why participants in ICF sector tables came mainly from international organisations and donor agencies and only a few belonged to NGOs, though participation was not formally restricted (ibid.).

... To the Need for a Global Humanitarian System in Haiti

The implementation of the cluster system, which is formally deployed in 2006 (but not activated), as a second central element of United Nations humanitarian reform further incorporates the aid-steering mechanisms into humanitarian logics. The cluster system becomes only fully operational in 2008, after it is activated during Hurricanes Fay and Gustav and tropical storm Hanna. Unlike the system of sector tables, its focus is explicitly on humanitarian aid. It is the United Nations Office for Coordination of Humanitarian Affairs (UN-OCHA) which is responsible for its implementation (IASC, 2015).

At the international level, the humanitarian reforms initiated by the United Nations in 2005 were intended to strengthen coordination mechanisms between crisis and disaster management, civil–military, and humanitarian interventions. The crisis in Darfur in 2004 and the delayed implementation of a humanitarian response led emergency agencies and notably the emergency coordinator and the under-secretary of humanitarian affairs to rethink the United Nations crisis management. Following an evaluation period, the Inter-Agency Standing Committee proposed in 2005 the 'sectoral accountability' approach, aimed at establishing the cluster coordination system, to create a new mandate for the humanitarian coordinator accompanied by Humanitarian Country Teams (HCT), to create new funding instruments, and to create a platform for partnerships with non-UN humanitarian actors. The drafting of the reform coincided with the emergence of new crises in Haiti, which made the country a 'test site' for its implementation.

The process described shows that the loss of legitimacy of the Haitian state after the coup in 2004, together with the redirection of resources towards NGOs as well as the importation of coordination tools applied in conflict situations, leads to a reconfiguration of power relations among emergency management professionals in Haiti during the second half of the 2000s. First, state agents are still present in coordination efforts but they do not have the lead role in the system anymore, especially since one of the explicit objectives of the ICF is to control the compliance of the Haitian government with the democratisation process through conditionality. Second, the cluster system, from 2008 on, gives a decisive role to donors, the United Nations resident humanitarian coordinator, and the HCT. Finally, the increasing presence of humanitarian organisations, which arrived wave after wave on the ground, consolidated the system in this evolving situation, and they became important players in the larger aid system. Therefore 'humanitarian aid' became institutionalised through a complex process of inclusion of new actors and exclusion of the Haitian state, as well as of development assistance agencies that had been working in the country since the 1980s and 1990s, and whose former relevance was gradually eroded.

This process shows how humanitarian reform at a global level had local effects in the provision of a centralised institutional toolset. This helped to create expectations about a universal humanitarian mandate in Haiti. During the 2000s, the objective was first to regulate the relation between state and non-state actors and second to regulate civil–military relations in the context of emergency. The liberalisation of the Haitian state and the creation of coordination mechanisms for international aid resulted in the establishment of humanitarian action as hegemonic professional logic. This process had already been completed before the 2010 earthquake and shaped perception of the morality of humanitarian aid as the governing instance in Haiti.

Institutional reform was thus essential in the transformation of the sector, but, in addition, it is relevant to understanding how the professional practices of humanitarian actors also contributed to making the humanitarian logic prevail while eroding a shared perspective on the morality of humanitarian action.

2010 – How the Coordination of Humanitarian Agents Transformed into a Need for Humanitarian Coordination

The earthquake that hit Haiti on 12 January 2010 profoundly altered the way in which the above-described system operated. The crisis led to an unprecedented increase in humanitarian aid by various measures. Funds raised by national governments, international and intergovernmental organisations, as well as NGOs reached the sum of 9.49 billion dollars, while tens of thousands of actors arrived in the 'field'. At the same time, many of the organisations that had been based in the country had evacuated their staff to the Dominican Republic or to their countries of origin. More specifically, the personnel of organisations that defined themselves as development organisations temporarily left the country or redirected their projects to humanitarian objectives and were therefore overshadowed by humanitarian actors. The arrival of a substantial number of young humanitarian professionals without 'field' experience had an impact on the perceptions of aid actors as well as on the relative positions of humanitarian agencies such as UN-OCHA and MINUSTAH. Since the end of the 1990s, and especially after the 1998 hurricanes, improvised coordination meetings had been held by humanitarian actors in the field. These meetings were supposed to solve logistical problems encountered by humanitarian actors in the field and were therefore not necessarily visited by development agencies. This is how the regional coordinator of a development agency that specialised in agriculture describes it:

> We have been involved in Haiti since the 1980s. And we know the country very well. Of course we also led emergency projects whenever needed. We did during the hurricanes at the end of the 1990s and we did it in 2010. It is important to criticise organisations and humanitarian aid, but such a critique should be differentiated. We, for example, have always remained in contact with officials of the Ministry of Agriculture. Of course, our partners changed quite a bit, but at the departmental level the administration is more stable [...] Before 2010, barbecues at the embassy helped to coordinate between heads of mission, or we went for a beer together with other organizations on the ground to discuss important issues. (Guenther, 2011)

The interview extract shows that the practices of coordination between aid workers in development agencies and between them and Haitian state agents were working in accordance with a sector logic (here the agricultural sector is mentioned) and were based on informal social networks linked to the long contract duration of aid personal. Seniority in the field was considered an asset, because it allowed for the building of personalised relationships, albeit informal, but perceived as effective.

This leads me to make two observations: on the one hand, we can see that those aid professionals who were already in Haiti did not perceive the Haitian state as a block, but distinguished the local scale (a scale understood as relatively stable, allowing for the development of a long-term, continuous framework of joint action) from the national level. On the other hand, those professionals distance themselves from 'humanitarian' organisations, to divert blame for the perceived malfunction of the aid system observed since the influx of humanitarian organisations in the late 1990s. Differentiating between short-term humanitarian and long-term development aid enabled actors to cope with their own participation in a morally challenged aid system.

In any case, the arrival of humanitarian workers from abroad was already perceived as problematic prior to the earthquake in 2010. After the earthquake, the exchange or temporary displacement of staff on the ground is also criticised. The following interview extract from an aid agent who was evacuated to the Dominican Republic exemplifies this type of criticism:

> We spent weeks and weeks sending them care packages from Santo Domingo, to distribute them where we worked before. It was annoying and frustrating. Most of those humanitarians had never set foot in Haiti. (Heigl, 2016)

The criticism came mainly from NGOs that had long been working in the country, such as development agencies that specialised in agriculture, Médecins Sans Frontières or Clio, an alliance which formalised exchanges between local and international NGOs like Oxfam or Doctors of the World. One of my interviewees, from a group of NGO team leaders who met on a regular basis before the earthquake, pointed out what he perceived as an inversion of hierarchical processes in decision-making due to the massive arrival of new staff and the installation of a new HCT Team as a central coordination instance (Interviewee A, 2011). The power relations, formally created by seniority, were not only questioned but a new verticality was implemented and shaped by humanitarian professionals, and humanitarian coordination began to coordinate mostly humanitarian organisations, which led to the partial displacement of development agencies and the Haitian state.

Perception of a Broad and Universally Engaged 'Humanitarian System'

Since 2010, the local population began to refer to aid as something which had been 'deployed' or 'arrived' or which 'leaves' the country. This popular perspective underlines the change in the perception of aid actors as a homogeneous and coherent global actor within a specific timeframe. I use the term 'humanitarian system' to describe this perspective because this notion is commonly used in the grey literature and in the field by humanitarian actors and humanitarian experts (ALNAP, 2016; Binder, 2013; Davey, Borton and Foley, 2013; Taylor et al., 2012; The Humanitarian Coalition, 2016). The notion is based on the idea that there is a set of distinct but interconnected institutions that produce concrete operational norms, which guide humanitarian action on the ground and allow it to be coherent. However, the way in which this system is defined varies considerably according to the authors. In some cases, the humanitarian system refers to what could be more precisely described as a humanitarian government, with reference to the definition of Fassin and Agier. It can be understood in a broad sense as all attempts at controlling the population in a Foucauldian sense, and in a strict sense as institutions that work to rationalise and centralise decision-making processes in the context of a humanitarian crisis (Agier, 2014, 2013; Fassin, 2010; Fassin & Pandolfi, 2013).

In Haiti, the broad sense prevailed. Thus, respondents tended to include bilateral aid negotiations and diplomatic exchanges with the Haitian government in the humanitarian system. The humanitarian system also sometimes included hybrid institutions such as the 'Interim Haiti Recovery Commission' that existed between 2010 and 2011 and incorporated both Haitian and international actors (Willems, 2012). However, most foreign NGOs were viewed as part of the system, while 'local' organisations were generally not seen as such. In this context, the 'international community' was often used as a synonym of the 'humanitarian sector'.

This perspective was even more convincing for aid actors as it corresponded to that of the local population. The terms Kreyol, 'Internasional', or 'blan' designate all non-Haitians in a similar way and tend to designate all foreigners as humanitarian actors (few foreigners in the country are not associated with the professional field of aid) and of humanitarian actors as a coherent block. That is why anthropologists such as Olivier de Sardan think that, from the point of view of beneficiaries, it makes no sense to distinguish between development organisations and humanitarian aid organisations (while on the contrary the North–South divide is relevant, for instance) (Olivier de Sardan, 2011).

But this shared perception of the existence of a humanitarian system should not distract us from the need to study existing practices of distinction between aid professionals, particularly in their self-presentation or their relationships to donors. At the same time, the

Haitian case also encourages us to account for the entanglement of different logics of humanitarian action. For instance, the fact that different types of aid actors on the ground conceive their actions as being part of a humanitarian aid system corresponds less to a situation in which the boundaries between local and global, development and humanitarian, short-term and long-term are blurred, and more to the perspective of practitioners who locate their practices in a broader context, structured by the need to cope with a permanent emergency and the institutionalisation of humanitarian coordination on the ground.

Demanding More Humanitarian Coordination to Deal With Humanitarian Failure

Lack of knowledge about the reality on the ground, the short duration of humanitarian contracts, and the demand for increased aid efficiency after the negative media coverage of aid in the Haitian case, led actors to perceive their working environment as an especially difficult and complex one. Grievances about working conditions were common, but mostly directed towards the performance of the overall aid system. Humanitarian agents were favourable to the existence, and especially to the reinforcement, of a central coordination instance. While the dominance and dysfunctionalities of the system were ethically challenged, the moral and practical need for more coordination was constantly highlighted.

Orientation Through Coordination

Thus, while the hegemony of the HCT was sometimes perceived as a threat by international NGOs in the field, this was not the case for OCHA. Their new centrality after the earthquake was rather well perceived. This centrality was linked to the location of OCHA in Port-au-Prince. Located at the beginning on the MINUSTAH logistics base, in the immediate vicinity of the airport that formed the main entry point for humanitarian aid and the border passing with the Dominican Republic, OCHA benefited from the fact that the 'logbase' had become the central area for the logistical and human coordination of aid, as planned in OCHA's mandate. Thus, humanitarian workers used to first register with OCHA, upon arrival, to access information and to participate in cluster meetings. One of the interviewees describes his arrival in the following terms:

When I arrived, I didn't know how things were organized in Haiti.
The guys from OCHA knew their stuff. They had maps and addresses,
you could go to the meetings. That was impressive. I first thought the
system worked. (Interviewee B, 2011)

Most newcomers stressed the importance of information exchange
and welcomed interactions, which they perceived as horizontal and
inclusive. The '3W' system (Who does What and Where), an inven-
tory of aid agencies and their localised actions produced by OCHA,
reinforced this positive impression of the work done by the humanitarian professionals of the UN representing a working machinery. When
criticism of failing relief efforts became stronger, aid professionals
did not perceive the cluster system overall as a problem. Rather, they
focused on problems of efficiency, with specific clusters that 'worked'
and others that did not (Martel, 2014).

When there was criticism, participants complained of the chaotic
conditions they experienced during meetings, caused by too many
attendees, although the existence of these meetings was considered
crucial, as was the provision of information online. When asked for
suggestions, interviewees overwhelmingly demanded more coordination and an even more proactive role for OCHA.

The Need for a Permanent and Stable Source of Information

This request for centralisation addressed to the United Nations
can be explained by the volatility of the humanitarian professional
space after the earthquake. By analysing the contract situation of
humanitarian workers, using data from the internet as well as resumés
available online on LinkedIn, a sharp decrease in contract duration
before and after the earthquake is clearly visible. On average, people
were contracted for at least a year prior to the earthquake. This situation
changes with the earthquake when most contracts are short term, from
a few weeks to a few months. Even after the emergency period between
January and May 2010, most positions are offered for a duration of
about six months on average

As part of its mandate to coordinate humanitarian action, OCHA
transformed into a central hub for arriving humanitarian agencies during
the emergency phase since MINUSTAH had been hit hard by the
earthquake (eighty-two dead, thirty-two missing, major infrastructure
losses). The UN peace mission was therefore unable to take the

leading role inside the humanitarian government after the earthquake. Moreover, the Haitian state authorities were also decimated by the disaster and therefore very disorganised, and regained their capacity to act only very gradually. The SNGRD was, for example, not activated before President Préval declared the state of emergency, two weeks after the earthquake.

A civil–military Joint Operation Tasking Center (JOTC) was therefore put in place to create an immediate coordination structure between military liaison officers from the United States and Canada and the UN coordination instances to facilitate the exchange of information and the orientation of military services towards humanitarian needs. The role of OCHA coordination staff was central, as the following quote from a member of the HCT shows.

> One of the most obvious conclusions that can be drawn from the operation in Haiti – and one which reinforces current practice is the need to engage with the military *before* a disaster strikes, so that humanitarian agencies have the opportunity to shape military planning, rather than simply reacting to it. (Butterfield, Reario, and Dolan, 2010)

Even though the ambition to directly supervise military operations was not turned into reality as the quotation shows, OCHA staff were able to incorporate the military forces into the humanitarian system. The humanitarian aid system immediately after the earthquake in Haiti therefore gave the MINUSTAH as well as OCHA a central place in Haiti and reinforced the perception that there existed a unified humanitarian system which overlapped and integrated all aid actors in the country. The scope of the crisis and the massive influx of new aid organisations, however, transformed the power structure that had been put into place during previous crises. While humanitarian professionals were only one group of actors among others in 2008, they became central in structuring aid management after 2010, while MINUSTAH lost its ability to play a role as an independent actor (with its parallel structure of coordination) and was integrated into the humanitarian system. Finally, thanks to coordination meetings and information sharing, newcomers from different organisations had the feeling they shared the same experience and commitment. This legitimised centralised coordination as a morally justified process.

Aid Illegitimacy and Shared Experience of Humanitarian Failure

The satisfaction expressed by humanitarian staff regarding the creation of coordination mechanisms changed, during 2010, to increasing criticism. UN coordination staff were criticised for not implementing the recommendations of the Global Humanitarian Platform created in 2006 (after the humanitarian reform of 2005), which underlined the importance of building partnerships between humanitarian and local actors. In particular, the cluster system should be co-managed between an international organisation and local government (Martel, 2014). Although this objective was regularly mentioned by OCHA, it was never completely achieved. Haitian state agents were also critical of institutional arrangements, which further undermined the legitimacy of the humanitarian system.

Although there was no explicit logic of exclusion, the system suffered from the fact that it had been built on top of pre-existing structures without integrating them, as was also exemplified by other international coordination structures.

The main mechanisms for humanitarian coordination were meant to coordinate between organisations and agencies and therefore did not foresee a proactive integration of state actors. As we can understand from the previous quote, the dynamics of exclusion were based on existing disparities in terms of operational resources and participation in decision-making meetings.

This loss of legitimacy among international actors also led local aid professionals to distance themselves from the field of humanitarian aid. Indeed in 2011 some of the Haitian interviewees still self-identified as humanitarian, but as of 2012, most professionals described themselves either as government officials or Haitian civil society.

The Cholera Epidemic as Legitimacy Problem and Ethical Challenge

The situation further deteriorated in late 2010 with the cholera epidemic and an election crisis. In October 2010, ten months after the earthquake, the deposit of human faecal matter from a MINUSTAH camp in the Artibonite River led to a massive cholera epidemic in the country. At the end of October, the first press reports accused MINUSTAH of having imported the disease. When, in November, the US-American Center for Disease Control made a statement comparing the type of cholera bacteria present in Haiti to that found in Asia, MINUSTAH, with troops from Nepal, was designated as responsible for the epidemic (Piarroux, 2011). The cholera outbreak coincided with the presidential elections, which took place despite the difficult context. The Special Representative of MINUSTAH, Edmund Mulet, was afraid that a political void would lead to social unrest. He and the 'Core Group' (a multilateral coordination group which includes Brazil, Canada, Spain, the United States, France, the UN, the OAS and the EU) exerted pressure on the Haitian government to ensure that the electoral calendar was respected. For this reason, when allegations of election fraud emerged, and were subsequently confirmed, the legitimacy of MINUSTAH was again questioned. Demonstrations demanded the departure of the UN mission, and across Port-au-Prince one could see graffiti saying: 'down with MINUSTAH'. In 2011, more and more humanitarian actors distanced themselves from the peace mission.

Two interviews that I conducted in 2012 with two cluster managers show that after a period marked by shared perceptions about the existence of a common humanitarian response, aid professionals distanced themselves from MINUSTAH, the former coordination instance.

One cluster coordinator told me: 'We are meeting here at the Logbase but we are not from MINUSTAH. I am fairly critical of their record and I am not sure that we need the military to do humanitarian aid. We have seen the results' (Interviewee C, 2011). He pointed at the Logbase and stated, 'We do not work the same way.' During another interview, a few hours later another cluster coordinator performed the same gesture, explaining to me that, 'Camp management is a work that goes beyond humanitarian logic. It's long term work. Many do not understand this' (Interviewee D, 2011).

At the same time, MINUSTAH tried to distance itself from its security and stabilisation mandates. On its website, the relative lack of military or security references was particularly striking between 2012 and 2015. Humanitarian efforts, on the contrary, were presented as central. The head of civil affairs of MINUSTAH had for instance told me with melancholy that the mission had been welcomed by Haitians dancing in the streets when it was deployed in 2004, and that MINUSTAH's commitment had been directed towards humanitarian projects to regain the confidence of the population (Rosendahl, 2011).

Humanitarian actors presented themselves as distinct from MINUSTAH, because they did not want to be associated any longer with a discredited military actor after the importation of cholera. On the other hand, some other UN actors did not want to be associated with a humanitarian logic, while MINUSTAH by contrast wanted to appear as a humanitarian actor.

Both MINUSTAH and OCHA adjusted, in 2011 and 2012, to regain their legitimacy. As for NGO professionals, they sought to distance themselves from humanitarian aid and presented themselves from 2012 onward more as sector specialists than as humanitarian actors. In my interviews, humanitarian aid became a category used to describe the other. And finally, the crisis of legitimacy of the humanitarian space also triggered a process of dissociation between Haitian actors and international actors.

In this game of institutional competition, it became risky to be part of a humanitarian system associated with international aid failure, while MINUSTAH, a civil and military actor, nonetheless tried to embrace a humanitarian framework for its actions in order to legitimate its actions after the loss of legitimacy linked to the importation of cholera. To insist on a humanitarian profile rather than on its security and stabilisation mandate enabled them, furthermore, to be perceived as an actor of disaster management rather than as an enabling factor for disaster. Professional sub-distinctions become important once again. United Nations humanitarian personnel positioned themselves as intermediary transition actors prior to the reappearance of the Haitian state as a coordination instance. Development actors were re-embracing a development identify themselves and disaster risk management and prevention became a central reference from 2011/2012 for NGOs on the ground. The sedimentation of coordination mechanisms allowed professionals to redefine themselves by using elements of institutional environments.

Continuous Emergencies and the Continuous Need for Coordination

From 2011 onward the focus of coordination instances was towards the transition to Haitian state actors. This was frequently referenced in different types of coordination meetings from cluster meetings on the national level to meetings of embassies or NGO coalitions. This transition proved however to be difficult. Haitian governmental authority was blocked by a stalemate between parliament and president, which resulted in frequent turnover of government positions. The position of prime minister was particularly unstable and ministerial positions, as well as the corresponding cabinets, changed on average more than once per year during the period between 2010 and 2016. Hurricane Sandy in 2012, a drought ongoing since 2014, the deportation of Haitians from the Dominican Republic since 2015, and the ongoing political crisis, which materialised in 2015 and 2016 as an electoral crisis, provided several further emergencies that justified the prolongation of the presence of a humanitarian coordination system. Cluster coordination staff themselves highlight that the utility of the centralised coordination mechanism justified its prolonged existence:

> The cluster system had to finish one day, but we realized that having nothing is not possible. What we have is not called cluster anymore, but it's the same thing. The goal of a cluster is to prepare for the time when there are no more clusters. But you still need coordination, it's just that it's less urgent. That's the only difference. Because between the food security cluster and the food security working group there is no big difference. (Charpentier, 2016)

From 2014 onward so-called working groups were put in place after the cluster system was deactivated. Once introduced, the humanitarian coordination mechanisms could not easily disappear and still coexist today with other coordination instances from aid coalitions and national actors as well as initiatives from the Haitian state. MINUSTAH however finishes its mandate in October 2017 and will be replaced with a new non-military peace mission, the United Nations Mission for Justice Support in Haiti (MINUJUSTH) (United Nations Security Council, 2017).

Conclusion

The objective of this chapter was to show the importance of historical and local context for understanding the conditions under which ethical questions about aid efficiency and failure are formulated. I analysed, therefore, how a relatively fragmented professional field, including actors in development aid and local actors (government agencies as well as civil society organisations), became unified under one overwhelming narrative of humanitarian aid, which created a consensus of a moral need for centralised coordination instances.

This transformation is linked both to the humanitarian reform carried out in 2005 by the UN, which introduced the coordination mechanism associated with a 'humanitarian system', and to the conditions imposed on the Haitian state by the US government and major donors that resulted in the channelling of funds away from the public sector and into the private sector.

At the same time, this consensus of shared values and a shared humanitarian mission did not prevail for long under the pressure of scandals linked to inefficiencies in international crisis management. It became costly for NGOs as well as for OCHA to be identified as part of the humanitarian system, which opened a debate about long-term aid versus short-term relief and a moral pressure to get back to a development-based system.

However, it should be stressed that the widely shared consensus of the failure of humanitarian aid clearly demonstrates the extent to which the concept of participating in a humanitarian system remained strong among the staff of organisations involved in crisis management between 2010 and 2015, and reflects the continuity of the value attached to coordination between organisations, rather than with state authorities.

The analysis shows, for this reason, the importance of understanding the power structures of aid before we can consider the ethics of aid efficiency. The moral of the humanitarian failure narrative is a demand for further professionalisation and increasing aid management. This may even result in more efficient relief and recovery, but at the risk of becoming self-referential and gradually excluding those it wants to help from decision processes. Furthermore, the ethical dilemma of the efficiency gain of a more rigid system versus the flexibility to adapt to changing (political) conditions on the 'ground' can only be decided based on precise knowledge of pre-existing aid structures. Finally, this makes organisational and institutional memory an ethical need.

References

Agier, M. 2013. Espaces et temps du gouvernement humanitaire. *Pouvoirs* 144 (1): 113.

Agier, M (ed.). 2014. *Un monde de camps.* Paris: La Découverte.

ALNAP. 2016. The state of the humanitarian system. Accessed August 2017. http://sohs.alnap. org/#introduction.

Atlani-Duault, L & Dozon, J-P. 2011. Colonisation, développement, aide humanitaire. Pour une anthropologie de l'aide internationale. *Ethnologie Française.* Vol. 41 (3): 393.

Binder, A. 2013. Is the humanitarian failure in Haiti a system failure? A comment on Jean-Marc Biquet's critique 'Haiti: between emergency and reconstruction. An inadequate response'. *Revue Internationale de Politique de Développement*, No. 4.3.

Biquet, J-M. 2014. Haiti: between emergency and reconstruction: an inadequate response. *Revue Internationale de Politique de Développement*. No. 4.3.

Butterfield, A, Reario, R & Dolan, R. 2010. The United Nations humanitarian civil–military coordination (UN-CMCoord) response to the Haiti earthquake. Accessed August 2017. *Humanitarian Practice Network*, August. http://odihpn.org/magazine/the-united-nations-humanitarian-civil%C2%96military-coordination-un%C2%96cmcoord-response-to-the-haiti-earthquake/.

Campeau, L. 2006. Haiti: Lessons from the Interim Cooperation Framework (ICF) from 2004–2006 & the extended and revised ICF from 2006 onward. World Bank. http://pcna.undg.org/index.php?option=com_docman&Itemid=26.

Charpentier, C. 2016. Interview on the food security working group.

Dauvin, P & Siméant, J. 2002. *Le travail humanitaire: les acteurs des ONG du siège au terrain*. Paris: Presses de Sciences Po.

Davey, E, Borton, J & Foley, M. 2013. A history of the humanitarian system. Western origins and foundations. *HPG Working Paper*, 1–50.

Farmer, P, Gardner, A, Hoof Holstein, CVD & Muckherjee, J. 2012. *Haiti after the earthquake*. New York: PublicAffairs.

Fassin, D. 2010. *La raison humanitaire: une histoire morale du temps présent*. Hautes Études. Paris: Gallimard : Seuil.

Fassin, D & Pandolfi, M (eds). 2013. *Contemporary states of emergency: the politics of military and humanitarian inventions*. 1. Paperback edn. New York, NY: Zone Books.

Faubert, C. 2006. Evaluation of UNDP assistance to conflict affected countries. Case Study Haiti. UNDP Evaluation office.

Ferreyra, A. 2008. *Best Practices in the implementation of the Brussels programme of action for the least developed countries for the decade 2001–2010*. New York: United Nations.

Gros, J. 2012. *State failure, underdevelopment, and foreign intervention in Haiti*. Routledge Studies in North American Politics 4. New York: Routledge.

Guenther, D. 2011. Interview on the role of German Aggro Action in Haiti.

Heigl, K. 2016. Interview on the professional situation of aid workers in rural development in Haiti.

Humanitarian Coalition, The. 2016. The humanitarian system. Accessed February 2016. http://humanitariancoalition.ca/the-humanitarian-system.

IASC. 2015. Reference module for cluster coordination at the country level. New York: IASC.

Interviewee A. 2011. Interview on the transformation of aid in Haiti. [Recording in possession of author].

Interviewee B. 2011. Interview on the condition on the ground for humanitarian workers. [Recording in possession of author].

Interviewee C. 2011. Interview with logistic cluster staff. [Recording in possession of author].

Interviewee D. 2011. Interview with CCM cluster staff. [Recording in possession of author].

Karunakara, U. 2010. Haiti: where aid failed. *The Guardian*, October 28.

Katz, J. 2013. *The big truck that went by: how the world came to save Haiti and left behind a disaster*. New York: Palgrave Macmillan.

Martel, A. 2014. Coordination humanitaire en Haïti : le rôle des clusters dans l'externalisation de l'aide. *Mondes en développement* 165 (1): 65.

Mathieu, L. 2012. *L'espace des mouvements sociaux*. Sociopo. Bellecombe-en-Bauges: Éditions du Croquant.

Ministère de l'Intérieur et des Collectivités Territoriales. 2001. Plan national de gestion des risques et des désastres. Accessed August 17. www.preventionweb.net/files/29734_plannationaldegestionrisquesetdesas.pdf.

Morton, A. 1997. Haiti. NGO sector study. World Bank.

Olivier de Sardan, J-P. 2011. Aide humanitaire ou aide au développement ? La « famine » de 2005 au Niger. *Ethnologie française* 41 (3): 415.

Piarroux, R. 2011. Understanding the cholera epidemic, Haiti. *Emerging Infectious Diseases* 17 (7): 1161–68.

Revet, S. 2011. Penser et affronter les désastres : un panorama des recherches en sciences sociales et des politiques internationales. *Critique Internationale*. Vol. 52 (3): 157.

Rosendahl, H. 2011. Interview on MINUSTAH and aid relations.

Sauveur, P-E. 1997. *Invasion des ONG*. Port-au-Prince: Editions du CIDIHCA.

Schneiker, A. 2015. *Humanitarian NGOs, (in)security and identity: epistemic communities and security governance*. Global security in a changing world. Farnham, England/Burlington, USA: Ashgate.

Schuller, M. 2008. Invasion or infusion? Understanding the role of NGOs in contemporary Haiti. *Journal of Haitian Studies* 13 (2): 96–119.

Taylor, G, Stoddard, A, Harmer, A, Haver, K & Harvey, P. 2012. The state of the humanitarian system. ALNAP/Overseas Development Institute.

Thomas, F (ed.). 2013. *L'échec humanitaire: le cas Haïtien*. Charleroi: Couleur Livres.

UNDG. 2004. Cadre de Coopération Interimaire. Accessed August 2017. http://haiticci.undg.org/index.cfm?Module=ActiveWeb&Page=CategoriesList&CategoryID=352.

UNDG. 2006. PCNA review: Phase One Haiti Needs Assessment case study.

United Nations Security Council. 2004. Resolution 1529. https://undocs.org/S/RES/1529(2004).

United Nations Security Council. 2017. Resolution 2350. http://unscr.com/en/resolutions/2350.

Verlin, J. 2014. Haïti: état failli, état à (re) construire. *Cahiers Des Amériques Latines*. Vol. (75): 25–40.

11 | ETHICAL ENCOUNTERS AS A HUMANITARIAN PSYCHIATRIST

Peter Hughes

Humanitarian Psychiatry and Ethics During Crises

Deciding when and how to treat mental illness in different cultural contexts is challenging as it raises many normative questions. Given that biomedical frameworks for understanding mental illness have primarily been developed among Western populations, the translation and transferring of concepts surrounding psychological trauma and depression, for example, have been critiqued as forming a 'category fallacy'. In other words, an initial ethical consideration is whether psychiatric categories appear as universal around the world. There are some strong critics of this notion, most notably, psychiatrist Derek Summerfield who argues that 'to case Western knowledge as universal, whereas indigenous knowledge is merely local and ignorable, is to propagate a new imperialism. Global mental health workers are the new missionaries' (Summerfield, 2012). Furthermore, the history of psychiatry has been turbulent in its relationship with ethics and has been accused of failing to sufficiently account for societal changes (Welsh and Deahl, 2002). Thus, when practising psychiatry in humanitarian crises, these ethical challenges are magnified and are set against the backdrop of cultural and religious beliefs relating to mental illness that conflict with Western diagnoses and treatments.

Introduction

I am a UK-based psychiatrist who for the past ten years or so has been travelling around the world to support mental health delivery in low- and middle-income countries (LMICs). In this chapter, I contextualise my practice in the debate pertaining to global mental health, and more specifically, the exercise of humanitarian psychiatry during crises. There is a disjoint between academics and practitioners with direct experience of the ethical issues, and this is highlighted in the chapter.

The ethical issues of global mental health, for example, focus on the theoretical implications of a universal application of psychiatric categories and the mainstreaming of the dominant biomedical framework of psychiatry globally. However, in the case of the scenarios that are contributed in the second half of the chapter, the nuances of the ethics that emerge and that are present in humanitarian crises regarding the practising of psychiatry or the addressing of mental health needs highlight the psychosocial landscape of mental distress and suffering. The chapter concludes with recommendations for further development of humanitarian psychiatry and ethics during crises.

Contextualising Global Mental Health

In this section, I provide a background to global mental health, then review of literature in terms of humanitarian crises.

The use of the term 'global mental health' is a relatively recent concept, which has further become popularised as a movement of sorts, or a global initiative on agendas of health organisations to improve mental health resources and infrastructure. Furthermore, references to mental health in humanitarian emergencies are even more recent. Global mental health has now become a specialist and exciting energised area with humanitarian crises being an area of great interest. The World Health Organization's aphorism 'there is no health without mental health' is now taking its place in health service delivery but progress is, nevertheless, slow.

There is a huge disparity in resources for mental health. Globally only 20 percent of world resources for mental health are attributed to LMICs. The lack of redress and accountability for ensuring mental health treatment is dealt with in terms of breaches of human rights legislation, which is further infused with a catalogue of abuses and violations of individuals who suffer from mental illness worldwide. For example, in many impoverished countries, the treatment gap can be over 90 percent.

Ethical issues are present throughout the chain of delivery of mental healthcare in LMICs. A significant problem is that even when treatment is provided it can be incorrect. This is despite much evidence on the efficacy and cost effectiveness of treatments for mental health. Underlying this phenomenon is a heavy stigmatisation of mental health, which is systematic through societies, including healthcare systems. As a consequence of such stigmas, health professionals are reluctant to specialise in mental health and the severe shortage of trained psychiatrists means that treatment is administered inaccurately.

Chaining or shackling of the mentally ill is common place and a severe violation of human rights. To try to combat the negative ways in which individuals suffering from mental illness are treated, there has been a development of user groups and advocacy, which is driving service delivery.

Mental Health: A Global Burden of Disease

Globally, 14 percent of the global burden of disease is attributable to neuropsychiatric disorders. Mental disorders can be factors in the increase of non-communicable and infectious diseases. There is a clear increase of depression for many physical health conditions, for example, tuberculosis, HIV, diabetes, myocardial infarction. Following the Ebola epidemic in West Africa in 2014, there was a surge of post-traumatic stress disorder (PTSD) cases.

Mental health problems have been recognised since the beginning of historic records. There have been mental health hospitals since the ninth century in the Islamic world. What is also clear is that mental health has long been a neglected area and even now only a minority of world countries have dedicated mental health policies and budgets. Those budgets are miniscule and are often focused on a national asylum with virtually no coverage for the rest of the country.

The presence of mental health problems is clear in all LMICs in the psychotic homeless indigents that one can see in the marketplaces; and it must be noted that due to stigma and lack of treatment, family members affected by mental illness are typically locked indoors. However, it has only been with more clear epidemiological studies that an accurate understanding has been produced of the extent of the global burden of mental illness. The global Burden of Disease surveys first showed how significant was the burden of mental illness in 1993 and 2010. The burden due to mental health problems was 8 percent. It showed the burden of invisible conditions such as depression and anxiety. The concept of looking at Disability Adjusted Life Year (DALYs) rather than a simple mortality figure enabled this highlighting of the burden of mental illness. DALYs capture an element of mortality but also record the morbidity of the illness. In this way, days of disability demonstrated the huge socio-cultural and economic effect of mental illness. Every survey since then shows that mental health problems form five of the top ten most disabling health conditions worldwide. There was a misconception that mental illness was the provenance of the Western countries. This has subsequently been debunked and we now see that there are similar figures for mental illness in all countries of the world, for example, following the International Pilot Study of Schizophrenia (IPSS) in 1973. There was an interest in some of the esoteric culture-specific problems such as Koro, but not in the general mental health problems of low- and middle-income countries.

The World Health Report from 2001 recommends that mental health is delivered at a community or primary care level predominantly, which leads to a need for task shifting so that non-mental healthcare specialists can deliver mental healthcare as well as physical healthcare. This is economically viable and non-stigmatising, and enables greater accessibility.

The WHO Mental Health Action Plan is an important policy direction signed by all member states with remarkable levels of agreement. There are four main objectives:

- strengthen effective leadership and governance for mental health;
- provide comprehensive, integrated and responsive mental health and social care services in community-based settings;
- implement strategies for promotion and prevention in mental health; and
- strengthen information systems, evidence and research for mental health.

This in principle directs response in humanitarian crises especially, as there is a principle of long-term development and emphasis on integrated mental health at primary care level.

Post-traumatic Stress Disorder: Fact or Fallacy?

There remains some controversy around conditions such as PTSD, which some argue are a Western social construct. A pivotal critique of PTSD as a diagnostic category has been laid out by Summerfield, one of the originators of the PTSD debate. In the paper 'Invention of post-traumatic stress disorder and the social usefulness of a psychiatric category', Summerfield writes:

A central assumption behind psychiatric diagnoses is that a disease has an objective existence in the world, whether discovered or not, and exists independently of the gaze of psychiatrists or anyone else. In other words, Neolithic people had post-traumatic stress disorder as have all people in all epochs since. However, the story of post-traumatic stress disorder is a telling example of the role of society and politics in the process of invention rather than discovery. (Summerfield, 2001, p. 95)

Other psychiatric conditions such as eating disorders seem less common in low- and middle-income countries. What is clear is the need to understand the nuances of psychiatric categories, which is difficult because mental health is a term used in all diagnostic categories within this area of health. When mental health is applied globally, then, it fails to speak to the varying phenomenologies of mental illness around the world, which are subjected to and shaped by pre-existing social processes. For example, experiencing melancholy in some societies will primarily be viewed as a spiritual or religious phenomenon whereas in other societies it is constructed as a health issue for which the sufferer will seek treatment and help from a healthcare professional.

Tackling global health requires a systematic analysis and understanding of two aspects, namely, the treatment resources and facilities, and, fundamentally, the experience of an individual and harms incurred as a direct result of being perceived as mentally ill. In this sense, 'mentally ill' is a description that is blurred with other stigmatising references to people such as accusations of witchcraft, or spirit possession, or as victims of curses.

The mentally ill face problems of lack of resources, abuse of human rights, stigma and injustice. The mentally ill have diminished access to equal healthcare, education, housing and employment. We know now that the mentally ill die up to fifteen to twenty years younger than the rest of the population. This acknowledges that the problems are worldwide even in the more affluent countries. Where there are mental health services, they are typically centralised to a national mental health hospital with very limited community services.

However, there have been major milestones in the past few years that form an architecture of how to deal with mental health in LMICs, which, in turn, has a bearing on how mental health during humanitarian emergencies and crises is approached.

Global Mental Health in Humanitarian Emergencies

The neglect of mental illness becomes more apparent in humanitarian crises where there are poor societal reserves to deal with emergencies. Most of the world's humanitarian crises occur in LMICs with some notable exceptions such as Hurricane Katrina.

Mental Health and Psycho-Social Support (MHPSS) has been an ongoing theme that becomes accentuated during humanitarian crises. The focus of MHPSS has tended to be weighted heavily on the aspect of psychosocial support, instead of looking at the issues of severe and common mental health problems.

The methodology of dealing with humanitarian crises is that the correct approach is evidence-based dealing with all four levels of the Inter-Agency Standing Committee (IASC) guidelines for mental health and psychosocial support in emergency settings, including dealing with the lower two levels of self-help, family/community support, and basic needs. There is a risk that the needs of the severely mentally ill are overlooked due to the huge demand for management of psychosocial difficulties. What is clear from research on humanitarian disasters is the resilience of people, including children, in dealing with the most adverse situations. This negates the argument for trauma-focused interventions but emphasises the need for a broad-based approach that covers all the IASC pyramid levels.

Nevertheless, clearly humanitarian crises have a direct impact on the mental health of the population, which is not entirely predictable, or managed, due to resilience factors. The effects can be wide ranging. We know that there is a doubling of the prevalence of severe and moderate mental illness as well as the magnifying of negative social processes such as domestic violence or traditional harmful practices, which potentially results in further psychological distress. Distress can be endemic among individuals but occurs within specific socio-cultural frameworks where there are vulnerabilities already in place. Whether in crises or in peace times, treating psychosis can deliver the greatest improvement compared to other conditions, which can be less dramatic in response.

There is a significant focus and prioritisation on PTSD in humanitarian crises. There is some consensus that there is a variability of prevalence. Acute stress can appear identical to PTSD symptomology. Pooled surveys show a figure of 15.4 percent (3 ref book). Similar pooled data showed a depression rate of 17.3 percent. There has been a higher figure for children in the Middle East. PTSD can increase in situations of cumulative stress exposure, torture and prolonged exposure, which could explain some of the findings from areas in the Middle East that have been subjected to chronic conflict. There may be issues of checklist ratings that are not culturally appropriate or locally validated. There is a risk of normal distress being medicalised into the mental health condition of PTSD. In other words, considering how to apply PTSD as a diagnostic category globally and in extreme situations, has a normative bearing – it employs a judgement on when an individual's suffering transcends from *normal* to *abnormal* in the sense that it constitutes a pathology.

Ethics and Evidence: Developing Guidelines in Response to Lessons Learned from Humanitarian Situations

Many mistakes have been made in humanitarian situations in addressing mental health. Two major guidelines have been developed to ensure that there are some basic principles in humanitarian response that will lead to evidence-based interventions with a view to pre-planning in emergency and post-emergency phases.

Exposure to extreme stressors is associated with a disruption of social structures and even governmental infrastructure, which can, in turn, exacerbate psychosocial distress. Informal care as well as formal care can be disrupted depending on the crisis.

A key message in humanitarian crises is that stress conditions tend to be self-limiting and eventually fade without any formal interventions. Debriefing has been proven to be potentially harmful, with a risk of increasing traumatisation if people do not wish to discuss their traumatic experiences. Psychological First Aid (PFA) is a preferable approach and allows people to speak when they wish at their own pace.

Ethics of Social Transformation During Humanitarian Mental Healthcare

Opportunity can also arise from disasters, as described in 'Building Back Better' (WHO, 2013). This details a selection of case studies from ten countries/areas that made use of the opportunity of a disaster to develop better health services in the long term. Mental health-oriented research is crucial during humanitarian contexts, and is lacking, but at the same time invites significant ethical issues regarding consent and how to respond to any diagnosable psychiatric conditions, or distress, on a short-term basis, when there are limited resources. There are also gaps in how to respond to stigma, which may result in the affected individual being subjected to forced traditional treatments such as exorcisms; there are significant gaps between the biomedical or even the psychosocial framework of mental illness and societal or cultural perceptions and it is extremely challenging to grasp the context and be equipped with the skills to manage potential harms on an emergency basis.

The IASC is a committee of UN and non-UN organisations providing expert guidelines on mental health and psychosocial responses to humanitarian crises. The Sphere handbook is another major guideline, detailing the Humanitarian Charter and Minimum Standards for Disaster Response and is the product of an expert consensus of NGOs.

Both IASC and Sphere provide very clear guidelines on how to deal with mental health in emergency settings. Key areas are coordination among health and non-health sectors, needs assessment, monitoring and evaluation, human rights/protection, self-help, person-centred and human resources. It is vital for healthcare professionals and humanitarian actors to receive good authoritative information when responding to a humanitarian disaster. There is also a need to link families and community as early as possible. Basic needs must be met, which broadens the mental health remit of MHPSS to cover psychosocial support. Even for the severely mentally ill, there is a need to ensure basic needs are met. In the Sphere guidelines, psychosocial support cross-cuts all other chapters and includes both mental and social aspects of care. Humanitarian mental health responses, then, are complex and interdisciplinary, involving clinical and sociological or anthropological approaches and cross over to altering fundamental conceptualisations about mental health and stigma throughout society.

Targeting Mental Health Human Rights Violations

In terms of service delivery, MHPSS should be predominantly met at primary care level with secondary care support using tools such as PFA and mhGAP (mental health Global Action Programme). There are eight principles that govern contingency planning before the crisis, namely, 1) needs assessment, 2) development of long-term strategy, 3) immediate response, 4) intersectoral collaboration, 5) treatment at primary care level rather than parallel service, 6) access to services for all, 7) training, and 8) supervision and monitoring indicators.

In addition, it is important to protect human rights, to operate on the 'do no harm' principle and to include the active participation of beneficiaries in development of projects. It is important to avoid parallel services but instead to enhance and support already existing systems. It is advisable to avoid vertical programmes and those that are targeted towards a specific group, but instead to have a broader focus. A multi-layered intervention is favoured. This includes economic development and livelihoods for those affected. Ongoing supervision and outreach is needed. Trauma-focused work should be integrated into general services. Community-based self-help and support groups are important in managing psychological distress during humanitarian crises. Within these guidelines, there is potential to work with traditional healers to fulfil their requirements. Policy development should go arm in arm with recovery from a humanitarian crisis.

Overall there is a crucial need for further research on interventions particularly at the two lower levels of the intervention pyramid, where the greatest impact of a humanitarian crisis will be apparent. In humanitarian crises, it is important to encourage normal social activities such as schools, religious activities, funerals, etc. to promote social cohesion and support, although these may be difficult to resume or carry out and are often overlooked in terms of their importance. Religious activities and bereavement rituals, for example, played a symbolic role in aiding grief and psychological distress in the aftermath of the Sri Lankan tsunami in 2004.

The Sustainable Development Goals (SDGs) for 2016–2030 have a health goal that includes mental health. This again is helping to ensure that mental health becomes part of an integrated comprehensive health package. Yet, there remains an ethical imperative to motivate further attention to mental health and the response to mental health during humanitarian crises.

WHO mhGAP: Closing the (Ethical) Gap Between Humanitarian and Development Mental Health Interventions?

The WHO launched its mhGAP programme in 2008. The mhGAP programme is the response to a huge gap between mental health need and capacity. In part, the treatment gap results from the huge shortfall of mental health workers. There are many countries where there are just a handful of psychiatrists, and a similar lack of psychologists, psychiatric nurses and psychosocial workers. The global action programme aims to strengthen non-specialist health workers in mental health skills through the mhGAP training manual. The principle is to provide training and supervision to non-specialist health workers to deliver and integrate mental health treatment at a primary care level.

The WHO mhGAP training manual has now been used in over ninety countries. The manual is derived from rigorous review of evidence-based interventions from all global literature. It does involve a phase of national adaptation to acculturate and to formulate the local context. Providing ongoing supervision to ensure the standard of delivery coupled with an expert secondary care level for advice and referral for complex cases is essential. The mhGAP training manual deals with conditions coined in the phrase Mental, Neurological including epilepsy, and Substance abuse (MNS). There are a range of accompanying support documents to mhGAP including those dealing with implementation, supervision, monitoring and evaluation.

In 2015, the mhGAP humanitarian version of the implementation guide was released. This is a shortened version of the mhGAP Implementation Guide, and has more emphasis on conditions associated with stress. PFA was released in 2011. This is a guide to responding to and providing psychological first aid to people experiencing stress following a humanitarian crisis. The guide covers good communication, information and linking families together as well as stress management. It is an important tool for first responders and for those in direct contact with people in stress.

Lived Experience of Mental Health Across Cultures

Despite an increasingly global focus on mental health, the emphasis is on its burden of disease. What is lacking is the bringing together of lived experiences and cultural narratives that depict the meanings and phenomenologies of different interpretations of mental illness. In addition, arguably, there is no such thing as global mental health as all principles that apply in the affluent West should be in place in impoverished areas. It is when there is injustice, and contrasting values regarding medicalised views of mental illness, that ethical issues emerge.

For a Western health worker with a privileged background working in the United Kingdom's National Health System (NHS), there is an ethical bias from the very moment of arriving in the field in the aftermath of a humanitarian crisis.

As a Western, white, middle-class, middle-aged male, the representation of my identity is difficult to disguise. The image intensifies when arriving to join a team of humanitarian actors and frequently joining similar people secure behind secure fences in comfortable accommodation with generators and running water (most of the time).

The ethical issues arise painfully and unexpectedly from this very identity, carrying a potential badge of neo-imperialism, of the humanitarian actor as a saviour from the day-to-day struggles of life. However, conceptualising ethics in global mental health requires addressing the local as global as well; failure to grasp the inclusiveness of those who are suffering from poor mental health constructs the *Other* and creates stigma. Ethical issues and injustices can be seen in a Western country like the UK, for example, where there is a treatment gap between services provided and needed in mental health. I encounter the same issues of poverty, bad housing, social injustice, and lifestyle problems that I am faced with in other, poorer, regions of the world.

Personal Reflections: Ethics of Humanitarian Psychiatry on the Frontline

I will give some examples from the field to flesh out some of the ethical issues of humanitarian work.

Case Scenario One: Chad

I started in this field naïve and unaware of the various humanitarian issues that faced me. Yet, as a healthcare professional I was considered to possess the necessary skills to transfer the way I treat mentally unwell patients in the UK to other contexts regardless of the situation. I soon encountered the ethical blockade that this creates in relation to being able to engage with and integrate ethical analysis into my practice; I was expected to know what to do.

Eastern Chad has had refugee camps from the mid-1990s. I went there to work in a mental health clinic in some of these camps. This was a difficult living environment for me, without regular electricity and running water. Refugees were registered and received benefits following their registration. At times, local Chadians would pretend to be refugees to also receive the benefits. Unquestionably, it has been the poorest area I have ever worked in. I can remember the groups of children with ragged clothes and no shoes. We had a children's group with about ten toys to share for thirty, with headless dolls and broken cars. We were trying to treat patients with epilepsy. It is very important to have a regular supply of medication for this condition. Yet, our supply of medication was not secure. I recall one man walking for three days to come to the clinic for the medicines for his son's epilepsy. I had none. He thanked me and left and said he would return when we had our supply back.

I saw a child in a Chadian village. This was an eight-year old girl whose father worked in the camp. I diagnosed a brain tumour that was easily treatable in the West. Even in the camp, the child would have been moved and resettled with the family to a place where they could receive treatment. I discovered that the father was consulting with traditional healers when we could do nothing. I do not need to ask to know what happened to that child. In this case, not being a refugee placed this child at a severe disadvantage. What I loved about the camps was that we trained refugee workers to deliver mental healthcare in the camps. This was one place where the 'us' and 'them' could be diminished somewhat.

Case Scenario Two: Haiti

I got called to Haiti through a friend just after the 2010 earthquake. At the time, I did not know what to expect. Many mental health professionals in UK said that I would be dealing with PTSD symptoms. I managed to fundraise in a short time a large amount of psychiatric medication including 1000s of diazepam tablets that I could use to treat anxiety and acute stress in the aftermath of the disaster. I arrived to the peculiar effects of earthquake, with some buildings intact and many not. However, it was clear that there was utter devastation and disruption of the ability to live an everyday life.

The first few weeks were the time of bodies on the streets, impassable roads, and funerals. There were countless helicopters and a flurry of Non-Governmental Organisations (NGOs) and UN organisations. We were the providers of largesse, food, and security. In fact, what provided security was the United States military, who were dispatched after the earthquake. We felt quite impotent in the face of the huge need.

I had been given a tent by a friend in the UK to take with me. I soon realised that the driver who was taking me around was sleeping on the street and had a young baby. Thus, one of my first actions as a psychiatrist humanitarian aid worker was to donate my tent to the family of my driver. I had ready access to tents where I stayed in our secure house in the nice part of town. We could not stay indoors overnight due to the risk of a further earthquake but we were comfortable.

We found out as much as we could about what mental health services there were in the country. There was a psychiatry hospital in the centre of town. The walls had fallen, and its staff were either deceased, grief stricken, or unable to travel to work. The remaining patients had no food or water. The US military helped us by supplying food and water to the hospital.

There was a small camp of Haitians living in the grounds of the hospital either with tents or without shelter. Our remit of support extended to cover the basic needs of the people in this camp. We observed, as expected, an increase of cases of mental illness at the hospital. I saw a man being brought in by his young son who was grief stricken by loss of his mother, his siblings, and their home. The man was in a state of mania. He was laughing and joking – such behaviour appeared utterly bizarre in the presence of such grief.

Our other work during this trip was seeing people in distress in the main psychiatric hospital. The hospital had lost its management, as in the nature of humanitarian crises, and appeared to be controlled by external actors with the involvement of US, Canadian and other volunteers. We saw patients who were facing amputations, grief stricken and homeless, all suffering varying states and degrees of an indistinguishable psychological distress.

As time progressed in the aftermath of the disaster, we treated more and more women who had been raped. Haiti was a very violent society and one of the world's kidnapping hotspots. During the instability of the humanitarian crisis, these extreme situations escalated due to the fragility and weakness of infrastructure and lack of available protection. An ethical issue is that protocols, guidelines, and training from a gender lens were required, but the conceptual analysis of vulnerability and mental health remains scientifically bound and without a sufficient sociological basis.

Despite our lack of treatment resources, we worked on meeting the basic needs of the rape victims during this immediate time. At any point that I saw women who had been raped, my priority was making sure we could prioritise getting a tent for the woman that night, at the very least. My work was not about PTSD, which I saw very rarely and only after sexual violence, but about reassuring people that they were not 'mad' but normal and doing amazingly well dealing with intolerable stresses. I was challenged by the normativity with which I assessed the human lives and suffering that presented throughout the phases of this humanitarian crisis. My role needed to be adapted as I analysed and became further aware of the requirements of those I had travelled to and come to treat.

The 1000s of diazepam tablets that I had brought with me became redundant; a medicalised response to such human distress was not necessary nor appropriate. We had psycho-education as our tool. As a psychiatrist, I spent less and less time doing direct clinical management of severe mental illness and more on training local health workers to deliver psychological services. One day, during a consultation, I met a young man with an intellectual disability and a probable form of autism that had never been diagnosed before. He had suffered the deaths of many of his family in the earthquake. He was living on the street. He was biting chunks out of his arms. His mother had tied him up with rope which was cutting into his skin. I was presented with an extreme ethical challenge regarding the decision to continue to restrain my patient. I did so as there was absolutely nothing else I could do and my action directly contravened my training and the way I practice psychiatry in the UK. I helped the mother tie up her son with bandage but doing so in a way that would not cut into his skin and so he would not bite his arms. I helped the family get a tent and hopefully provide some stability in this man's life during this crisis, when he could barely understand what was happening around him. The mother thanked me but I wonder what I was doing ethically and for human rights here. Another task I participated in that was outside of my general boundaries was helping at and facilitating funerals when there was nobody. Of course, this was not something I could lead on but we got in a religious leader and it was a valuable intervention for mediating the psychological bereavement process of the families of the deceased.

We had plenty of money as Haiti was in the news. I gave interviews to world newspapers every other day of the week. The money poured in. A child found in the rubble alive whose image and story was broadcast to the rest of the world meant that money would come in. There was an absence of the Haitian government during the emergency, which, ultimately, effectively and paradoxically, helped us to implement programmes more easily.

We lived comfortably in Haiti as time went on. The first few months we were living in tents but then we moved to the nice part of town and stayed in beautiful homes. This made us all quite uncomfortable with the stark difference between our lives and the lives of the beneficiaries of our services. There was one rule for us internationals and another for the local people. Never did I feel more neo-colonial than this. The feeling extended even beyond the frameworks of psychiatry that are of concern to the critics of global mental health. At the same time, I was protected from kidnap, a perilous other edge to my clear identity.

We had funding to continue our programme for eighteen months. As the government regained control, we handed over our primary care mental health clinics. We ran out of money when the world forgot about Haiti and the promised money never arrived. We left and our clinics closed. Did we make it worse by coming in and parachuting in to serve and then leave without a clear service continuing? This raised a difficult ethical issue. I like to think that we invested so much in human capital, in our training and the development of skills and knowledge that our intervention had positive impacts over the long term.

Case Scenario Three: Sierra Leone and Ebola

I remember the maps of the region in the technical expert centre in WHO, Geneva. Monrovia, Liberia and Freetown, Sierra Leone were angry large red spots on the maps. Ebola was at its most terrifying when I arrived in Freetown. My brief as to where I would be was open-ended. Overall, on reflection, it is probably true that more people died from malaria and poverty-related problems than from Ebola. Ebola created financial revenue and resulted in the presence of humanitarian organisations and foreigners like myself. Interestingly, I had taken over from an anthropologist in developing a psychosocial response to Ebola. Again, similarly to Haiti, one of my most important tasks was working on funerals. So much of my work globally has been about funerals and very practical things rather than direct mental healthcare, even within the capacity of being there as a psychiatrist. It was a joy to work with so many local partners rather than in the 'us' and 'them' scenario. Rather uncomfortably, I felt very much one of the locals after being in contact myself with Ebola; in this sense I was wholly submerged in the crisis. However, I ultimately had support and good education, which provided an understanding of the situation, and access to evacuation strategies if the worst happened. Thankfully, it never happened.

At this stage, survival rates in Sierra Leone were poor in contrast to the excellent rates after treatment in a Western healthcare centre. I met some people who ignored the risk of Ebola saying that God would protect them. In fact, churches and mosques and especially funerals were dangerous places for the spread of Ebola. During those dark days, I recall winding my way past the terrified patients waiting for a bed outside the front of the hospital. I stumbled on some discarded clothing on the ground and was terrified for days after that.

The anxiety, stress, and fear of contracting Ebola was endemic. My work as psychiatrist became about practical help, meeting basic needs, and education. Training in hand washing was vital. I asked a group of health workers about the effect of Ebola on their lives. They were terrified. Some of those working with Ebola were ostracised from their communities and lost their accommodation. I spoke to a survivor of Ebola who had been treated in an Ebola treatment unit. He said the worst part, even worse than the deaths of those around him, was the dehumanisation. Staff were terrified of him. They gave him food at the end of the bed and did not use his name. There remains the ethical question of why Ebola penetrated so deeply into the local society and whether the response from humanitarian organisations was sufficient.

Case Scenario Four: The Middle East

The Middle East has always been political but it is visceral and the tension is felt in the blood. It is present every second of the day. The sense of injustice is palpable. I arrived in the West Bank and someone told me about their mother being shot dead. The anger is overpowering. As a humanitarian worker, I try to be impartial wherever I am but in Palestine this is almost impossible. Gaza is considered the largest prison in the world. We can support mental health in these places, but how can there be good mental health when you live in a virtual prison or need permission to travel ten kilometres up the road? These are ethical questions that can be resolved only through international legal and human rights discourses. The limitations posed by my ethical reflections and analysis, though, presented insurmountable consequences that were impossible to shift. Working within contexts of humanitarian crises due to conflict is some of the most challenging work – because the crises are preventable and unnecessary.

In Syria, the political fracturing is profound. I did some work in Damascus, which is effectively supporting the government but I then worked in southern Turkey and Iraq with the opposition side. To a significant extent, health is both beyond politics and imprisoned by it, and as a healthcare professional treating the effects of mental distress that results from political conflict, my ethical challenge was to locate my positionality and manage my values professionally.

My personal ethical dilemmas arise from coming as an outsider to places I am not familiar with but also from the joy of learning about new cultures and realising that in the end all human beings are similar; this has made me realise how much I value the human spirit in transcending all manner of evils and misfortune. What is extraordinary is not how many people are mentally ill but rather how many are *not* mentally ill, considering the circumstances, which is a hugely significant ethical observation for how victims of humanitarian crises are conceptualised and treated. I feel that I now am very familiar with different cultures, but my role is purely to facilitate and strengthen those in local situations.

Conclusion

Global mental health is a burgeoning area with increased research and policy focus, and an increasing manifestation of great need. Humanitarian crises, disasters or conflicts can be the tipping point for fragile health systems. Yet, they can also be an opportunity for 'Building Back Better'. Mental health workers have clear guidelines now on what to do in emergencies. We know now that treatment is effective and, in the long term, it is also cost effective. We need to stretch ourselves in ensuring good intersectoral coordination, and advocacy for the marginalised and the impoverished. In humanitarian crises, it is the mentally ill who become the most vulnerable to adversity such as homelessness, physical illnesses, societal breakdown, and medication supply loss, as well as stigma and abuse. Adequate preparation and the following of the principles of the IASC pyramid are key prevention and response strategies for humanitarian crises. Any humanitarian response to mental health must be both evidence based and human rights based, but as illustrated in my case scenarios, due to the lack of global mental health infrastructure, severe ethical problems arise in trying to treat mentally ill patients in the worst scenarios with no viable recourse other than to cross ethical boundaries. Response should also be based on existing health systems as much as possible. Parallel health systems and vertical programmes must be avoided. Health response must be primary care based. Gender-based violence needs to be part of the health system and not bracketed as a social issue. Both mental healthcare and psychosocial support need to be aspects of any humanitarian response to accommodate the importance of the clinical needs of the severely mentally ill as well as societal distress. Important messages to remember and pass on are to recognise resilience and informal systems in many societies. Acute stress conditions tend to be self-limiting. PTSD is relatively unusual and is usually self-limiting despite the reductive view of humanitarian crises resulting in severely traumatised populations. In terms of research, surveys during times of humanitarian crises are futile and more effort is needed to develop a systematic needs assessment that is based on a standard humanitarian needs assessment.

What I have seen in my professional global work is the improvement in disaster response from Haiti to Sierra Leone and to conflicts of the Middle East. There is a greater awareness of how to manage mental health during humanitarian crises, but the ethical issues I have outlined in this chapter remain and struggle to be brought to the surface. These are, in their essence, ethical questions that emerge from the existential situation in the difficulty or challenge itself. In other words, I could not have and did not perceive these ethical issues until I was actually present in the field. The training that I have tried to give to local health workers, regardless of whether they specialised in mental health or not, has been a mode of disseminating ethical analysis, yet formalised structures for the ethics of global mental healthcare during humanitarian crises remain underplayed.

Furthermore, resources such as training can be present for a disaster but in the longer term we see that the money does not last and it is a challenge to ensure development and to follow the principles of 'Building Back Better' where there may be a lack of sustainable funding beyond the crisis period. The mental health crisis, then, persists, even after the immediate humanitarian crisis has subsided.

Models to be used are stepped: care with primary and secondary care, expert advice and treatment when necessary for complex cases. Finally, further research is needed on mental health interventions in humanitarian crises but this will require the development of ethical guidelines and analysis and the expansion of the discipline of humanitarian psychiatry within global mental health.

References

Inter-Agency Standing Committee. 2007. *IASC Guidelines on Mental Health and Psychosocial Support in Emergency Settings*. Geneva.

Kleinman, A. 1987. Anthropology and Psychiatry. The Role of Culture in Cross-Cultural Research on Illness. *British Journal of Psychiatry*, 151(4), pp. 447–454.

Patel, V & Prince, M. 2010. Global Mental Health: A New Global Health Field Comes of Age. *JAMA*, 303(19), pp. 1976–1977.

Sphere Project, The. 2011. Humanitarian Charter and Minimum Standards in Disaster Response. Geneva.

Summerfield, D. 2001. Asylum-Seekers, Refugees and Mental Health Services in the UK. *Psychiatric Bulletin*. Vol. 25: 161–163.

Summerfield, D. 2012. Afterword: Against 'Global Mental Health'. *Transcultural Psychiatry*, 49(3–4), pp. 519–530.

Welsh, S & Deahl, MP. 2002. Modern Psychiatric Ethics. *The Lancet*, 359(9302), pp. 253–255.

World Health Organization. 2013. *Building Back Better: Sustainable Mental Health Care After Emergencies*. World Health Organization.

12 | ONE FOR ALL, OR ALL FOR ONE: THE ETHICAL IMPLICATIONS OF INDIVIDUAL HUMAN RIGHTS-BASED AND PUBLIC GOOD-BASED FRAMEWORKS IN EMERGENCY MENTAL HEALTH

Liyam Eloul and Claire F O'Reilly

Abstract

The humanitarian field is plagued with ethical crises. Historically, humanitarian institutions arose and developed spontaneously across multiple regions in response to both man-made and natural crises. However, the modern humanitarian system only began to take form in the aftermath of World War Two (WWII), developing around a framework of universal principles that attempted to unify across boundaries of territory, politics, culture, ethnicity, and class. Many of these principles developed reactively, in response to experience, while others require ongoing exploration and affirmation. One such principle is the universal application of Individual Human Rights (IHR) as the foundation for humanitarian action. While currently viewed as vital to ethical humanitarian practice, the implications of this principle in the field are the subject of growing criticism, particularly in relation to the delivery of health interventions. In this paper, we contrast the implications of an IHR approach with that of a Public Good (PG) perspective in mental health and psychosocial support (MHPSS) programming, and explore the ethical challenges of each approach from our perspective as field-based mental health clinicians working in humanitarian crises.

Public Good and Individual Human Rights Frameworks

Historically, the concept of (IHR) – the assertion that there is a set of universal and inalienable rights applicable to all human beings (Mazower, 2004) – only garnered widespread popular attention following the devastation of WWII, which was blamed in part on European nationalist co-optation and abuse of the concept of Minority

Rights upheld by the League of Nations (Mazower, 2004). The United States led a push for the international institutional recognition of individual rights, with the wry caveat that this objective should not be framed in any way that could pose a challenge to national sovereignty. Thus, in 1946 the UN Commission on Human Rights was convened under the guidance of US First Lady Eleanor Roosevelt and a charter was drafted; in 1948, the UN General Assembly passed the Universal Declaration of Human Rights. Since then, IHR have been written into a variety of guiding documents, from high-level policy to the specific implementation plans of United Nations (UN) agencies and international non-governmental organisations (INGOs).

In contrast to IHR, another concept arose in the wake of the world wars: the concept of a Global Public Good (GPG), or 'a good which it is rational, from the perspective of a group of nations collectively, to produce for universal consumption, and for which it is irrational to exclude an individual nation from consuming, irrespective of whether that nation contributes to its financing' (Smith & MacKellar, 2007). GPG was championed by health sector workers in an attempt to stimulate greater buy-in from high-income countries for international humanitarian aid (Mazower, 2004). The aim of framing health interventions as GPGs was to illustrate to wealthy countries the benefit of improving healthcare in low- and middle-income countries (LMICs), thereby diminishing transmission of health risks in a globalising world. As UK Foreign Secretary Ernest Bevin famously quipped, 'while the Channel could be used to stop the German [sic], it cannot stop germs' (Steinert, 2008). The fearful self-interest of donor countries was used as leverage to trigger political support, as was the case with the drive to eliminate certain infectious diseases such as poliomyelitis and later HIV, and with the support for global vaccination campaigns, which gained traction in the 1980s. In the current era of economic austerity, donor government support for programmes as GPGs has waned, leaving non-state actors (both the private sector and INGOs) to take greater leadership, albeit without the same authority to compel fundraising (Moon, Røttingen & Frenk, 2017).

Both IHR and GPG are frequently, and sometimes interchangeably, cited as justification for and frameworks under which to offer emergency humanitarian health services. Particularly in the relatively new and burgeoning field of Mental Health and Psychosocial Support (MHPSS), where stigma towards mental illness has significant impact on access to services (Padmavati, 2014), and where the wider public health risk is not as immediately evident, there remains space for debate. As field clinicians working in emergency mental health, we have encountered both the positive and negative aspects of IHR and GPG when used to frame MHPSS interventions. In its recognition of the rights of the individual, IHR necessarily raises the inherently political questions of: 'who is responsible for fulfilling this right?' and 'to what extent?' The GPG framework's utility lies in its ability to mobilise resources by emphasising not only the benefits bestowed upon the recipient, but also on the community at large, including the giver. However, this direction of focus leaves space to drift from the original humanitarian principles, and in turn raises the question: 'who determines whether something is in the public good?'

By examining how these approaches are applied, and with the use of an illustrative case study derived from our field experience, we intend to contrast the IHR and GPG frameworks and demonstrate the very real impact that these concepts can have on individual clients and how treatment decisions are made. It is our hope that field clinicians will recognise the value and necessity of an exploration of the advantages and shortcomings of these frameworks, and actively advocate for an approach, or combination of approaches, that best responds to their clients' contextualised needs.

Historical Overview of MHPSS

MHPSS sits at a unique nexus in humanitarian response: at the intersection not only between emergency response and development, but also of protection and health. The result is an ambiguous space demanding of both responsibility and operationality, which in turn amplifies the need for ethical frameworks to guide practice. It is important to note that the term MHPSS encompasses a range of target populations and needs in practice, from psychosocial distress due to displacement and loss, to coping with the experience of trauma, and serious and persistent mental illness. (IASC, 2010) The term also incorporates an array of interventions, from single-session, acute Psychological First Aid (PFA), to a more comprehensive core component of long-term peace-building and conflict-resolution efforts. Interventions may be more individual and medicalised (i.e. in the top tier of the Inter-Agency Standing Committee (IASC) pyramid) or more socially targeted, and integrated within other forms of aid (IASC,

2007). Efforts to identify a pragmatic and appropriate programme from this range of possible responses is the source of ongoing tension in the mental health field.

The development of MHPSS marked the move away from a psychiatric conceptualisation of post-traumatic responses, which had dominated since post-traumatic stress disorder (PTSD) was coined as a diagnostic term after WWII, to a broader recognition of the potent impact of conflict and disasters on social and societal wellbeing (Meyer, 2013). The mass displacement of Cambodians between 1975 and 1979, many of whom later emigrated and came into contact with mental health services in their countries of refuge, prompted the first significant recognition of the MHPSS needs of refugees. By 1988, a critical mass of ad hoc observations led to a high-level meeting between the UN, INGOs and the Thai government to address the deteriorating wellbeing of camp-based refugees in Thailand (Mollica et al., 1993). One of the primary factors that drove greater attention to MHPSS in humanitarian response was increasingly long-term displacement in chronic crisis contexts. Crises in the 1990s, particularly following the breakup of the former Yugoslavia, drew critical attention to MHPSS needs and highlighted the need for their inclusion in humanitarian response. Nevertheless, such initiatives lacked consistent guidance and remained disorganised (Abramowitz & Kleinman, 2008). Despite the continued application of the principle of 'Do No Harm' in humanitarian work, as one of the foundational elements of medical ethics (Mackenzie et al., 2007), the distancing of mental health from the medical model has often also resulted in a distancing of medical practice from its ethical frameworks.

MHPSS is now widely recognised as a vital and cross-cutting element of humanitarian response (Alonso et al., 2014; Jones et al., 2009; Meyer, 2013; Wessells & van Ommeren, 2008). The World Health Organization's (WHO) Mental Health Action Plan elevated this issue on the health agenda in 2013, while, according to the 2016 Global Burden of Disease Studies, mental health is now the leading cause of disability globally (Whiteford, Ferrari & Degenhard, 2016). The resultant increases in allocated funding have led to the inclusion of MHPSS in projects across a variety of crisis responses, from the 2010 Haitian and 2015 Nepali earthquakes, to the mass displacement of Syrians during the country's civil war, and more recently of much of the population of Mosul, Iraq. Mental health ethics have developed in parallel, often in reaction to the complex situations faced in emergency settings. A Psychosocial Working Group was established in 2003, while recognition of the many questionable 'psychosocial' activities imposed on survivors of the 2004 Indian Ocean Tsunami led to the establishment of an IASC task force in 2005 (Opaku & Biswas, 2014). This concerted effort resulted in the development and dissemination of a set of guidelines for MHPSS interventions in emergency contexts in 2007, in an attempt to define ethical standards of practice for the field. It is notable that one of the six core principles of MHPSS interventions named in these guidelines is IHR (IASC, 2007).

Intersection of Clinical Work and Theoretical Frameworks

As field practitioners and humanitarian health professionals, we must define our goals in order to assess the fit of theoretical frameworks and approaches underpinning implementation at both individual and programmatic levels in a variety of settings. While wrestling with the theoretical applicability of a specific framework for service delivery may seem to many of our clinical colleagues far from the practical task of sitting with a patient, in reality these conceptual issues affect not only the implementation of programmes, but also concerns related to the sustainability of initiatives, and the degree of their acceptability to the recipients of a service. In doing so, conceptual issues directly impact the effectiveness of mental healthcare.

This framing ultimately has trickle-down effects on clinical decision-making. Given the realities of humanitarian work, we must accept the necessity of compromise and that 'less than ideal' is often the default setting. Herein lies one of the shortcomings of the IHR approach in emergency contexts: from an individual human rights perspective, complete treatment should aim to achieve a state of total, holistic wellbeing, as defined by WHO (1946). However, the resources and time needed to achieve such a state in an individual who has experienced trauma, and who continues to live in a state of uncertainty, would necessarily preclude the treatment of many of their compatriots (and in some cases, may be entirely impossible until greater contextual stability has been achieved). In contrast, the decision to treat as many individuals as possible so as to achieve a level of functionality, thus serving a wider pool of those in need, follows a PG-driven approach. However, the ethics of such a triage-driven style of intervention hinges on the assumption that further services will be accessible once the situation stabilises and national mental healthcare systems are (re-) established.

Not infrequently, funding imperatives mean that original programmatic goals may be redefined in order to appear more appealing to donors. Smaller-scale specialised MHPSS organisations and local community-based organisations (CBOs) that do not have the influential capacity with donors that larger INGOs do are particularly susceptible to this 'branding' issue. There is a practical moral dilemma at play here, as service providers see the absolute need for MHPSS services, while recognising the reality that certain recipient groups are more appealing to donors than others. In the case of MHPSS, there is a tension when field staff are convinced of the value of treating one group, while a proposal focused on another group may be perceived as more readily fundable. There is often a circular relationship between how programmatic or headquarters staff may present a project, and how field and clinical staff leverage their power to influence how the organisation's work at a project level is perceived internally.

Resources will almost always be insufficient relative to population needs, which raises the recurrent question of who should be prioritised for treatment. A decision might be made to prioritise individuals with the lowest level of functionality, making the argument that they would benefit most from treatment. Alternatively, decisions could centre a community-bolstering approach. Much like the analogy of a flight attendant instructing an individual to engage their own oxygen mask prior to aiding others, such an approach aims to prioritise those best able to provide care and support to others, thus amplifying treatment impact, particularly in high-risk settings where a programme may have to close unexpectedly. A plethora of decisions, stemming from these often-divergent value stances, highlight how acknowledging the appropriateness and shortcomings of IHR- and PG-based approaches enables clinicians to recognise when a particular concession may be an unacceptable compromise, undermining the desire for client-focused goals.

This is where the designation of 'vulnerability' is engaged: a conceptual framework based on a very particular cultural and value-driven point of view. Vulnerability as a means to direct humanitarian programming emerged in the wake of World War One. British NGOs deliberately publicised their work providing food aid to German schoolchildren, as it was felt that programmes that served adult German men would be considered unacceptable by the British public (Davey, Borton & Foley, 2013). Children were perceived as both innocent and inherently vulnerable, and therefore 'deserving' of support.

Vulnerability, however, is an amorphous concept and definitions vary. Although more complex and relevant frameworks for vulnerability assessment have been developed (notably the Vulnerability Assessment Framework (VAF) in Jordan in 2015), current designations often still opt for what at first glance may seem to be an intuitive prioritisation: children, the elderly, female-headed households, and the like. Designating 'vulnerability' is, in effect, a value judgement of who is more deserving of help. Human rights, and the individualistic focus they inspire, when applied to our clinical decision-making, can overlook cultural roles and systems of care-taking. We have seen male clients respond very well to mental health interventions, and then bring the knowledge they gained back to their homes, positively impacting the whole family; an outcome that could be lost if adult men were designated insufficiently vulnerable to warrant intervention.

'Vulnerability' comes to the fore when deciding whom to serve or prioritise as it provides a measuring tool within the IHR framework with which to make decisions 'ethically', even if this still remains a value judgement, originating from an individualistic cultural perspective (Graz, 2003).

The prominent example in our work of the pressure to shift away from a focus on the provision of services to men, particularly those of fighting age in conflict settings, unless subject to a Countering Violent Extremism (CVE) rationale, and instead to base interventions around children or female-headed households, results in one of two outcomes. First, such men are no longer a 'target' under the terms of the funded project, undeniably ignoring their right to be considered in terms of their individual needs and vulnerabilities. Secondly, they continue to be included, but become the unseen beneficiaries, as the media and broader conversations focus on more 'acceptable' recipients. This is ethically objectionable as it denies the opportunity to raise awareness and to realise a wider public good as the result of treating those most frequently seen as perpetrators rather than victims. A CVE justification would shift towards the focus to men, and by contrast arguably employs a greater PG perspective. However, the CVE angle as a motivator for humanitarian interventions generates alternative grey areas, as providing treatment to help someone recover from terror differs fundamentally from the provision of treatment in the hope that this will prevent them from committing acts of terrorism, due in part to underlying assumptions about the potential future actions of the target group.

With the use of a composite case study, we aim to exhibit the necessity of identifying an approach (IHR or PG), and demonstrate, particularly for the benefit of other 'field'-based practitioners, that it is worthwhile to make this distinction clearly and to advocate for the best programme orientation for our clients.

Composite Case Study

The following composite case study represents many of the common themes we have seen in our clients. Names and details have been altered or amalgamated to preserve confidentiality, but the circumstance reflects field realities. We will cover the clinical decision-making and prioritisation typical within either an IHR or a PG approach.

Mohammad is a 47-year-old man, married to Fatima (38), with three children, Ahmad (14), Leila (8), and Mirium (5). The family is from a village near Damascus, Syria. Mohammad (high-school educated) owned a shop, which was doing well before the war; they lived in their own house and had a car. The two older children were in school.

When tensions started to rise in 2012 the village became restive, and shelling and open conflict in the streets became frequent. Mohammad's shop was heavily damaged and he was detained and questioned several times; on one occasion, he was held for several days. His family did not know where he was and Fatima was terrified. After he returned he refused to speak about what happened, but he had marks all over his body from beatings. Finally, he stopped going to work.

Eventually the conflict became so intense that the family could not safely leave the house and struggled to get food. The malnourishment during this time had an impact on Mirium's early development and she began to frequently fall ill. In early 2014, the family decided they needed to leave and went to stay with relatives in a more rural area. In 2015, the town that they were staying in was shelled. Mohammad's wife and son were outside at the time and his son was injured.

After this, the family decided to seek asylum in Jordan. They came to Zaatari refugee camp, but after eight months became frustrated with the lack of protection from the extreme weather, and the lack of privacy provided for Fatima.

The family left the camp and moved into an illegal apartment in the city of Zarqa, Jordan. The conditions were difficult, and Mohammad had no legal right to work, so Ahmad left school and began working illegally in a machine shop to earn enough money for rent and food.

Now, his parents notice that Ahmad has become quiet and withdrawn., He keeps getting into fights with other boys in the area, and has begun talking about returning to Syria to fight. Leila, who was attending school, was teased badly by the other children for being Syrian and now refuses to go back. She has developed night-time enuresis and often wakes in the night crying.

Mohammad has become increasingly despondent, sleeping or staying in the dark bedroom most of the day. Once an energetic, humorous man, he has begun having fits of rage, often hitting Fatima and sometimes Ahmad as well. Fatima feels isolated and says she spends all day crying and cannot manage her children's needs. She feels guilty when they ask her for anything and becomes irritable with them. She cannot hold Mirium, who continues to be ill and has started fussing more often, and often leaves her to cry. After each interaction with her children she feels even more guilty and hopeless. The family does not talk about their time in Syria because it is too painful for Mohammad to remember what happened to him and what they have lost.

One day Fatima meets another woman who suggests that she take Leila to an MHPSS centre in the area that provides services for children and adults. Fatima arrives and completes an initial assessment, describing the changes she has seen in her family.

How Each Framework Would Have Impacted Clinical Decision-making for this Family

Individual Human Rights

Determining an intervention for this family from an IHR approach, the practitioner would look at each person eligible for treatment as an individual unit, with a right to health and wellbeing. In most programmes, it would be difficult to commit to treating all five family members, thus the programme's decision-making would be guided by prioritisation according to functional impairment and vulnerability. Vulnerability, at its core, is a protection category; however, it is used across the humanitarian and development fields to determine an individual or group's level of risk and access to services (Graz, 2003). There are a number of formats for vulnerability assessments, and many organisations develop their own, either officially or from within the organisational culture. However, most are guided by assumptions related to gender ('women are more vulnerable than men'), age ('children and the elderly are more vulnerable') and special groups ('those affected by poverty, illness or who belong to ethnic, religious or social minorities should be prioritised'), as formalised in the 2011 Age, Gender and Diversity Policy (Meyer, 2013). For the purpose of this case study, we have opted to use this framework.

Using this framework, the children would be targeted, particularly Leila and Ahmad since they are out of school, along with Fatima as a 'woman at risk' (i.e. exposed to domestic violence in the country of asylum). Since Ahmad is a minor who is not attending school, is engaged in child labour, and is at risk of joining an armed group, his vulnerability would be considered high, and he would be prioritised for individual or group therapy. Leila might be brought into a children's psychosocial group to increase her socialisation and to teach her basic coping skills to help manage her symptoms. Fatima could be selected for a woman's therapeutic group, which would provide her with social support and psycho-education, as well as information on how to manage her symptoms and help her children with their own. She may also be offered additional individual therapy depending on her assessed level of trauma and/or depression. As an adult man who is not a single parent and without a clear physical disability or a known history of torture, Mohammad is likely to be the last family member to receive treatment, despite his history of detention and impaired functioning.

This framework attempts to ensure that the family members who are more likely to be disenfranchised are able to access treatment, based on the assumption that they a) may require it more due to their vulnerability, and b) may have more difficulty accessing such treatment. This could be a useful metric if Mohammad, as the patriarch, is resistant to the family accessing services due to a need to control his family as his life spins out of control (a common response in this context), or due to the perceived social stigma of requiring mental health support. It is important to note the individuals with pre-existing serious mental illness are considered particularly vulnerable and would receive priority for treatment (Mollica et al., 2004; WHO, 2013).

Thus, in designating intervention priorities for this family from an individual rights-based perspective, guided by prioritisation according to supposed levels of vulnerability, a practitioner would likely bring the two older children into treatment and perhaps Fatima as well. Only if resources allowed, might Mohammad also be considered for treatment.

Public Good

In contrast, a PG approach may lead a practitioner to assess for whom treatment could be used to leverage the greatest impact for the family as a whole, and perhaps even the wider community. In the case of a patriarchal culture boasting strong family systems, treating Mohammad directly, and the resultant reduction in household violence from such treatment (if efficacious), would be a higher priority. Our clinical experience in the Middle East and North Africa (MENA) region has led us to the conclusion that due to intra-familial power dynamics, and those of wider social systems, the treatment of a father often results in the greatest change within a family. Men take leadership over their family's wellbeing. As such, when a husband or father has undergone treatment that he found to be beneficial, he will frequently encourage his wife or other family members to engage in treatment, or to practice new, effective coping strategies at home. This contrasts with the common pattern of a husband or father who has not experienced such treatment, and is actively discouraging of a wife or family member engaging in treatment either due to perceived shame and stigma, or because it draws an individual away from family duties at home. In some instances, men have become enthusiastic about the new skills that they have learned, and have started to facilitate healthier practices in their homes. These practices do not require long-term specialist support; we see them take the form of regular walks, grounding (returning to the 'here and now'), or breathing exercises when a family member experiences anxiety.

Furthermore, the current evidence base for trauma treatment in children demonstrates that MHPSS work that supports the stabilisation of the parents or caregivers is significantly more effective than work directly targeting children in distress (Aisenberg & Ell, 2005). Thus, work with Mohammad and Fatima to alleviate their symptoms and develop healthier coping strategies will likely have a wider impact on the functioning of their children. Providing psycho-education (e.g. teaching parents about the symptoms that they are seeing in their children and how to help their children to manage) can be highlighted. Attendance at a parents group to provide such information in a normalising environment would be recommended, along with possible additional therapeutic group support for Fatima to help her build a social support system. A potential final focus of treatment could be inclusion in an adolescent support group for Ahmad, which would allow him to build healthy relationships and coping skills, with the goal of reducing his feelings of powerlessness and aggression.

Beyond the family, a GPG perspective allows for the programmatic targeting of community members who will have greater influence on stigma reduction and the provision of increased social and community support (Stuart, 2014). When it comes to mental health, stigma is a powerful barrier not only to accessing services, but to a commitment to treatment and recovery, even in those already receiving services (Cameron, 2014). Notably for MHPSS work in humanitarian response, particularly in situations of civil conflict or displacement, social support is vital to recovery (IASC, 2010). Prioritising the engagement of community or religious leaders in psycho-education or treatment sessions expands the awareness and acceptance of MHPSS work within a community, and can have a significant impact on the effectiveness of outreach work, treatment and wider social support for more vulnerable individuals. We recognise similar multi-component approaches with other GPG-framed public health issues, such as HIV interventions, which incorporate both treatment and educational campaigns.

In summary, using a PG approach allows for a broader interpretation of vulnerability in the case of Mohammad and his family, wherein the vulnerability and suffering of all members of the family can be acknowledged, and decision-making is directed to increase the stability of the overall family system. Thus, targeting Mohammad himself, rather than his wife or children, could be more easily justified by the clinician as an entry point to ultimately improve the status of the entire family. Adopting a GPG approach in this instance would allow us to think differently about who to target, and how to allocate our resources, emphasising the key points of impact in the family or community, with the intention of amplifying the outcome of the intervention.

Advantages and Disadvantages of the IHR Approach

Since 1994, and following the popularisation of the phrase 'rights-based approach to development' (Rights and Humanity, 1994), the individual human rights-based approach has demonstrated a particular utility with disenfranchised groups such as those living with severe mental illness.

'Beneficiaries' in their many forms are not passive recipients of our goodwill. This has been repeatedly demonstrated to the authors during numerous interactions with patients in the Middle East, where the populace of middle-income countries in particular are often well-informed and vocalise their opinions regarding from whom they may or may not be willing to receive assistance. Perceptions of hypocrisy between an organisation's stated goals and the political motivations of donors can complicate an individual's confidence in the services they are receiving. This is all the more important in our field, due to the trust and development of relationships required in MHPSS treatment, which is vital for a successful intervention and outcome. If an organisation declares its intention to realise human rights, but then does not – or cannot – act to do so, beyond a very narrow definition, this can erode a patient's trust in their clinician's ability or interest in doing what they say they will.

A rights-based approach to the delivery of humanitarian mental healthcare has an ethical advantage in that it can redress to some extent the significant power imbalance between provider and recipient. If enacted thoroughly, a rights-based approach can recalibrate this dynamic, by enforcing a process of accountability for the person or organisation fulfilling the right, and promoting agency on the part of the individual who seeks to realise their rights. However, individuals may still struggle to access the services available, as the steps involved in navigating complex systems (e.g. registration, paperwork, and in-person attendance) can be overwhelming, while structures for redress are few and often challenging to access. Therefore, we must accept that, in reality, many barriers remain even when services exist, and as such, providers have a duty to continue to improve the accessibility of their programmes.

Notably, human rights-based approaches have been described as 'anti-state' (Darcy, 2004), and humanitarian MHPSS providers must consider this as they endeavour to avoid the creation of parallel health structures, and to consider the long-term and post-crisis needs in affected regions. IHR elevates the rights of the individual above the primacy of the state, such that attainment of the right is the priority, without regard for the identity of the provider – whether the state or otherwise. IHR also encourages agency of the part of the 'receiver', entitling them to advocate for the full realisation of their rights. Therefore, defining the duty bearer is a prerequisite to the fulfilment of any individual right, followed by the need to hold accountable either state (e.g. Ministry of Health) or non-state (e.g. CBOs/INGOs, local ruling powers) actors. Any attempt to undermine or bypass state bodies, whether perceived or actual, in order to ensure that IHRs are recognised may have negative repercussions during the post-crisis phase if the state has been discredited by such an approach.

A more sinister fear is that couching an intervention in the language of human rights sets the stage for an incremental shift away from the central humanitarian principle of impartiality – a commitment to assist individuals foremost on the basis of their degree of need – towards the 'delivery' of rights as justification for political interventionism.

Finally, given the culturally thorny nature of emergency mental health, humanitarian organisations may find that they need to choose between access and advocacy. When stigma or other socio-cultural or political issues prevail, governments may obstruct or deny access, or potential clients may choose not to seek treatment due to fear. Where a state abuses its citizens, and will deny access to an organisation providing services if they identify these transgressions, how can such an organisation claim to a commitment to human rights if it says nothing as a way to remain in service? Similarly, but at the opposite end of this spectrum, the authors have experienced situations where permissions to operate have been denied unless the organisation can guarantee to offer a service to *all* those in need, despite resource limitations. This is a particularly sensitive issue in situations where refugees have overwhelmed the already fragile health systems of host nations. Host governments cannot be accused of failing to represent the right of their citizens to obtain such healthcare services. Nonetheless, this application of IHR then denies services to any of those in need by requiring an impossible commitment on behalf of the organisation offering the service. Perhaps dialogue between host nations and organisations could be rendered more constructive with the use of an alternative operational framework, namely that treating those most at risk of suffering from severe mental distress, or treating those most able to then provide care for others, is beneficial to society in a wider sense.

Advantages and Disadvantages of the Public Good Approach

As crises become more protracted (Spiegel et al., 2010) and commentators continue to call for the seamless transition of emergency aid into development assistance, so too have elements of humanitarian healthcare shifted from a focus on immediate needs to the adoption of longer-term perspectives. This is recognisable as language regarding resilience or intergenerational trauma, once confined within specialist circles, becomes more present in the broader humanitarian lexicon. The GPG framework, which incorporates the strengthening of health systems and a focus on the wider health sector, along with raising public awareness, also aligns with this trend.

While an IHR approach may fit better with development-oriented programmes, where national systems are already in place and accessible, in situations of widespread trauma exposure where resource access is restricted, GPG may offer a more pragmatic approach. Particularly with the broadening of the mental health field to include less specialised psychosocial (PSS) interventions, a PG framework may make more sense as it more easily incorporates activities aimed at the wider community and the repair of the social fabric. The increasing use of community-based trauma-centred MHPSS interventions for reconciliation and peace-building, as well as a desire to address the intergenerational transmission of trauma, are also more easily approached and funded by employing a PG perspective (Abramowitz & Kleinman, 2008). In this way, a PG framework allows for the incorporation of preventative measures as well as treatment and recovery.

The number of non-state actors fulfilling global health governance roles is on the rise, with the influence of the WHO, other UN agencies, and INGOs well recognised (Gartner, 2012). However, unlike states, non-state actors engaged in health governance lack the authority to directly demand funding from a citizenry (i.e. in the form of taxation) (Smith et al., 2003). Thus, a constant need to fundraise restricts the implementation capacity of non-state actors. With this in mind, the GPG framework has been seen as a way to supplement public interest and available resources. However, a shortcoming of the GPG approach in relation to MHPSS remains the observation that fear and empathy and other such emotions are more difficult to elicit in the case of mental health: the 'invisible illness'. Complicating this is the pervasiveness of stigma, recognisable not only in recipient communities but also among donors (Stuart, 2014). As a first stumbling block, public support for mental health programming as a global public good is difficult to generate, and opting to utilise fear – as evident in CVE-derived approaches – raises its own complicated ethical issues.

A GPG perspective allows for a focus on the destabilising effect of widespread post-trauma reactions – such as increased arousal and aggression, or isolation and depression, which strain the social fabric, decrease individual and community functioning, and delay societal recovery post-disaster or conflict – with the aim of promoting national stability and facilitating international security. Increasingly visible in recent times is the way in which humanitarian MHPSS as a global public good has been re-framed in the language of 'countering violent extremism', which has received greater attention from American and European donors. The restricted scope of CVE is such that these initiatives fail to capture the full diversity of MHPSS activities that are required in the wake of a humanitarian crisis. The limited purview of CVE initiatives, alongside self-evident ethical concerns for the potential branding of all recipients of MHPSS support as prospective terrorists, should serve to caution us from shifting towards a GPG framework at the expense of IHR. As such, a key question remains that must be carefully considered in each context: what might be the impact on clinical programming and decision-making if re-envisioned to serve the public good as opposed to individual human rights?

Summary

The disconnect between academic research and field implementation is frequently criticised within the humanitarian sector. In our experience, field practitioners instinctively malign the slow pace of academia as irrelevant to the process of emergency implementation. Their impatience, while understandable given the practicalities of their work, is regrettably short-sighted. Field clinicians ignore at their peril considerations such as the theoretical frameworks explored in this chapter.

Most modern humanitarian programming follows practices that derive from an individual human rights (IHR) tradition. While the field has benefited from this approach, as it provides a platform to advocate for the provision of essential services to all constituents, it can become unwieldy in emergency settings. Problems arising in situ can give rise to shorthand frameworks, such as over-simplified vulnerability frameworks. Thus, we caution against the instinctive application of IHR, particularly in relation to MHPSS. In this chapter, we have contrasted IHR and PG perspectives in relation to MHPSS programming, and have explored the ethical challenges and implications associated with both approaches. Our aim in using a composite case study to illustrate these decisions was to bridge the divide between theory and practice, and between academic and practitioner, by demonstrating that irrespective of the extent to which either party chooses to engage with the realities of the other, the effects of organisational value orientation will inevitably trickle – quite rapidly and tangibly – down to individual recipients of a service.

The PG approach provides a rationale for broader action and for interventions that can utilise scarce resources in order to reinforce existing structures for health and social support. We have argued for a pragmatic, mindful selection of appropriate elements from IHR and GPG, and against a blind attachment to strict disciplinary ideologies. Examining the downstream effects of implementing either framework, particularly on those receiving services, can help us not only to make the best decisions, but also to understand how we set out upon paths that lead us to make specific choices in humanitarian practice. There remains a clear responsibility to understand, question and refine the value system(s) we uphold.

Declaring oneself a member of a human rights organisation, or fundraising in accordance with a mandate to act in the public good, naturally affects the values and actions that shape organisational practice. Such distinctions also affect donors (both individual and governmental), who may have complex reasons for their engagement with, or avoidance of, concepts such as human rights. However, central to our argument, and our experience as field clinicians, is the concrete effect that this positioning has on the clinical interaction between therapist and client.

This effect is not only evidenced in the alternating treatment choices outlined in the case study above, but also through our experience of clients' reactions to our work. Their perspective should be a key consideration in any modern humanitarian response, but it is of particular importance in relation to MHPSS, where recovery is predicated upon engagement and reciprocal relationships which transcend the inadequate distinction between active giver and passive receiver. Those individuals who present to the clinics where we work judge our services not only in accordance with their efficacy but also their assumed motivations. We must be clear about exactly what these are.

References

Abramowitz, S & Kleinman, A (2008), Humanitarian intervention and cultural translation: a review of the IASC Guidelines on Mental Health and Psychosocial Support in Emergency Settings. *Intervention*. Vol. 6 (3): 219–27.

Aisenberg, E & Ell, K (2005), Contextualizing community violence and its effects: an ecological model of parent–child interdependent coping. *Journal of Interpersonal Violence*. Vol. 20 (7): 855–71.

Alonso, J, Chatterji, S, He, Y & Kessler, RC (2014), Burden of illness. Pp. 11–26. In: Okpaku, SO (ed.), *Essentials of global mental health*. Cambridge: Cambridge University Press.

Cameron, E (2014), Internalized stigma. Pp. 72–7. In: Okpaku, SO (ed.), *Essentials of global mental health*. Cambridge: Cambridge University Press.

Darcy, J (2004), Human rights and humanitarian action: a review of the issues. HPG Background Paper prepared for the workshop on Human Rights and Humanitarian Action convened by the IASC Sub-Working Group, Geneva. London: Humanitarian Policy Group, ODI.

Davey, E, Borton, J & Foley, M (2013), *A history of the humanitarian system: Western origins and foundations*. London: Humanitarian Policy Group, Overseas Development Institute.

Gartner, D (2012), Global public goods and global health. *Duke Journal of Comparative and International Law*. Vol. 22 (303): 303–18.

Graz, L (2003), A question of vulnerability: theory into practice. The Magazine of the International Red Cross and Red Crescent Movement.

IASC (2007), *IASC Guidelines on Mental Health and Psychosocial Support in Emergency Settings*. Geneva: Inter-Agency Standing Committee.

IASC Reference Group for Mental Health and Psychosocial Support in Emergency Settings (2010), *Mental health and psychosocial support in humanitarian emergencies: what should humanitarian health actors know?* Geneva: Inter-Agency Standing Committee.

Jones, L, Asare, JB, El Masri, M, Mohanraj, A, Sherief, H & van Ommeren, M (2009), Severe mental disorders in complex emergencies. *The Lancet*. Vol. 374 (9690): 654–61.

Mackenzie, C, McDowell, C & Pittaway, E (2007), Beyond 'do no harm': the challenge of constructing ethical relationships in refugee research. *Journal of Refugee Studies*. Vol. 20 (2): 299–319.

Mazower, M (2004), The strange triumph of Human Rights, 1933–1950. *The Historical Journal*. Vol. 47 (2): 379–98.

Meyer, S (2013), *UNHCR's mental health and psychosocial support for persons of concern: global review*. Geneva: United Nations High Commissioner for Refugees Policy Development & Evaluation Service.

Mollica, RF, Cardozo, BL, Osofsky, HJ, Raphael, B, Ager, A & Salama, P (2004), Mental health in complex emergencies. *The Lancet*. Vol. 364 (9450): 2058–67.

Mollica, RF, Donelan, K, Tor, S, Lavelle, J, Elias, C, Frankel, M & Blendon, RJ (1993), The effect of trauma and confinement on functional health and mental health status of Cambodians living in Thailand–Cambodia border camps. *JAMA*. Vol. 270 (5): 581–6.

Moon, S, Røttingen, JA & Frenk, J (2017), Global public goods for health: weaknesses and opportunities in the global health system. *Health Economics, Policy and Law*. Vol. 12 (2): 195–205.

Okpaku, SO & Biswas, S (2014), History of global mental health. Pp. 1–10. In: Okpaku, SO (ed.), *Essentials of global mental health*. Cambridge: Cambridge University Press.

Padmavati, R (2014), Stigmatization and exclusion. Pp. 85–92. In: Okpaku, SO (ed.), *Essentials of global mental health*. Cambridge: Cambridge University Press.

Rights and Humanity (1994), A rights based approach to social development: what does it have to offer? Report of a Rights and Humanity Workshop, London, 21 April 1994, in preparation for the World Summit for Social Development, Copenhagen, Denmark, March 1995. IS/Dev/Publ.8/1994.

Smith, RD, Beaglehole, R, Woodward, D & Drager, N (eds) (2003), *Global public goods for health: a health economic and public health perspective*. Oxford: Oxford University Press.

Smith, RD & MacKellar, L (2007), Global public goods and the global health agenda: problems, priorities and potential. *Globalization and Health* 3(9).

Spiegel, PB, Checchi, F, Colombo, S & Paik, E (2010), Health-care needs of people affected by conflict: future trends and changing frameworks. *The Lancet*. Vol. 375 (9711): 341–5.

Stuart, H (2014), Definition and process of stigma. Pp. 78–84. In: Okpaku, SO (ed.), *Essentials of global mental health*. Cambridge: Cambridge University Press.

Wessells, M, van Ommeren, M (2008), Developing inter-agency guidelines on mental health and psychosocial support in emergency settings. *Intervention*. Vol. 6 (3): 199–218.

Whiteford, H, Ferrari, A & Degenhard, L (2016), Global burden of disease studies: implications for mental and substance use disorders. *Health Affairs*. Vol. 35 (6): 1114–20.

WHO (1948), *Constitution of the World Health Organization*. Basic Documents. Forty-fifth Edition, Supplement, October 2006. Geneva: World Health Organization.

WHO (2013), *Mental health action plan 2013–2020*. Geneva: World Health Organization.

13 | ETHICS OF CULTURAL CONCEPTS AND CONFLICTS SURROUNDING DISCLOSURE OF GENDER-BASED VIOLENCE IN HUMANITARIAN SETTINGS

Ayesha Ahmad

Introduction: Gender-based Violence, Cultural Concepts, and Conflict Contexts

Historic and contemporary examples of atrocities that have occurred in areas such the DRC, Rwanda, Afghanistan, and Bosnia, and current events in Iraqi Kurdistan and Syria, demand humanitarian intervention for the prevention of and as a response to sexual violence during conflict. For example, I recall a recent reflection from a Congolese medical doctor, a woman who had trained and undergone her medical education in South Africa, a country that has some of the highest rates of sexual violence in the world. She had travelled to the Democratic Republic of the Congo (DRC) and was treating victims of war. Many of these victims were men, and they were suffering from chronic and atrocious injuries related to sexual violence that had been perpetuated man to man as a systematic act of using *rape as a weapon of war* during the decades-long conflict. She says she simply did not know how to help them; there was no training, no protocols, and very little awareness among humanitarian healthcare workers that men were also victims of sexual violence during conflict. Her response was to undertake an MSc in Global Health and Development, and to write a thesis entitled *The Invisible Man: Challenges to healthcare responses to male victims of sexual violence in the DRC.*

This is how I came to have this conversation with Dr Vanessa Okito Wedi (whose chapter follows on from this), as she recalled her experience during one of our supervision meetings. So pressing was the need to both help and know how to help that she decided to forge the way ahead herself. Dr Wedi's discussion will continue in the next chapter and the rest of this chapter will critically highlight the nuances in disclosing gender-based violence during humanitarian crises.

Disclosure of Gender-Based Violence (GBV) is paramount for the evidence base on the prevalence of GBV as well as the individual and collective response. However, there are significant barriers that inhibit the disclosure of GBV. Some of these barriers are structural or cultural, some may be a coping strategy to protect a woman both physically and psychologically. These all invoke ethical issues related to health inequalities and injustice yet also an ethical issue of whether greater accommodation is needed in the humanitarian response to GBV to offer alternative screenings and assessments for identifying GBV-related health needs without mandating either a verbal or written disclosure.

Furthermore, the global context of GBV and specifically GBV during humanitarian crises reveal staggering statistics regarding affected individuals – who are vulnerable, for reasons that will be discussed during this chapter, to being left alone when requiring treatment, help, and support. This is the overarching ethical premise for this chapter, namely, that when considering the ethical challenges of disclosure of GBV there should also be recognition that there are many victims who remain silent or who are silenced.

Ethical Considerations of Conceptualising GBV During Humanitarian Crises

The ethical issues related to treating and responding to GBV during humanitarian crises fundamentally have their roots in the conceptual framework that embodies the context of GBV. Understanding GBV requires 'understanding the roots of unequal gender treatment, and thus the cultural setting of a community' (Colombini, 2002, p. 167). In terms of how humanitarian organisations are to respond, the need to factor in complex social phenomena to an intervention that is primarily responding to an acute emergency or crisis, and that cuts across cultural boundaries, requires interdisciplinary and multi-sectoral approaches.

In the conduct of academic field research in post-disaster and post-conflict settings, there is a challenging overplay between the role of gathering and analysing data and the real-time nature of the violence in the lived experience of the participants. GBV signifies structural gender inequalities, and disclosures of GBV may pose significant risk for the individual and at times the researcher or practitioner, and include disclosure of the identities of perpetrators from all aspects of society.

In this chapter, the nuances of cultural concepts and conflicts surrounding the disclosure of GBV in humanitarian settings will be unpacked and their bearing on ethical issues regarding the approach to GBV disclosures in humanitarian settings analysed.

Gender-based Violence: A Global Disaster?

Gender-based violence (GBV) is a global phenomenon and has remained a pressing public health issue since 1996 when declared so by the World Health Assembly. GBV has significant health consequences and thus it is vital that healthcare settings develop both preventative and responsive measures. GBV has a strong correlation with humanitarian crises, with both conflicts and disasters and often their overlap serving as foundations for increased incidences of GBV. Yet, GBV remains poorly responded to during humanitarian emergencies (Marsh and Purdin, 2007).

Since the World Health Assembly in 1996, gender-based violence has remained a public health issue. A predominant focus within GBV is violence towards women and girls (VAWG) but this form of GBV is by no means unique, and at times, the preventative and response efforts to VAWG obscure and polarise GBV towards men and boys.

An estimated one in three women experience one or multiple forms of GBV globally in their lifetime. Due to the stigma and lack of resources for strengthening women's rights and responding to GBV, there is significant underreporting. Similarly, as regards the response to GBV from health professionals, including humanitarian actors, which will be the primary focus for this chapter, dealing with GBV is challenging; it is continuously present yet elusive and difficult to treat within symptomatic and diagnostic clinical frameworks that have restricted application to social processes such as structural violence.

GBV occurs both in peace time and during humanitarian emergencies. In contexts of conflict, 'sexual and gender-based violence in armed conflicts lacks visibility and is not fully understood as it is often labelled as a woman-only issue. Its gendered nature extends beyond the actual period of conflict, into the period of rehabilitation and reconstruction, carrying with it many physical and psychological problems' (Colombini, 2002). In this sense, humanitarian health responses need to 'understand the roots of unequal gender treatment, and thus the cultural setting of a community becomes essential when dealing with the phenomenon of sexual violence' (ibid.). However, there is a tension, which in turn presents another ethical aspect, namely that there is a need to ensure that there are healthcare facilities for GBV victims. In other words, GBV needs to be framed as an area of healthcare, which, in the context of a humanitarian emergency where the saving of lives is prioritised and there is insufficient knowledge about the occurrence of GBV, is difficult to achieve. Furthermore, even when GBV is situated in healthcare frameworks, 'multi-dimensional and gender-sensitive healthcare' (ibid.) is needed, but this psychosocial approach transcends traditional approaches to health, where, it may be added, the patient bears the responsibility to consult with and disclose their symptoms to their healthcare provider. GBV, especially in cross-cultural settings during crises and traumatic events, presents a conceptual challenge, with consequences for harm if not adequately responded to, and thus presents grave ethical challenges.

Why Is GBV in Humanitarian Crises Becoming an Ethical Issue?

Given our enhanced understanding of disaster settings and the humanitarian crises that unfold, the kinds of situations that present vulnerabilities have also broadened. Considering disasters outside of the boundaries of an event means that other circumstances can now be included, such as migrant journeys, which refer to human experiences rather than the locale of specific events, although an event/s may be a trigger. This means that humanitarian responses to GBV are complex and sensitive.

Health facilities and guidelines lack awareness of the manifestation of GBV prior to, during, and in the aftermath of humanitarian crises. The consequences of GBV, left untreated, are long term and include chronic physical conditions and psychological effects. Responding to GBV in humanitarian crises requires the foresight of planning health systems and delivery from a sustainable and culturally appropriate public health and primary care vantage point. Tackling GBV is difficult because its social origins and presentation as a health issue further mean that multi-sectoral approaches are required – stigma, cultural values that reinforce unequal gender norms, and structural elements such as policy and legislation for the protection of GBV victims, must be treated too. A humanitarian response to GBV bears significant ethical weight for the immediate victim and future vulnerability to GBV.

Cultural Contexts of GBV

Gender refers to the 'socially constructed roles, behaviours, activities, and attributes that a given society considers appropriate for men and women' (WHO, 2017). Although there are comparable patterns globally of certain forms of GBV, such as VAWG, gender is not a universal object or category that can be assumed to be the same in all cultures. Furthermore, violence is also characterised by cultural variations. Violence is understood through narrative – it is a distinctly cultural process (Wood, 2007). The rhetoric of gender and of violence is translated through various mediums within a society. Such cultural processes create concepts and circumstances where an act of violence that is committed from a gender-based motivation will occupy certain 'symbols, ideas, or images' (Juergensmeyer, 2003). There is, then, a phenomenology attached to GBV that is inescapable for the victim and needs to be recognised by those operating in a therapeutic capacity, such as healthcare professionals.

The act of sexual violence against and murder of Ozgecan Aslan, a twenty-year-old woman returning home from college on a public bus in southern Turkey, was reflected on by the mother of the subsequently convicted rapist and murderer, twenty-six-year-old Ahmet Supho Altindoken. In a Turkish media article, she stated: 'No child is born a murderer, a thief, or a terrorist. Everyone is born an angel. There are many things behind what has turned him into this.' Such words may indeed be a veil to excuse the actions of her son, but, nevertheless, they present a complex experience of the cultural narration of GBV in a context that is subject to chronic conflict, ethnic tensions, prevailing ideas of honour and shame, and a refugee crisis following the conflict in neighbouring Syria.

In terms of Syria, soon after the conflict began, accounts of sexual violence chronicled the experiences of Syrian women and fears of sexual violence also created mass movements of refugees. In this arguably GBV crisis, humanitarian healthcare efforts needed to serve a population where disclosures of GBV carried significant risks and cultural expectations in respect to the way a raped woman, for example, would be perceived and treated.

Yet, in the World Health Organization guidelines for the medico-legal treatment of victims of sexual violence, culture is rarely mentioned. There are more references to culture in the context of obtaining specimens for the testing of sexually transmitted infections (STIs) than discussions of culture in terms of beliefs or practices that will shape the psychological trauma, risk and vulnerability, and decision-making about disclosure. For example, some suggested strategies and techniques for dealing with victims of sexual violence are to 'aim for an attitude of respectful, quiet professionalism within the boundaries of your patient's culture' and to 'maintain eye contact as much as is culturally appropriate' (WHO, 2005). There is no detailed or direct discussion of the way in which that culture impacts on disclosure, which presents an ethical issue given that healthcare providers have been identified as the professionals who victims of sexual violence are most likely to trust and disclose to, and who can play a unique role in facilitating disclosure (WHO, 2013).

The crux of the ethical issue in the cross-cultural humanitarian healthcare response is that in prioritising the facilitation of disclosure to obtain gateways for medico-legal responses and treatment, the choice to remain silent is negated. While there are efforts now to develop screening and assessment tools for identifying victims of sexual violence in cases of non-disclosure to enable access to healthcare, the wider ethical issue is that disclosure represents, to some extent, a further form of force. This is perhaps a narrative-based force in relation to revealing and exposing the internal, albeit in this case, the internal experience of suffering as well as, potentially, an intimate examination. The internal or private body, and mind, are compromised by physical and psychological needs that were caused, ultimately, by the perpetrator/s. From a cultural perspective, then, disclosure relates to bodily identity as well as beliefs surrounding the meaning of and representation of suffering in a certain context. The translation of cultural meanings of this understanding of disclosure is vulnerable to overlooked nuances of the victim's experience and the challenges of translating cultural bearings and burdens.

Sexual Violence During Conflict: Untold Traumas

Sexual violence is invisible unless disclosed by its victims, and disclosure is at the 'heart of the difficulty' regarding attempts to both respond to and prevent sexual violence during conflict (Alcorn, 2014). Stigma is recognised as a dominant factor in preventing disclosure.

The act of sexual violence during conflict represents another form or strategy of overpowering and capturing the enemy. The risks and consequences of sexual violence committed during conflict persist following both the physical act and any further threat – the aftermath of the humanitarian crisis resulting from sexual violence during conflict, then, is extensive and expands over contexts as well as beyond the immediate effects (Shanks and Schull, 2000).

Sexual violence as a systematic strategy of conflict exists in tandem with taboos and stigmas related to victims of sexual violence that pre-exist in the affected society during peacetime. A long-term aim of the perpetuation of sexual violence towards both men and women is to eradicate family and community bonds. Wartime rape as a weapon of war is a 'social act' that is 'marked by gendered power' (Kirby, 2012). The metaphorical meaning of the body, the gendered body, during conflict and in the aftermath of an act of sexual violence, transcends the medicalised form of the human body. This observation is critical for considering how to engage with *victims* of sexual violence during conflict who are subsequently *patients* in humanitarian medical clinics.

Humanitarian medical and healthcare professionals are, then, potential witnesses to the effects of human rights violations and war crimes. In the clinical treatment of a patient who has experienced sexual violence, there are ethical obligations towards the individual and the wider, collective society. The individual can play a role in contributing to the evidence base for bringing perpetrators of sexual violence during conflict to justice through the information that their medical examination and testimony can bring. The International Protocol on the Documentation and Investigation of Sexual Violence in Conflict, first published in 2014, is a training tool for humanitarian and other healthcare actors to ensure that all disclosures and medical examinations are handled so to allow them to be used as valid evidence. The importance of this evidence is underscored by a need to counteract impunity, both as a justice-based response to the suffering of victims and as a preventative measure against sexual violence during conflict. Disclosure, therefore, carries ethical weight, but there are many reasons why a victim of sexual violence may refuse to disclose.

Furthermore, interestingly, collecting data related to sexual violence in humanitarian emergencies is also part of the role of the humanitarian response to the health needs of survivors (Marsh et al., 2007). Humanitarian frameworks for disclosure, therefore, need to consider the ethical weight of the disclosure – the consequences and boundaries of sexual violence accounts and testimonies bear wider societal symbolisations than merely instrumentalising the clinical navigation of health needs. Even mental health in the context of trauma related to forms of GBV during all stages of conflict and humanitarian emergencies reflects potential space for addressing gender inequality, social transformation, and peace processes. However, is it the case that full disclosure of an experience of sexual violence is necessary as part of humanitarian interventions for the prevention of and response to GBV? The next section will look further at the meaning and representation of GBV disclosures during humanitarian emergencies, and the surrounding ethical discourse.

Autonomy, Narrative, and Silence

Psychological healing following trauma is typically centred around disclosure. The traumatic event needs to be recounted and the trauma narrative analysed and examined. The aim is for an individual to reconstruct their narrative. Disclosure of traumatic experiences is thus situated within a therapeutic framework. On the one hand, the therapeutic framework relates to clinical aspects, yet on the other hand, there is the transnational justice paradigm. Disclosure is a link between the clinical and the societal, which means that sexual violence features multiple ontologies and thus understanding of any disclosure must be aware of cultural concepts and conflicts involved in the disclosure decision-making.

In the following case scenario, a 35-year-old woman attends a medical clinic in a refugee camp complaining of headaches and stomach cramps. The woman is Kurdish and speaks Arabic, and the doctor is a humanitarian aid worker from Greece. The woman reached the refugee camp alone with her three children following exposure to the torture and killing of her journalist husband. During this time, she had also been raped in front of her children, but this was not disclosed at the initial consultation. The doctor observed her to be in a highly agitated state, and, following an abdominal examination, which was all clear, the woman began to weep and ask for tests without specifying which tests she was referring to. Due to the experience of the doctor in previous humanitarian settings dealing with patients who are refugees from war, she took the cue from the patient's behaviour that she was indeed referring to a pregnancy test.

The doctor faced an ethical challenge: if she suggested a pregnancy test, she knew her patient would refuse outright to consent because accepting the offer would amount to a form of disclosure. In this case, silence was imperative. The patient was widowed, and a pregnancy in the refugee camp would result in her being ostracised and potentially at risk of other forms of gender-based violence. Her brothers were also in the refugee camp. The implications for her honour, a culturally bound concept, as a pregnant rape victim, could result in her being killed or forced to commit suicide by the cultural expectations placed on rape victims.

Yet, from the doctor's perspective, the patient's consent, or assent, was crucial for the ethical conduct of the consultation. Furthermore, the doctor and the patient were dancing in an unspoken dialogue – the fear of pregnancy and the trauma of rape were present, yet absent. The woman was silenced by her cultural context, and she had not disclosed, but neither was she silent. Yet, in this case, the disclosure was denied by both the patient and the doctor. The doctor's ethical reflection on this was a fear that she was colluding in her patient's harmful cultural beliefs about her status as a rape victim. In parallel, though, by being mindful of the structural elements – the socio-cultural determinants – of the patient's silence, the doctor is enabling trust and protection for her patient. The dilemma of how to conduct the pregnancy test remained.

The doctor responded to the inherent and nuanced complexities of the cultural phenomenon of disclosing rape by offering a range of tests for a standardised and general health check, given that this was the patient's first clinical consultation since arriving at the refugee camp. Thus, the clinical consultation was geared around the non-disclosure of rape, but the diagnostic assessment of symptoms and the treatment protocols were focused and premised on disclosure.

Limitations on resources also present ethically problematic constraints for treating and caring for victims of sexual violence or other forms of GBV. For example, in a study investigating the prevalence of intimate partner violence (IPV) among women visiting healthcare centres in Palestinian refugee camps in Jordan, it was found that physical, emotional, sexual, and economic controlling behaviours by partners were reported by the participants (Al-Modallal et al., 2015). IPV also tends to occur more frequently during humanitarian emergencies than does wartime rape and sexual violence perpetuated by individuals outside of the home (Stark and Ager, 2011).

Understanding of such gender dynamics and vulnerabilities is necessary in the healthcare context for anticipating the nature of potential GBV disclosures, as well as the type of resources that are required. In the context of a refugee camp, with security conditions such as poor lighting and overcrowding, women are at heightened risk, and male companions provide protection from other forms of GBV.

Therefore, a disclosure of IPV to a healthcare provider in a refugee camp when safe relocation is not a viable option is ethically challenging.

After Disclosure: The Aftermath of Violence

The emergency nature of a humanitarian crisis creates a sense of urgency and finitude, and the sense that events such as conflict or other disasters are temporary. In this vein, and due to the acute physical consequences of various forms of GBV for both men and women, the humanitarian response, in virtue of the nature of a humanitarian intervention, is an immediate response. The legacy of GBV continues beyond bodily needs, and the psychological impact of atrocities such as GBV is still not fully understood. The phenomenological aspect of GBV is not integrated into the biomedical framing of GBV. Furthermore, in the context of humanitarian crises, GBV is not the only trauma that individuals will have been exposed to. Experiencing trauma during a humanitarian crisis when societal structures are breaking down, and there is displacement to other cross-cultural settings, places the trauma on a continuum. At this point, there is no *post*-trauma stage as the traumas continue to occur and be experienced.

Judith Herman, a clinical specialist in psychological trauma, reflects that the 'ordinary response to atrocities is to banish them from consciousness. Certain violations of the social compact are too terrible to utter aloud: this is the meaning of the word unspeakable.' She then adds that 'atrocities, however, refuse to be buried' (Herman, 2016). Any resultant disclosure, then, will be shaped by such psychological processes, and Herman (ibid.) further notes that 'people who have survived atrocities often tell their stories in a highly emotional, contradictory, and fragmented manner, which undermines their credibility'. The implications for an individual's attempt to disclose their physical or mental state are clear; in other words, this is a further ethical issue to be considered by humanitarian health actors in terms of defining expectations and understandings towards disclosures of GBV. It is not a clear-cut binary between non-disclosure and disclosure, and the nuances of this need further exploration especially when developing screening and assessment tools for treating victims of GBV in a humanitarian crisis.

In the context of conflict-related humanitarian emergencies, contemporary understandings of conflict refer to the identification 'new wars' (Kaldor, 2013). These are increasingly protracted conflicts, often related to other forms of humanitarian crises, such as natural disasters, and exhibit extreme forms of violence targeting civilians. Exposure to and witnessing of such violence, motivated by localised and cultural gender dynamics and structures, in turn impact on the intensity of trauma that is experienced. From a global mental health perspective, there is a greater understanding of the mental health burden on societies in low- and middle-income countries (LMICs), where the greatest majority of humanitarian emergencies are situated. In a survey of 998 households in the DRC, 67 percent of households reported incidents of conflict-related human rights abuses, such as forms of GBV against men and women; 41 percent met the symptom criteria for Major Depressive Disorder (MDD); and 50.1 percent met the symptom criteria for post-traumatic stress disorder (PTSD) (Johnson et al., 2010). At the time of developing mental health infrastructure and systems globally, especially in post-conflict rebuilding of societies, cultural and narrative expressions are important for contextualising humanitarian mental health, for example, among refugee or internally displaced populations.

Some critics of global mental health, though, have argued that 'because concepts such as Post-Traumatic Stress Disorder (PTSD) implicitly endorse a Western ontology and value system, their use in non-Western groups should be, at most, tentative' (Bracken et al., 1995). Thus, ethical consideration needs to be given to the very concepts and discourses of trauma that are used to respond to violence in wars and disasters before we can understand the content of a disclosure, especially because, for victims of violence, 'it is difficult to find a language that conveys fully and persuasively what one has seen' and for an individual to speak about their experience of violence is 'to invite the stigma that attaches to victims' (Herman, 2016). Trauma, or, in a wider scope, suffering, is culturally formed, and situated in language and identity, and is not a benign transferrable object that can be immediately transferred in a GBV protocol across humanitarian emergencies. There needs to be systematic and multi-factorial analysis and gender-oriented healthcare that is engaged with alternative discourses to biomedical and Western-oriented approaches to mental health.

Conclusion

This chapter represents a current recognition of the need to develop GBV-centred protocols for use in humanitarian emergencies by healthcare providers. Disclosure is a crucial element in the approach to both the health and legal response to GBV, and the role of justice, for example, can also play a role in therapeutic recovery for victims of war crimes such as rape as a weapon of war. Yet, disclosure of GBV presents significant ethical challenges and reflections on cultural concepts and conflicts that affect the way in which stigma or trauma, as well as barriers to healthcare, is shaped.

The importance of GBV has intensified with greater understanding of the nature of the humanitarian crises that result from disasters and conflict. Yet, there is a requirement for further understanding of the cultural concepts that are embedded in GBV and the pre-existing gender inequalities and societal traditions that impact on the prevalence of GBV and barriers to reporting.

Most significantly for this chapter is the ethical notion of ways to treat a victim of GBV, and the discussion needs to evolve with a dialogue between medicalised or health approaches to GBV, with the role of the healthcare provider as a crucial mediator and facilitator for disclosure of GBV, and wider humanistic discourses of society and suffering. Finally, the definition of disclosure is complex and tricky to formulate, and there may need to be a shift from prioritisation of the verbalisation of GBV, or, rather, speech, to other expressions of GBV, with adequate development and dissemination of training for humanitarian health actors to follow.

References

Alcorn, T. 2014. Responding to Sexual Violence in Armed Conflict. *The Lancet*, 383(9934), pp. 2034–2037.

Al-Modallal, H, Abu Zayed, I, Abujilban, S, Shehab, T and Atoum, M. 2015. Prevalence of Intimate Partner Violence Among Women Visiting Health Care Centers In Palestine Refugee Camps in Jordan. *Health Care for Women International*, 36(2), pp. 137–148.

Bracken, PJ, Giller, JE and Summerfield, D, 1995. Psychological Responses to War and Atrocity: The Limitations of Current Concepts. *Social Science & Medicine*, 40(8), pp. 1073–1082.

Colombini, M. 2002. Gender-Based and Sexual Violence Against Women During Armed Conflict. *Journal of Health Management*, 4(2), pp. 167–183.

Curran, SR, Shafer, S, Donato, KM and Garip, F. 2006. Mapping Gender and Migration in Sociological Scholarship: Is It Segregation or Integration? *International Migration Review*, 40(1), pp. 199–223.

Gerritsen, A, Bocquier, P, White, M, Mbacke, C, Alam, N, Beguy, D, Odhiambo, F, Sacoor, C, Dang Phuc, H, Punpuing, S and A Collinson, M. 2013. Health and Demographic Surveillance Systems: Contributing to an Understanding of the Dynamics in

Migration and Health. *Global Health Action*, 6(1), p. 21496.

Herman, JL. 2015. *Trauma and Recovery: The Aftermath of Violence--From Domestic Abuse to Political Terror.* Hachette UK.

Johnson, K, Scott, J, Rughita, B, Kisielewski, M, Asher, J, Ong, R and Lawry, L. 2010. Association of Sexual Violence and Human Rights Violations with Physical and Mental Health in Territories of the Eastern Democratic Republic of the Congo. *JAMA*, 304(5), pp. 553–562.

Juergensmeyer, M. 2003. The Religious Roots of Contemporary Terrorism. *The New Global Terrorism: Characteristics, Causes, Controls*, pp. 185–193.

Kaldor, M. 2013. *New and Old Wars: Organized Violence in a Global Era.* John Wiley & Sons.

Marsh, M, Purdin, S and Navani, S. 2006. Addressing Sexual Violence in Humanitarian Emergencies. *Global Public Health*, 1(2), pp. 133–146.

Padilla, MB, Del Aguila, EV and Parker, RG. 2007. Globalization, Structural Violence, and LGBT Health: A Cross-Cultural Perspective. In: *The Health of Sexual Minorities* (pp. 209–241). Springer US.

Shanks, L and Schull, MJ. 2000. Rape in War: The Humanitarian Response. *Canadian Medical Association Journal*, 163(9), pp. 1152–1156.

Stark, L and Ager, A. 2011. A Systematic Review of Prevalence Studies of Gender-Based Violence in Complex Emergencies. *Trauma, Violence, & Abuse*, 12(3), pp. 127–134.

Summerfield, D. 1999. A Critique of Seven Assumptions Behind Psychological Trauma Programmes in War-Affected Areas. *Social Science & Medicine*, 48(10), pp. 1449–1462.

Wood, JC. 2007. Conceptualizing cultures of violence and cultural change. In *Cultures of Violence* (pp. 79–96). Palgrave Macmillan, London.

World Health Organization. 2003. Guidelines for Medico-Legal Care of Victims of Sexual Violence.

World Health Organization. 2005. *Sexual and Gender Based Violence Guidelines.* World Health Organization.

World Health Organization. 2013. *Responding to Intimate Partner Violence and Sexual Violence Against Women: WHO Clinical and Policy Guidelines.* World Health Organization.

World Health Organization. 2017. *Gender Definition.* World Health Organization.

14 | THE INVISIBLE MAN: THE SHROUDING OF ETHICAL ISSUES RELATED TO SEXUAL VIOLENCE AGAINST MEN IN THE HUMANITARIAN RESPONSE IN THE DEMOCRATIC REPUBLIC OF CONGO

Vanessa Okito Wedi

Introduction

Sexual violence has been a pervasive feature of conflict throughout history. In the Democratic Republic Congo (DRC), sexual violence has been one of the most prolific weapons of the civil war aimed at 'the complete physical and psychological destruction of communities with implications for the entire society' (Meger, 2010). As a South African medical doctor who has worked in remote regions of the DRC, I have witnessed first-hand the complete devastation and demoralisation of entire communities in the wake of the country's decades-long conflict. Many times, I was left with a feeling of great hopelessness whenever I encountered victims of sexual violence, not only because of the profound atrocities the patients themselves had suffered, but because I, as a healthcare professional, did not know how to truly help them. This ethical challenge has shaped the course of my future work.

Emerging reports from around the world confirm the widespread and systematic use of sexual violence against civilian populations. However, in the discourse on sexual violence in armed conflict, violence against men and boys has seemingly been forgotten, receiving relatively little to almost no attention from global civil society. Media and service provider reports have focused heavily on violence against women and girls, while the issue of sexual violence against men and boys is still largely neglected in humanitarian and development aid (Arieff, 2011; Oosterhoff et al., 2004).

Sexual violence is associated with negative physical, sexual and reproductive health, and can have profound long-term mental health consequences (Harris et al., 2011). It can also impair economic and social post-war recovery at both an individual and community level (Elbert et al., 2013). A review of the literature on sexual violence against men in conflict reveals many gaps in the discourse. I argue that the gendered experience of sexual violence in conflict, as well as the barriers preventing the development of adequate and appropriate healthcare services for male victims of sexual violence, must be understood in relation to social constructs of masculinity. Communities and humanitarian organisations are not equipped to deal with the issue of male victims of sexual violence as it undermines these social constructions of masculinity.

Sexual Violence in War

Of all the secrets of war, there is one that is so well kept that it exists mostly as a rumour. It is usually denied by the perpetrator and his victim. Governments, aid agencies and human rights defenders at the UN barely acknowledge its possibility. Yet every now and then someone gathers the courage to tell of it. (The Rape of Men, Storr, 2011)

Sexual violence has been a defining characteristic in recent conflicts worldwide, including in the Great Lakes regions of Sub-Saharan Africa (Eriksson Baaz & Stern, 2010; Solangon & Patel, 2012). The widespread and systematic use of sexual violence in armed conflict has spurred international outcry and has frequently been described as a 'weapon of war' used to devastate individuals, family structures and communities, particularly in societies with strong patriarchal organisation (Elbert et al., 2013). Rape was formally recognised as a weapon of war and a crime against humanity during the International Criminal Tribunal for the former Yugoslavia (ICTY) in 1991 (Weitsman, 2008). Since then, sexual violence in armed conflict has received greater attention from the international community, seen primarily as a crime against women and girls (Carpenter, 2006). The World Health Organization (WHO) defines sexual violence as, 'any sexual act, attempt to obtain a sexual act, unwanted sexual comments or advances, or acts to traffic women's sexuality, using coercion, threats of harm or physical force, by any person regardless of relationship to the victim, in any setting' (2007). However, for the purpose of this chapter, sexual violence is defined as 'any act, attempt, or threat of a sexual nature, that results or is likely to result in physical, psychological and emotional harm' (ibid.).

In recent years, greater international attention has been placed on sexual violence in conflict and post-conflict settings primarily against women and girls, while sexual violence against men and boys has been hidden from international – and particularly international human rights – consciousness (Couturier, 2012; Solangon & Patel, 2012). For this reason, male rape has been labelled 'the forgotten method of torture' (OCHA, 2008). Between 1998 and 2008 alone, sexual violence against men has been recorded in over twenty-five armed conflicts across the world including in Northern Ireland, Guatemala, Burundi, and the DRC (Sivakumaran, 2010). The UN Security Council officially recognised men and boys as victims of sexual violence in conflict in UNSCR 2106 of June 2013 (UNSCR, 2013). Forms of male sexual violence (MSV) that have been recorded include: rape, mutilation of genitals, total/partial castration, forced incest, enforced sterilisation, sexual enslavement, sexual humiliation, and forced rape (Carpenter, 2006; Solangon & Patel, 2012).

Reports indicate that child soldiers, prisoners of war, civilians, military conscripts, refugees, and internally displaced persons (IDP) are particularly vulnerable to male-directed sexual violence in conflict-affect regions (Sivakumaran, 2007). It has been argued that wherever sexual violence is thoroughly investigated, 'male sexual violence has been recognized as regular and unexceptional, pervasive and widespread' (Sivakumaran, 2010). In some conflicts, such as the Bosnian war, more that 80 percent of the 5000 men in Sarajevo Canton concentration camp were reportedly raped (Russell, 2007). OCHA reports estimate that over 4000 Croatian men were sexually abused by Serbian militants, although this number is probably higher due to underreporting (OCHA, 2008). Yet, despite these accounts, relatively little research has documented the long-term health and psychosocial impact of male-directed sexual violence on individuals and communities that have been affected by this devastating atrocity (Sivakumaran, 2007; Solangon & Patel, 2012).

In addition, there remains a reticence among governmental and non-governmental organisations (NGOs) to fully engage with the realities and consequences of male-directed sexual violence. In 2002, it was reported that of the 4076 NGOs that focused on sexual violence, only 3 percent addressed the issue of sexual violence against males, and 25 percent unequivocally denied that sexual violence against men was a serious problem (Del Zotto & Jones, 2002). The international and humanitarian community have exacerbated ignorance considerably by not recognising the full scope of sexual violence in conflict.

Sexual Violence in Conflict in the Democratic Republic of Congo

The DRC has been the scene of insurgency, rebellion and conflict for many years. One of the poorest countries in the world, the DRC is ranked 176 of 188 countries in the latest United Nations Human Development Index (HDI) (UNDP, 2016). The 1994 Rwandan genocide, together with the collapse of the Mobutu regime, triggered over two decades of armed conflict, resulting in the widest interstate war in modern African history. Over 5.4 million civilian deaths were recorded between 1998 and 2003, with the death toll increasing by 45,000 a month according to one study by the International Rescue Committee (Truscott, 2008). The conflict is often referred to as 'Africa's World War', and is considered the deadliest conflict since World War Two (Cain, 2015).

Although empirical evidence on sexual violence in conflict is quite limited, significant country-based evidence on the prevalence of sexual violence in the DRC has been reported. A recent epidemiological study by Johnson et al. reported that 64.5 percent of all men in a random sample in Eastern DRC have been victims of conflict-related sexual violence of which 20.2 percent reported rape (2010). In the North Kivu and South Kivu sample areas, it is approximated that almost 760,000 men are in need of sexual violence-related care (ibid.). Other studies from the DRC report that Congolese men and boys comprise 4 percent to 10 percent of the total number of victims of sexual violence who seek medical treatment (Gettleman, 2009; McGreal, 2007).

The Refugee Law Project at the Makerere University in Uganda has conducted quite extensive research on sexual violence against males across Uganda, documenting cases of fathers who were forced to rape sons, and sons to rape mothers (Dolan, 2014a). In the news article 'Symbols of unhealed Congo: Male rape victims', Gettleman highlights the difficulties male victims encounter in seeking help in Goma, DRC, as well as the exclusivity of GBV programmes targeting women and girls (2009).

In an article published by *The Guardian*, Will Storr states that sexual violence against men is 'the darkest secret of war' (2011). He goes on to tell the story of a man who was raped more than three times a day, every single day, for three years by rebel forces during the civil war in the DRC (ibid.). He profiles another young man who was anally raped by eleven soldiers and sodomised (Storr, 2011). Countless stories of rape, mutilation and sexual emasculation have been told, one no less tragic than the other. Yet the real tragedy lies in the fact that these victims' stories have fallen on deaf ears.

Health Responses to Male Victims of Sexual Violence in War

There is a growing body of literature, including governmental and non-governmental reports, that focuses on the various forms, causes and consequences of sexual violence against men in conflict and post-conflict settings (Arieff, 2011; Courtenay, 2000; Del Zotto & Jones, 2002; Solangon & Patel, 2012). However, there is little formal public health and social science research that explicitly focuses on the realities and challenges of health and psychosocial support for male victims of sexual violence in the DRC. By reframing the issue of sexual violence against men in conflict and post-conflict settings from a primarily global health perspective, I hope to induce a shift in the treatment of sexual violence as a central and systematic tactic of war, and not just an unfortunate secondary by-product (Chinkin & Kaldor, 2013). This chapter aims to advance our understanding of the complex dynamics and challenges of sexual and gender-based violence (SGBV) against males in conflict and post-conflict settings, such as the conflict in DRC, with a view to adding depth to our understanding for future health response.

Analytical Framework

In this section, I apply a social constructionist view of gender to sexual violence against men in conflict to reveal an ethical issue in relation to the many gaps in health and humanitarian discourse. In brief, social constructivism is considered a theory of knowledge concerned with the way in which meaning is created (Nightingale & Cromby, 1999). Emerging from criticism of objectivity, social constructivism proposes that there are many things that people know, or take to be reality, that are at least partially, if not completely, socially constructed (Courtenay, 2000; Gergen, 1985). A constructionist account of gender lends itself to an understanding of masculinity not as a set of innate characteristics influenced by universal biological factors but rather as a socially and culturally constructed phenomenon that is neither stable nor constant (Connell & Messerschmidt, 2005; Courtenay, 2000; Nightingale & Cromby, 1999).

Through an analysis of sexual violence in the DRC, this chapter addresses a theoretical concern that the current framework used to define sexual and gender-based violence in conflict may have negative impacts for service delivery to male victims. This may also limit public health and social science research that only examines the experience of female victims, which in turn impacts on the data and evidence available for humanitarian actors.

Finally, this work engages with the gendered experience of what Mary Kaldor calls 'New Wars', as it focuses on the construction of gender in contemporary conflicts (2013). Looking at sexual violence in conflict through a gendered lens gives us insight into not only the nature of sexual violence in conflict and post-conflict settings, but also the nuanced experience of sexual violence against males, and in doing so can guide policy-makers in the development of healthcare responses that cater to the specific reproductive and psychosocial needs of victims of sexual violence.

Consequences of Male-directed Sexual Violence

Physical and Mental Consequences

Male survivors of sexual violence suffer severe and numerous physical, mental and social consequences. Reported physical health problems include bruises, lacerations, weakness, genital pain during urination, genital infections, impotence, testicular pain and sexually transmitted diseases such as HIV (Oosterhoff et al., 2004; Schopper, 2014). However, as severe as the physical and social consequences of sexual violence may be, the psychological consequences often far outlive physical effects (Russell, 2007). The WHO (2007) reports that male victims are likely to suffer from a range of psychological consequences, both in the immediate and long term.

Many male victims describe feelings of shame, humiliation, anger, fear, and powerlessness (Harris et al., 2011). They may also experience psychological problems such as depression, suicide, substance abuse, anxiety and post-traumatic stress disorder (PTSD) (Harris et al., 2011). Additional studies suggest that there is an association between adolescent males who have been raped, and substance abuse, violent behaviour, stealing, and absenteeism from school (WHO, 2007).

A population study in the eastern province of the DRC found that populations with a high prevalence of sexual violence also report high levels of mental health disorders (Johnson et al., 2010). In the same study it was reported that among the represented population, 41 percent met the symptoms criteria of Major Depressive Disorder (MDD) or PTSD (ibid.). The cumulative effect of sexual violence may result in the destruction of gender identity and confusion of sexual orientation (Dolan, 2014a).

Psychosocial Consequences

Sexual violence can destroy the fabric of families and communities, which is often the inherent purpose of sexual violence as a strategy of conflict. Male victims report feelings of shame and humiliation as a result of no longer being considered a man in their community (Christian et al., 2011). For example, in the Congo when men report being raped, they are instantly ostracised from community and public life, ridiculed, shunned and left alone (Gettleman, 2009). Often derisively referred to as 'bush wives', male victims would rather leave their wives, homes, families and communities than face the shame and discrimination associated with sexual violence (Solangon & Patel, 2012).

In the immediate aftermath of a sexual assault, male victims have reported not being able to work and thus contribute to the household income as a result of physical and mental health problems, leaving the wife with the sole responsibility of earning the entire household's income in order to support the family (Christian et al., 2011). This generates further tension and conflict within families, often resulting in a lack of funds to meet basic household needs such as food, shelter, medication, and education for the children (ibid.). These effects become more pronounced in cases of repeated and prolonged exposure to conflict coupled with unstable political conditions, such as is the case in the DRC.

In the Congo, male victims report that they either hide away from friends and neighbours and/or assume different roles in the home such as cooking, cleaning, or taking care of the children: the 'traditional' roles of a woman and wife (ibid.). Male victims report that prior to an assault, they were involved in mining or animal husbandry (the raising and breeding of chickens, goats, and cows), or maintained small businesses. Whether as a result of physical trauma that prevents victims from working strenuous jobs, or due to the assumption that domestic work is commensurate with their status as someone who has been the object of violent male sexuality, these household changes in gender roles impact not only the victims themselves but also the family and wider community (ibid.).

Challenges to Effective Healthcare Responses: Reporting and Data Collection

Concepts of hegemonic masculinity that underlie the potential causes of sexual violence in conflict settings overlap with the many reasons why comprehensive information is neither offered by male victims or accurately collected by healthcare professionals. Due to gaps in the data there has been an underestimation of the extent of the problem by global civil society (Couturier, 2012; Dolan, 2014c; Sivakumaran, 2010). This collective ignorance further complicates the formulation of comprehensive policy and advocacy responses, and reinforces unpopular concepts and myths surrounding MSV (Cain, 2015).

Men's and boys' reluctance to share their experience of violence can be attributed to the value that hegemonic masculinity places on self-reliance, emotional strength, and endurance (Connell & Messerschmidt, 2005; Onyango & Hampanda, 2011). It is argued that to talk about your problems as a 'man', particularly in societies where men are prohibited from talking about their emotions, contravenes the male expectation of silence and stoicism in times of adversity (Onyango & Hampanda, 2011). For many male victims the simple acknowledgement of male rape brings into question the legitimacy of their masculine identity. Sivakumaran notes that 'incompatibility between this understanding of masculinity and victimization occurs both at the level of the attack itself –should have been able to prevent himself from being attacked – and in dealing with the consequences of the attack – to be able to cope "like a man"' (2007).

Reliance on traditional, heteronormative stereotypes of masculinity further perpetuate misconceptions about sexual violence against men and boys, assuming that if the victim was engaged in a male-on-male sexual act and had an erection during the rape, which, unknown to both themselves and the perpetrator, is a normal physiological response and not a sign of sexual arousal, then surely he must be homosexual (Christian et al., 2011; Dolan, 2014a; Sivakumaran 2010). In the DRC, homosexuality is still taboo, while stigma generates a risk of persecution (i.e. another form of gender-based violence). Many Congolese refugees flee to Uganda, where homosexual acts are punishable by life imprisonment, which makes men even more reluctant to come forward and report their experience if they are unable to prove that it was non-consensual (Cain, 2015; Dolan, 2014c). The consequences of this are two-fold: the male victim is burdened with the perceived disgrace of homosexuality, and must then choose between excommunication from his family and community, or suffering in silence, both of which would be a triumph for the perpetrator (Couturier, 2012).

Feminist movements have rightfully argued that in regard to female sexual violence, absolute numbers should not be the main concern as there are many factors that can lead to underreporting by female victims, such as shame, humiliation, and overwhelming stigma (Dolan, 2014c). Studies show that in the Eastern DRC, rates of non-reporting among female victims at the time of seeking medical care are estimated to be as high as 75 percent (ibid.). Women's rights activists argue that since the number of male victims will never equate to, or exceed, the number of female victims of sexual violence in armed conflict, we should focus most of our efforts and resources to women (Couturier, 2012).

However, one may argue that the lack of male activist campaigning against SGBV, and the social construct of masculinity in patriarchal societies such as the DRC, leave men even more vulnerable to stigma and humiliation due to not having fulfilled their masculine role, preventing them from disclosing their experience, which in turn leads to a gross underestimation of the prevalence of MSV (Linos, 2009). This is to show that a general absence of statistics does not equate to an absence of incidents (Dolan, 2014a). Sivakumaran remarks, 'As far as sexual violence is concerned, it is not, nor should it be, a matter of numbers' (2010). Sexual violence against men is still sexual assault and should be addressed regardless of the absolute number of people affected.

Furthermore, actively seeking to address gender specificities within studies of sexual violence, and implementing systemic screenings of populations of concern to humanitarian multilaterals and NGOs, notably refugees and ex-combatants, may lead to a more nuanced discussion about the roles of men and women in conflict (Dolan, 2014c; Elbert et al., 2013). If women's rights activists move to dispel the essentialisation of women as weak, submissive, and always viewed as 'the victim', we need to adopt the same language and reasoning for men and boys by rejecting the monolithic and invariably negative portrayal of men as perpetrators and villains. This may facilitate a more dynamic process about the way in which questions are formulated and to whom they are posed, which is vital to the final data that is collected, not to mention to its interpretation (Dolan, 2014a; Dolan, 2014b).

Challenges to Medical and Institutional Responses

I didn't know that a man could be raped. (Unknown physician; Gender Against Men (Refugee Law Project, 2009))

Scholars postulate that NGOs and humanitarian agencies offer a welcome first step on the path to physical healing and recovery for male victims of sexual violence, due to the traditional socialisation of masculine physicality, where greater awareness and regard is placed on the physical body than on the mental state (Connell & Messerschmidt, 2005; Courtenay, 2000). However, I argue that illness itself is an affront to hegemonic masculinity, which prizes control, invulnerability, and physical strength. Acknowledging the existence of illness is often perceived as an attack on the individual's masculine identity: an admission of defeat. Health is perceived as a feminine domain as it is characterised by the hegemonic ideology of women in the 'traditional' care-giving role (Lichtenstein, 2004). In a news article for the BBC, Stephen Kigoma, a Congolese rape victim, describes being taken to see a doctor who treated survivors of sexual violence, where he was the only man in the entire ward: 'I felt undermined. I was in a land I did not belong to, having to explain to the doctor how it happened. That was my fear' (Mutengi, 2017). The feminised male no longer fits within the borders of traditional gender roles and so undermines their dominant ideals, which results in the refusal of the male victim to subordinate to the doctor's instructions, thus constructing a veil of secrecy and denial in a final attempt to preserve a sense of autonomy and masculine identity (Couturier, 2012; Onyango & Hampanda, 2011).

In the immediate aftermath of a sexual assault, healthcare professionals and humanitarian field workers play a crucial role in the provision of urgent medical and psychiatric assistance to victims of sexual violence (Harris et al., 2011). They are the first point of contact for most men and women who have experienced sexual violence, and this has a profound impact on whether or not the victim will continue to engage with the healthcare system, and further with the judicial system (Sivakumaran, 2007). States are legally obligated to provide medical and psychosocial care to victims of sexual violence in times of conflict (IASC, 2005). WHO guidelines for the medico-legal care for victims of SGBV aim to, 'improve professional health services for all victims of sexual violence by providing: healthcare workers with the knowledge and skills that are necessary for the management of victims of sexual violence; standards for the provision of both healthcare and forensic services to victims of sexual violence' (2007).

I would argue that healthcare responses to GBV are still too reductionist and manage GBV inadequately, particularly GBV against males. Despite the centralised nature of sexual violence in contemporary armed conflict, GBV is still prioritised as secondary for treatment and care. Herein lies a major discrepancy between reality and response, which is made even more apparent by WHO guidelines that state that no direct questions should be asked when interviewing a victim or other person who may have experienced sexual violence, for fear of re-traumatising the individual (2007). While understanding that disclosure is sensitive and risk-inducing, there need to be other ways to assess for SGBV that allow for the victim to be treated, especially given the gendered barriers to access to healthcare services, when such services are available.

There has been a shift in the perception of GBV as a purely human rights/social issue to GBV as a health problem. The health risk and consequences of GBV are well-evidenced and the need to treat GBV in healthcare settings is recognised (Linos, 2009). However, healthcare professionals who do not know how to deal with the problem of GBV are ill-equipped to manage and treat these individuals. The literature suggests that there is a lack of awareness among healthcare professionals of the problem of MSV in conflict and post-conflict settings (Cain, 2015; Solangon & Patel, 2012). Healthcare professionals are not equipped with the training or knowledge needed to adequately respond to male victims (Dolan, 2014c). It is no wonder that the seeking of health and psychosocial support in conflict-affected areas causes great anxiety for not only the men and boys affected by sexual violence, but also for the healthcare providers who are supposed to render these services.

The doctors in Panzi Hospital in Eastern DRC report that they do not know how to 'deal' with the issue of sexual violence against males, and often feel pressured when expected to do so (Bott et al., 2005; IASC, 2005). A study by Oosterhoff and colleagues found that many healthcare professionals found it difficult to discuss the topic of sexual violence with their patients and would either skim over the topic or ignore the matter altogether (2012). The inability of healthcare professionals to examine and identify male victims of sexual violence demonstrates not only their lack of preparedness but also 'the strength of gender norms in governing the workings of society and the danger of leaving these standards unquestioned' (Couturier, 2012).

With the complete collapse of the Congolese healthcare system (Cain, 2015), service providers are still struggling to adequately resource the work with women and girls who have suffered sexual violence in the DRC (Dolan, 2014b). Consequently, many humanitarian workers are reluctant to move the focus off women and on to men, as it may draw already limited resources away from the women and girls who supposedly need it the most (Cain, 2015; Sivakumaran, 2007). However, Sivakumaran asserts that 'looking at the issue of male sexual violence will not take away from female sexual violence, for ultimately it is part of the same issue' (2010). A feminist consciousness seeks to deconstruct and reorganise harmful perceptions of feminine gender roles in society, particularly as they relate to men and boys (Couturier, 2012). Nevertheless, because the rape of males imposes these very same gendered attributes through the 'feminisation' of the subordinated individual, male-directed sexual violence forms part of the same narrative (ibid.). An exclusive focus on the rights and victimisation of women, without acknowledging the monolithic impact sexual violence has on men and boys further alienates male victims.

Support for male victims of sexual violence is virtually nonexistent, including among medical service providers in the DRC, who themselves have internalised heteronormative ideals, and are not given the intellectual, material or social capital to fully engage with the issue of MSV with the necessary nuance and sensitivity required (Couturier, 2012).

An Ethical Challenge of Misclassification

As stated earlier, the different forms of sexual violence against men and boys are extensive, and the full extent of which is still unknown due to the underreporting and stigma associated with MSV (Solangon

& Patel, 2012). Healthcare professionals might only focus on anal rape to the exclusion of other forms of MSV due to their familiarity with sexual violence against women and girls, while classifying violent acts such as genital mutilation and castration as torture (Cain, 2015; Solangon & Patel, 2012).

This view is made very apparent when examining non-governmental and intergovernmental reports, and reinforces the view that men are not susceptible to sexual violence in conflict (Sivakumaran, 2007). The misclassification of abuse by healthcare professionals is significant because those specific cases of sexual violence are not recorded as such in reports and data. This contributes to the obscure picture investigative bodies have painted of the subject of MSV in the DRC, as the numbers of people affected remain unclear and there is a dearth of material and information on the issue (Dolan, 2014a).

Many scholars are of the belief that trying to determine whether male rape in the DRC constitutes torture is not a worthwhile exercise (Ferrales et al., 2016; Schopper, 2014). I argue that that the implications of not making a clear distinction between sexual violence and torture are potentially far-reaching, as it creates a serious hurdle for both healthcare providers and healthcare users to adequately address the problem, and acts as a stumbling block for male survivors in expressing what they themselves have experienced.

Gender, New Wars, and Health

War and conflict play an important role in the way gender and identity are constructed and 'fixed' for both men and women (Chinkin & Kaldor, 2013). The way men and women conceptualise and experience war is fundamentally different, particularly in regard to the way they experience violence as a result of their sex or gender (ibid.; Linos, 2009). New wars, as described by Kaldor, are conflicts that are currently taking place in different parts of the world such as the Eastern Democratic Republic of Congo. Predominately fought by men in the name of a political identity, new wars usually have a significant gender dimension, in contrast to the geopolitical and ideological wars of the early twentieth century, otherwise known as 'old wars' (2013).

The literature would suggest that identities constructed in war tend to be closely linked to gender binaries, whereby traits associated with masculinity such as physical strength, stoicism, and aggressiveness are valued, while, correspondingly, traits associated with femininity such as caring and emotion are undervalued (Chinkin & Kaldor, 2013; Couturier, 2012; Onyango & Hampanda, 2011). Concepts of humiliation, shame, and sexuality that are attached to male and female bodies in peacetime, compounded by the prolonged disintegration of social order in war, are key to understanding the establishment of supremacy and a claim to power on the basis of a particular identity (Couturier, 2012; Kaldor, 2013). This would explain why a lot is achieved through particular forms of violence. The use of sexual violence involves going to the heart of the individual and collective sense of self. It is more than just an attack on the physical body: it is an attack on identity.

Kaldor's framework contributes to our understanding of sexual violence in conflict as deliberate and systematic, and not just a side effect of war (2013). Her contemporary work on gender and conflict seeks to deconstruct the strict male–female perpetrator–victim dichotomy by challenging essentialist views that equate men with violence and women with peace, enabling the conceptualisation of women as perpetrators as well as men as victims.

A gendered analysis enables us to see that the motive for sexual violence in conflict is the disruption of society. As such, if health systems are only a reflection of the communities in which they are embedded, and if humiliation, stigma, patriarchy, and distrust have destroyed the fabric of the community itself, healthcare institutions will most likely reflect this too. Barriers to the provision of healthcare in the DRC, such as a lack of data, reduced health-seeking behaviour by male victims, a lack of resources, and a lack of knowledge among healthcare professionals, all add to the 'success' of sexual violence in conflict as a 'tactic of war'. Disability, unemployment, and psychological trauma are but a few of the long-term health and societal impacts designed to remain after the conflict ceases (Harris et al., 2011). By failing to adequately respond to the health and psychosocial needs of male victims of sexual violence, victims are further marginalised: a great accomplishment in a patriarchal society.

By acknowledging the pivotal role gender plays in contemporary armed conflict, we can appreciate the need for first responders, especially humanitarian agencies, to develop healthcare services that utilise a gendered framework in order to understand the experience of GBV in conflict and post-conflict settings (similar to the framework Kaldor (2013) uses to understand the nature of sexual violence in conflict). Men who have suffered sexual violence in conflict and post-conflict settings have distinct sexual, social, and psychological needs that require gender-sensitive consideration (Linos, 2009). For practitioners and policy-makers responding to health and SGBV needs in conflict, a more nuanced consideration of the gendered experience of sexual violence, called for by Kaldor, is central to ensuring that both men and women receive adequate and appropriate care.

Conclusion

Sexual violence against men in the DRC – and globally – has been under-detected, under-reported, and underrepresented due to deeply entrenched beliefs about stereotypical gender roles and masculinity that influence and shape societal and policy processes. Underpinning every act of sexual violence is an attack on gendered identity and its associated hierarchy. The subordinated male victim is fundamentally stripped of his masculine identity by the feminisation and emasculation associated with sexual violence. The physical, mental, and psychological damage experienced by male and female victims of sexual violence make it even more imperative that global civil society addresses sexual violence in the DRC and elsewhere in a gender-inclusive manner which supports the health and psychosocial needs of both men and women in the immediate and long term. Now is a precarious moment for investigative bodies to realise their emancipatory potential, for the benefit of all of those affected by violence. Sexual violence in conflict-affected areas moves beyond physical and mental wounds: it is a social phenomenon that transcends cultural and territorial boundaries. Healthcare providers, NGOs, and humanitarian organisations need to change their perception of sexual violence as a by-product of war to sexual violence as a central feature of armed conflict, if they wish to develop effective primary GBV response programmes which will not only begin a process of healing for male victims and their communities, but also ignite a hope that the 'invisible' male victims of sexual violence will once again be seen.

References

Arieff, A (2011), Sexual violence in African conflicts. *Current Politics and Economics of Africa*. Vol. 4: 351.

Bott, S, Morrison, A & Ellsberg, M (2005), Preventing and responding to gender-based violence in middle- and low-income countries: a global review and analysis. Washington, DC: World Bank.

Cain, M (2015), *Hope in the shadows: male victims of sexual assault in the Democratic Republic of the Congo*. Humanity in Action.

Carpenter, RC (2006), Recognizing gender-based violence against civilian men and boys in conflict situations. *Security Dialogue*. Vol. 37: 83–103.

Chinkin, C & Kaldor, M (2013), Gender and new wars. *Journal of International Affairs*. Vol. 67 (1): 167–87.

Christian, M, Safari, O, Ramazani, P, Burnham, G & Glass, N (2011), Sexual and gender based violence against men in the Democratic Republic of Congo: effects on survivors, their families and the community. *Medicine, Conflict and Survival*. Vol. 27: 227–46.

Connell, RW & Messerschmidt, JW (2005), Hegemonic masculinity: rethinking the concept. *Gender & Society*. Vol. 19: 829–59.

Courtenay, WH (2000), Constructions of masculinity and their influence on men's well-being: a theory of gender and health. *Social Science & Medicine*. Vol. 50: 1385–1401.

Couturier, D (2012), The rape of men: eschewing myths of sexual violence in war. *On Politics*. Vol. 6: 2.

Del Zotto, A & Jones, A (2002), *Male-on-male sexual violence in wartime: human rights' last taboo*. Annual Convention of the International Studies Association (ISA), New Orleans, 23–27 March 2002.

Dolan, C (2014a), *Into the mainstream: addressing sexual violence against men and boys in conflict*. Briefing paper prepared for a workshop held at the Overseas Development Institute, London, 14 May 2014.

Dolan, C (2014b), Has patriarchy been stealing the feminists' clothes? Conflict-related sexual violence and UN Security Council Resolutions. *IDS Bulletin*. Vol. 45: 80–4.

Dolan, C (2014c), Letting go of the gender binary: charting new pathways for humanitarian interventions on gender-based violence. *International Review of the Red Cross*. Vol. 96: 485–501.

Elbert, T, Hinkel, H, Maedl, A, Hermenau, K, Hecker, T, Schauer, M, ... Lancaster, P (2013), *Sexual and gender-based violence in the Kivu provinces of the Democratic Republic of Congo: Insights from former combatants*. Washington, DC: World Bank.

Eriksson Baaz, M & Stern, M (2010), *Understanding and addressing conflict-related sexual violence: lessons learned from the Democratic Republic of Congo*. Uppsala: Nordiska Afrikainstitutet.

Ferrales, G, Nyseth Brehm, H & McElrath, S (2016), Gender-based violence against men and boys in Darfur: the gender-genocide nexus. *Gender & Society*. Vol. 30: 565–89.

Gergen, KJ (1985), The social constructionist movement in modern psychology. *American Psychologist*. Vol. 40: 266.

Gettleman, J (2009), Symbol of unhealed Congo: male rape victims. *New York Times*, 4 August 2009.

Harris, L, Freccero, J & Crittenden, C (2011), *Sexual violence: medical and psychosocial support*. Berkeley, CA: Human Rights Center.

IASC (2005), *Guidelines for gender-based violence interventions in humanitarian settings: focusing on prevention of and response to sexual violence in emergencies*. Geneva: Inter-Agency Standing Committee Task Force on Gender and Humanitarian Assistance.

Johnson, K, Scott, J, Rughita, B, Kisielewski, M, Asher, J, Ong, R & Lawry, L (2010), Association of sexual violence and human rights violations with physical and mental health in territories of the Eastern Democratic Republic of the Congo. *JAMA*. Vol. 304: 553–62.

Kaldor, M (2013), *New and old wars: organised violence in a global era.* Hoboken, NJ: John Wiley & Sons.

Lichtenstein, B (2004), Caught at the clinic: African American men, stigma, and STI treatment in the Deep South. *Gender & Society.* Vol. 18: 369–88.

Linos, N (2009), Rethinking gender-based violence during war: is violence against civilian men a problem worth addressing? *Social Science & Medicine.* Vol. 68: 154–51.

McGreal, C (2007), Hundreds of thousands of women raped for being on the wrong side. *The Guardian*, 12 November 2007.

Meger, S (2010), Rape of the Congo: understanding sexual violence in the conflict in the Democratic Republic of Congo. *Journal of Contemporary African Studies.* Vol. 28: 119–35.

Mutengi A (2017), 'We need to talk about male rape' DR Congo survivor speaks out. BBC, 3 August 2017.

Nightingale, D, Cromby, J (1999), *Social constructionist psychology: a critical analysis of theory and practice.* New York City, NY: McGraw-Hill Education.

OCHA (2008), *Discussion paper 2: the nature, scope, and motivation for sexual violence against men and boys in armed conflict.* Use of sexual violence in armed conflict: identifying gaps in research to inform more effective interventions. OCHA Research Meeting, 26 June 2008.

Onyango, MA & Hampanda, K (2011), Social constructions of masculinity and male survivors of wartime sexual violence: an analytical review. *International Journal of Sexual Health.* Vol. 23: 237–47.

Oosterhoff, P, Zwanikken, P & Ketting, E (2004), Sexual torture of men in Croatia and other conflict situations: an open secret. *Reproductive Health Matters.* Vol. 12 (23): 68–77.

Refugee Law Project (2009), Gender against men [documentary]. Great Lakes Region, Africa.

Russell, W (2007), Sexual violence against men and boys. *Forced Migration Review.* Vol. 27: 22–3.

Schopper, D (2014), Responding to the needs of survivors of sexual violence: do we know what works? *International Review of the Red Cross.* Vol. 96: 585–600.

Sivakumaran, S (2007), Sexual violence against men in armed conflict. *European Journal of International Law.* Vol. 18: 253–76.

Sivakumaran, S (2010), Lost in translation: UN responses to sexual violence against men and boys in situations of armed conflict. *International Review of the Red Cross.* Vol. 92: 259–77.

Solangon, S & Patel, P (2012), Sexual violence against men in countries affected by armed conflict. *Conflict, Security & Development.* Vol. 12: 417–42.

Storr, W (2011), The rape of men: the darkest secret of war. *The Guardian*, 17 July 2011.

Truscott, A (2008), Congo ceasefire brings little relief for women. *Canadian Medical Association Journal.* Vol. 179 (2): 133–4.

Weitsman, PA (2008), The politics of identity and sexual violence: a review of Bosnia and Rwanda. *Human Rights Quarterly.* Vol. 30: 561–78.

UNDP (2016), Human development for everyone: briefing note for countries on the 2016 Human Development Report, Congo (Democratic Republic of the). The Human Development Report.

WHO (2007), *WHO ethical and safety recommendations for researching, documenting and monitoring sexual violence in emergencies.* Geneva: World Health Organization.

15 | HUMANITARIAN ETHICS IN MÉDECINS SANS FRONTIÈRES/DOCTORS WITHOUT BORDERS: DISCUSSING DILEMMAS AND MITIGATING MORAL DISTRESS

Rachel Kiddell-Monroe, Carol Devine, John Pringle, Sidney Wong and Philippe Calain

Abstract

Médecins Sans Frontières/Doctors Without Borders (MSF) faces pervasive ethical issues in its pursuit of medical humanitarian action. Humanitarian aid workers often find themselves in unfamiliar contexts, vulnerable and isolated while making difficult decisions about a particular course of action. In violent and insecure contexts such as Syria, South Sudan and Nigeria, we encounter ethical challenges beyond the scope of medical ethics while knowing that our decisions will have a lasting impact on the people we try to assist. We make decisions related to: 'acceptable' levels of risk for our staff and whether we should continue to work in places where our facilities, and the local populations they serve, are attacked with impunity, while during the West Africa Ebola crisis we struggled with whether or not to use coercive public health measures.

MSF has decided to address ethical challenges with greater purpose and accountability. In keeping with our culture of self-reflection, we are making efforts to create spaces in which to discuss core ethical dilemmas and operational challenges. This chapter will: 1) discuss what humanitarian ethics means for MSF as a medical humanitarian organisation; 2) present case studies that illustrate the types of ethical challenges and dilemmas we face, both on the ground and institutionally; and 3) discuss some of the efforts made within MSF to improve our understanding of, and decision-making processes in relation to, ethical issues at all levels of MSF. We hope that sharing our experiences and efforts to actively develop ethical humanitarian reasoning in MSF will contribute to a greater awareness and understanding of dilemmas inherent in the provision of medical humanitarian assistance in these chaotic and deeply challenging times for people living through crisis worldwide.

Introduction

> Every humanitarian organisation should make a commitment like this!
> (Ross Upshur, Special Advisor to the MSF Ethics Review Board)

Ethical issues are pervasive in humanitarian action. Médecins Sans Frontières/Doctors Without Borders (MSF) has faced such issues since the organisation was founded. These ethical issues are not a theoretical pastime for MSF: they have a real and lasting impact on the people we try to assist, as well as on our project and headquarters staff. Yet, medical and non-medical humanitarian aid workers find themselves in unfamiliar contexts, often vulnerable and isolated in the process of making difficult – and sometimes what feel like impossible – decisions about which course of action to take.

Brought to a head by experiences during the West Africa Ebola crisis, in 2016, MSF's International General Assembly (IGA), the organisation's highest governance body, acknowledged the 'profound moral challenges inherent in humanitarian action' (see Box 15.1). The IGA resolved to take concrete steps to address ethical dilemmas more openly, more effectively, and with more purpose and accountability.

Box 15.1 MSF International General Assembly (IGA) Humanitarian Ethics Motion (2016)

'MSF Association acknowledges the profound moral challenges inherent in humanitarian action. These challenges have repercussions for the people we assist and result in moral distress of our field workers. Therefore, the Association requests the Board to commit to reflections, discussions, and concrete measures that will promote ethics dialogue for our humanitarian action, with the goal of 1) making fair and open decisions towards those we strive to serve, and 2) reducing the moral distress of our field workers.'

Today, MSF is trying to consciously promote and create space for ethical dialogue, and to develop tools intended to reduce moral distress among project staff. By passing this deliberative motion, MSF seeks to ensure more coherent and tangible mechanisms for the ethical analysis of challenges and dilemmas, as well as practical support for all of our staff, from recruitment to post-mission. By creating spaces for ethical discussions, the intention is to implement a more systematic approach to humanitarian ethics in MSF by understanding how to identify ethical dilemmas and challenges, by making choices and decisions that respect our core humanitarian principles, and by ensuring that we put our patients first.

Humanitarian Ethics in MSF

When we speak of humanitarian ethics at MSF, we are not referring simply to medical ethics. While medical ethics is a core component of humanitarian ethics given that MSF is a medical organisation, our ethical decision-making invariably extends far beyond the frameworks for ethical reflection defined by medical ethics. While medical ethics guides the medical practitioner–patient relationship, humanitarian ethics incorporates all aspects of humanitarian action. Humanitarian ethics overlaps with global health ethics, public health ethics, and elements of professional ethics. It involves ethics *in* humanitarianism (operational, in-the-project challenges), ethics *of* humanitarianism (societal and policy issues), and ethics *for* humanitarianism (substantive normative ethics) (Pringle, 2015). In particular, medical humanitarian ethics deals with the challenges and dilemmas that appear at the intersection between medical practice and humanitarian action, as guided by the humanitarian principles of impartiality, independence and neutrality (Mackintosh, 2000; Schenkenberg, 2015). These humanitarian principles, together with our founding documents (that guide how we work to apply those principles),[1] underpin our humanitarian ethical reasoning.

Since 'ethical' and 'moral' are often used interchangeably, we wish to emphasise that we are do not seek to discuss morality. Ethics represents a field of study based on philosophical and critical reasoning, whereas morality relates to personal or societal belief systems that stipulate right and wrong. For MSF, the primary purpose of ethical reflection is to understand and justify reasons, values, and choices, and to learn from them.

Humanitarian ethics inherently acknowledges that those who receive, or are in need of, assistance maintain diverse views, and are guided by differing morals and principles, which in turn generates a wide range of individual experiences. MSF recognises the importance of making decisions based on the needs of the people we support, which in turn means embracing the specificities of context, culture, and individual preferences. As a result, there is a growing appreciation of the need to ensure the participation of recipients of humanitarian assistance in various aspects of humanitarian response. MSF continues to consider ways to make dialogue with people receiving assistance in our projects more inclusive, and to address the absence of data concerning the ways in which such populations perceive aid.[2]

Dilemmas in Real Time

The response to the 2014–2016 West Africa Ebola crisis represents a stark example of attempts to deal with profound ethical dilemmas in real time. As we will discuss in Case Study 1, many ethical issues that required rapid resolution arose in such a short space of time that the organisation was barely able to keep up. Such issues included questions over whether MSF should use coercive public health measures to ensure that potentially Ebola-infected people were corralled to the organisation's treatment centres, or whether people should be left to make such decisions for themselves. Other questions related to whether MSF should medivac national staff, expatiate staff, or both or neither. As the outbreak progressed, MSF explored whether experimental treatments should be used, and if so, who should receive them (Rid & Antierens, 2017). Further concerns were raised over how to triage patients when hospital capacities were exceeded, and whether MSF might be seen as complicit in repressive quarantine practices.

The impact of decisions with a clear ethical dimension exist far beyond the decision-making moment; to this day, decisions made during the Ebola crisis have residual consequence for decision-makers (Calain, 2016). In violent contexts such as Syria, Iraq, South Sudan, Nigeria or the Central African Republic, we face ethical challenges that fall outside the scope of medical ethics on a regular basis, with such scenarios often repeated across different contexts. We are forced to make decisions pertaining to acceptable levels of risk for our staff, and on whether to selectively assign project staff based on gender, age and cultural background in order to minimise the risk that people are targeted on the basis of demographic qualities. We must decide whether to work remotely or not at all in some particularly dangerous places, and whether we should work in environments where our facilities and the local populations they serve are attacked with impunity. On occasion, we have to decide whether to continue to work in places where there has been a diversion or misappropriation of aid, or where we witness discrimination or violence against local populations (Magone, Neuman & Weissman, 2011). We have also been pressed to consider where the boundary lies between humanitarian action and complicity as we respond to the needs of refugees and migrants kept in inhumane detention centres (Sheather & Wong, n.d.).

Moral Distress

Moral distress in humanitarian action has been recognised for many years (Terry, 2002).[3] It is well established that psychological trauma is pervasive in contexts of war, disasters, and other public health emergencies. In their response to crises, humanitarian aid workers are witness to tragic and inhumane situations. They are often subject to innumerable hazards and endure high levels of psychological distress. Burnout and post-traumatic stress is not uncommon (Gilbert, 2017). Related to, but distinct from, psychological distress is *moral distress*. Troubling ethical experiences induce stress and stress-related disorders among project staff. Primarily studied in healthcare workers, moral distress has been described as the manifestation of 'traditional negative stress symptoms that occur due to situations that involve ethical dimensions and where the healthcare provider feels she/he is not able to preserve all interests and values at stake' (Kälvemark et al., 2004).

In humanitarian action, moral distress can be experienced in a number of ways, in the form of moral uncertainty, a moral dilemma, or moral distress by association. Moral uncertainty can result from situations in which aid workers find it difficult or impossible to identify the morally right course of action due to a lack of pertinent empirical information. Moral dilemmas emerge from situations in which aid workers face limited options and are compelled to make what feels like an impossible choice. Moral distress may also be experienced by association, when aid workers feel morally compromised when working or interacting with problematic individuals or organisations (Campbell, Ulrich & Grady, 2016).

Moral distress takes a heavy personal toll. It also takes a toll at the organisational level. In the absence of an appropriate venue in which aid workers can share and reflect on their experiences, their lessons will fail to be captured and conveyed within and between organisations. Without these lessons, those who come after them will inevitably repeat the same mistakes: they will feel that their ethical challenges are new, and that their situations are exceptional. Decisions will be made as if for the first time with all the accompanying stress that this entails. Poor institutional memory means that aid workers will feel at fault. Isolation and self-doubt lead to attrition. Low retention rates lead to poorly informed organisational policies and practices, which in turn becomes a downward cycle. Breaking this cycle requires sharing moral burdens across the collective.

The many challenging contexts in which MSF works have always exposed, and will continue to expose, our staff to morally difficult and complex situations. These challenges, and the difficult decisions they prompt, have an important impact on the lives of both patients and staff. Addressing the multiple sources of moral distress can ultimately help to improve the organisation's effectiveness.

Case Studies: Humanitarian Ethical Challenges and Dilemmas in Practice

MSF Case Study 1 – Contact Tracing: Public Health Measures and Ethical Obligations

The West Africa Ebola crisis of 2014–2016 (see Box 15.2) raised multiple ethical dilemmas that continue to reverberate in the present day. The crisis illustrated the many ethical dimensions of public health strategies used to control disease outbreaks (Calain & Poncin, 2015). Some of the ethical dilemmas that MSF faced included, but were not limited to: the balance between coercive public health measures and patient autonomy; public health and clinical management priorities; inequalities in treatment options between expatriate and national staff (e.g. the possibility of medical evacuation or access to experimental treatments); the lack of a pre-established scheme for clinical triage when hospitalisation capacities were exceeded.

MSF project staff self-reported moral distress. During the early days of the crisis, some were troubled by the absence of a concerted international response, even after MSF had raised concerns at the highest level (MSF, 2014a).[4] Staff were deeply affected by their own inability to meet the needs of their patients, the reality of having to turn away victims from treatment centres, and the need to strike a compromise between the quality and quantity of care that could be provided (Watson-Stryker, 2016). In the following extract, Brett

Adamson, MSF's Field Coordinator in Monrovia in August 2014, describes some of these challenges, and their effect on the team.

> I'm horrified by the scale of the centre we're constructing and the horrible conditions inside, what people are enduring. It's horrible what our staff are having to do, with the risk and the heat. We're struggling to deal with the number of patients. We're trying to adapt and build as the need increases, but we're not keeping up. We feel tremendous guilt and shame that we can't adequately address the needs of the people. (MSF, 2015)

The atmosphere was one of terror: death was omnipresent and accusations of exaggeration and rumours were pervasive. Some of MSF's staff suffered severe stigma, often ostracised by family and neighbours, while at the same time remaining at risk of infection (MSF, 2015). By the end of the outbreak, twenty-eight MSF colleagues had fallen ill with Ebola Virus disease: fourteen recovered and fourteen died (MSF, 2017b).

Box 15.2 MSF and the 2014–2016 West Africa Ebola Crisis

The 2014–2016 crisis was the worst Ebola outbreak in history and the largest Ebola outbreak to which MSF has responded. Ebola is recognised one of the most deadly diseases in the world, with a case fatality rate of between 25 and 80 percent (MSF, 2017a). In West Africa, the disease emerged and spread rapidly in affected communities generating fear, panic, mistrust, stigma, and misinformation, causing many tragic deaths (Hofman & Au, 2017). In March 2014, MSF declared the outbreak unprecedented due to the extent of its geographic spread (MSF, 2015). Despite the organisation's calls for support, the international response was slow and inadequate, revealing many weaknesses in existing global health infrastructure, and the fragility of regional mechanisms for emergency health response. The outbreak went on to claim over 11,000 lives including those of 500 healthcare workers. From March 2014 to December 2015, MSF handled more than 85 percent of all hospitalised cases in Guinea, Liberia and Sierra Leone (the three worst affected countries), and admitted one-third of all WHO-confirmed cases to its Ebola management centres (MSF, 2016).

Reflecting on ethical dilemmas faced by the organisation during the response to the Ebola crisis, Calain & Poncin (2015) describe the delicate balance between 'persuasion and subtle coercion, between veracity and deception'. During contact tracing, which is recognised as one of the six central Ebola control strategies,[5] public health workers 'conduct and promote thorough tracing of those who have been in contact with Ebola-infected people' in order to support other public health activities and prevent the spread of the disease (MSF, 2015). During the Ebola outbreak, case finders and contract tracers had the dual function of carrying out restrictive public health measures to contain the rapid spread of the disease, and observing medical ethics. These functions were in tension as public health legislation imposed mandatory isolation for suspect cases and quarantine for those exposed. These measures violated civil liberties and respect for autonomy, particularly informed consent. Exacerbating these tensions was the fact that isolation in Ebola treatment centres did not ensure survival, and quarantine was not accompanied by basic necessities such as sufficient food, water, and compensation for lost work. These failings undermined the utility of isolation and quarantine as methods to quickly control the outbreak. On reflection, MSF was not certain that the isolation of cases was 'an absolute and constant necessity in the course of the epidemic', while the imposition of isolation may have had the effect of sending people with symptoms into hiding (Calain & Poncin, 2015).

There were instances of overt hostility from community members when health workers sought suspected Ebola patients (MSF, 2015). Case finders and contract tracers faced the dilemma of having to employ different strategies that teetered between 'force, persuasion and appeals for self-sacrifice' (ibid.). The tracer often asked the patient to leave his or her home immediately to limit the risk of contagion posed to unprotected relatives. As such, trust, respect and diplomacy became essential components of engaging with communities.

A doctor with MSF working in Guinea, Dr Tim Jagatic, described the reaction of communities as the numbers of Ebola cases continued to rise. He said it was hard to counter the rumour mill: local populations had been suspicious of MSF for some time despite MSF's attempts at community engagement. 'The reason for this is best explained as follows: one day someone got sick and died. The next day MSF came dressed in space suits and started spraying ... around the village (the disinfection process) and soon a lot more people started dying. Therefore

MSF is spraying us with Ebola' (MSF, 2014b). More recent work by MSF and non-MSF contributors has highlighted how 'patients and their care were not sufficiently prioritised as security and containment not solidarity became the biggest prerogative of governments and organisations supporting the response' (MSF, 2017c).[6]

However, contract tracers remained agents who could help to manage expectations, ease tensions with communities, and offer some form of mediation between communities and health authorities. What was needed was training on the ethical dimensions of their role, and the steps to take in difficult circumstances. If trained to offer a variety of possible choices to patients, public health workers could help to prevent families from hiding cases, or from refusing disease control measures. Ensuring informed consent and providing psychological support for families during such a difficult time could have helped to promote trustworthiness, reciprocity, and proportionality (see Box 15.3).

MSF has since made recommendations that combine ethical principles and pragmatic observations to help humanitarian workers both improve contact tracing and public health, and at the same time deliver respectful and dignified care for Ebola patients and their families during Ebola outbreaks (see Box 15.3). These recommendations

---

Box 15.3 Practical Ethical Guidance for Outreach Teams

Calain and Poncin (2015) recommend the following practical guidance for outreach teams:

1 Trustworthiness:
- Veracity: openness about the exact reasons – with their burdens and benefits – for isolation;
- Clarity of roles: separation from law enforcement authorities;
- The inclusion of Ebola survivors in outreach teams.

2. Reciprocity:
- Material and psychological support for families;
- The provision of basic health services.

3. Proportionality and Least Infringement:
- The offering of genuine choices: possible alternatives to facility isolation, including home-based care.

serve as an example of a practical tool that can be used to ensure that responses are both effective and ethical.

MSF Case Study 2 – Barriers and Moral Distress for Humanitarians Denied Access: Paul's Story

Paul is an experienced emergency medical practitioner with MSF.[7] He has completed multiple missions in conflict zones and unstable regions where mortality and morbidity is invariably high among affected populations. While sharing the moral dilemmas he faced, Paul does not wish to disclose details of the particular country or context due to the sensitive political situation: 'We have to protect the people we are trying to assist and our field teams.'

He and his team were blocked from reaching thousands of people with both suspected and reported humanitarian needs. The government cited security concerns, yet the team was concerned for this large population, residing in an 'apocalyptic' place with little humanitarian assistance. 'As health care workers, we had an amazing team of emergency trained national medical staff, we had all the resources: we just didn't have access. That's morally distressing.'

In this 'very political situation', Paul's team tried daily to gain access to this particularly vulnerable population. They had conversations around access, strategising, and negotiating with the government. However, it should be noted that MSF also had teams working in other parts of the country and did not want to jeopardise those projects. On this, Paul noted that, 'We have to maintain neutrality and when we do advocate or speak out, we have to do it carefully, like a delicate political dance. We were always hopeful, thinking maybe next week we'll get access.'

One incident raised an ethical dilemma and exacerbated Paul and team's moral distress. The team heard reports of a child whose situation was likely a medical emergency. The team received an image of the child but they were unable to fully assess the child's medical situation without a clinical assessment. The government gave MSF permission to provide medical care to this child, and to proceed with a medical evacuation if necessary. While Paul wanted to go and assess the child, another emergency medical professional on the team thought that an attempt to reach and evacuate one patient would jeopardise MSF's impartial stance. Nevertheless, Paul felt that 'we should be able to evacuate the child if necessary and use our advocacy position to say, "This is what we're doing, there are other people there in need, we need access to the population." We could use this example as leverage.' The dilemma faced by the team ultimately related to the need to make a choice between assessing and potentially saving the life of one child, and on the other hand maintaining the security of the mission and the ability to continue working in the same context, and the desire to eventually access the whole population. 'It wasn't a logistical question it was more about the higher-level strategy. Yes, we could go there and see this child: we have a driver, vehicle, medicine and equipment, we have an emergency nurse and doctor.' This assertion was contrasted with a strategy of, 'Let's be careful now, we want good relations with the country we don't want to push too much.'

Initially, Paul was conflicted, 'It's hard not to have an emotional response and think this is what we are here to do.' Gaining access became an obsession for the team, as they remained in the same place for many weeks, with little else to do but wait. 'Every day we were asking, How many water trucks got through today? What's happening with the food delivery? It wasn't allowed this week.' Eventually Paul was able to resolve this tension, with support from a colleague. 'I came around eventually. We had really good conversations about the situation. I was with someone who was so grounded and very experienced. I trusted and respected her. She helped me understand it wouldn't be the right decision to try to help only one person. There was no perfect decision but at the same time I think about other missions where we compromise our values to a certain extent to still be allowed to have some humanitarian and medical presence. Sometimes that risk is worth the benefit to provide medical care.'

Paul's team were ultimately unable to secure access during his mission. They hoped that the child recovered because they did not hear about her again. 'In the end, the process of "do we go or not" became important. If the child died because we didn't go then we'd likely look back wondering if we should have done something differently.' Reflecting on his mission Paul later contemplated,

> Were we right to try to get to the people? Yes. Should we have
> continued to have advocated for access? Absolutely. Being there
> without doing any medical activity, we were still advocating through
> our humanitarian presence and pushing for access to medical care. I

think we did the best job possible but we were limited by the politics. I think many people can't appreciate that we have these barriers. I've been in other situations where we are able to treat patients but it's the government's decision to allow us access, and that access can be taken away anytime. Sometimes we're very limited in what we can speak about.

Paul's case has contextual specificity, yet at the same time, the challenges he describes echo other dilemmas that MSF has faced, and will undoubtedly face again.[8] On reflection, he found it invaluable that his team was able to openly voice and discuss the dilemmas they faced, and that all members of the team were able to participate in decision-making processes. The team was able to generate open dialogue related to ethical questions, but also to seek advice from staff at headquarters who had experienced ethically complex situations, but who also shared a concern for macro-level issues. Creating this shared space within the team ultimately reduced Paul's experience of moral distress: 'I was blessed to have a small, inclusive team where we could all speak openly.'

On reflection, Paul recognised that, 'There are these moral dilemmas in the field, and it's easy to look back and question what you did, whether your decisions were right. These dilemmas are so complicated and the decisions are weighted. It's layered. I think it's so important to have these conversations in the field, to have buy-in from the team on hard decisions. Lastly, I think the moral distress not only comes from dealing with circumstances in the field but also the somewhat isolating aftermath. Due to the often-delicate political nature of our work, there are scenarios we are unable to really talk about when we reintegrate into our lives back home. MSF of course has opportunities to debrief and provides counselling support post-mission but this highlights for me the link between moral distress and mental health support, which is a major issue for humanitarian ethics.'

Identifying Ethical Dilemmas and Making Decisions

Humanitarian ethics is a dynamic and developing topic. We continue to learn as we practice, though we do know that if we do not address ethical issues appropriately, they can cause problems both for humanitarian workers, and for the people we hope to assist. Decision-making that is impulsive, decisions that are not openly discussed, and rationales that are not clearly justified or shared with the necessary stakeholders, can undermine MSF's humanitarian action and damage the organisation's reputation.

It is increasingly clear that established sources of ethical guidance, such as biomedical ethical frameworks or professional codes of conduct, do not capture the complexity of humanitarian situations in which ethical challenges arise. As such, it is imperative that we consider new contextual circumstances, values, and constraints. Notably, when the outcome of an ethical decision-making process is disputed, it is often still judged from the perspective of 'misconduct', reflecting a narrow interpretation of ethics (Calain, 2015).

The repercussions of ethical dilemmas have a profound impact on MSF's operational mandate. MSF has long reflected on the meta-level ethical dilemmas that touch on our core principles, as raised by project-level realities. Some examples currently under discussion include MSF's duty of care towards patients, staff, and non-MSF visitors to projects; the role of MSF in the broader humanitarian system; the ethical dimensions of *témoignage* (i.e. witnessing and speaking out) (Calain, 2013); the place of universal versus relative ethics; and the issue of complicity in humanitarian action (Sheather & Wong, n.d.); and questions about MSF's role in the provision of maritime search and rescue during the global migration crisis.

Paul's dilemma of waiting for access to vulnerable populations with important needs is reminiscent of the distress MSF volunteers faced in September 1999 while trying to secure access in East Timor. The organisation had been expelled from the country. Violence had ensued after the referendum for independence from Indonesia and many people were forcibly displaced from the country and into West Timor. Eventually MSF achieved access, but this waiting game was excruciating for staff, who knew that people were suffering.[9]

Identifying ethical challenges requires a continuous attentiveness at the level of individual projects. Developing the awareness and sensitivity of project staff to ethical issues will allow them to become more practised in recognition of issues that require an adapted and more sensitive decision-making approach. Recognising ethical dilemmas requires an additional order of awareness and, while dilemmas can quickly become apparent, addressing such situations requires the insight to recognise that dilemmas lack, by their nature, a clearly right or wrong course of action.

While every dilemma is qualitatively different, Paul's dilemma of whether to help one patient when his team did not have access to the whole population is reminiscent of MSF's stance in South Africa during the period of AIDS denialism. At this time, HIV was a death sentence for many people living with the virus. The chairman of a drug company visited an MSF project and met with Dr Eric Goemaere, MSF's General Director at the time. By chance, Eric was giving a consultation and invited the executive along. He recalls, 'I hadn't prepared this, but there was a young boy ... slowly but surely dying from HIV.' The chairman offered to pay for the boy's treatment. Goemaere replied, 'it might be possible, there were thousands of children like this, dying slowly from HIV, and that only generic antiretrovirals would make it affordable. One child's care wasn't the issue' (MSF, 2014c).

While there are many different and context-specific ethical challenges faced daily by MSF staff and patients, MSF has thus far prioritised some general areas of concern. These include: establishing the boundaries of authorised medical procedures; establishing competencies according to qualifications (e.g. nurses, clinical assistants, medical doctors); improving the level of confidentiality maintained during clinical care, public health activities, and clinical research; ensuring the equitable management and treatment of our staff, irrespective of their nationality or geographic location; promoting informed consent; and addressing moral distress by ensuring that ethical challenges are handled appropriately, with adequate follow up for staff (with the involvement of human resources, psychologists, and peer support networks as deemed necessary).

Creating Ethical Spaces

In the course of our ethical reflection, we have identified the creation of spaces for ethical deliberation as one way to facilitate discussion and reflection in a safe and non-judgemental manner. MSF now recognises the potentially harmful and exclusive effect of imbalances of power and mishandled inter-cultural dynamics, and acknowledges the need to ensure that previously unheard voices and opinions are afforded attention. Creating these 'spaces' implies that all opinions are respected and – within the parameters of MSF's guiding principles – that open debate remains central to the vitality of the organisation. These spaces take various forms, as we outline in the following section.

Harnessing MSF's Culture of Debate and Reflection

Ethical issues are often highlighted during the annual field associative debates held at MSF projects in many of the sixty countries in which we work. By focusing our collective attention on the ethical issues faced by teams, we can learn important lessons from the rich reflection generated at the project level, which in turn helps to shape our ethical reflection at a national and international level. The annual general assemblies of our twenty-four MSF associations plus the IGA are key moments at which to raise these ethical issues, and to debate how they might impact MSF's mandate, principles, and the form of its humanitarian action.

We have found that the inclusion of an ethicist, either from within or external to the organisation, has been helpful during the course of these ethical deliberations. As an action-oriented emergency organisation, our reflex is to find answers first and pause to ask questions later. An ethicist experienced in the framing of ethical discussions, and with some knowledge of MSF and humanitarianism, can help the organisation create time and a space firstly to identify ethical issues, and secondly to guide the non-judgemental exploration of such issues, accounting for a variety of different perspectives and points of view. Depending on the magnitude of the issue at hand, this can either be quick and relatively straightforward, or a more extensive and time-consuming process. Such reflection invariably paves the way for a more open and transparent decision-making process, where all stakeholders are able to actively participate and share their different views, with the eventual effect that everyone feels that they were consulted ahead of a final decision.

Management Training

In some MSF operations, discussions related to ethical challenges and dilemmas are included as part of management training. By exposing our management staff at both the project and headquarters level to guided discussions during their training courses, they become better equipped with the skills required to identify ethical issues and awareness of the ways in which spaces can be created to foster debate within project teams. Other MSF operations have also included ethical reflection during annual conferences organised for management staff.

MSF Ethics Review

The consistent growth in both the volume and complexity of MSF's human participant research led to the creation of the MSF Ethics Review Board (ERB) in 2001 (Schopper et al., 2015). The MSF ERB is an independent board with expertise in research ethics, and attentive to vulnerable populations in humanitarian contexts. It ensures that research conducted by MSF responds to the unique ethical challenges inherent to MSF's humanitarian response, which may not be captured by research ethics guidelines developed for primary application in stable, non-crisis contexts. The MSF ERB has since set a strong precedent for research ethics during humanitarian crises (Schopper et al., 2017).

In addition to human participant research ethics, MSF recognises the need to be more attentive to the ethical aspects of innovation in MSF projects. MSF developed and is now piloting a self-guided ethics framework for use in MSF. The MSF Ethics Framework for Humanitarian Innovation is intended to encourage critical reflection and discussion about the different ethical considerations involved in innovative project implementation (Sheather et al., 2016).

Informal Discussion Platforms

Several informal platforms have been created in MSF between association members and executive staff in order to discuss ethical issues. One such group was formed to support the IGA motion detailed in Box 15.1. This group, which includes people living and working in ten countries, with both executive and associative roles within MSF, represents a new informal space to reflect on the ways in which MSF deals with ethical issues, to exchange experiences, to inspire action, and to collaborate on articles and analysis intended to further provoke debate within MSF.

Another informal mixed group has formed to approach the issue of improved accountability to the crisis-affected people we try to assist. This is an open platform for anyone within MSF, which functions as a means to organise thinking and reflection for dissemination to the wider MSF movement.

Towards an Ethical Framework for Decision-making

Ethical reflection is formed of two distinct stages: the identification of ethical dilemmas and challenges, and the creation of space to discuss such issues. One option currently under consideration within MSF is the creation of a simple framework for ethical reflection that can be easily used at both project level and headquarters alike.[10] Such a framework could help to generate the safe space needed to deal with complex and often emotional issues at all levels within the organisation. In light of real-time constraints at the project level, such a framework must be efficient so as to generate ethically informed decisions within a short space of time.

In relation to the process of decision-making in MSF, the seminal work on 'accountability for reasonableness' by Daniels and Sabin continues to provide a relevant conceptual framework. The four conditions outlined in the framework emphasise the need to: 1) justify decisions based on evidence or principles that are considered relevant by all parties to a decision; 2) ensure open and transparent publicity of all decisions and their associated justification; 3) create a mechanism to challenge and revise decisions in the event that there is disagreement or that new evidence emerges; and 4) ensure the means exist with which to uphold conditions 1 to 3. Such a framework has clear utility in relation to many of the operational decisions made at all levels within MSF (Daniels, 2000).

Conclusion

Ethical debates exist at the core of MSF. Ethical dilemmas and challenges touch on our identity and our interpretation and application of the humanitarian principles. The two interconnected and interdependent faces of MSF, our Association and Executive, both play important roles in stimulating and guiding ethical discussions and identifying practicable solutions.

Humanitarian ethics is to be neither ideological nor judgemental. A process of humanitarian ethical reflection must provide a space within which different complex ethical positions can be articulated, developed, and challenged. This ethical space allows us to discuss key issues, take decisions or adopt a particular position, and to follow up with clear reasoning and justification. Whether or not consensus is ultimately achieved, it is imperative that all of those involved in decision-making processes should understand how and why a decision was taken.

Much of our work is guided by a form of ethical intuition: an 'ethical GPS' developed within the organisation over the course of the last forty-six years. Nothing can replace that intuitive capacity. However, this does not detract from the need to engage with a process of more rigorous ethical reflection in relation to humanitarian action. Ethical reflection requires us to identify dilemmas before seeking solutions, to consider the various different interpretations of ethical issues, and to be open to different worldviews before making affirmative decisions.

As more and more people are displaced by war and social upheaval, as access to safe and dignified places to seek sanctuary are denied, and as urgent needs go unmet, the ethical issues faced by MSF and other humanitarian organisations are surely set to intensify. We hope that by sharing our experiences and outlining efforts taken by MSF to actively develop its humanitarian ethical reasoning capacity, the organisation can contribute to a greater awareness of the inherent dilemmas and challenges associated with the provision of medical humanitarian assistance, with the ultimate aim of improving humanitarian action for the benefit of the people we seek to assist.

Notes

1 These foundational documents are the MSF Charter, read together with the Chantilly Agreement of 1995, and the La Mancha Agreement of 2005.

2 For one such example of MSF's attempt to better understand how its work and its principles are perceived by those who receive its emergency medical care, see C Abu-Sa'Da (ed.) (2012), *In the eyes of others: how people in crises perceive humanitarian aid.*

3 For examples of empirical research see: Schwartz, L, et al. (2010), Ethics in humanitarian aid work: Learning from the narratives of humanitarian health workers, *AJOB Primary Research*; and Hunt, MR, Sinding, C, Schwartz, L (2013) Tragic choices in humanitarian healthcare practice. *Journal of Clinical Ethics.*

4 Personal communications.

5 Six core pillars are recognised as elements of an Ebola control strategy: 1) isolate and care for patients, 2) make burials safe, 3) engage communities, 4) conduct disease surveillance, 5) trace contracts, and 6) re-establish healthcare

systems. As Pagano and Poncin (2016) note, 'engaging in one without another will fail to bring Ebola under control, particularly neglecting to gain the trust of the affected communities.'

6 The quoted passage derives from an article that refers to: Hofman, M, Au, S (eds) (2017) *The politics of fear: Médecins Sans Frontières and the West African Ebola epidemic.*

7 Paul is a pseudonym.

8 For additional examples see MSF (2014c), *No valley without shadows: MSF and the fight for affordable ARVs in South Africa*; and Weissman F (ed.) (2004), *In the shadow of 'just wars': violence, politics and humanitarian action.*

9 This was particularly difficult as journalists were able to achieve access first, before medical personnel or humanitarian supplies.

10 The Humanitarian Health Ethics Analysis Tool (HHEAT) is an example of one such framework. For more details, see: https://humanitarianhealthethics. net/home/hheat/hheat/.

References

Abu-Sa'Da, C (ed.) (2012), *In the eyes of others: how people in crises perceive humanitarian aid*. New York: MSF, Humanitarian Outcomes, NYU Center on International Cooperation.

Calain, P (2013), Ethics and images of suffering bodies in humanitarian medicine. *Social Science & Medicine*. Vol. 98: 278–85.

Calain, P (2015), *Syllabus: preparing for ethical challenges in humanitarian medicine*. Facilitator's manual. First edition. Geneva: Unité de Recherche sur les Enjeux et Pratiques Humanitaires (UREPH), Médecins Sans Frontières.

Calain, P (2016), The Ebola clinical trials: a precedent for research ethics in disasters. *Journal of Medical Ethics*. Published online 29 August 2016.

Calain, P & Poncin, M (2015), Reaching out to Ebola victims: coercion, persuasion or an appeal for self-sacrifice? *Social Science & Medicine*. Vol. 147, 126–33.

Campbell, SM, Ulrich, CM & Grady, C (2016), A broader understanding of moral distress. *American Journal of Bioethics*. Vol. 16 (12): 2–9.

Daniels, N (2000), Accountability for reasonableness. *BMJ*. Vol. 321 (7272): 1300–1.

Hofman, M & Au, S (eds) (2017), *The politics of fear: Médecins sans Frontières and the West African Ebola epidemic*. Oxford: Oxford University Press.

Hunt, MR, Sinding, C & Schwartz, L (2013), Tragic choices in humanitarian healthcare practice. *Journal of Clinical Ethics*. Vol. 23 (4): 338–44.

Gilbert, E (2017), Burnout in the field [online]. Available from: https:// medium.com/msf-passport/burnout-in-the-field-2dcaf47do1eb (accessed 25 August 2017).

Kälvemark, S, Höglund, AT, Hansson, MG, Westerholm, P & Arnetz, B (2004), Living with conflicts – ethical dilemmas and moral distress in the healthcare system. *Social Science and Medicine*. Vol. 58 (6): 1075–84.

Mackintosh, K (2000), *The principles of humanitarian action in international humanitarian law*. HPG Report 5. Humanitarian Policy Group, Overseas Development Institute.

Magone, C, Neuman, M & Weissman, F (eds) (2011), *Humanitarian negotiations revealed: the MSF experience*. London: Hurst & Co. Publishers.

MSF (1999), With lives at stake, MSF is denied access to East Timor [online]. Available from: www.msf.org/en/ article/lives-stake-msf-denied-access-east-timor (accessed 9 August 2017).

MSF (2014a), United Nations special briefing on Ebola by MSF International President Dr. Joanne Liu [online]. Available from: www.msf.ca/ en/node/43606 (accessed 26 August 2017).

MSF (2014b), Ebola: a Canadian reflects on his second mission to West Africa [online]. Available from: www.msf.ca/ en/article/ebola-canadian-reflects-his-second-mission-west-africa (accessed 9 August 2017).

MSF (2014c), *No valley without shadows: MSF and the fight for affordable ARVs in South Africa*. Brussels: Médecins Sans Frontières.

MSF (2015), *Pushed to the limit and beyond: a year into the largest ever Ebola outbreak*. Geneva: Médecins Sans Frontières.

MSF (2016), *Ebola 2014–2015 facts & figures*. Geneva: Médecins Sans Frontières.

MSF (2017a), Medical issues: Ebola [online]. Available from: www. doctorswithoutborders.org/our-work/medical-issues/ebola (accessed 26 August 2017).

MSF (2017b), Ebola [online]. Available from: www.msf.org.uk/issues/ebola (accessed 10 August 2017).

MSF (2017c), The politics of fear [online]. Available from: www.msf.org/en/article/politics-fear (accessed 29 August 2017).

Pagano, H & Poncin, M (2016), Treating, containing, mobilizing: the role of Médecins Sans Frontières in the West African Ebola epidemic response. In: Halabi, SF, Gostin, LO & Crowley, JS (eds) *Global management of infectious disease after Ebola*. New York: Oxford University Press.

Pringle, J (2015), Charity medicine for the global poor: humanitarian ethics and the Nigerian lead-poisoning outbreak. p. 16. Doctoral thesis, University of Toronto. Available from: http://hdl.handle.net/1807/69439.

Rid, A & Antierens, A (2017), How did Médecins Sans Frontières negotiate clinical trials of unproven treatments during the 2014–2015 Ebola epidemic? Pp. 133–74. In: Michiel, H & Au, S (eds), *The politics of fear: Médecins sans Frontières and the West African Ebola Epidemic*. Oxford: Oxford University Press.

Schenkenberg van Mierop, E (2015), Coming clean on neutrality and independence: the need to assess the application of humanitarian principles. *International Review of the Red Cross*. Vol. 97 (897/898): 295–318.

Schopper, D, Dawson, A, Upshur, R, Ahmad, A, Jesani, A, Ravinetto, R, ... Singh, J (2015), Innovations in research ethics governance in humanitarian settings. *BMC Medical Ethics*. Vol. 16: 10.

Schopper, D, Ravinetto, R, Schwartz, L, Kamaara, E, Sheel, S, Segelid, MJ, ... Upshur, R (2017), Research ethics governance in times of Ebola. *Public Health Ethics*. Vol. 10 (1): 49–61.

Schwartz, L, Sinding, C, Hunt, M, Elit, L, Redwood-Campbell, L, Adelson, N, ... De Laat, S (2010), Ethics in humanitarian aid work: learning from the narratives of humanitarian health workers. *AJOB Primary Research*. Vol. 1 (3): 45–54.

Sheather, J, Jobanputra, K, Schopper, D, Pringle, J, Venis, S, Wong, S, Vincent-Smith & R (2016), A Médecins sans Frontières ethics framework for humanitarian innovation. *PLOS Medicine*. Vol. 13(9), e1002111.

Sheather, J & Wong, S (ND), *Complicity*. Pending publication.

Watson-Stryker, E (2016), Psychosocial care for Ebola patients: the response of Doctors Without Borders/Médecins Sans Frontières. Pp. 167–73. In: Kuriansky, J (ed.) *The psychosocial aspects of a deadly epidemic: what Ebola has taught us about holistic healing*. Santa Barbara, CA: ABC-Clio.

Weissman, F (ed.) (2004), *In the shadow of 'just wars': violence, politics and humanitarian action*. London: Hurst & Co. Publishers.

16 | STOP MISSING THE POINT: MANAGING HUMANITARIAN ACTION WELL

Caroline Clarinval

Introduction

In 2012, wars and disease outbreaks generated an attractive 8.23 billion USD in business by way of humanitarian response (Scott, 2015). At the same time, humanitarian actors aim to meet basic needs of affected populations, and do so by deploying human and financial resources to assist the most vulnerable. To illustrate the magnitude of the business model, the United Nations High Commission for Refugees (UNHCR) requested over 7.5 billion USD to meet the needs of their operations in 2016 (UNHCR, 2017). For 2017, the International Committee of the Red Cross (ICRC) appealed for a budget exceeding 1.8 billion Swiss francs to cover its headquarters and field operations costs (ICRC, 2016). In the same year, the United Nation's humanitarian organisation for children, UNICEF, aimed to mobilise close to 1.5 billion USD.

In 2016, over 65.6 million people were forced to leave their homes, with this trend projected to increase (UNHCR, 2016). Humanitarian interventions implemented by national and international aid organisations have proliferated with a diversification of modalities of response, ranging from the provision of basic food assistance to elaborate cash programmes, and the delivery of specialised medical care to premature neonates.

The overarching objective of humanitarian action is to meet the needs of people affected by crises such as wars, natural disasters, or a combination thereof. Terry (2002) reiterates that 'the humanitarian imperative declares that there is an obligation to provide humanitarian assistance wherever it is needed and is based on the right to receive, and to offer, humanitarian aid'.

Aside from securing financial resources, a significant challenge for humanitarian actors is not related to fundraising, but to the deployment of the right people to the right place at the right time and to the process of ensuring that they have the tools required to be fully operational (i.e. to ensure that financial support is managed effectively and used to the best of its potential to improve the lives of those during, and in the aftermath of, humanitarian emergencies). As such, ensuring that the right people are present in the right place is imperative, given that peoples' lives and wellbeing are at stake.

In response to wars and environmental disasters that affect large populations, the number of humanitarian actors continues to grow as international and national organisations flourish across the globe. In the name of saving people's lives, directed (in some cases) by the guiding humanitarian principles, and with belief in the subtle power of human rights law or international humanitarian law, humanitarian workers engage in an 'off-road' type of life in order to assist people in need. Many leave or abandon their own families and friends to help the 'distant in distress'. Philosophers have debated whether there is a moral obligation to assist the 'distant' (Singer, 2004). Nevertheless, for those engaged in humanitarian response, the answer to this debate seems clear. These ongoing discussions considered, in this chapter I assume that we have a moral obligation to assist people in need without exposing ourselves or others to harm.

While much humanitarian action is now overshadowed by business models, the historical development of its underlying ethical values cannot be sidelined or ignored; there remains a need to ensure actions are ethically justified in the context of a humanitarian intervention. Notably, despite the fact that humanitarian work has professionalised and become more technical, the ethical challenges encountered by humanitarian workers have become more multifaceted as a consequence of humanitarianism's corporate dimension, and engagement with global investors.

To this day there remains a lack of agreement on the most appropriate profile and skill set humanitarian workers ought to have before they are deployed to an emergency situation. The dichotomy between being technically savvy, or an outstanding manager who graduated from a renowned management school, stands unresolved. Ideally, managers should embody both profiles, but due to the lack of skilled humanitarian workers, aid organisations often have to accept a trade-off.

On the one hand, humanitarian agencies desperately look to fill certain posts, often in the most rural areas. On the other, there are a number of people who desire to become humanitarian professionals, exploring their options, and attempting to understand where they can make a significant contribution, and for whom they should work. Reis and Bernath (2016) argue that prospective staff, when faced with many job options, need to consider several elements such as the job level, geographical area, sectoral focus, required skill set, and function. As Slim (2015) highlights:

> Humanitarian ethics has long been torn between the passion of voluntarism and the importance of professional qualifications. Driven by the universal moral value of humanity, humanitarianism hopes for a world in which everyone is motivated by humanitarian impulses to care for and protect each other. Entry into humanitarian aid work is primarily vocational, impulsive and urgent. It is a voluntary response to a moral call that we feel and share, as immediate neighbours and global neighbours. In this sense, humanitarian help is the great domain of the amateur: literally, the lover of something, which in this case is our fellow human beings ... many humanitarian workers have mixed motives for doing what they do.

The humanitarian aid industry has evolved in such a way that the days when people engaged in the profession solely motivated by altruism, willing to participate in any task required of them, and accepting of deployment to any location, have changed.

In summary, the needs of large populations remain unmet, while the international community has yet to reach a consensus on who is best equipped to efficiently manage large-scale relief operations. Recruiting and deploying the right people at the right time to the right place is difficult and remains a challenge for most human resources units. One of the key issues is the need to find and mobilise people that are able to run humanitarian operations – and thus to meet needs 'on the ground' – and are also capable of dealing with ethical dilemmas and unclear courses of action. This chapter provides two real-life anonymised cases that illustrate some of the difficulties and ethical challenges faced by humanitarian actors.

Managing Bedlam

Humanitarian action by its nature is rooted in a degree of chaos, as humanitarian actors are pressed to trace numbers of people displaced or injured, and those who have died. Operating in war zones and in the aftermath of natural disasters bears a number of risks that must be explored. It is acknowledged that humanitarian aid workers engage in humanitarian activities either as a genuine form of altruism, as a desire to aspire towards a comfortable life, or as a combination thereof, while still exposing themselves to threats such as the risk of being looted, kidnapped, raped or killed.

Experienced humanitarian aid workers are conscious of the risks they take and accept that they operate in contexts characterised by uncertainty. However, no standard norms exist to ensure that staff are safe in the 'field', and individual organisations continue to manage their security risks independently of one another. Some organisations are more amenable to taking risks and staying in areas affected by active conflict until a cessation of hostilities is achieved, while others retrieve their staff at a much earlier stage. Nevertheless, Neuman and Weissman (2016) assert that 'the alternative to the dominant security culture means trusting the practical wisdom of humanitarian workers and helping it flourish by relating and analysing their experiences with danger'.

Besides security threats, humanitarian workers have to assess and continuously evaluate other key issues as well. As such, a lack of understanding of the needs that exist 'on the ground', a lack of cultural awareness, a lack of operational readiness, and a lack of coordination are all problematic when attempting to establish an appropriate response. While humanitarian organisations have put a great deal of effort into training their staff, there is currently no widely accepted curriculum that teaches how to effectively, efficiently and promptly respond to disasters.

Unfortunately, despite repeated efforts to prepare communities for worst-case scenarios, when a disaster does occur it often drastically outdoes any table-top or simulation exercise. The common denominator of any disaster is that needs outweigh response capacities at a local level. Often first-line crisis responders comprise members of the affected community, while those that pay the price are ultimately the most vulnerable: those people buried underneath 'layers of vulnerability' (Luna, 2009). In this sense, by virtue of the nature of a disaster, large populations are left without access to basic services, and humanitarian aid workers are quickly overwhelmed by the perplexing situation with which they are faced. Consequently, the humanitarian aid sector nearly always delivers a delayed, disorganised and ill-equipped initial response. Following the 2004 tsunami in South East Asia, the

2010 earthquake in Haiti, and more recently the latest cholera outbreak in the Horn of Africa, donors, humanitarian actors and affected communities agree that there is room for improvement in the analysis and response to the initial phases of a disaster. Aside from the practical issues related to appropriateness of emergency response, ethical challenges also exist, which present an additional burden that humanitarian actors must learn to manage. In this chapter, I highlight specific cases with an ethical dimension faced by humanitarian workers.

The following two cases illustrate several ethical issues affecting contemporary humanitarian action. The aim of the cases is to highlight that many problems are not of a technical or managerial nature *per se*, but that they represent ethical challenges that need to be further scrutinised and discussed at a managerial level in order to allow teams 'on the ground' to engage in an appropriate course of action. The cases are anonymised in order to convey the ethical essence of each case more clearly.

Case Studies

Case 1: Allocating Limited Resources Fairly: Whose Life Ought to Be Saved?

An international organisation receives funding to work in a conflict-affected country. Millions of people have left this country and are seeking asylum or refuge in neighbouring countries, or further afield. The neighbouring countries are unable to host such large numbers of displaced and have closed their borders, asking the international community for assistance. Aid organisations are engaged in the provision of life-saving goods to the refugees. Fortunately, international donors are keen to assist the displaced populations and provide over 50 million USD to be spent in several countries. How shall these limited resources be shared across host countries, and in the conflict-affected country? Which programmes should be supported? Should all countries receive an equal share, or should the share be adjusted such that it is proportional to the number of displaced people hosted in each country?

Today, aid organisations struggle to secure funding and as soon as funding is received, they need to coordinate their responses to avoid a duplication of efforts. However, the moment that multiple parameters are at play, it becomes extremely challenging to make well-considered decisions, as no organisation has the tools or resources at hand to do so, which presents a severe ethical shortcoming in organisational structure. Making fair and just decisions in the context of an emergency requires the following components:

1. A forum to meet and discuss the ethical issues at stake;
2. An agreed decision-making process;
3. Established roles and responsibilities among decision-makers regarding the process;
4. Consensus on who is ultimately part of, and entitled to, make decisions;
5. An agreed understanding of the ethical principle of justice to guide the decision-making process;
6. A review mechanism to explore the decision-making process and its consequences.

At present, none of the above components have been adequately established and decisions regarding fair processes of resource allocation still lack transparency and accountability simply because there is no mechanism in place that would guarantee a consistently appropriate decision-making approach.

Case 2: Ethical Issues when Partnering with For-Profit Businesses in a Not-For-Profit World

An international organisation decides to provide medical support close to the frontline of a conflict. To do so, the organisation establishes a partnership with a for-profit partner. This partner agrees to provide multi-million USD of supplies and services close to the frontline. The proposed cost significantly exceeds the average cost of similar supplies in other contexts, but since there appears to be no other partner willing to engage, the international organisation agrees to the collaboration with the for-profit business with the aim of saving people's lives. No ethicist was invited to be participate in the discussions and after lengthy deliberation the managers of the organisation decide to pursue the collaboration with the partner despite the associated cost and ethical implications.

Such collaborations have the potential to do more harm than good. For example, these decisions can carry a reputational risk for the entire organisation, which may have greater consequences than would nonintervention. In this case, the allocated funds could have been used to conduct other projects and still save lives. From a utilitarian point of view, I would argue that more people's lives could likely have been saved had these efforts been diverted to assist other groups.

Managing large-scale humanitarian operations demands a strong sense of justice. Questions such as how limited funds should be distributed fairly across populations, countries, agencies, and ultimately different aid programmes require ethical consideration since decision-makers are required to weigh up several parameters when proposing a possible solution.

'Appropriateness' in Humanitarian Response

Both cases illustrate that determining 'appropriateness' in human-itarian response remains difficult and above all requires a protected space that allows humanitarian aid workers to debate openly and to question whether their actions can be deemed right or wrong. Today, such a space exists only if created by individual managers. Otherwise, humanitarian agencies seem to rely on the fact that their staff are all driven by semi-altruistic motives, which in turn makes their actions objectionable. For example, some organisations continue to receive limited funds. In certain contexts, they might agree to accept funding from countries that are actively involved in conflict in the country in which they wish to provide assistance. A legitimate question to ask in such a circumstance would be whether it is ethically justifiable that humanitarian agencies accept funds from countries that at the same time impose sanctions or engage in hostilities in the country in which they deliver humanitarian aid? Are there limitations to the amount of funding that it is ethically justifiable to accept? Making appropriate decisions in contexts where bombs continue to explode is inevitably problematic. As detailed earlier, the unanswered question remains that of the ideal profile and skill mix of a humanitarian worker. Should this be a general manager with limited technical expertise, or a techni-cal specialist with limited managerial skills? Or perhaps a combination thereof? If the latter is the case then what would be this person's essen-tial characteristics?

Overall, the management of humanitarian aid programmes is a daunting task insofar as the ideal world continues to clash with reality. For example, shipping medicines from point A to point B is expected to follow a simple logistical process that would be a straightforward task in a stable context. However, this is a challenging task in conflict settings or in the wake of a natural disaster, in the context of widespread infrastructural damage. As such, context, geopolitical considerations, funding and human resource capacities matter when attempting to decide what is a right or wrong course of action in humanitarian crises. Depending on the context, very quickly aid organisations can either be accused of prolongation of a conflict (Terry, 2002) or of being unable to meet needs 'on the ground'. Despite the best of intentions, it is clear that responding to emergencies in contexts affected by a man-made or natural disaster requires a specific skill set.

Managing Large-scale Humanitarian Aid Operations

In this section, I explore the advantages and inconveniences of the standard profiles of humanitarian aid workers. The common argument that general managers embody the appropriate profile for the management of a humanitarian response is valid only insofar as they have sufficient experience of the technical requirements, and are fully supported by technical staff. However, as we have seen, aid organisations are unable to deploy experienced and well-trained staff fast enough. In the absence of a sufficient number of qualified technical experts to support the managers responsible for making informed decisions, organisations are unlikely to be able to guarantee an appropriate response, and to alleviate suffering 'on the ground'.

Nevertheless, humanitarian action is a different type of business. Many humanitarian aid workers do not embrace such career perspectives for the money or the adrenaline rush. Rather, they do so because – similarly to Peter Singer (2004) – they are convinced that people's lives and wellbeing matter; even if they live thousands of miles from such individuals, distance should not be used as an argument not to intervene.

On the earlier assumption that humanitarian workers recognise a moral obligation to assist during humanitarian emergencies, which characteristics and skill sets should the ideal candidate embody? I have argued that there are broadly two types of humanitarian aid workers: the managers, and the technical experts. In the section that follows, I will discuss which profiles humanitarian aid workers require when responding to acute crises with high rates of mortality and increasing morbidity among the affected population. Subsequently, I will suggest an appropriate skill mix for humanitarian 'leaders'.

Based on the hypothesis that humanitarian response differs significantly from the approach of the private sector, I argue that humanitarian aid workers learn their skills essentially while undertaking the job. This is fundamentally due to the fact that no full-time bachelor's or master's degree can prepare prospective candidates for the diverse situations they will be confronted with in real life. In the absence of an appropriate curriculum to train humanitarian aid workers for their diverse career paths, this gap must be filled in order to enable field professionals to successfully steer multifaceted operations, and, in turn, to ultimately meet the needs of crisis-affected populations. For instance, the skill set of technical specialists focusing on protection, health, agriculture, or animal health differs significantly from that of general managers, human resource specialists, or administrators. The critical question is who has the power to make decisions, and who will be required to execute them? Here, opinions across agencies differ, and are still debated.

In light of a lack of consensus, donors have changed their approach to funding for humanitarian projects. In accordance with Scott's observations (2014), business models for the delivery of humanitarian assistance must remain fit for purpose, which requires the sector to a) move away from one-size-fits-all response models, b) adapt to new programming tools and concepts and, c) clarify whether responses are effective. Scott (ibid.) concludes that 'most of the proposed options for improved effectiveness will require collective efforts and change, across the entire humanitarian system'. The need to improve decision-making processes in order to optimise the impact of programme outputs is essential, simply because of the sheer number of people that are affected by crises every year, and the cumulative financial sum required to meet their needs. Humanitarian actors must provide an ethical forum and continuously review programme indicators, monitor progress regarding the implementation of the program response, and measure the impact of the provided aid. In addition, to achieve all of the above in a timely manner, agencies rely on deploying the right people to the right place at the right time.

Transversal Learning

The for-profit sector and the not-for-profit sector fundamentally differ. Humanitarian action is embedded in humanistic, non-profit-based values, whereas the for-profit industry primarily adheres to commercial values and is strongly profit-driven. But do these differences significantly affect the quality of humanitarian response?

Theoretically, the boundaries between both areas are distinct. However, in practice, not-for-profit organisations have engaged with the for-profit industry to develop innovative interventions, which ultimately serve humanitarian actors by improving their response. These recent developments have led to a blurring of boundaries. For example, UNHCR and the IKEA Foundation have established a joint venture to develop improved housing for camp settings (UNHCR, 2017). In this case, the development of innovative solutions for camps is a win-win for both parties, as the humanitarian sector benefits from the know-how of the private sector. Nevertheless, while there are some positive initiatives, certain issues have yet to be resolved. For instance, when examining the issue of access to medicines, the focus of the pharmaceutical industry remains the maintenance of high prices for medicines. As MSF continue to reiterate, 'The truth is that high prices are stifling access to medicines, not promoting innovation for public health priorities and causing deadly consequences everywhere' (2017). The blurring of boundaries between the for-profit and the not-for-profit sector occurs as soon as it becomes difficult to ascertain that people in need ultimately benefit the most from this type of collaboration.

Embodying Core Values

Recalling that the core values of humanitarian action are humanity, impartiality, independence, and neutrality, these principles differ fundamentally from the drivers of the for-profit industry, where profit and market share eclipse any form of altruism. Generally, to remain in business, profit matters more than the end user in the for-profit industry, contrary to the not-for-profit sector.

Acknowledging this fundamental difference between the sectors, further questions are raised of whether the profile of managers in charge of humanitarian operations should also differ, and if so, what their profiles should look like, and where they should be trained. What staff profiles should humanitarian organisations pursue in order to be 'successful'? What core values should be transferred to their staff? Lastly, who is held accountable when things go wrong?

Operationalising Ethical Decision-making to Address
Humanitarian Dilemmas

Although several humanitarian organisations have started to rely on project management tools such as dashboards, cockpits, and control and command systems, which certainly help to maintain oversight of their operations, these tools fall short in assisting humanitarian aid workers to make the right decisions when confronted with ethical dilemmas. Referring to the cases above, I understand that dealing with questions where values collide and contradict each other faces a further ethical challenge in terms of any attempted reductionism. There are simply no dashboards with flashing lights that can send an alert to managers as soon as an ethical issue arises. Yet, unless these issues are identified and addressed, operational responses 'on the ground' can have disastrous effects, and ultimately jeopardise the reputation of an entire organisation. If, for example, a for-profit business has links with the arms industry, or to a specific political party, or to a country that is actively engaged in combat, a humanitarian organisation will face a hard time convincing others that it still abides by the fundamental humanitarian principles of impartiality and independence.

With this in mind, it is paramount that humanitarian aid workers are trained to identify and address ethical issues, as the consequences of a lack of, or inadequate, training directly impact on the way critical decisions are applied in the 'field'. For example, exploring the trade-off between principles such as solidarity and do no harm is difficult. We need trained humanitarian aid workers who can guide the decision-making process and ensure that the right decisions are made in an informed and transparent manner.

There Is More to Managing Well than Good Intentions

Doing the right thing and doing things right in contexts affected by humanitarian crisis is problematic and unclear. Terry (2002) underlines that tensions may arise in the application of principles, and that the disparate multitude of humanitarian organisations respond very differently according to their own values and principles. With this in mind, good intentions and the traditional humanitarian values of humanity, impartiality, independence, and neutrality are insufficient to guide humanitarian aid workers when it comes to making difficult decisions. In order to embody these values, humanitarian aid workers require a pluralistic knowledge framework, which includes technical, managerial, geopolitical, and ethical expertise. Therefore, the development of a mixed skill set for humanitarian actors is critical. First, they must understand and adhere to the humanitarian values. Second, because humanitarian actors operate in highly volatile contexts, they must embody key leadership skills such as an ability to:

1. Observe and understand the broader system;
2. Master the art of intervening in the system;
3. Orchestrate collaboration in the system;
4. Foresee and manage system-wide risks; and
5. Lead with a new mind set. (Reeves et al., 2017)

Such skills will enable humanitarian actors to adjust operations in rapidly changing and dynamic contexts. However, in order to make the best use of the limited financial and human resources that humanitarian actors have at their disposal, I would like to add a third element, which is that of formal training in ethics. This is most pertinent as the greatest challenges to be solved are related to ethical dilemmas such as those illustrated in the cases above, while international and national humanitarian organisations continue to neglect the need to train their decision-makers in ways to address ethical issues.

Conclusion

Despite recognising that there is a moral obligation to assist the 'distant', and realising that receiving help and responding to needs are rights for both recipients and aid organisations, the international community has yet to determine which individuals are best equipped to manage large-scale relief operations.

Managing aid operations in contemporary humanitarian emergencies is demanding and humanitarian actors clearly require a specific skill set. Harm to others should always be minimised, and it is for precisely this reason, at a time where humanitarian action has become a multi-billion USD business, that it is critical to review the skills that humanitarian actors have in order to reduce the risk of doing harm.

Presently, if humanitarian aid workers are keen to further develop their professional skills, they must take the initiative themselves and participate in specific curricula that several schools have started to offer in lieu of the mandatory training required by aid organisations. Yet, the risk remains that ill-trained aid workers will continue to operate in highly volatile environments. Notably, the issue of whether or not this field of work should be further regulated in order to minimise harm has yet to be debated in full.

As illustrated in the cases above, the ethical dilemmas humanitarian aid workers are now faced with are often 'new', given the complex and often context-specific factors at play in contemporary humanitarian emergencies. It is unlikely that a universal solution will be found to address all such ethical issues. Prior preparation will need to be nuanced, focused, and multifaceted, which in turn requires a significant amount of time and resources.

Ideally, humanitarian aid agencies should hire staff who are technically sound, geo-politically aware, and trained in methods of ethical deliberation, in order to optimise their decision-making capabilities. I have also argued that such a mixed skill set will allow managers to understand the technical issues they face, while also considering contextual challenges, and addressing possible ethical dilemmas that occur frequently in this line of work. In particular, questions around the allocation of limited resources and the application of the humanitarian principles arise constantly, and repeatedly challenge organisations' current *modus operandi*.

In any case, humanitarian aid organisations still lack a platform where ethical dilemmas can be raised and discussed. There is an urgent need to establish such a forum, where space is afforded to question the status quo, and for humanitarian aid professionals to define what is right from what is wrong.

References

ICRC (2016), *Appeals 2017 overview.* Geneva: International Committee of the Red Cross.

Luna, F (2009), Elucidating the concept of vulnerability: layers not labels. *International Journal of Feminist Approaches to Bioethics.* Vol. 2: 121–39.

MSF (2017), Proposed executive order puts Pharma interests over people's lives [online]. Available from: www.doctorswithoutborders.org/article/proposed-executive-order-puts-pharma-interests-over-peoples-lives (accessed 12 August 2017).

Neuman, MA & Weissman, F (eds) (2016), *Saving lives and staying alive. Humanitarian security in the age of risk management.* London: Hurst Publishers.

Reeves, M, Levin, S, Harnoss, JD & Ueda, D (2017), The five steps all leaders must take in the age of uncertainty [online]. Available from: http://sloanreview.mit.edu/article/the-five-steps-all-leaders-must-take-in-the-age-of-uncertainty/ (accessed 2 August 2017).

Reis, C & Bernath, T (2016), *Becoming an international humanitarian aid worker*. Oxford: Butterworth-Heinemann.

Scott, R (2014), *Imagining more effective humanitarian aid: a donor perspective*. OECD Development Co-operation Working Paper 18. Paris: OECD.

Singer, P (2004), Outsiders: our obligation to those beyond our borders. Pp. 11–32. In: Chatterjee, DK (ed.), *The ethics of assistance: morality and the distant needy*. Cambridge: Cambridge University Press.

Slim, H (2015), *Humanitarian ethics: a guide to the morality of aid in war and disasters*. London: Hurst & Co. Publishers.

Terry, F (2002), *The paradox of humanitarian action: condemned to repeat?* Ithaca, NY: Cornell University Press.

UNHCR (2016), UNHCR – Figures at a Glance [online]. Available from: www.unhcr.org/figures-at-a-glance.html (accessed 24 July 2017).

UNHCR (2017), 2017 global requirements – programmed activities [online]. Available from: http://reporting.unhcr.org/financial#_ga=2.213228308.1852794148.1503769548–247947265.1500857882 (accessed 26 August 2017).

UNHCR (2017), Private sector supporters – main partners: IKEA Foundation [online]. Available from: www.unhcr.org/ikea-foundation.html (accessed 2 August 2017).

17 | AN ETHIC OF REFUSAL: THE POLITICAL ECONOMY OF HUMANITARIANISM UNDER NEOLIBERAL GLOBALISATION

John Pringle and Toby Leon Moorsom

Though the rich of this earth find no difficulty in creating misery, they can't bear to see it. (Bertolt Brecht (1898–1956), socialist playwright and poet)

Abstract

A central concern of humanitarian organisations today should be the question of whether their actions challenge or maintain structures of political power that depend on massive global inequality, and that continually recreate conditions that demand humanitarian response. The principles of impartiality, neutrality and independence, central to the Dunant tradition of humanitarianism, are challenged if the organisation's purported neutrality in fact serves to uphold and reify imperialist orders dependent upon uneven geographies of development. While humanitarians uphold neutrality as a fundamental necessity for access to victims across and outside of state boundaries, this is very different from suggesting their actions are apolitical. In fact, we argue that humanitarians today must consider the ways in which their organisations are impacted by a particular class project and – through an ethic of refusal – reaffirm the humanitarian act as one of defiance and solidarity.

This chapter begins with a discussion of the origins of humanitarianism alongside the rise of capitalism and the Westphalian nation state system. Second, we examine the rise of neoliberal economic thought and the concurrent political project that served to increasingly, and then overwhelmingly, guide political and economic decision-making throughout the world since the 1970s. It is this body of thought that manifested itself most brazenly in the Structural Adjustment Programs (SAPs) imposed upon much of the world following the oil price hikes of the early 1970s, the period of rising interest rates during 1979–1981, and the resulting debt crisis of the 1980s. Third, we contextualise humanitarian emergencies in this economic context and examine the changes to humanitarian doctrines in response to them. In particular, we describe what has been termed *philanthrocapitalism*. Fourth, we propose that an essential response of humanitarian organisations is to assert an ethic of refusal that resists the ideological assimilation of our organisations into this common sense. Lastly, we encourage humanitarian actors to consider their own class relation to the humanitarian project: to act in solidarity rather than to treat affected populations as targets of charity.

Introduction

At a Médecins Sans Frontières (MSF) annual general meeting, discussion turned to the continued and unprecedented growth of the MSF organisation. Tongue in cheek, the speaker declared that MSF is on its way to becoming the ministry of health for the world.[1] What was intended as sarcasm had the opposite effect. Many, particularly the association's younger members, were excited by the growth of the organisation and the potential it afforded. But older members issued a word of caution; MSF is meant to be an emergency medical organisation, one that addresses immediate needs until other organisations, such as ministries of health, are capable of responding. MSF was not meant to be a private contractor of healthcare for the world's poor. This exchange embodies a fundamental tension. On one side, there is ambition, a desire for growth and dominance of the humanitarian sector. On the other, there is want for a world in which local governments are equipped – and willing – to provide adequate and accessible healthcare to all of their people. If healthcare were properly regarded as a human right, humanitarian organisations would exist only for the most extreme and exceptional of circumstances.

The two visions do not have equal footing. The fend-for-yourself ethic of neoliberal globalisation has translated into policies that deprive the poor of healthcare and other essential services. Through deregulation, privatisation, and the clawing back of public spending, healthcare work, particularly in low- and middle-income countries (LMICs), is precarious. Shelves in hospitals and clinics sit empty. Sometimes going months without pay, frontline healthcare workers are forced to emigrate, transfer to more lucrative trades, or supplement their income by other means. On a day-to-day basis, the gutting of public services causes grief and torment for much of the world's population. However, when ineffectual public health systems result in outbreaks of emerging, re-emerging, and vaccine-preventable diseases, suffering reaches new heights. International humanitarian organisations – if they do respond – tend to respond late in the epidemic curve and are unable to provide much more than a modicum of case management. Their vertical programmes are meant to address the outbreak and little more. Then aid organisations pack up and leave, the charitable response is lauded, the situation is labelled 'unprecedented', lessons are 'learned', and suffering returns to baseline.

The story does not end there. Having responded to public health crises precipitated by policies of neglect, non-governmental organisations (NGOs) can showcase their heroic actions in a free-market battle for brand recognition and donations. In a sector with hundreds – if not thousands – of NGOs competing for the same hearts and minds, fundraising campaigns are delivered medicalised and decontextualised. Reductionist public messaging creates the illusion that more donations will fix the problem. This leaves service provision for the poor vulnerable to further austerity while private charitable organisations flourish, and the cycle continues. Breaking the cycle aptly dubbed 'philanthrocapitalism' (*The Economist*, 2006) demands an *ethic of refusal*: the reaffirmation of the humanitarian act as one of defiance. This requires a clear conceptual understanding of contemporary humanitarianism and how it is situated historically.

Capitalism, Dispossession, and the Historical Stages of Humanitarianism

The concept of humanitarianism arose from the emergence of capitalism in Europe. As technological capacities for material progress greatly increased, they did so at the expense of new forms of impoverishment and enslavement that was increasingly global in scope. This is not to deny the long tradition of Islamic Zakat (alms to the poor) and numerous forms of communal aid and reciprocity that exist in various cultures throughout the world. It is, rather, to point to a dominant strain of humanitarianism that arose within the capitalist nations of Western Europe (Barnett, 2011). Most pre-capitalist societies maintained a variety of mechanisms by which they could assist those facing hardship. In fact, even as capitalism and the ethic of possessive individualism emerged in England, older institutions to help people in need, such as the parish system, remained in place until very late in the process (albeit in increasingly condescending and oppressive terms).[2] Contemporary humanitarianism was then, and continues to be, a relation of power.

Along with the emergence of capitalism in Europe, the concept of humanitarianism arrived as an extension of liberal political thought. Emerging from the Renaissance, liberalism has professed the fundamental value of the individual and the individual's personal liberty. It did so largely in terms in which the individual to be valued was narrowly defined (male property holders), and alongside racial and gender discourses that simultaneously dehumanised the majority of the human population (Losurdo, 2014). This is not to deny, however, the revolutionary aspects of liberalism, which worked to limit the power of monarchies through the powers of a constitution, to end serfdom, and to produce the theoretical basis upon which claims could be made about the fundamental value of human life.

Political scientist Michael Barnett (2011) periodises the history of humanitarianism into three stages: imperial humanitarianism (1800–1945); neo-humanitarianism (1945–1989); and liberal humanitarianism (1989–present). Early imperial humanitarian doctrines, beginning in the early eighteenth century, were imbued with racial discourses in which Europeans were burdened with a civilisational mission to uplift the colonised from supposed heathenism and barbarity. The best strains among them fought to abolish slavery, but then only in terms that further entrenched the commodification of human labour, which was then destined to be sold to a class of property owners. At the same time, many abolitionist leaders promoted Christianity and colonialism as a way of supposedly helping people otherwise seen as 'children' in need of guidance. In general, humanitarianism of this sort was ultimately paternalistic in that interference with one person's liberty of action was 'justified by reasons referring exclusively to the welfare, good, happiness, needs, interests, or values of the person whose liberty is being violated' (Barnett, 2011: 34).

For Barnett, the second stage of humanitarianism, or 'neo-humanitarianism', saw a shift from the civilisational mission to nationalism, development, and sovereignty. He places this stage as emerging post-World-War-Two (WWII), with the third stage, 'liberal humanitarianism' – the era of liberal peace, globalisation, and human rights – beginning around 1990 after the fall of the Soviet Bloc. In the following section we discuss these shifts, which coincide with dramatic events in the global political economy. For the moment, however, it is worth making a few broader points. The first is that, by virtue of existing amid these political–economic periods, humanitarian thought has invariably been impacted. Some see humanitarianism as unwittingly playing the ideological function of dampening the most extreme impacts of capitalist imperialism. At the same time, others point out that there are disparate strains of thought and action among humanitarian organisations and actors, and that many seek to pose a fundamental challenge to the existence of highly unequal and unjust global conditions, which regularly induce periods of extreme trauma upon populations. Barnett further distinguishes between two broad types of humanitarianism that have dominated thought and practice: an emergency branch that focuses on symptoms, and an alchemical branch that includes the ambition of removing the root causes of suffering. Yet acts of intervention, no matter how well intended, are also acts of control. For this reason, Barnett suggests that humanitarianism ultimately seeks to establish a form of governance that imposes limits upon the destructive powers of people, governments, and militaries, while also attempting to provide care to meet the necessities of life of populations seen as incapable of helping themselves.

Most importantly, humanitarianism emerged alongside the construction of a global civilisational core and a periphery of those in need of help. If we were to incorrectly assume that the world outside of Europe and North America was static prior to the colonial era, in a perpetual, pre-existing state of poverty and barbarism, then the growth of humanitarian thought could be seen as a process of growing compassion that emerged within Europe and North America as it became evermore aware of the world outside its boundaries. In political science terms, this would be considered classic Hegelian idealism that sees the world evolving towards a state of perfect freedom as human knowledge and reason is improved. This reasoning was, and remains, fundamentally racist, positioning Western Europe as the guiding light that the rest of the world must follow. The reality, as many historians, sociologists, and anthropologist have shown, is that the seemingly enormous global inequalities that gradually became apparent to Europeans, especially in the nineteenth century, were in fact produced in the colonial process, as societies of enormous material and cultural complexity came under attack. Thus, 'underdevelopment' was constructed and imposed on peoples. At the same time, a 'moral economy of suffering' emerged in Europe and America in conjunction with a political economy of need in the colonies (Barnett, 2011: 9, 227; Reid-Henry, 2013: 754).[3]

A useful additional concept when thinking about the history of capitalism and the humanitarian reaction arrives from the work of Karl Polanyi, who proposed the concept of the 'double movement'. As WWII raged, Polanyi tried to understand the underlying economic rationale that led to such horrendous devastation. He came to argue that it was the result of a capitalist economy. The self-regulating market system, he asserted, was a utopian ideal dependent upon fictitious commodities: land, labour and money, which ultimately became 'disembedded' from social control (2001).[4] Polanyi correctly pointed out that prior to the nineteenth century, for most of the world's population, the market played only a peripheral function in societies. The majority of people were able to meet their basic needs without having to resort to trade. This stands in stark contradiction to the popularised work of Adam Smith. The discipline of classical economics draws heavily from selective portions of Smith's work, which suggests that humans have a natural tendency to 'truck, barter and trade' (Smith, 1776). Polanyi draws from anthropological and historical research to argue that this was a fallacy. In most of human history, he argues, markets were tightly regulated and 'embedded' in society in a manner that tempered their harmful capacities. For example, he believed that if left to itself ('*laissez-faire*'), the self-regulating market could 'not exist for any length of time without annihilating the human and natural substance of society' (Polanyi, 2001: 3).

In the years since Polanyi wrote these words, the weight of historical research has shown that the penetration of the market into most societies was actually a very violent process: people sell their labour only when all other options are exhausted. Karl Marx described this as the 'so-called primitive accumulation', by which capitalism permeates first by creation of the working class: people kicked off the land and unable to feed themselves, but for the sale of their labour (Marx, 1987).[5] Human labour had to be commodified and the function of markets achieved that state, as communal access to land was gradually eroded or 'enclosed' and turned into private property. These processes of dispossession continue in various ways throughout the world.[6] Polanyi's concept of a 'double movement' posited that certain segments of society – 'those most immediately affected by the deleterious action of the market – primarily, but not exclusively, the working and landed classes' (2001: 138) – would create protective legislation, restrictive associations, trade unions and other 'collectivist' responses in an effort to curb the destructive impact of the market, in a sense re-embedding the market within society. However, Polanyi rejected the idea that 'laissez-faire' is in fact 'free'. In contrast, he showed how this was historically and socially constructed with the use of legislation and state power (ibid.: 147). Yet, 'if laissez-faire was planned, planning was not'. In other words, state-planning and interventions that introduced developments such as Medicare, worker's compensation, and restrictions on child labour, arose as an unexpected response to the tragedies and disorder unleashed by the market (ibid.: 151–6).[7]

Prior to World War One (WWI), major economic thought promoted free trade and financial deregulation. Classical economic liberalism suggested that the state should play a minimal role in society beyond maintaining the police and judiciary in order to uphold private property rights, and the armed forces to protect the sovereignty of the nation. 'With limited exceptions, individuals were on their own during hard times; they might find comfort from their neighbors, their churches, and their fellow citizens, but not the state' (Barnett, 2011: 99).

From World War Two: Keynesian Economics and the Rise and Fall of Developmentalism

In many ways, World Wars One and Two can be seen as a product of capitalist crisis in which capitalist blocs temporarily resolved their conditions of 'overproduction' (and therefore declining profits) with the near-destruction of humanity itself. Overproduction refers to a tendency for capitalists to produce more than available markets can consume, which is simultaneously a crisis of unemployment and impoverishment in the imperialist nation as factories are pressed to reduce labour costs when sales decline (Harvey, 2004). The recession of the late nineteenth century was resolved in the post-war era, when public spending and capital controls were reintroduced. In the wake of WWII, there arose a series of initiatives to re-regulate national economies in order to rebuild and stimulate new economic growth under conditions of peace. The most important of them were the Bretton Woods Agreement and the Marshall Plan, which were both heavily influenced by the economist John Maynard Keynes. 'Keynesian' economics proposed that the nation state could stimulate the economy with investment in public infrastructure and that peace could be maintained between nations if they agreed to some basic economic rules that included fixed exchange rates for national currencies pegged to the US dollar (whose value was in turn backed up by the 'gold standard'), and commitments to regulated bond and stock markets. Although the promotion of free trade was a goal of post-war economic policies, countries encouraged national industries and played a role in their economic management. At the same time, a bargain was made between capital (business owners and bankers) and labour that was to ensure that the working classes would receive a greater proportion of benefits from capitalist profits. Features such as free education and universal healthcare were introduced in capitalist countries, along with unemployment insurance and welfare programmes. To some degree, the dominant thinking was that this would curtail movements towards either fascism or socialism among the poor and working classes (Helleiner, 2014; Negri, 1994: 23–50).

The Bretton Woods Agreement was negotiated among forty-four Allied nations, with significant leadership from the US and Britain, and was predominantly attended by countries of Western Europe. The Soviet Union and its allies did not participate. From the Agreement was formed the International Bank for Reconstruction and Development (today known as the World Bank) and the International Monetary Fund (IMF). It also led to the General Agreement on Tariffs and Trade, out of which would eventually form the World Trade Organisation. The World Bank was initially intended to make funds available to European nations that needed to rebuild after the war, but its attention was quickly turned towards the project of 'developing' nations of the 'Global South', many of which had only recently gained independence from colonial rule (Helleiner, 2014). Its purpose was to act as a mediator – or guarantor – of loans to poorer nations that would otherwise be considered too high a risk for investors largely based in the United States. The IMF was to step in to assist in the repayment of debts when faced with short-term balance of payment problems and in turn, to prevent countries from competitively devaluing their currencies as a means of boosting exports by rendering their goods cheaper on the global market (a process that was seen as one of the causes of WWII). All of these institutions were dominated by the US, in a large part because the US had not participated in WWII until its final year.

The rise of development economics in the post-war era represented, in many respects, an urge to control change, and to manage the forms of displacement that capitalism inevitably unleashed. The independence-era leaders of former colonised nations also saw evidence of rapid economic development in the Soviet Union, which showed that public investment could yield results. Plans to rebuild Europe also saw the need for a massive boost in primary commodities, which they hoped to acquire from trade with former colonies. Throughout the 1960s and into the 1970s, less developed countries were thus enticed to take on huge debts to modernise their economies and to promote industrialisation with the profit made from primary commodity exports. Many countries boasted some impressive achievements in social policy, creating health and education infrastructure that had not existed in the colonial era. Too often, however, the struggles for independence turned into bloody battles between local elites trying to wrest control over the organs of the state, which could in turn be used to bolster their particular regional and ethnolinguistic constituents, and political clients.

The early 1970s then introduced a number of crises that would cripple the industrialisation efforts of poorer nations and would lay the foundation for many of the humanitarian emergencies we see today. This included a recession in the US (i.e. a state of 'overproduction'), in part brought on by economic recovery in Japan and Germany, which led to increased competition for manufactured goods. During this period, the US also had to manage inflation, in part precipitated by the massive public debts incurred to pay for the Vietnam War. In turn, the huge supply of US dollars into sovereign accounts throughout the world greatly surpassed US gold reserves. To prevent a run on the bank as countries tried to convert their US reserves into gold, in 1971 President Nixon unilaterally abandoned the gold standard fixed exchange rate system established by the Bretton Woods Agreement. This in turn caused the currency to decline in value, again in part because the US was printing money to pay for the Vietnam War. These problems were compounded by the OPEC oil crisis of 1973, which then massively increased the cost of the state expenditures of less developed nations, and sent US dollars flowing towards the oil-producing nations.

In the Less Developed Countries (LDCs) of the 'Global South', export-oriented commodities rapidly lost their value while the cost of production soared. States responded by drawing more debt, much of it from predatory private banks awash with stagnant US dollars, as well as from the IMF, both of which maintained painful terms of repayment. Then, between 1979 and 1981, the US retracted its money supply in efforts to reduce inflation, drive up their interest rates, and attract some of the petro-dollars back into their economy. This became known as the 'Volcker Shock', named after the then-chairman of the federal reserve, Paul Volcker. Rapidly rising interest rates sent the debts incurred by LDCs rocketing upward, leading to what has become known as the 'lost decade of development' in the 1980s: a period during which public spending was redirected into debt payments.

Some believe the Volcker Shock formed part of a broader initiative by the US to 'systematically discipline the Third World' and to find markets for financial institutions that had exhausted lending opportunities in the North (McNally 2002: 163). Between 1971 and 1980, 'Third World' external debt grew from $70 billion to $560 billion (Bracking & Harrison, 2003). By 1991, total external debt in the 'developing world' amounted to $1.362 trillion, equivalent to 126.5 percent of the countries' total exports of goods and services in that year. The ratio of debt servicing to the gross domestic product of the 'developing world' reached 32.4 percent and would continue to rise in the following decades (Ferraro & Rosser, 1994).

In order to understand the debt crisis as an aggressive economic strategy led by the US, one has to consider the enormous number of wars and covert actions that the US was involved with at this time: from Vietnam to Afghanistan, El Salvador, Nicaragua, Argentina, Chile, Mozambique, Angola, and South Africa to name just a few. Many of these wars were directed against poor nations that were trying to develop public services and climb out of poverty. Many independence struggles, determined to bring about more egalitarian economic systems, faced such heavy retaliation from the US that countries were forced to turn to the USSR for assistance. In the midst of this period, humanitarian efforts became heavily politicised and were often seen by the US as an opportunity to hold back the spread of communism.

We must avoid constructing caricatures of socialist and anti-capitalist thought and activism during these years. Most active socialists and anarchists throughout the 1980s shared concerns with humanitarian organisations, and many were grassroots organisers against imperialist military aggression. They defended refugees, agitated against apartheid in South Africa, and opposed the US/South African proxy wars, as well as those in Central and South America. The Left was perhaps more aware than others that the pursuit of radically democratic and egalitarian societies in these countries was severely restricted by relations with the Soviet Union and the 'Comintern'. The latter imposed coercive, even imperialist, economic policies and suppressed democratic processes during the revolutions. While humanitarians tend to ascribe to the principles of independence and political 'neutrality', in certain contexts in Southern Africa it became impossible to avoid choosing sides; one side supported the extension of public infrastructure and a distribution of the benefits of the modern nation state to all, regardless of the colour of their skin, while the other fought for the perpetual servitude of the black majority under white minority rule. Moreover, the US and its proxies viciously sabotaged efforts to create alternatives in places like Mozambique, where newly built schools, hospitals and bridges were bombed by South African and US mercenaries.

Barnett reminds us that although humanitarians strive for neutrality, they inevitably must act amid messy and complex circumstances in which these ideals are always challenged, and may even be impossible to maintain. In fact, humanitarians' goals become highly politicised insofar as they ultimately seek to bring about a 'revolution in the ethics of care' (2011: 18). Moreover, if our concerns about the inherent value of human life are genuine, we must support the conditions in which human needs can be met, and humanitarian disasters protected against.

The Rise of Neoliberalism

As we have shown, the international economic institutional mechanisms that were meant to maintain peace, which were established by the Bretton Woods system, were gradually eroded throughout the 1970s. This timeframe coincides with the rise of a new economic doctrine that became known as neoliberalism. If the Keynesian post-war period represented an attempt to re-align the market with rules established by society (and a regulatory response to prevent world war) then neoliberalism was its opposite: an attempt to re-impose the logic of the market as the central governing logic for humanity (Toussaint, 2005: 89). It was, perhaps, the market's 'counter-offensive' (ibid.: 263).[8] Drawing from the ideas of Frederick Hayek and Milton Friedman, neoliberalism is a theory and set of political and economic policy prescriptions that proposes that human wellbeing can be best advanced by 'liberating individual entrepreneurial freedoms and skills within an institutional framework characterised by strong private property rights, free markets and free trade' (Harvey, 2005: 2). According to neoliberal theory, the role of the state is to create and preserve the institutional framework appropriate for such practices. While state social services are reduced to a minimum, the military, police, and legal structures of the state are required to secure private property rights and to guarantee the functioning of markets. 'Furthermore, if markets do not exist (in areas such as land, water, education, healthcare, social security, or environmental pollution) then they must be created, by state action if necessary. But beyond these tasks the state should not venture' (ibid.).

It was according to this neoliberal logic that the World Bank and the IMF designed and imposed Structural Adjustment Programmes (SAPs) upon African countries. SAPs were a response to the debt crisis and short-term balance of payment problems, and a means to secure repayment of loans (Toussaint, 2005: 222). The rise of neoliberalism brought an end to the era of development theory, which sought to end inequalities and allow the 'Third World' to rise out of poverty and 'catch-up' with the industrialised West. The world was told, in the words of Margaret Thatcher, that 'There is No Alternative'. The state was no longer to play any role in the development of countries in the 'Global South'. Instead, these countries were to open themselves up to the global market and export products with which they had a comparative advantage. This represented a re-emergence of the system of 'free-market imperialism' that dominated global production prior to World Wars One and Two. In hindsight, the Keynesianism of the 1950s and 1960s can be seen as an anomalous period for global capitalism, with neoliberalism representing a return to its 'normal' state (Leys, 1996: 25; Wood, 2002).

SAPs devastated the people and economies of LDCs (Moorsom, 2010; 2016; SAPRIN, 2002). They destroyed emerging manufacturing sectors by flooding them with cheap imports and removing access to credit facilities. They crippled the public sector, including education and healthcare. They destroyed marketing networks and agrarian production, which in turn precipitated famine conditions. Unemployment rose, while those who maintained work were subject to job insecurity and harsh restructuring that saw them lose benefits as real wages fell. In turn, child labour increased as families sought every possible means of survival. By the new millennium, 'approximately 80 percent of malnourished children in developing countries' could be found in countries 'where farmers have been forced by structural adjustment policies to shift their agricultural production from subsistence to export production for industrialized nations' (Kawewe & Dibie, 2000). In many countries, especially those in Africa, SAPs coincided with the growth of the HIV epidemic in a context where state capacities to respond had been wiped out. SAPs ultimately reproduced what Mike Davis described as 'state decapacitation' (2001: 310), prompting humanitarian and other non-governmental organisations to respond to the HIV epidemic.[9]

From the 1980s, and with the imposition of SAPs, political instability and repression increased in part because those in control of the state had fewer resources to placate rival factions, but also because political elites plundered resources and benefited from privatisation, while conditions for the majority worsened. In some cases, SAPs led to outright state failure. They ushered in unprecedented levels of migration, displacement and urbanisation (Freund, 2010; Mbembe, 2001). The latter occurred without a corresponding investment in urban infrastructure such as water and sanitation. As states retreated, NGOs began filling the void, but 'only in the context of emergency' (Ticktin, 2011: 74). The result has been the *humanitarianisation* of socio-political crises and the *NGO-isation* of global public health (Pringle, 2015: 313).

A fundamental premise of SAPs was that they would allow nations to pay off their debts to the banks. Public schools and agricultural support programmes were rendered luxuries, while healthcare was transformed into a commodity to be bought and sold (Qadeer & Baru, 2016). It is not surprising, therefore, that rather than helping to pay off debts, SAPs caused said debt to rise further. By 2002, the total debt of 'developing countries' was $2,338,848,000,000 (2.3 trillion), with a servicing ratio to GNI (income) of 39 percent (World Bank, 2004).

Furthermore, while the term 'globalisation' has been used to describe a massive rise in international trade, this distorts the fact that the majority of transactions actually occur within companies structured across borders, so as to avoid the payment of taxes. The deregulation of global finance has also led to forms of 'predatory', 'casino' or 'vulture' capitalism, whereby the wealthiest 'investors' resort to speculation 'dedicated to the appropriation and devaluation of assets, rather than to building them up through productive investments' (Gill, 2015a; Harvey, 2004: 72). This system has consolidated enormous levels of wealth among the largest corporations, while the divergence of wealth and poverty within and between nations has reached an obscene level, to the point that only eight men now own the same wealth as the 3.6 billion people who make up the poorest half of humanity (Oxfam, 2016).

Neoliberals have been extremely successful at advocating for the rights of the wealthy. This reached grotesque levels when their betting on complex financial products (derived from the value of people's housing) caused the near wholesale collapse of the global financial system in 2007. At the time, the banks responsible for the crisis were bailed out with public funds that exceeded the combined debt level of the so-called 'developing countries'. This demonstrated that funds can be found to protect billionaires but not the global poor. Thus, it is sickeningly ironic that billionaires are then lauded when they donate to charities, call themselves humanitarians, and profess to know how to end global poverty.

The aftermath of the global financial crisis sent shock waves through LDC economies, sending food prices rocketing. This was largely due to speculation and a growth in 'futures' and derivatives markets, as capitalism increasingly commodifies virtual space and time. The result was an acceleration of a process of dispossession that was already underway (Bryceson, 2009; Clapp & Cohen, 2009). At the same time, the trend of militarisation continued to vastly expand the destructive capacities of capitalist societies, with more people than ever before witnessing the destruction of their livelihoods amid war and economic deprivation. This has precipitated 'the largest and most rapid escalation ever in the number of people being forced from their homes' (Booth, 2017). At the time of writing, more than 65 million people have been forcibly displaced (ibid.). This global migration crisis incorporates a constellation of crises involving sexual violence, enforced prostitution, human trafficking, extortion, kidnapping, detention, torture, and death by exposure or drowning. Nevertheless, these crises have received official indifference from Western governments, and outright hostility from anti-immigrant forces. In contrast, the humanitarian response has been innovative and brave, incorporating maritime rescue to the provision of care for victims of sexual violence. The global migration crisis, however, is only symptomatic of a much deeper crisis routed in neoliberal capitalism. The latter is one in which rates of profit continue to fall and capitalist producers seek out spatial fixes for their state of overproduction (or overaccumulation) – at tremendous human cost. The tendency to *humanitarianise* crises of capitalism severs such crises from their policy origins. It obscures causality and effectively absolves responsible parties. Nefariously, it goes further by opening the door to philanthropic power.

Philanthrocapitalism and the Commodification of Humanitarian Aid

I consider humanitarian response not as an exogenous reaction to adverse shocks, but as part and parcel of humanitarian crises, as deeply embedded in today's disaster and war economies. (Gilles Carbonnier, 2015)

The term philanthrocapitalism 'encapsulates a new force in global health funding' in which some of the world's wealthiest are donating enormous sums in hopes of 'harnessing the market to make their giving more efficient and achieve better results' (Clark & McGoey, 2016). This is not unlike the earlier capitalist phase of 'free-market imperialism' in which major capitalist barons such as Rockefeller, Carnegie, and Mellon applied their business strategies to find solutions to certain global health problems. For example, finances from the Rockefeller Foundation contributed to the development of a vaccine for yellow fever, and promoted the introduction of 'green revolution' technologies in agriculture (*The Economist*, 2006). They then went on to significantly influence the mandate of the World Health Organization (Birn, 2006), as remains the case with current philanthrocapitalists (Qadeer & Baru, 2016). In the current era of neoliberal globalisation, individuals such as Warren Buffett, Bill and Melinda Gates, and Richard Branson are doing much the same, but often on a much larger scale. Bill and Melinda Gates have pledged to respond to HIV/AIDS and create new vaccines, and have enlisted dozens of billionaires to join their cause. Similarly, Mark Zuckerberg and Priscilla Chan have also announced that they are on a mission to 'cure, prevent or manage all diseases' by 2100 (Solon, 2016), while George Soros announced in 2016 that he plans to invest $500 million to help refugees (Reuters, 2016). While this might understandably sound like a positive step for humanitarian organisations that are often dependent on donations, there are a number of concerning dimensions to these initiatives.

First among them is the obvious fact that these philanthrocapitalists and the organisations they support lack any form of democratic oversight or public accountability. In many cases they have no obligation to disclose full details of their activities. Instead, their agendas are based on their own personal interests and biases rather than on evidence. Moreover, the creation and implementation of their agendas may in fact replicate forms of discrimination that maintain global inequalities. Clark and McGoey, for example, point to a 2009 *Lancet* study on the Gates Foundation, 'which showed that only a small proportion of global health grants went to researchers based in the global south' (2016). Moreover, their funds tend to be channelled to emergencies deemed sufficiently worthy by prime-time news networks, and their interventions limited to quick technical fixes rather than intended to achieve meaningful change. Philanthrocapitalism further emboldens states and public bodies to neglect their obligations towards their citizens (ibid.). This can occur in both donor and recipient nations; in the 'Global North', governments are steadily rescinding their aid promises, while in the 'Global South' attention is drawn away from the need to build national governments that can serve their populations' needs and prepare for emergencies.

As developmentalism has fallen out of favour, humanitarianism has risen in its place. As the capitalist class becomes ever wealthier, it receives incentives to donate, and to leverage power through philanthropy. As taxes are reduced, as public services languish, as social commons are expropriated, private charitable foundations thrive. Philanthrocapitalists finance the aid industry to serve as a 'cordon sanitaire', distancing and protecting capital from 'surplus populations' portrayed as dangerous and burdensome. Yet, capital itself can remain wholly indifferent, for it 'is not focused upon the promotion of global health but on the accumulation of capital via the profit system. Capital will profit from obesity as well as from hunger' (Gill, 2015a; see also: Patel, 2007).

The benefits that wealth derives from charity are vast. For one, charity obscures and distracts from the fact that the same policies that enrich donors also generate the needs that charities seek to address. This is highlighted by Levich (2014) in his critique of the Bill and Melinda Gates Foundation (BMGF):

> Gates' willingness to carry the torch for the world's billionaires reflected an understanding that his Foundation plays an important

ideological role within the global capitalist system. Apart from the promotion of specific corporate interests and imperialist strategic aims, BMGF's expertly publicised activities have the effect of laundering the enormous concentration of wealth in the hands of a few supremely powerful oligarchs. Through stories of Gates' philanthropy we are assured that our rulers are benevolent, compassionate, and eager to 'give back' to the less fortunate; moreover, by leveraging their superior intelligence and technocratic expertise, they are able to transcend the bureaucratic fumblings of state institutions, finding 'strategic, market-based solutions' to problems that confound mere democracies. This apotheosis of Western wealth and know-how works hand in hand with an implicit contempt for the sovereignty and competence of poor nations, justifying ever more aggressive imperialist interventions.

Moreover, as Clark and McGoey (2016) note, philanthrocapitalism serves to elevate 'moral authority in global health and development to perceived technological wizards'. Yet the real work of global health development 'takes place on the ground – in the cultural and economic realities of people's lives, in ways that cannot be wholly quantified' and in circumstances where much more than business acumen is needed (ibid.: 2459).

Philanthrocapitalists seek to apply market mechanisms and business principles to purportedly make their giving more efficient, and to achieve better results. However, this assumes that markets can actually provide solutions for public needs. It neglects to consider the ways in which markets are predatory upon public goods, closing off options for equitable distribution.[10] This occurs within the context of a global shift in perspective where monetary efficiency, profit maximisation and the commodification of health has taken precedence over public health, collective wellbeing, and environmental preservation. At the same time, notions of assistance and cooperation are contorted by the interests of those seeking to penetrate and control new market spaces (Qadeer & Baru, 2016). Healthcare provision becomes a 'service' within the market, rather than a public good, with public sectors restructured to this end.

Left to themselves, capitalists will turn humanitarianism into one more vehicle upon which they can open up ever-greater spaces of commodification. In a world where everything is commodified, philanthrocapitalism can itself be seen as a commodity for which billionaires will seek effective returns on their payments. This can occur through the generation of patents (Thompson, 2014), but also extends to what Klein (2007) has described as the 'disaster capitalism' complex, whereby powerful global engineering firms gain lucrative contracts to disperse aid. More importantly, these efforts continue to bolster free-market capitalist solutions to the problems of capitalism (Pringle, 2015). This in turn perpetuates the perception that the grand exploiters of capitalism are in fact not that, but rather givers: those who support life, coming to the rescue to resolve problems that have seemingly divine causes.

In this way, discourses around philanthrocapitalism function in the same ideological manner as that in which Wai describes discourses around military intervention in Africa on supposedly humanitarian grounds, by defining 'social reality on the continent in terms of crisis and disorder endogenously produced by the internal dysfunction of African societies blamed solely on its corrupt political classes' (2014: 496). Far from being neutral, humanitarianism intertwined with philanthrocapitalist financing is thus highly political in nature and therefore something that should concern principled humanitarian actors.

An Ethic of Refusal

> For MSF, this is the humanitarian act: to seek to relieve suffering, to seek to restore autonomy, to witness to the truth of injustice, and to insist on political responsibility. (James Orbinski, International President of Médecins Sans Frontières, Nobel Peace Prize Lecture, Oslo, December 10, 1999)

Contemporary humanitarianism was founded by Swiss businessman Jean-Henri Dunant. While on a business trip, Dunant happened upon the gruesome aftermath of the Battle of Solferino in 1859, in what is now northern Italy. Appalled by the situation, he marshalled an improvised team of volunteers to provide first aid and to comfort the dying. He refused to accept that victims of war ought to be left unattended, and from this experience he helped to establish the International Committee of the Red Cross (ICRC) in 1863, and the Geneva Convention of 1864. In 1901, Dunant became the first recipient of the Nobel Peace Prize (Boissier, 1985; Hutchinson, 1996).

Over a century later, humanitarianism was transformed again by the *sans frontières* movement as embodied by the founding of *Médecins Sans*

Frontières (MSF). Much has been written about the history of MSF, from its inception by a ragtag group of French doctors and journalists in 1971, to being the world's largest medical humanitarian organisation, as it is today.[11] The movement globalised and democratised humanitarian action. Its increasingly ambitious and provocative projects gave MSF notoriety, but also legitimacy. Less than ten years into its mandate, MSF received official endorsement: it was invited by the UNHCR to provide medical care in refugee camps (Orkin, 2010).

MSF's assent coincided with the decay of, and counter-revolutionary assault upon, national independence movements, and the corresponding rise of neoliberal ideology. As explained earlier in the chapter, divestments in social services across the 'Global South' in the 1980s precipitated social upheaval and political crises, which necessitated humanitarian response and entrenched the humanitarian sector. Correspondingly, the *sans frontières* movement became increasingly institutionalised. Aaron Orkin identifies a telling sign within MSF: a change in taxonomy from '*je suis un médecin sans frontières*' (I am a doctor without borders) to '*je suis un membre de Médecins sans frontières*' (I am a member of Doctors Without Borders). The difference is subtle but significant, representing a shift from movement to institution (ibid.: 26). As MSF became a larger organisation, radical politics were muted in favour of professionalism and efficiency. Polman describes this as involuntary collaboration, whereby rebellious humanitarians are assimilated into the international aid industry (2010: 160).

The humanitarian movement was never intended to serve private interests or assuage the egos of the uber-wealthy. At its core, it is about saving lives, alleviating suffering, and restoring dignity in the wake of large-scale emergencies and disasters (Pringle & Hunt, 2015). Humanitarian organisations mobilise when local forms of resilience are overwhelmed or non-existent. Humanitarian action responds to populations in danger, communities in distress, and groups subjected to social exclusion or repression. Humanitarian actors provide direct assistance in the form of materials, services and medical care. Dunantist organisations are guided by the humanitarian principles of neutrality, impartiality and independence. Neutrality means not partaking in military operations or taking sides in hostilities. Impartiality means providing assistance according to need alone and without discrimination. Independence means not having ties to parties in conflicts or stakes in their outcome. The point here is that humanitarian actors strive to serve people in need, and not ideological or commercial interests.

Dunantist humanitarian organisations such as MSF have argued that neutrality and independence situate them outside of the political realm (Barnett & Weiss, 2008). However, French philosopher Michel Foucault, who was influential in the *sans frontières* movement, cautioned against illusions of neutrality and independence:[12]

> It seems to me that the real political task in a society such as ours is to criticize the workings of institutions that appear to be both neutral and independent; to criticize and attack them in such a manner that the political violence which has always exercised itself obscurely through them will be unmasked, so that one can fight against them. (Foucault, in Foucault & Chomsky, 1971)

Central to the *sans frontières* movement is the ethic of refusal. Articulated in MSF's 1999 Nobel Peace Prize speech, an ethic of refusal disallows 'moral political failure or injustice to be sanitized or cleansed of its meaning' (MSF, 1999). An ethic of refusal requires resisting ideological assimilation and exposing philanthropic modes of power. It means acknowledging that neoliberal globalisation is inherently prone to crisis and that the inequalities it produces render societies incapable of coping with disasters. An ethic of refusal defies philanthrocapitalist attempts at sanitising social injustices and obfuscating structural violence.

Humanitarian organisations accrue moral legitimacy through their actions (Calain, 2012). To preserve their legitimacy, humanitarian organisations need to reassert that healthcare and the provision of public services must be defended against the market.[13] This may not be an easy place for humanitarians to tread politically, but opposition to the valorisation of capital can occur in the form of social movements rather than political parties (in the manner in which MSF came into being). We agree with Gill, who argues, 'the principal challenge for the progressive political forces and political economists in the coming decade' is to mobilise 'forces and arguments – as well as policies and governance proposals – to create a new "common sense" that can address the global organic crisis' of capitalism (2015a). As the *sans frontières* movement has shown, neutrality need not equate to complicity.

Closing Words

This chapter approached humanitarianism as an unfinished project, one that is contested and historically situated. We have focused our attention on relations between humanitarian values and social power, acknowledging that values are not based in nature, but determine and are determined by how societies exercise control. Contemporary humanitarianism continues to evolve as a regime of practice with profound significance for the lives of crisis-affected populations (Pringle, 2015). In a world [dis]order that is 'contested, transient and governed by violence' (Gill, 2015b), an ethic of refusal remains an essential feature of principled humanitarian action.

The MSF Nobel Peace Prize speech asserts that 'humanitarianism occurs where the political has failed or is in crisis' (1999). We have argued that rather than having failed, 'the political' is succeeding, furthering a capitalist agenda through cycles of crisis and charity, wealth accumulation and philanthrocapitalism. The cycle destabilises societies, suppresses dissent, and generates repression locally and globally.[14] Through their work, humanitarian actors witness this directly in what we label humanitarian emergencies. An ethic of refusal requires that we use our privileged positions to substantiate the effects of harmful social and economic policies, and speak out against them. This is in keeping with the MSF Nobel Peace Prize speech, which affirms a need to bear witness to the truth of injustice and which insists on political responsibility. An ethic of refusal requires that we critically examine our own relationships of class, race, and gender, and consider the ways in which these influence our relationships with those we serve (Cole, 2012).[15] In these ways, an ethic of refusal provides a conceptual reference for principled humanitarian actors, from which they can assert their independence from structures of political power that generate massive global inequality and that recreate the very conditions that necessitate humanitarian response. With this refusal, we can reaffirm the humanitarian act as one of defiance and solidarity.

Notes

1 MSF seems well on its way; according to MSF's International Financial Report (2017), MSF's total income in 2016 was 1.516 billion Euros, representing 41% of the WHO proposed programme budget of 3.69 billion Euros (2016–2017) (WHO, 2015). What is more, 96.4% of MSF's income in 2016 came from individual donors and private funders, with just 3.6% from public institutional funding.

This affords MSF precious independence from the whims and politicking of WHO member states.

2 England is widely considered the birthplace of capitalism, or at least the 'classic case' whereby capitalism emerged in its most articulated form, with the bulk of transformations taking place between 1790 and 1832 (McNally, 1988; Thompson, 1968; Wood, 2002).

3 There is an enormous critical literature on the creation of underdevelopment in the 'Global South', but one of the most appropriate examples that should be cited here is Mike Davis' *Late-Victorian holocausts, El Niño famines and the making of the Third World* (2001).

4 As he states, 'the origins of the cataclysm lay in the utopian endeavor of economic liberalism to set up a self-regulating market system ... the peculiarity of the civilization the collapse of which we have witnessed was precisely that it rested on economic foundations' (Polanyi, 2001: 31).

5 One of the best histories of its early stages exists in the last section of Rosa Luxemburg's *Accumulation of capital* (2003).

6 In *The shock doctrine: the rise of disaster capitalism* (2007) Naomi Klein suggests this is a new phase of capitalism, but we argue, along with Ellen Meiksins Wood (2002), that this is a fundamental aspect of capitalism that was temporarily dampened by the post-war Keynesian order.

7 Marx and Engels stated that capitalists create their own grave-diggers, with the formation of the working classes. Polanyi made a similar observation: 'For if market economy was a threat to the human and natural components of the social fabric, as we insisted, what else would one expect than an urge on the part of a great variety of people to press for some sort of protection?' (Polanyi, 2001: 156).

8 In economic discourse, markets tend to be portrayed as natural entities, functioning in near-mystical manner. It is important to keep in mind, however, that the overwhelming majority of transactions they refer to take place between corporations and investors: in other words, people who own the factories, industrial farms, mines and all the means by which the production of goods and services takes place. So when we say something is 'good for the market', we are really saying that it is good for property owners, whose interests it cannot be assumed are synonymous with those of society more broadly.

9 This is evidenced by MSF's initially reluctant integration of HIV/AIDS treatment into its programmes in 2000–2001; it would later become a cornerstone activity. For a well-substantiated account, see Fox (2014).

10 As Qadeer and Baru (2016) note, 'the global health market in trade spans health care services, drugs, medical instruments, information technology, insurance systems, and manpower training, as well as loans and aid'.

11 For more on this, see work by Renée C Fox, Peter Redfield, and Michael Barnett.

12 The founding president of MSF, Bernard Kouchner, wrote that Foucault's '"The Birth of the Clinic" was our bible' (1985).

13 A successful and ongoing example of this is the MSF Campaign for Access to Essential Medicines, or 'Access Campaign', launched in 1999, which argues that 'medicines shouldn't be a luxury'. See: *www.msfaccess.org*.

14 This is well substantiated in Naomi Klein's *Shock Doctrine* and David Harvey's work on accumulation by dispossession.

15 For example, Teju Cole (2012) describes a 'white-savior industrial complex' that valorises those with power and infantilises those suffering. The

following is taken from his seven-part Twitter essay: 'The white savior supports brutal policies in the morning, founds charities in the afternoon, and receives awards in the evening.' Instead, we must

seek out forms of solidarity that are grounded in humility and conviction, and that are not reduced to yet another product that one can purchase (Chouliaraki, 2013).

References

Barnett, M (2011), *Empire of humanity: a history of humanitarianism*. Ithaca, NY: Cornell University Press.

Barnett, M & Weiss, TG (2008), *Humanitarianism in question: politics, power, ethics*. Ithaca, NY: Cornell University Press.

Birn, A-E (2006), *Marriage of convenience: Rockefeller international health and revolutionary Mexico*. Rochester, NY: University of Rochester Press.

Boissier, P (1985), *History of the International Committee of the Red Cross: from Solferino to Tsushima*. 2nd edition. Geneva: Henry Dunant Institute.

Booth, E (2017), Global migrant and refugee crisis [online]. Available from: http://newirin.irinnews.org/global-refugee-crisis (accessed 21 August 2017).

Bracking, S & Harrison, G (2003), Africa, imperialism and new forms of accumulation. *Review of African Political Economy*. Vol. 30 (95): 5–10.

Bryceson, DF (2009), Sub-Saharan Africa's vanishing peasantries and the specter of a global food crisis. *Monthly Review*. Vol. 61 (3): 48–62.

Calain, P (2012). In search of the 'new informal legitimacy' of Médecins Sans Frontières. *Public Health Ethics*. Vol. 5 (1): 56–66.

Carbonnier, G (2015), *Humanitarian economics: war, disaster and the global aid market*. London: Hurst & Co. Publishers.

Chouliaraki, L (2013), *The ironic spectator: solidarity in the age of post-humanitarianism*. Cambridge, UK: Polity Press.

Clapp, J & Cohen, MJ (eds) (2009), *The global food crisis: governance challenges and opportunities*. Waterloo: Wilfred Laurier University Press.

Clark, J & McGoey, L (2016), The black box warning on philanthrocapitalism. *The Lancet*. Vol. 388 (10059): 2457–59.

Cole, T (2012), The white-savior industrial complex. [Online]. The Atlantic. Available from: www.theatlantic.com/international/archive/2012/03/the-white-savior-industrial-complex/254843 (accessed 21 August 2017).

Davis, M (2001), *Late Victorian holocausts: El Nino famines and the making of the Third World*. London: Verso.

Economist, The (2006), The birth of philanthrocapitalism: the leading new philanthropists see themselves as social investors. *The Economist*, 23 February 2006.

Ferraro, V & Rosser, M (1994), Global debt and Third World development. Pp. 332–55. In: Klare, M & Thomas, D (eds) *World security: challenges for a new century*. New York: St. Martin's Press.

Foucault, M & Chomsky, N (1971), *The Chomsky-Foucault debate: on human nature*. Dutch Television.

Fox, R (2014), Part IV: in South Africa. Pp. 121–97. In: Fox, R, *Doctors Without Borders: humanitarian quests, impossible dreams of Médecins Sans Frontières*. Baltimore: Johns Hopkins University Press.

Freund, B (2010), The social context of African economic growth, 1960–2008. Pp. 39–59. In: Padayachee, V (ed.), *The political economy of Africa*. London: Routledge.

Gill, S (2015a), Global organic crisis and geopolitics [online]. Available from: http://stephengill.com/news/2015/08/global-organic-crisis-and-geopolitics.html (accessed 21 August 2017).

Gill, S (2015b), An archaeology of the future, to be excavated by the post-modern prince? In: Kreps, D (ed.) *Gramsci and Foucault: a reassessment*. London: Routledge.

Harvey, D (2004), The 'new' imperialism: accumulation by dispossession. *Socialist Register*. Vol. 40: 63–87.

Harvey, D (2005), *A brief history of neoliberalism*. Oxford: Oxford University Press.

Helleiner, E (2014), *Forgotten foundations of Bretton Woods: international development and the making of the postwar order*. Ithaca, NY: Cornell University Press.

Hutchinson, J (1996), *Champions of charity: war and the rise of the Red Cross*. Oxford: Westview Press.

Kawewe, SM & Dibie, R (2000), The impact of economic structural adjustment programs [ESAPS] on women and children: implications for social welfare in Zimbabwe. *Journal of Sociology & Social Welfare*. Vol. 27 (4): 79–107.

Klein, N (2007), *The shock doctrine: the rise of disaster capitalism*. Toronto: Alfred A Knoff Canada.

Kouchner, B (1985), Un vrai samouraï. In: Badinter, R (ed.), *Michel Foucault: un histoire de la vérité*. Syros.

Levich, J (2014), The real agenda of the Gates Foundation [online]. Available from: http://liberationschool.org/real-agenda-gates-foundation (accessed 21 August 2017).

Leys, C (1996), *The rise and fall of development theory*. London: James Currey.

Losurdo, D (2014), *Liberalism: a counter-history*. London: Verso.

Luxemburg, R (2003: 1913, trans. 1951, reprint), *The accumulation of capital*. London: Routledge.

Marx, K (1987), *Capital*. Volume 1, unabridged. New York: International Publishers.

Mbembe, A (2001), *On the post-colony*. Berkeley, CA: University of California Press.

McNally, D (1988), *Political economy and the rise of capitalism: a reinterpretation*. Berkeley, CA: University of California Press.

McNally, D (2002), *Another world is possible: globalization and anti-capitalism*. Winnipeg: Arbiter Ring.

Moorsom, TL (2010), The zombies of development economics: Dambiso Moyo's Dead Aid and the fictional African entrepreneurs. *Review of African Political Economy*. Vol. 37 (125): 361–71.

Moorsom, TL (2016), *Black settlers: hybridity, neoliberalism and ecosystemic change among Tonga farmers of Southern Zambia, 1964–2008*. PhD Thesis. Queen's University.

MSF (1999), Nobel lecture by James Orbinski, Médecins Sans Frontières, Oslo, December 10, 1999 [online]. Available from: www.nobelprize.org/nobel_prizes/peace/laureates/1999/msf-lecture.html (accessed 21 August 2017).

MSF (2017), *MSF international financial report 2016*. Geneva: MSF International.

Negri, A (1994: originally published 1968), Keynes and the capitalist theory of the State. In: Hardt, M & Negri, A (1994), *Labor of Dionysus: a critique of the state-form*. London: University of Minnesota Press.

Orkin, AM (2010), *Enacting nonmodern doctorhood: Médecins Sans Frontières and the birth of the medico-*

humanitarian profession. Unpublished Master of Sciences in History of Science, Medicine & Technology. University of Oxford.

Oxfam (2016), Just 8 men own same wealth as half the world [online]. Available from: www.oxfam.org/en/pressroom/pressreleases/2017-01-16/just-8-men-own-same-wealth-half-world (accessed 21 August 2017).

Patel, R (2007), *Stuffed and starved: markets, power and the hidden battle for the world's food system*. London: Portobello.

Polanyi, K (2001, 1944, reprint), *The great transformation: the political and economic origins of our times*. Boston: Beacon Press.

Polman, L (2010), *War games: the story of aid and war in modern times*. London: Penguin Books.

Pringle, J (2015), *Charity medicine for the global poor: humanitarian ethics and the Nigerian lead-poisoning outbreak*. Doctoral Thesis. University of Toronto.

Pringle, J & Hunt, M (2015), Humanitarian action. Pp. 1562–70. In: Ten Have, H (ed.), *Encyclopedia of global bioethics*. New York: Springer.

Qadeer, I & Baru, R (2016), Shrinking spaces for the 'public' in contemporary public health. *Development and Change*. Vol. 47 (4): 760–81.

Reid-Henry, S (2013), Review essay: on the politics of our humanitarian present. *Environment and Planning D: Society and Space*. Vol. 31. (4): 753–60.

Reuters (2016), Billionaire Soros to invest $500 mln to help migrants, refugees [online]. Available from: www.reuters.com/article/us-europe-migrants-soros-idUSKCN11QoWX (accessed 21 August 2017).

SAPRIN (2002), *The policy roots of economic crisis and poverty: a multi-country participatory assessment of structural adjustment*. Washington, DC: Structural Adjustment Participatory Review International Network.

Smith, A (1776), *An inquiry into the nature and causes of the wealth of nations*. W Strahan & T Cadell: London.

Solon, O (2016), Priscilla Chan and Mark Zuckerberg aim to 'cure, prevent and manage' all disease. *The Guardian*, 22 September 2016.

Thompson, CB (2014), Philanthrocapitalism: appropriation of Africa's genetic wealth. *Review of African Political Economy*. Vol. 41 (141): 389–405.

Thompson, EP (1968), *The making of the English working class*. London: Penguin.

Ticktin, MI (2011), *Casualties of care: immigration and the politics of humanitarianism in France*. Berkeley, CA: University of California Press.

Toussaint, E (2005), *Your money or your life: the tyranny of global finance*. Chicago: Haymarket Books.

Wai, Z (2014), The empire's new clothes: Africa, liberal interventionism and contemporary world order, *Review of African Political Economy*. Vol. 41 (142): 483–99.

Wood, EM (2002), *The origins of capitalism: a longer view*. London: Verso.

World Bank (2004), *Global development finance, 2004*. Washington, DC: World Bank.

World Health Organization (2015), *Programme budget, 2016–2017*. Geneva: World Health Organization.

AFTERWORD: THE ETHICS OF COMPILING A BOOK ON HUMANITARIAN ETHICS

James Smith

Ethics: doing the right thing. So was my over-simplified introduction to field of moral philosophy. Such simplicity was not to last long, not least once 'ethics' met 'humanitarianism'. For those newly acquainted with humanitarian ethics it is unlikely to take long before someone refers to Hugo Slim's paper by the same title: 'Doing the Right Thing: Relief Agencies, Moral Dilemmas and Moral Responsibility in Emergencies and War' (1997). Published at a time of intense introspection across much of the professional humanitarian sector, this seminal paper established a foundational basis for a substantial proportion of the academic and operational reflection that followed over the course of the subsequent two decades.

A quick online search of 'humanitarian' and 'doing the right thing' now returns thousands of results, with news articles, reports, and peer-reviewed papers detailing how more robust evidence, better accountability mechanisms, improved coordination, more assertive politicians, greater financial independence, and a plethora of other factors, will supposedly allow the modern-day humanitarian to more effectively 'do the right thing'. Applying an ethical lens to the desire to 'do right' in contexts in which one can very quickly find oneself 'doing wrong' allows for a more considered exploration of the values and principles that shape the individual humanitarian act, while also allowing for a deeper engagement with questions of cause and effect.

However, has this perhaps gone too far? Is it not enough to say that the desire to 'do right' is at least as important if not more important than 'doing right' in practice? In a two-part MSF blog series Julian Sheather, ethics adviser to both the British Medical Association and MSF, called for humanitarian actors to 'abandon the language of complicity' (2017a), while in the latter blog he cautioned against the practice of 'moral narcissism' in relation to difficult and oftentimes compromising humanitarian encounters (2017b). A somewhat similar

THE ETHICS OF COMPILING A BOOK ON HUMANITARIAN ETHICS | **309**

sentiment was shared by MSF Germany's General Director, Florian Westphal, at the 2017 Berlin Humanitarian Congress:

> We shouldn't be beating ourselves about the head, and being ...
> in any way ashamed or embarrassed about being ... people from
> Western Europe, or the Global North, who do feel a very strong sense
> of solidarity, and who do want to ... remain involved, and who do
> want to help, and don't do this as some ... part of [a] neo-colonialist
> project. So, let's be self-critical, but let's also not put too much ash on
> our heads. (Humanitarian Congress, 2017)[1]

Despite the suggestion that humanitarians and their organisations have taken self-criticism too far, there clearly is something more than tokenistic self-flagellation in such continued critical engagement with humanitarian practice, both past and present. Humanitarianism is, and likely forever will be, characterised by complexity and contradiction, for which statements of complicity, neo-colonialism, and other such claims must be taken seriously. Attempts to reassert an 'untouchabililty' to humanitarianism, as has already been skilfully critiqued by Didier Fassin (2011), must be viewed with a careful caution. Such 'morally untouchable' assertions impede the ability to engage critically, relieving humanitarian actors of the obligation to defend their actions on the presumption that simply by identifying as 'humanitarian' one is automatically 'doing the right thing'. A similar word of caution should be extended to forms of ethical enquiry. Much like 'humanitarian', the language of 'ethics' is perceived by many to be intrinsically value-positive. Thus, to describe an act, process, or decision as 'ethical' can have far-reaching implications.

With this in mind, the process of compiling a book on Humanitarian Action and Ethics presented its own challenges. How does one prioritise the inclusion of certain contributions, and thus which narratives to elevate? In our case, and in the interest of complete transparency, it is important to note that no chapter submissions were refused during the call for contributions. The final seventeen chapters offer both theoretical and empirical insights drawn from contemporary humanitarian crises worldwide, many of which are underrepresented in mainstream discourse, but from which profound injustices are clearly recognisable.

Additional challenges relate to the tension that can develop when a described practice or process clashes with one's own judgement of right and wrong. For example, a series of discussions were dedicated to concerns over the inclusion of a paper that describes the return of Syrian patients to conflict-affected Syria from Israel (Chapter 9), a practice that narrowly avoids accusations of *refoulement* on the basis of a loophole in legal definitions. The specific context in question is the Golan Heights, a region between Syria and Israel with an intensely complex geopolitical history. As Plotner (2014) has outlined in a short report on the region in relation to the ongoing Syrian conflict, given the fact that the Golan Heights is still recognised by the international community as Syrian territory, the arrival of Syrians displaced by the conflict would legally constitute internal displacement, and thus displaced individuals would not be subject to the same protective processes that are enshrined in international law. Nevertheless, the static facility from which the chapter's ethical challenges are reported, Ziv Medical Center, resides in Galilee, twelve aerial kilometres from the western boundary of the Golan Heights, beyond the geopolitical demarcation of which, an individual fleeing the Syrian conflict would constitute a refugee as per the internationally recognised definition (Amnesty International, 2012).

Perhaps it can be argued that the inclusion of a chapter that describes the supposedly voluntary return of patients to conflict-affected Syria, controversial as this practice clearly is, would be less problematic were it not for the fact that the narrative of Syrian patients is not captured in this edited volume, and thus there is no voice to either counterbalance – or complement – that of the Israeli medical professionals. Despite six chapters related either directly to the ongoing conflict in Syria, or to the mass displacement that followed, Syrian contributors are notably underrepresented as authors in their own right. This was not an active omission, but it certainly has a bearing on the way in which unchallenged narratives are shaped and understood. Nevertheless, it was ultimately felt that it was not the place of the editors of this volume to deny readers the opportunity to critically engage with any particular chapter.

As such, pertinent in relation to the development of this volume have been questions of the tension between the need to elevate a multitude of voices and minimise the suppression of others, while at the same time avoiding any implied endorsement of practices that do not sit comfortably based on our own ethical judgement. With this in mind, it is clear that book editors, journal editorial committees, those who lend financial support to research proposals, and so on, wield substantial power in the way that they are able to shape both academic and popular discourse.

Allowing the preceding chapters, and these editorial musings, to speak for themselves, what has such a book to offer? Recognising that a growing catalogue of print publications now identify in one way or another with the language of humanitarianism – be it a dual focus on psychiatry, architecture, medicine, security, or law – we hope that this latest contribution succeeds in conveying the value and importance of ethical reflection as applied to humanitarian action, while illustrating the cumulative benefit of a comparative reading of the many diverse narratives and perspectives captured herein. It is intended that such a pluralism of perspectives, methodologies, and contextual insights will assist in the continued desire to identify and do the right thing.

Notes

1 'Ash on our heads' refers to the practice of placing ash on the forehead on Ash Wednesday, as a symbol of penance and remorse for one's sinful actions.

References

Amnesty International (2012), *Israel: government urged to allow all from Syria seeking refuge to enter Golan Heights*. Amnesty International Public Statement. AI Index: MDE 15/043/2012. London: Amnesty International.

Fassin, D (2011), Noli me tangere. The moral untouchability of humanitarianism. In: Redfield, P & Bornstein, E (eds), *Forces of compassion: humanitarianism between ethics and practice*. Santa Fe: School of Advanced Study Press.

Humanitarian Congress (2017), Closing remarks. 19th Berlin Humanitarian Congress [online]. Available from: www.youtube.com/watch?v=X3G8HhamJhI (accessed 28 November 2017).

Plotner, C (2014), If Israel accepted Syrian refugees and IDPs in the Golan Heights. *Forced Migration Review*. Vol. 47: 32–4.

Sheather, J (2017a), Time to abandon the language of complicity. MSF Opinion and Debate [online]. Available from: www.msf.org.uk/article/opinion-and-debate-time-abandon-language-complicity (accessed 28 November 2017).

Sheather, J (2017b), Moral narcissism and MSF. MSF Opinion and Debate [online]. Available from: www.msf.org.uk/article/opinion-and-debate-moral-narcissism-and-msf (accessed 28 November 2017).

Slim, H (1997), Doing the right thing: relief agencies, moral dilemmas and moral responsibility in political emergencies and war. *Disasters*. Vol. 21 (3): 244–57.

ZED

Zed is a platform for marginalised voices across the globe.

It is the world's largest publishing collective and a world leading example of alternative, non-hierarchical business practice.

It has no CEO, no MD and no bosses and is owned and managed by its workers who are all on equal pay.

It makes its content available in as many languages as possible.

It publishes content critical of oppressive power structures and regimes.

It publishes content that changes its readers' thinking.

It publishes content that other publishers won't and that the establishment finds threatening.

It has been subject to repeated acts of censorship by states and corporations.

It fights all forms of censorship.

It is financially and ideologically independent of any party, corporation, state or individual.

Its books are shared all over the world.

www.zedbooks.net
@ZedBooks